1995

BODY WORK

Body Work

Objects of Desire in Modern Narrative

Peter Brooks

Harvard University Press
Cambridge, Massachusetts
London, England   1993

Library of Congress Cataloging-in-Publication Data

Brooks, Peter, 1938–
  Body work : objects of desire in modern narrative / Peter Brooks.
    p.   cm.
  Includes bibliographical references and index.
  ISBN 0-674-07724-5 (acid-free paper)
  ISBN 0-674-07725-3 (pbk.)
  1. Body, Human, in literature.   2. Sex in literature.
  3. Narration (Rhetoric)   4. Literature, Modern—History and
  criticism.   5. Body, Human, in art.   I. Title.
PN56.B62B76   1993
809′.933538—dc20
92-34163
CIP

To the Fellows of the Whitney Humanities Center, 1980–1991

Contents

Illustrations

Preface

IN THIS BOOK I consider the body as an object and motive of narrative writing—as a primary, driving concern of the life of the imagination. I do so in a generally historical framework (with occasional violations of chronology in order to pursue my argument) and focus mainly on literary works. As I go along, I pay increasing attention to visual representations of the body, since viewing the body is of persistent importance in literature as well as other arts. My main concern throughout is with the creation of fictions that address the body, that imbed it in narrative, and that therefore embody meanings: stories on the body, and the body in story. In an earlier book, *Reading for the Plot*, I delineated a dynamics of desire animating narrative and the construal of its meanings; here my attention is directed toward the objects of desire, both within the text—the focus of its narrative logics—and of the text, that is, the objects which may be the obsessive motive of the writing project. I'm not entirely sure what genre this book belongs to. What I have produced might best be called an essay, if one could reactivate in that moribund word some of its original implication of a trying out of ideas, and some of the generic respectability it still has in French, where a book that does not claim to be either history or philosophy can seek honorable refuge under the banner of the *essai*.

As I began working on this book, I quickly discovered that I was not alone in my concern with the subject. The past decade has seen an outpouring of books, mainly in history and literary criticism, that evoke the body in one form or another. The new cultural history, originally associated with the *Annales* school but now far broader, has renewed attention to the daily lives and practices of ordinary people, to the private sphere as opposed to political events, and has necessarily made conceptions and rituals of the body a concern. Such history is indebted to the renewal of anthropology in our time, and its investigations of the ways in which natural bodies are marked, organized, and produced as cultural bodies. In literary studies, the coming of "new historicism" has meant that literary discourse is increasingly recontextualized in other social and cultural discourses, including those—medical, penal, sexual—that speak of the body. The work of Michel Foucault on madness, on the medical institution, on penology, and on sexuality has had a profound impact in historical and literary studies, both in the setting of intellectual agendas and in the conceptualizing of a sociohistorical *episteme* as the object of analysis. But perhaps most telling has been the work of feminist studies in a variety of disciplines: in their efforts to recover the experience of women, often silenced by traditional histories, to rediscover the published and unpublished texts that voice that experience, and to reconceive the place of the feminine in Western culture, feminist scholars have redirected our attention to bodily experience, including the stereotypes of the feminine perpetuated in much literature and art in a male-dominated tradition.

I address the question of the body in different modes, allowing a broad semantic range for "body"—biological entity, psycho-sexual construction, cultural product—since I believe that it is all of these, often all at once, to writers and readers. While resisting the (impossible) task of saying exactly what the body is, throughout I ask why and how bodies have been imagined and symbolized, and particularly how they have been made key tokens in modern narratives—"modern" starting sometime in the eighteenth century. What meanings are to be found in the massive writing project developed on the body? As I shall argue, modern narratives appear to produce a semioticization of the body which is matched by a somatization of story: a claim that the body must be a source and a locus of meanings, and that stories cannot be told without making the body a prime vehicle of narrative significations.

Much of my own discussion of the body draws on psychoanalysis. This is no doubt from a personal affinity with psychoanalytic thinking, and a conviction that psychic process and literary process are mutually illuminating. In the context of this book, psychoanalysis seems an almost inevitable point of reference since its understanding of the psyche passes so centrally through the body, both as the place where psychic conflict writes itself—as in hysteria—and as the source of human symbolism. I shall argue, following Freud, Melanie Klein, and Jacques Lacan, that the body furnishes the building blocks of symbolization, and eventually of language itself, which then takes us away from the body, but always in a tension that reminds us that mind and language need to recover the body, as an otherness that is somehow primary to their very definition. Psychoanalysis presents a shuttling between real and phantasized bodies which very much defines my own understanding of the body as at once a cultural construct and its other, something outside of language that language struggles to mark and to be embodied in.

The body that interests me most is, as in psychoanalysis, the body defined radically by its sexuality. By this I do not mean simple genitality, but rather the concept of the self as a sexual being, both deriving from and producing issues of gender difference, origins, and self-definition. Sexuality belongs not simply to the physical body, but to the complex of phantasies and symbolizations which largely determine identity. Sexuality develops as a swerve from mere genital utility, driven by infantile phantasies of satisfaction and loss; it involves a dynamic of curiosity that is possibly the foundation of all intellectual activity, which I describe under the rubric of "epistemophilia." The dynamic of the narratives that I discuss derives in large part from their curiosity about the body, their explicit or implicit postulation that the body—another's or one's own—holds the key not only to pleasure but as well to knowledge and power.

The chapters of the book develop a generally historical framework. In Chapter 1, I give brief mention to what a full history of the body in literature might look like, while acknowledging my own inability to write that full history and arguing that there is some justification in starting in the eighteenth century, where, I claim in Chapter 2, a particularly modern problematics of the body emerges, along with the predominance of narrative, especially in the relatively new form of the novel. The chapters that follow trace some destinies of the body in nineteenth-century narratives, primarily in the realist tradition, which makes an unprecedented use of description directed to the external world, of which the body is seen to be a part. In Chapters 5 and 6 especially, I bring into juxtaposition with literary texts some examples from the visual arts. Chapters 4 and 8 address most directly the theoretical issues raised by my project, charting between them a major tradition and its discontents. The reader who is distressed by the largely patriarchal model displayed by the texts discussed in Chapters 3 through 6 is respectfully urged to read on, since Chapters 7 and 8 bring some reversals of perspective. The final chapter makes forays into various twentieth-century manifestations of the narrative body, without attempting to give a full conspectus of a vast field. Clearly, the subject of this book has no natural limits, and any choice of materials must appear somewhat arbitrary. I cannot claim that my examples are representative. I simply hope that they serve to delineate some of the interest of the field.

In thinking and talking about this topic over a period of some years, I have accumulated a number of intellectual debts, which it is a pleasure to acknowledge, though I can do so only in this summary and partial form. For helpful dialogue, critical response, and the suggestion of texts and issues for exploration, let me single out for special thanks Ronald Bryden, Candace Clements, James Clifford, Evelyne Ender, Philip Fisher, Michael Holquist, Linda Hutcheon, Hilary Jewett, Juliet Mitchell, Toril Moi, Laura Mulvey, Linda Nochlin, Elaine Scarry, Natasha Staller, Sarah Winter, and Margaret Brooks. I was the grateful recipient of a National Endowment for the Humanities Fellowship in 1988–89. And over the course of the years I was thinking about and writing much of this book, I had the good fortune to serve as Director of the Whitney Humanities Center, which put me in continuing contact with an extraordinarily interesting and generous group of colleagues from within and without Yale University. To them I owe more than I can ever define precisely. Hence the dedication of this book.

Earlier versions of parts of this book appeared in the pages of *New Literary History, Critical Inquiry, Romantisme, Yale Journal of Criticism, Tidskrift för Litteraturvetenskap,* and *Paragraph;* in *Fictions of the French Revolution,* edited by Bernadette Fort (Northwestern University Press), and in *The Expanding Discourse,* edited by Norma Broude and Mary D. Garrard (HarperCollins). I am pleased to thank the various editors for their support and for the permission to reprint.

BODY WORK

1 Narrative and the Body

OUR BODIES ARE with us, though we have always had trouble saying exactly how. We are, in various conceptions or metaphors, in our body, or having a body, or at one with our body, or alienated from it. The body is both ourselves and other, and as such the object of emotions from love to disgust. To psychoanalysis, it is the object of primary narcissism. To religious ascetics, it is a dangerous enemy of spiritual perfection. Most of the time, the body maintains an unstable position between such extremes, at once the subject and object of pleasure, the uncontrollable agent of pain and the revolt against reason—and the vehicle of mortality. As such, it is always the subject of curiosity, of an ever-renewed project of knowing. If this project lies most obviously within the sphere of medical science, from gross anatomy to molecular biology, it clearly involves all human sciences. In imaginative literature the body has always been an object of fascination, at once the distinct other of the signifying project—which, as an exercise of mind and will on the world, takes a stand outside materiality—and in some sense its vehicle (this living hand that writes), perhaps even its place of inscription. The question of the body in literature is particularly interesting because of the apparent distance and tension between the two, an irreducible tension between "nature" and "culture," that coexists with the sense that the two are interdependent. Getting the body into writing is a primary concern of literature throughout the ages. And conversely, getting writing onto the body is a sign of the attempt to make the material body into a signifying body. As Wallace Stevens says in *Notes Toward a Supreme Fiction:*

From this the poem springs: that we live in a place
That is not our own and, much more, not ourselves
And hard it is in spite of blazoned days.

2   If the "place that is not our own" and "not ourselves" is the world, it
can often seem that the body, our body, belongs to the world and not
to our ideally constructed selves. If the motive of poetry is an attempted
recuperation of an otherness, often that otherness is our own body.

How is identity related to the body? A famous example can be found
early in the Western literary tradition, in the *Odyssey*. When Odysseus
returns in disguise to his palace in Ithaka—now in the hands of the
profligate suitors of Penelope—he is first recognized by the old nurse
Eurykleia. It is not an intellectual recognition, but rather a dramatic
finding-out from and on the body itself:

> But Lord Odysseus
> whirled suddenly from the fire to face the dark.
> The scar: he had forgotten that. She must not
> handle his scarred thigh, or the game was up.
> But when she bared her lord's leg, bending near,
> she knew the groove at once.[1]

Homer at this point opens a narrative of around one hundred lines,
recounting how the young Odysseus received the scar during a boar
hunt on Parnassos—a narrative specifically concerned with the inscription on his body of the sign by which Eurykleia, decades later, now
recognizes him. Then we return to the present moment:

> This was the scar the old nurse recognized;
> she traced it under her spread hands, then let go,
> and into the basin fell the lower leg
> making the bronze clang, sloshing the water out.
> Then joy and anguish seized her heart; her eyes
> filled up with tears; her throat closed, and she whispered,
> with hand held out to touch his chin:
>   "Oh yes!
> *You are Odysseus!* Ah, dear child! I could not
> see you until now—not till I knew
> my master's very body with my hands!"

As in Aristotle's theory of tragedy—which is itself indebted to the Homeric poems—the moment of recognition is a dramatic climax, a coming into the open of hidden identities and latent possibilities. Here the recognition comes, as it often does in Greek tragedies, through a mark on the body itself. It is the body marked in a significant moment of the person's past history that enables recognition—a scenario that will be replayed throughout literature, and given its most formulaic version in the notorious *croix de ma mère* of melodrama, the token affixed to or engraved on the abandoned orphan which at last enables the establishment of identity.[2] It is as if identity, and its recognition, depended on the body having been marked with a special sign, which looks suspiciously like a linguistic signifier. The sign imprints the body, making it part of the signifying process. Signing or marking the body signifies its passage into writing, its becoming a literary body, and generally also a narrative body, in that the inscription of the sign depends on and produces a story. The signing of the body is an allegory of the body become a subject for literary narrative—a body entered into writing.

    The scene of Odysseus' recognition by way of his scar is discussed in the first chapter of Erich Auerbach's magisterial *Mimesis: The Representation of Reality in Western Literature*. A history of the place of the body in Western literature would in many ways run parallel to Auerbach's study, since representation of the body is part of representing "external" reality as a whole. Representation finds its most elaborated rhetorical form in description, the attempt to render the appearances of the visible world in writing; and such descriptive representation becomes most extensive, most important, in what we think of as "realism," that species of literature for which the careful registering of the external world counts most. Thus we may expect that the body in literary narrative will have its most developed presentations in "realist" literature, or more generally, in the era beginning in the middle of the eighteenth century and continuing through Romanticism and its aftermaths to our own time. And indeed, this is the period of the rise of the novel, of lengthy narrative fictions concerned most often with the individual in the social and phenomenal world. The body of that individual necessarily figures in the story, though with greatly varying degrees of explicitness. This literary history is overdetermined: one cannot establish unequivocal causal relations between the new importance given to the external world in the literature of the modern era and the modern concept of the individual and "personality," or new concepts of privacy and modesty, or modern medical science with its new concepts and technologies of the body. But there is a sufficient convergence of forces to make the body in modern literature, broadly understood, a newly important object of writing.

This is not to say, of course, that the body is not a central object of attention before the modern era, as the example from the *Odyssey* attests. In the *Iliad,* for instance, the heroic body has notable physical presence, as an essential integer of reality, especially in scenes of combat and slaughter.[3] In Greek tragedy, the body provides a number of signs of recognition, perhaps most famously the lock of Orestes' hair and his footprint that put Electra on the track of his identity in Aeschylus' *Libation Bearers,* a scene later imitated and parodied by Euripides in his *Electra.* In Sophocles' *Philoctetes,* the suppurating wounded foot of the archer becomes the very center of the play's action.

Then there is the central Christian story of the incarnation, of the word made flesh, repeated every time the Eucharist is celebrated. The insistence on the bodiliness of Christ is an endless source of narrative within the Christian tradition, since the adventures of the flesh on the way to the redemption of mankind provide a series of emblematic moments where spiritual significances are embodied. From the early Middle Ages through the Renaissance, writers in the West necessarily see sign and meaning in terms of embodiment and spirit. The status accorded to tragedy as a high—perhaps the highest—of literary modes derives in part from the ways in which tragedy resembles the Mass. Tragedy, says Northrop Frye, is a "mimesis of sacrifice," in which the audience participates as communicants, sharing symbolically the sacred body.[4] In Shakespeare, for instance, the body is omnipresent as both metaphor and physical presence, be it the anointed body of the king or the sweating, decaying body of Falstaff, and the organization of human society is regularly described in terms of a body, whole or sick. The secular or "carnivalesque" body that one finds most obviously represented in Rabelais in a sense parodies the tragic sacred body, claiming the final locus of significance—or anti-significance—in the body itself.

After the medieval and early modern periods the body became more hidden and more problematic in European culture. The work of Mikhail Bakhtin on Rabelais stressed the centrality of the body in the world-turned-upside-down of Renaissance carnival, and social historians have also shown how the body at this time is more openly displayed, in public encounters as well as in literary metaphors, and used to define what is human. As Francis Barker writes of Jacobean England, "A mode of discourse operates here which, basing itself in incarnation, exercises a unitary *presence* of meaning of which the spectacular body is both the symbol and the instance."[5] Barker reiterates a traditional historical scheme when he sees René Descartes as the symbolic moment of passage to the modern conception of the body. Cartesian "dualism"—positing a thinking essence distinct from corporeality—creates a body that is no longer "in" language but rather the object of discourse: "The Cartesian body is 'outside' language; it is given to discourse as an object (when it is not, in its absent moment, exiled altogether) but it is never *of* languaging in its essence" (99).

There is no doubt much truth in this history—and Norbert Elias's history of manners, which I shall discuss in a moment, bears it out—but perhaps also a certain romanticized nostalgia typical of some recent views of early modern Europe as a period of more unified sensibility, where bodily functions, sexuality, and death were more fully integrated in human consciousness as "natural" parts of life. We are prone to assume that we live after a Fall from a time of greater unity of consciousness, language, and being. In any event, we can think back to, or invent, such unity only through our present consciousness of division, our sense that the body can be recuperated to consciousness and language only by an effort—of which the narrative and descriptive project of realism is one example. Whatever it once was, the body is now problematic; and our sense that it was once less so may be a reflection of how much it now is.

A history of the body, or even a thorough conspectus of the literary body, would have to reach back to the beginnings, and to take account of many types—heroic, sacred, suffering, tragic (combining the previous three types), carnivalesque (revelling in bodiliness), pornographic, even moribund, since the primacy of the body may be most dramatically felt in its failure: the deathbed is a privileged literary place. I cannot attempt so much. My concern is with the body in modern narrative, and, within those chronological confines, mostly with the body in the erotic tradition, using "erotic" to designate the body primarily conceived, and primarily become significant, as the agent and object of desire. I want to talk mainly about bodies emblazoned with meaning within the field of desire, desire that is originally and always, with whatever sublimations, sexual, but also by extension the desire to know: the body as an "epistemophilic" project. The desire to know is constructed from sexual desire and curiosity. My subject is the nexus of desire, the body, the drive to know, and narrative: those stories we tell about the body in the effort to know and to have it, which result in making the body a site of signification—the place for the inscription of stories—and itself a signifier, a prime agent in narrative plot and meaning.

The erotic body may be the most venerable of all, since many of mankind's earliest attempts at art seem to be representations of fecund female forms and erect phalluses. The body as object of desire is the subject of much of the earliest poetry in the Western tradition, in the *Song of Songs,* and in Sappho and other poets of the Greek Anthology. It is the tradition that animates troubadour lyric and chivalric romance, and finds a particularly clear expression in the Renaissance "blazons" of the women's body, poems which elaborately describe and praise every feature in a game that can be played in the most courtly manner, and in its seeming parody, in poems of high obscenity. It is a tradition that also inevitably intersects with the political, since the erotic body both animates and disrupts the social order. The "laws" generated by human sexuality may themselves be foundational of social structure and regulation that police desire and make its place in civilization uneasy. To the extent that the body necessarily implicates sexuality—by which I mean not simple genitality, but the complex conscious and unconscious desires and interdictions that shape humans' conceptions of themselves as desiring creatures—it is always a restless captive of culture, including language.

Toward the end of his most probing study of narrative, *S/Z,* Roland Barthes makes the somewhat enigmatic claim that the "symbolic field"—the field of reference of the symbolic code, the one of his five codes of structure and meaning in narrative that refers to the text's overall rhetorical, thematic, and economic structurings—"is occupied by a sole object, from which it derives its unity . . . This object is the human body."[6] Are we to read this as a claim that the body is the referent of reference itself, the object for which reference, as a notion or an activity, exists? Is the body the ultimate field from which all symbolism derives, and to which it returns? Are we to conclude that ultimately the text itself represents the body, and the body the text? Without being wholly clear as to Barthes' meaning here, I find his remark suggestive of the close relations between narrative text and body. He intimates that the body is at least our primary source of symbolism—an intimation that anyone sympathetic to psychoanalysis will readily accept—and that literature, in its use and creation of symbols, ever brings us back to this source, as that which its representations ultimately represent. Barthes seems to say that the symbolic field and the body at some point converge:

that meaning, especially meaning conceived as the text's self-representations—its representations of what it is and what it is doing—takes place in relation to the body, and that we are forever striving to make the body into a text.

Let me try to be more precise. One tradition of contemporary thought would have it that the body is a social and linguistic construct, the creation of specific discursive practices, very much including those that construct the female body as distinct from the male. If the sociocultural body clearly is a construct, an ideological product, nonetheless we tend to think of the physical body as precultural and prelinguistic: sensations of pleasure and especially of pain, for instance, are generally held to be experiences outside language; and the body's end, in death, is not simply a discursive construct. Mortality may be that against which all discourse defines itself, as protest or as attempted recovery and preservation of the human spirit, but it puts a stark biological limit to human constructions. The body, I think, often presents us with a fall from language, a return to an infantile presymbolic space in which primal drives reassert their force. Yet the earliest infantile experiences—the sense of the infant's body in relation to its mother's, its orientation in space, its first attempts to achieve equilibrium—may be foundational of all symbolism. Prior even to primary narcissism, according to Freud, are the autoerotic instincts or drives that provide the earliest experience of the body. For Melanie Klein and her followers, the mother's body, and particularly the breast, provides the original object of symbolization, and then the field of exploration for the child's developing "epistemophilic impulse," the urge to know.[7] Klein, starting from Sándor Ferenczi's theory that "identification, the forerunner of symbolism, arises out of the baby's endeavour to rediscover in every object his own organs and their functioning," argues that "symbolism is the foundation of all sublimation and of every talent, since it is by way of symbolic equation that things, activities and interests become the subject of libidinal phantasies."[8] Bodily parts, sensations, and perceptions (including the notorious recognition of the anatomical distinction between the sexes) are the first building blocks in the construction of a symbolic order, including speech, play, and the whole system of human language, within which the child finds a libidinally invested place.

In this sense, the most highly elaborated symbolic structures and discursive systems no doubt ultimately derive from bodily sensations. Yet these structures and systems move us away from the body, as any use of signs must necessarily do. Representation of the body in signs endeavors to make the body present, but always within the context of its absence, since use of the linguistic sign implies the absence of the thing for which it stands. The body appears alien to the very constructs derived from it. However much it may belong to the process of socialization, and preside at the birth of intellectual curiosity, it nonetheless often appears to be on the far side of the divide between nature and culture, where culture ultimately has no control. It is perhaps most of all this sense of the body's otherness that leads to the endeavor to bring the body into language, to represent it, so that it becomes part of the human semiotic and semantic project, a body endowed with meaning. Conversely, language seeks to remotivate itself as a symbolism with an original referent in the body: to become a language embodied. Narratives in which a body becomes a central preoccupation can be especially revelatory of the effort to bring the body into the linguistic realm because they repeatedly tell the story of a body's entrance into meaning. That is, they dramatize ways in which the body becomes a key signifying factor in a text: how, we might say, it embodies meaning.

In modern narrative literature, a protagonist often desires a body (most often another's, but sometimes his or her own) and that body comes to represent for the protagonist an apparent ultimate good, since it appears to hold within itself—as itself—the key to satisfaction, power, and meaning. On the plane of reading, desire for knowledge of that body and its secrets becomes the desire to master the text's symbolic system, its key to knowledge, pleasure, and the very creation of significance. Desire for the body may appear to promise access to the very *raison d'être* of the symbolic order. Thus narrative desire, as the subtending dynamic of stories and their telling, becomes oriented toward knowledge and possession of the body. Narrative seeks to make such a body semiotic, to mark or imprint it as a linguistic and narrative sign. If the plot of the novel is very often the story of success or failure in gaining access to the body—and the story of the fulfillment or disillusionment that this brings—the larger story may concern the desire to pierce the mysteries of life that are so often subsumed for us in the otherness of other people. As Georges Bataille maintains, each individual feels himself or herself as discontinuous, and the erotic—the attempt to know another through breaching the lonely confines of one's own body—marks an effort to know, if only momentarily, a kind of continuity with others. Thus eroticism is for Bataille "the affirmation of life all the way into death." Its decisive moment, says Bataille, is the action of denuding, *la mise à nu,* since it is in this confrontation in nakedness that two human beings assume the risk of giving up their closed, discontinuous state in a momentary surrender to otherness.[9]

Bataille's speculations on the meaning of the erotic raise questions about our fascination with bodies and the means we deploy for knowing them. For Freud and Klein as for Bataille, the desire to know—the epistemophilic urge—is ultimately linked to sexuality: to the child's autoerotic exploration of its own body, and its perception of the anatomical difference between the sexes. The child's overwhelming question addressed to the world, and to its parents, is: Where do babies come from? The child never can receive a wholly satisfactory answer because the child's own physical development is inadequate to allow it to understand the nature of adult sexuality, and the meaning of sexual difference. The "diphasic onset" of sexuality, by which children awake to sexual curiosity—first of all about their own bodies—long before they reach sexual maturity, seems to insure that their primary investigation of knowledge shall be frustrated at its very roots, setting up a model of the desire to know as an inherently unsatisfiable, Faustian project. The drive for possession will be closely linked to the drive to know, itself most often imaged as the desire to see. For it is sight, with its accompanying imagery of light, unveiling, and fixation by the gaze, that traditionally represents knowing, and even rationality itself. Luce Irigaray complains that Freud's scenarios of sexual curiosity and difference are invariably visual, and indeed *Schaulust* or "scopophilia"—the eroticized desire to see—is a prime theme in Freud's writings, and closely tied to the *Wisstrieb,* epistemophilia.[10] But this is not accidental, nor can it simply be dismissed as one more ideological product of what Irigaray calls the "phallic gaze." The gaze may indeed be predominantly phallic, since the Western literary (and philosophic and artistic) tradition has overwhelmingly featured men looking at women. As a concept, however, the gaze appears to be a crucial element in any epistemological project, and certainly the privileging of sight in scenarios of knowing has been theoretically examined in psychoanalytic thinking. The investment of eroticism in the visual may pragmatically—in terms of the individual's development—be explained in the manner proposed by psychoanalyst Edith Jacobsen: "the prohibition of manual genital play, i.e., of 'touching,' is certainly responsible for the child's usual overcathexis of visual perception, particularly with regard to seeing the genitals of others as well as his own."[11] But Freud's own writings frequently return to the theoretical bases of eroticized seeing. In particular, he puts forward one theory about the origins of the privilege accorded to sight that is so

NARRATIVE AND THE BODY

curious and, in a mythic way, so persuasive that it is worth dwelling on for a moment.

Freud's theory is given its most detailed, but still very sketchy, exposition in a long footnote to a discussion in *Civilization and Its Discontents* (1930) of the genesis of the human family and the regulation of sexuality. In the footnote, Freud hypothesizes that "the fateful process of civilization . . . set in with man's adoption of an erect posture" (*Standard Edition* 21:99). For when humans stand upright, there is a repression of the sense of smell—previously the main source of sexual stimulation and knowledge—and a corresponding privileging of the sense of sight. In particular, when men and women stand erect the genitals are exposed to sight and become the object of visual inspection and curiosity. They also become more vulnerable than they had been, and thus thought to be in need of protection, which may be the origin of the sense of shame in the concept of the *pudenda*. If intellectual curiosity is based upon sexual curiosity, the moment at which the genitals are exposed—and therefore subject to covering—represents the emergence of sight as the intellectual faculty par excellence, the very figure of perception and discrimination. Smell, of course, remains particularly connected to sexuality, and Freud notes that many of the so-called perversions enact a partial failure of the "organic repression" of smell.[12] The shift to erect posture is connected with the formation of the family through another factor: the transformation of periodic moments of estrus, or "heat," characteristic of most mammals, into the human female's menstrual cycle. In the regimen of estrus, females are sexually available only at certain, often quite limited, times, whereas the human female (whether or not a given society may place taboos on intercourse during menstruation) is constantly available. That is, only in humans is there a "continuity of sexual excitation." And this continuity means that the male "acquires a motive for keeping the female, or, speaking more generally, his sexual objects, near him." In other words, the possibility of an uncontrolled female sexuality leads, in Freud's scenario, to the male's creating the structure of the family and his patriarchal authority (the nature of which, and the "laws" of which, Freud develops more fully in *Totem and Taboo* [1912–1913]). So it is that erect posture, the suppression of estrus, the continuity of sexuality, the founding of the patriarchal family, and the emergence of sight as the dominant faculty are all connected for Freud, and constitute the "threshold of human civilization."

Freud's scenario is only, as he puts it, "theoretical speculation," unfounded in observation, but probably about as good as most sociobiological theorizing, which generally invents narratives of origin in order to explain the primeval origins of contemporary conditions, as defined by the theorist. What is useful about Freud's scenario is that it "explains"— in the sense that it gives a mythic origin to—various attitudes and practices that have been common to Western culture. In particular, it persuasively links vision, desire, and the epistemophilic urge, which we repeatedly find conjoined in presentations of the body, and also suggests how vision, desire, and the drive toward knowledge become connected through narrative in a newly eroticized sense of time as the medium of desire and its possible realization.[13] The relation to another body is repeatedly presented in visual terms, and the visual as applied to the body is often highly eroticized, a gaze subtended by desire. The desire can be a desire to possess, and also a desire to know; most often the two are intermingled, sometimes indistinguishable. The *libido amandi,* the *libido dominandi,* and the *libido capiendi* (lust for love, for power, for knowledge)—to speak the language of the Church Fathers—have always been closely allied in Western philosophy and literature. What one might call the metaphysical Don Juan tradition gives an enduring instance: in Molière's seventeenth-century version, *Dom Juan,* and still to some extent in Mozart's *Don Giovanni,* and in Casanova's *Memoirs,* and in later avatars such as Kierkegaard's *Diary of a Seducer,* Don Juan pursues the conquest of his "catalogue" of women not merely from a desire for sexual satisfaction but just as much from a wish for mastery which is in essence a desire to know. Molière's figure is a libertine in the other (earlier) sense of the term as well: a freethinker who defies the dictates of church and state in his restless need to prove the emptiness of the heavens, the lack of transcendent law. His need to conquer women appears as a contradictory desire to know and to prove that there is nothing to know—much in the manner of (to cite only one modern instance) André Malraux's character Ferral, in *La condition humaine,* whose erotic encounters are both moments of the greatest plentitude and proof of the void.

Charles Pinot Duclos, a historian, memorialist, and minor novelist of the eighteenth-century, offered a bemused comment on this tradition: "I don't know why men have accused women of falsity, and have made Truth [*la Vérité*] female. A problem to be resolved. They also say that she is naked, and that could well be. It is no doubt from a secret love for Truth that we pursue women with such ardor; we seek to strip them of everything that we think hides Truth; and when we have satisfied our curiosity on one, we lose our illusions, and we run after another, to be happier. Love, pleasure, and inconstancy are perhaps only a consequence of the desire to know Truth."[14] We have only to think of representations in painting and sculpture to acknowledge that Truth, in our culture, is indeed a woman. She may be naked, or she may be veiled, in which case the veils must be stripped away, in a gesture which is repeated in countless symbolizations of discovery, which will often give a narrative similar to Duclos' "pursuit." In a patriarchal culture, uncovering the woman's body is a gesture of revealing what stands for an ultimate mystery.

Here, of course, we encounter another Freudian scenario: the danger of looking at woman naked. For the male child, the view of the woman's genitals creates the fear of castration, which may be represented as a threat to the eyes of the observer: Freud repeatedly posits an equivalence of blinding and castration, notably in his reading of the *Oedipus*. Freud finds a mythological representation of the scenario in the Greek myth of the Gorgon Medusa, the sight of whose head turns all observers to stone. The Medusa's head, with its snaky locks, represents the female genitals. The snakes may at the same time, however, represent a multiplicity of penises—an attempted reassurance against the threat of castration. And whereas turning to stone, like the decapitation of Medusa's head, evokes terror of castration, becoming stiff with terror also "means an erection," offering the observer the consolation that "he is still in possession of a penis."[15] Freud goes on to note that "this symbol of horror is worn upon her dress by the virgin goddess Athene. And rightly so, for thus she becomes a woman who is unapproachable and repels all sexual desires—since she displays the terrifying genitals of the Mother." In this manner, Freud extends the danger—as well as the desire—of seeing woman naked to the representation of the goddess of wisdom.

Freud's "castration complex" (and its corollary in woman's "penis envy") has been the object of intense criticism and revision from early in the psychoanalytic movement. Although we may reject the Freudian concept in its more naive and anecdotal forms, and in its patriarchal assumption that the development of the male is the norm, the more sophisticated view, associated especially with Jacques Lacan's rereading of Freud, cannot easily be dismissed. The Lacanian phallus, in the words of Jacqueline Rose, "symbolises the effects of the signifier in that having no value in itself, it can represent that to which value *accrues*."[16] It becomes, in other words, the signifier of a difference which refers to the anatomical difference between the sexes as simply the most obvious instance of difference as a mental category, that which enables the process of symbolization. The phallus comes to stand in for the object of desire which everyone, men as well as women, feels as necessarily missing. "If this is so," writes Juliet Mitchell, "the Oedipus complex can no longer be a static myth that reflects the real situation of father, mother, and child, it becomes a structure revolving around the question of where a person can be placed in relation to his or her desire. That 'where' is determined by the castration complex."[17] The castration complex brings an end to the Oedipal stage by instituting the Law, with the superego as its representative, promulgating the interdictions that retrospectively make the perception of anatomical sexual difference fundamentally significant; human desire emerges as rule-governed, subject to a basic "thou shalt not" that ensures that desire will be riven by lack, always be absolute, unsatisfied with its objects, inherently unsatisfiable. The castration complex makes human sexuality something other than mere genitality—makes it what Mitchell calls "psychosexuality."[18]

What is at stake in this conception of the castration complex—and in the need to "rescue" it from more anodyne theories of human sexual development—is well stated by Gregorio Kohon: *what makes sexuality in human beings specifically human is repression,* that is to say, sexuality owes its existence to our unconscious incestuous fantasies. Desire, in human sexuality, is always transgression; and being something that is never completely fulfilled, its object cannot ever offer full satisfaction." The theory of the castration complex means that sexuality is neither biologically nor sociologically determined, and that one's position as woman or man is not an essentialist given but something produced. Kohon says further: "What there is in the unconscious is *a danger and a threat* for the man, and *a desire and an envy* for the woman, and not—as is assumed—an overvalued penis and an undervalued vagina. A penis, just as much as a vagina, does not secure or guarantee anything for the subject about becoming a sexual human being. What the idea of bisexuality denotes is precisely the uncertainty of that process and the struggle through which all human beings *become* either a woman or a man."[19]

Hence the visual experiences of anatomical difference related by Freud are by themselves too simplistic, and should rather be considered manifestations of the complex structuring, by prohibitions, of human desire. The body as we want to know it—as the agent and the object of what we precisely call "carnal knowledge"—is itself a complexly constructed and multiply invested site. As part of, and motive of, the process of

NARRATIVE AND THE BODY

creating meaning in the world by way of symbols, the body is produced by the psychosexual thought of difference. And since this thought of difference is marked by dramas of desire and interdiction, the body is rarely simply a biological given. Phantasies project it forward in imaginary scenarios of fulfillment, pleasure, power, and backward to the unconscious infantile sources of phantasy. This temporal structuring has narrative consequences, making access to the body that has been chosen as the object of desire difficult, indirect, mediated, subject to delay, digression, and error: a process of becoming in which desire often mistakes its objects and its nature in the search for the significant, enlightening end to the story. The radical structuring of human nature by sexuality ensures that the body will always be a problem in meaning.

Relation to one's own body as well frequently has its symbolic manifestation in a privileged visual moment: self-reflection in the mirror. The story of Narcissus is replayed in endless variants, including Lacan's celebrated "mirror stage." The infant perceives his or her image in the mirror, and perceives it as unitary, whole, while the infant's inner sense of self remains incoherent, unformed, incompletely separated from its surroundings.[20] The ego recognized by the infant is not identical with the self; it is an imaginary identity, founding a system in which the ego is always other, and the other always an *alter ego*. Identity is thus alienated, the product of the gaze. The self-reflexive moment founds the imaginary order, one of deceptive specular identities. In other words, our early experiences of our own bodies may be not necessarily those of oneness or unity, but rather those of otherness and alienation: our selves as they are for others, a relation of displacement which notably affects relations of erotic love to others.

The story of the eroticized gaze at the body is also, from another perspective, the story of *pudeur*, modesty, of the hiding of those parts known as *pudenda*, shameful, or at least private. The development of civilization is for Freud in large measure a question of instinctual renunciation, learning to repress, sublimate, and delay various gratifications—a renunciation that takes a high toll, in that it virtually makes civilization synonymous with neurosis. Norbert Elias has traced what he calls "the civilizing process" as a lowering of the threshold of disgust, particularly in relation to the body and its products, a progressive hiding of bodily parts and functions.[21] The story told by Elias is in part one of an increasingly socialized body learning to discipline itself, to be more self-contained, controlled, autonomous, and private. It is also the story of an increasing psychologizing of mankind, where questions that originally pertain to the body—how one eats with others, when one farts or belches—become subsumed in more general psychological and ethical categories such as shame and modesty. While this story is not linear, and progresses differently for different social classes as well as for different cultures, it is in the main characterized by increasing privatization 15 and hiding. Recent historians of private life have demonstrated that privatization and hiding affect all aspects of existence: architecture, sleeping and eating arrangements, relations to servants, the raising of children—indeed, the "invention" of childhood as a separate stage of development needing isolation from adulthood, and especially from adult sexuality.[22] When the body becomes more secret, hidden, covered, it becomes all the more intensely the object of curiosity. As Michel Foucault has argued, modern societies have created a massive discourse of sexuality that produces sexuality as that which is hidden, secret, and therefore most desirable to know.[23] In this sense, discourse of the sexual body has perhaps replaced theological discourses of the arcane and the sacred for a desacralized era.

These generalities apply to both the male and the female body, but there are profound asymmetries in the specific treatments of the two genders. It appears that in patriarchal societies, the male body is ostensibly deproblematized, decathected as an object of curiosity or of representation, and concomitantly more thoroughly hidden. There is an apparent paradox here: if the male body in patriarchy becomes the norm, the standard against which one measures otherness—and thus creates the enigma of woman—one might expect the male body to be more openly displayed and discussed. But a moment's reflection allows us to see that the paradox is merely apparent. Precisely because it is the norm, the male body is veiled from inquiry, taken as the agent and not the object of knowing: the gaze is "phallic," its object is not. Barthes suggests that in our culture, narrative itself, as the eventual unveiling of truth, is a "staging [*mise en scène*] of the Father (absent, hidden or suspended)— which would explain the interdependence of narrative forms, familial structures, and prohibitions of nudity, all brought together, for us, in the myth of Noah covered by his sons."[24] In this view, the nakedness of the drunken patriarch Noah would be the central scandal of our culture, one that must at all costs be veiled since it reveals the very principle of patriarchal authority. Despite—or because of—the attention paid to viewing woman naked, the paternal phallus may be the ultimate taboo object of our culture. As the controversy aroused in 1989 by the exhibit of photographs by Robert Mapplethorpe confirmed, the erect penis is virtually the only object still rated obscene in contemporary American society—the very definition of "hard core"—and subject to restrictions.[25]

Here, however, we encounter a problem in thinking about the display and representation of the body. For when we go back to Greek art, it is clearly the male body that is the object of representation, completely naked (though not, in sculpture, sexually aroused, whereas it may be in vase painting); fig leaves are a later, Hellenistic addition. The female nude appears considerably later than the male—Kenneth Clark asserts that there are no female nudes in the sixth century B.C., and only rare examples in the fifth century—and is for a long time less common.[26] Clark alludes to various social and religious factors that seem to have made nudity much less acceptable for representations of women and of female divinities. Another common explanation (and one which Freud mentions in his piece on "Medusa's Head") is the homosexual ideal of Greek civilization, which made the young male body the measure of beauty. In the Christian Middle Ages of course the body of either sex is suppressed as an object of visual contemplation. But when the body re-emerges as a privileged object of representation in the Italian Renaissance, again the male body predominates, partially in imitation of Classical Antiquity, and also because it is considered the public body par excellence, the measure of the world. Renaissance costume puts the male body on display in ways that more recent customs have suppressed: witness the tights and prominent codpieces familiar to us especially from some of Bronzino's portraits. The combined force of Classical and Renaissance models is sufficiently strong to insure that the male body will continue to be the main artistic model up through the eighteenth century; it is only with the nineteenth century that the female emerges as the very definition of the nude, and censorship of the fully unclothed male body becomes nearly total. French academic training, which dominated European art for the first half of the nineteenth century, continued to emphasize life drawing from male models, but finished paintings normally bore testimony to the students' expertise in the use of windblown drapery to cover the genitals and to attenuate the outlines of the nude male body. Meanwhile, the female nude became the object of connoisseurship, art exhibits, and collecting.[27]

While I can propose no sure answer to the complex issues raised by the history of the nude, I would advance this hypothesis: the naked male body, in the art of the Renaissance and thereafter, is supposed to be heroic rather than erotic. It is regularly presented in postures of action, combat, or struggle, its muscles tensed and visible. Reinventions of the male body—I think particularly of Jacques-Louis David at the end of the eighteenth century—belong to the heroic tradition, as part of a conscious restatement of the combative, militant potential of man. Male nudity could exemplify strength and force, but the culture suppressed it as an ideal of beauty.[28] There are of course exceptions, such as (nearly contemporary with David's heroic canvases) A.-L. Girodet's languid and sexualized *The Sleep of Endymion* (1791), but in the main the male body is not the object of an overtly erotic gaze. Indeed, if spectatorship is gendered as male—as it certainly is throughout most of the modern Western tradition, when male spectators have set the terms of art appreciation and awarded commissions and prizes—then the male nude cannot ostensibly be looked at as an erotic object. Our erotic looking is not necessarily so strictly categorized, and may be more nearly androgynous: male spectators take pleasure in male nudes, women in female nudes. But this pleasure involves sublimations, of the type involved in the admiration of the heroic body, which are put into question by art that seems to invite an explicitly homoerotic gaze, such as Girodet's *Endymion,* for instance. The female nude, on the other hand, seems to be an object of male erotic looking nearly from the beginning. The heroic female divinity—such as Praxiteles' Athene in the Parthenon—is thoroughly draped; it is Aphrodite, given her classic statement in Praxiteles' Knidian Aphrodite of 330 B.C., who is completely nude. Beginning with the Hellenistic period (whose most influential works are the so-called Capitoline and Medici Venuses), the female nude assumes the form of the *Venus pudica,* caught in a gesture of modesty in which she partly covers her sex, and therefore may draw greater attention to it. Certainly in the Renaissance and thereafter the female nude is erotic, and associations with the biblical Eve assure that the state of nudity always implies nakedness, suggests that the protective veilings that characterize the fallen world have been removed. There is a further question why the female nude has traditionally been represented in an "airbrushed" fashion, minus pubic hair, which was never the case for the male nude. Perhaps complex, unarticulated cultural markings are at work here—hair connoting masculinity, smooth surface connoting femininity—along with an attempt, not uncommon in patriarchy, to rework the woman's body as a cultural rather than natural artifact.[29] Recourse to Freud might suggest why direct confrontation of the female sex is, to the male spectator, fraught with desire, fear, and a sense of the uncanny.

17

NARRATIVE AND THE BODY

The nature of women's genitalia is effaced, even uncertain, in the airbrushed nude. One finds here a strange, and long perpetuated, attenuation of female anatomy.

By the time of the modern—by which I mean, again, sometime beyond the middle of the eighteenth century—the female nude is well established as the erotic object of specifically gendered spectatorship, and representation of the nude has increasingly taken on characteristics of an invasion of privacy, as women are seen in moments of intimacy, at the bath or toilette, or exposed on a bed. Foucault argues that the rise of the bourgeoisie promoted the idea of sex—of genitality—over the aristocratic belief in blood: aristocrats measure their power through illustrious ancestors, but bourgeois place their faith in the future, in their family and posterity. Thus modern notions of privacy, hiding, decency are linked to a new valuing of what has, as a result, been hidden, ultimately the genitals themselves.[30]

Although the mythological references of Renaissance painting continue throughout the nineteenth century in academic practice—endless births of Venus, bacchantes, bathing Dianas, and so forth—they increasingly appear unmotivated, insincere, beside the point: narrative pretexts to permit the creation of the female nude. Inevitably there came a crisis in representation, beginning around the middle of the nineteenth century, when Realism, then Impressionism and its sequels, forced a consideration of the contexts in which nudity could plausibly be displayed, provoking an increasingly deep split between academic and countertraditional art. In popular culture, the development of technologies of spectacle as varied as the department store display window and photography has tended to produce a commodification of the nude—almost always female—that continues to dominate both entertainment and the selling of nearly everything produced in late capitalist societies.

Representation of the nude in the plastic and pictorial arts offers the clearest example of the constitution of modern canons of vision and desire; literature appears to follow a similar, if more tortuous, route. The eighteenth century produces a particularly rich collection of erotic literature, which is fascinated by that which is normally covered and kept private. The literary representations most often have a playful indirectness, naming the private body through series of substitutions, as metonymies and metaphors. They also very often describe the naked female body as if it were posed for artistic representation. A century later, the aesthetics of realism does not bring the more graphic and detailed report of the naked body, in literature that intends to be public rather than pornographic, that one might have expected. In part, this is because narrative literature increasingly sees the world, and objects of attention and desire, through the eyes of fictive persons, including a narrator who is himself (or, less frequently, herself) a person both in the created world and above it. Therefore the object of attention and desire—most obviously, the person of the beloved—is not detailed in its nakedness but rather approached by way of its phenomenal presence in the world, which means by way of the clothing and accessories that adorn and mask the body. The approach to the body of the beloved may strive toward unveiling (Barthes compares traditional narrative to a striptease) but it also tends to become waylaid in the process of this unveiling, more interested in the lifting of veils than in what is finally unveiled.[31] An interest in the way, rather than simply in the endpoint, is indeed virtually a definition of narrative.

19

Barthes' model of narrative as striptease refers to the "classic" (or "readable") text which works toward a progressive solution of preliminary enigmas, toward a full predication of the narrative "sentence," toward a plenitude of meaning. The desire to reach the end is the desire to see "truth" unveiled. The body of the object of desire is the focal point of a fascinated attention. Yet this attention, the very gaze of literary representation, tends to become arrested and transfixed by articles of clothing, accessories, bodily details, almost in the matter of the fetishist. What Kleinian analysts call "part objects" become invested with affect and meaning, as the text presents inventories of the charms of the beloved (as in the enormously influential Petrarchan tradition). The moment of complete nakedness, if it ever is reached, most often is represented by silence, ellipsis. Narrative is interested not only in points of arrival, but also in all the dilatory moments along the way: suspension or turning back, the perversions of temporality (as of desire) that allow us to take pleasure and to grasp meaning in passing time.

One could, once again, find in Freudian scenarios of the man's fear and fascination at beholding the woman's sex an explanation for the way narrative swerves from direct contemplation of the object of desire—from direct confrontation of the Medusa—and also for the necessity of its reaching eventually that uncanny place that is man's first home. It may be more useful, however, to consider that the castration complex, which dictates that post-infantile desire emerges subject to interdictions and repressions, founds a narrative "law" whereby direct access to the object of desire never can be unproblematic or linear, and indeed where knowing the vectors of desire and identifying its object is always complex, mediated, and subject to necessary error. The "eroti-cization of time," as a factor of human sexuality, also presides at the creation of narrative temporality. This temporality, like a force-field of desire, impels both fictive persons and real readers forward in a search for possession and truth, which tend to coincide in the body of the object that finally stands in the place to which desire tends. The greater reticence and indirection of the narrative text in depicting the body, as compared to painterly representation, has to do with the dynamic temporality of desire in narrative, the way in which narrative desire simultaneously seeks and puts off the erotic dénouement that signifies both its fulfillment and its end: the death of desiring, the silence of the text.

The history of narrative offers its own story of a hesitant unveiling of the body—an increasing preoccupation with bodiliness, and a certain, somewhat sly, shedding of reticence about the erotic body. In France, Honoré de Balzac, Gustave Flaubert, Emile Zola, and Marcel Proust represent stages in an increasingly explicit discourse of desire and its objects. In England, a greater weight of social repression affects representation of the body, but a displaced or censored eroticism is strongly registered by the reader of Charles Dickens, Charlotte and Emily Brontë, Henry James, or Thomas Hardy. A breakthrough in the uncensored, matter-of-fact representation of the body comes in our century, in James Joyce's *Ulysses,* with its portrayals of Leopold Bloom at stool and Molly Bloom in bed with her own body. Yet literature continues to display a greater reticence about the representation of the body than painting. While I have attempted to explain this reticence by way of the logic of narrative, there may be additional reasons having to do with the logic of writing itself as a self-conscious remaking of the world in signs. Literature may be less interested in contemplation of the naked body per se than in the body as the locus for the inscription of meanings.

Let me try to gloss this last remark. The development of "civilization" *(Kultur),* as both Freud and Elias contend in their different ways, consists in instinctual renunciation and a disciplining the body and its functions. Bodiliness, we might say, is assigned to certain places in life, just as undressing or excretion are assigned to specific spaces within the modern bourgeois dwelling. In the predominant philosophical tradition that we usually derive from Descartes, the body is the other of soul or mind, and its place in life, while highly important, is not the same as that of the self. We live at a certain distance of spirit from materiality, while recognizing that it is a false distance—that spirit, whatever it is, depends on matter. Such a condition is not without analogies to that of the writer, whose spiritual conceptions are dependent on the materiality of the letter. If the letter, according to Saint Paul, kills while the spirit gives life, writers and readers of texts know—have always known—that there can be no spirit without the letter, and that the story of incarnation is, among other things, an analogy of writing. Although the body often seems opposed to spirit, its other, the realm of unmeaning, it can also be spirit's very material support, as the letter is the material support of the message.

21

Writing is often aware of this situation, and frequently dramatizes it as the recovery of the letter for spirit, of the body for signification. That dramatization very often takes the form of a marking or signing of the body. That is, the body is made a signifier, or the place on which messages are written. This is perhaps most of all true in narrative literature, where the body's story, through the trials of desire and over time, often is very much part of the story of a character. The result is what we might call a narrative aesthetics of embodiment, where meaning and truth are made carnal.

The moment of the recognition of Odysseus' scar by Eurykleia provides an emblem of this narrative tradition. It is the signing of Odysseus' youthful body by the boar's tusk—and we are given a detailed narrative of the incident of marking itself—that allows Eurykleia, so many decades later, to recognize the rightful lord of Ithaka. There could, of course, be other ways to assure Odysseus' recognition; indeed, Penelope will set him tests to assure herself of his identity, including the famous test of knowledge of how their marriage bed was constructed. The existence of other possible means of identification makes it only the more significant that the marked body should be the key, and the most dramatic, token of recognition. It is on the body itself that we look for the mark of identity, as writers of popular literature have so well understood. At the close of Alexandre Dumas's thunderous melodrama *La Tour de Nesle*, Buridan rolls back the sleeve of the expiring Gaultier d'Aulnay to reveal to Marguerite de Bourgogne the cross cut into his shoulder by a knife before he was abandoned as an infant on the steps of Notre-Dame Cathedral—thus offering the final revelation that he, like his twin brother Philippe, is the child of Buridan and Marguerite, and that she has committed both incest and infanticide. The example from Dumas' popular play is just one instance of the countless moments in modern literature when recognition takes place through markings made on the body itself. Climactic moments of coming-to-consciousness about one's identity, about the very order of the moral universe, are played out on the body.

The bodily marking not only serves to recognize and identify, it also indicates the body's passage into the realm of the letter, into literature: the bodily mark is in some manner a "character," a hieroglyph, a sign that can eventually, at the right moment of the narrative, be read. Signing the body indicates its recovery for the realm of the semiotic. When Freud comes to read the bodily symptoms of the hysteric as signs of psychic conflict, he brings a specific semiotic analysis to a long tradition of literary as well as medical efforts to make the body signify. Hysterical symptoms are a writing on the body. There are many other forms of such writing, including the sentences inscribed on the body by the torture machine of Franz Kafka's *In the Penal Colony*. The body can be made to bear messages of all kinds. Even more interesting than reading the messages on the body may be the study of their inscription. For the texts that show us the process of inscription give a privileged insight into the ever-renewed struggle of language to make the body mean, the struggle to bring it into writing. Most interesting to me—and this interest has dictated my choice of examples—are those texts that explicitly or implicitly speak of or dramatize the marking or imprinting of the body with meaning, its recreation as a narrative signifier.

What presides at the inscription and imprinting of bodies is, in the broadest sense, a set of desires: a desire that the body not be lost to meaning—that it be brought into the realm of the semiotic and the significant—and, underneath this, a desire for the body itself, an erotic longing to have or to be the body. As Freud's theories of the birth of the epistemophilic urge from the child's curiosity about sexuality suggest, there is an inextricable link between erotic desire and the desire to know. Both converge in writing, and where it concerns writing a body, creating a textual body, the interplay of eros and artistic creation is particularly clear. Among many instances that particularly emblematize that interplay, and that strikingly dramatize the marking and imprinting of the body, perhaps the one with the greatest mythic resonance for the Western literary imagination is that of Pygmalion and Galatea. In Ovid's *Metamorphoses,* the story of Pygmalion is told by Orpheus, and thus is doubly about artistic creation. Pygmalion has turned away from women since he has found too many harlots among them, and devoted himself to a chaste existence. But when he creates a statue "lovelier than any woman born," he falls in love with his own creation.

Pygmalion's relation to the statue of Galatea is at first set within the imaginary order: a relation of *trompe l'oeil* deceptiveness, where he treats the statue as if it were alive: "Often he ran his hands over the work, feeling it to see whether it was flesh or ivory, and would not yet admit that ivory was all it was. He kissed the statue, and imagined that it kissed him back, spoke to it and embraced it, and thought he felt his fingers sink into the limbs he touched, so that he was afraid lest a bruise appear where he had pressed the flesh."[32] He then presents it with gifts and adornments, and places it on a couch, and calls it "his bedfellow." With the coming of the festival of Venus, he prays to the goddess that she give him "one like the ivory maid"—he doesn't dare say "the ivory maid"—as his wife. But Venus, understanding the true object of his desire, produces a metamorphosis of the statue itself. When Pygmalion returns home, and goes to kiss the statue on the couch, 23

> She seemed warm: he laid his lips on hers again, and touched her breast with his hands—at his touch the ivory lost its hardness, and grew soft: his fingers made an imprint on the yielding surface, just as wax of Hymettus melts in the sun and, worked by men's fingers, is fashioned into many different shapes, and made fit for use by being used. The lover stood, amazed, afraid of being mistaken, his joy tempered with doubt, and again and again stroked the object of his prayers. It was indeed a human body! The veins throbbed as he pressed them with his thumb [*Corpus erat! saliunt temptatae pollice venae*]. (10:289)

This moment when the statue becomes flesh—in a scene that will have its Christian version in the *hoc est enim corpus meum*—registers Galatea's coming into existence by way of the throbbing of the blood in her veins under the pressure of Pygmalion's thumb. The word for thumb, *pollice*, concludes a series of words having to do with Pygmalion's touching of the statue: the hands he runs over the statue *(saepe manus operi temptantes admovet)*; the fingers he thinks he feels sink into the limbs he touches, so that he is afraid he has created a bruise *(et credit tactis digitos insidere membris / et metuit, pressos ne veniat ne livor in artus)*; then, at the moment of transformation, the breast yielding to the touch of his hands *(manibus quoque pectora temptat)*; and then the image of his fingers making an imprint on the yielding surface of the breast, as on softening wax *(temptatum mollescit ebur positoque rigore / subsidit digitis ceditque, ut Hymettia sole / cera remollescit tractataque pollice multas / flectitur in facies ipsoque fit utilis usu)*. Hands, fingers, thumbs: they make no imprint on the ivory maiden, except in Pygmalion's momentary hallucination. But when she becomes flesh and blood, they leave their imprint, as in wax; and the thumb then feels the pulse throbbing beneath it.

The play of hands, fingers, thumbs images the artist's mark on his created work. The ivory virgin is of course Pygmalion's artistic handwork, but it remains other, inanimate, until desire is fulfilled by Venus. Then it bears the mark of his fingers, the sign of its shaping by human hands. So imprinted, Galatea opens her eyes and becomes Pygmalion's wife, and then the mother of Paphos, who in turn is the mother of Cinyras, who unwittingly becomes the lover of his own daughter Myrrha, engendering Adonis, who becomes the beloved of Venus. Galatea, then, joins the narrative world of the *Metamorphoses*. It is as if the human imprint on her cold, all-too-perfect and impenetrable body were the necessary marking or signing to make her come alive for narrative—become a vehicle of narrative signification. And she becomes this living, humanly imprinted body precisely because her perfect sculpted body has been the object of intense desire: it is Venus who presides at her animation.

The story of Pygmalion and Galatea has exercised a continuing fascination on the creative imagination because it magnificently represents a crucial wish-fulfillment: the bodily animation of the object of desire. It may suggest that in essence all desire is ultimately desire for a body, one that may substitute for *the* body, the mother's, the lost object of infantile bliss—the body that the child grown up always seeks to recreate.[33] As in the case of Pygmalion, that recreated body realizes simultaneously erotic desire and the creative desire to know and to make. Galatea is a fiction suggestive of that word's derivation from *fingere*, meaning both to feign and to make. She is the supreme fiction that becomes reality as the embodiment of the artist's desire.

The story of Pygmalion and Galatea is in a sense the antithesis of Ovid's story of Narcissus, where the desired body is a vain image in the mirroring pool, an impossible object of desire which leads to sterile narcissism and the desire for death. Pygmalion and Galatea is the story of life, of enlivening, where the object of desire is both created according to one's wants and also other, a legitimate object of desire (though the ensuing story of the incest of Cinyras and Myrrha suggests a kind of return of the repressed, as if a toll had to be exacted for this perfect realization of desire). It is the story of how the body can be known, animated, and possessed by the artist of desire, and of how the body marked, imprinted, by desire can enter narrative. In this manner, it is something of an allegory of the narratives that interest me in the following chapters, which mainly concern, in very differing ways, attempts by a desiring subject to imprint the desired body. That desiring subject may be in the narrative, and is always also the creator of the narrative, whose desire for the body is part of a semiotic project to make the body signify, to make it part of the narrative dynamic. An aesthetics of narrative embodiment insists that the body is only apparently lacking in meaning, that it can be semiotically retrieved. Along with the semioticization of the body goes what we might call the somatization of story: the implicit claim that the body is a key sign in narrative and a central nexus of narrative meanings.

When we move into the modern world, we come upon indications that the individual identity has become newly important and newly problematic, and that the identification of the individual's body is a subject of large cultural concern. The historian Alain Corbin notes that the nineteenth century, in particular, brings a greater diversity in persons' forenames, as if to insist on the distinctive identity of the individual, along with a new mass distribution of the mirror, for self-contemplation, and the democratization of the portrait, once the exclusive appanage of the rich or famous, with the coming of photography.[34] At the same time, societies become more concerned with the identification of individuals within the group, especially in the undifferentiated mass of city dwellers. The identification of malefactors and marginals, such as prostitutes, was an obsessive issue; prostitutes were inscribed on police registers and given a "card" if they were streetwalkers, a "number" if they were in a brothel. When *la marque*—the practice of branding convicts' bodies with letters signifying their sentence—was abolished in France in 1832, various other methods for singling out recidivists were invented: photography, "bertillonage"—the cranial measurements devised by Alphonse Bertillon—and the classification of criminal "types" by Cesare Lombroso. Eventually, fingerprinting—a technique long known to the Bengalis, and discovered by officials of the British Raj—would offer a surer indication of identity. In France and many other countries, various papers, employees' passports, and certificates of residence led to the creation of a national *carte d'identité,* textual authentication of the bearer's claim to a state-specified individuality.

NARRATIVE AND THE BODY

Along with the concern to make some version of the bodily mark—like that by which Eurykleia identified Odysseus—into a universal system of social semiotics and control goes a literature driven by the anxiety and fascination of the hidden, masked, unidentified individual. The invention of the detective story in the nineteenth century testifies to this concern to detect, track down, and identify those occult bodies that have purposely sought to avoid social scrutiny. The shadowy underworld supermen created by Balzac—especially the arch-criminal Jacques Collin, alias Vautrin, alias Reverend Father Carlos Herrera, who undergoes multiple metamorphoses in his war on society—and the demiurgic Abel Magwitch, hidden author of Pip's life in Dickens's *Great Expectations,* and Victor Hugo's Jean Valjean, in *Les misérables,* whose saintly present is always undermined by the return of his convict past, prepare the fiction of Edgar Allan Poe, Gaston Leroux, and Arthur Conan Doyle in which emphasis shifts to the professional decipherer of the hidden identity.

To know the body by way of a narrative that leads to its specific identity, to give the body specific markings that make it recognizable, and indeed make it a key narrative sign, are large preoccupations of modern narrative. If these preoccupations are most fully dramatized in the nineteenth-century novel, they need to be perceived first in the rise of the novel, along with the rise of the modern sense of individualism, in the eighteenth century. The work of social and cultural historians has more and more confirmed our commonsense view that the Enlightenment is the crucible of the modern sense of the individual, the individual's rights, and the private space in which the individual stakes out a claim to introspection, protection, and secrecy, including private practices of sexuality and writing. Modern notions of the individual entail a conception of privacy as that place in which a person can divest himself or herself of the demands of the public and cultivate the irreducibly individual personality. Within this private space, what often appears to be most problematic, interesting, anguishing is the body. It is no accident that the person most often held to offer at least symbolic entry into the modern—and most often held responsible for its catastrophes as well as its more benevolent achievements—is also the first person to write about his own body as a problem. While certainly other confessional writers, notably Saint Augustine and Montaigne, examine problems of the flesh, its concupiscence, its weakness in disease, Jean-Jacques Rousseau appears to me the first who recognizes his body as a problem in the determination of his own life's story, and sets himself the task of giving a narrative account of that problem. It is, then, toward Rousseau, especially his *Confessions,* that I now propose to work, first by way of a consideration of how the very private realm of the body becomes the object of publicity.

2 Invasions of Privacy: The Body in the Novel

> The greatest men, those of the first and most leading taste, will not scruple adorning their private closets with nudities, though, in compliance with vulgar prejudices, they may not think them decent decorations of the staircase, or salon.
>
> John Cleland, *Memoirs of a Woman of Pleasure*

THE RISE OF the novel is closely tied to the rise of the idea of privacy. The condition of privacy characterizes the reading and writing of novels. Perhaps as a consequence of this private production and consumption, private life was from the inception of the genre the novel's subject matter as well—or perhaps it was the other way round: the need to explore the relatively new concept of private experience entailed the invention of the novel. This privacy, as Ian Watt has shown in *The Rise of the Novel,* belongs to a conception of upper- and middle-class leisure and family life that emerged, first in England, and then in France, starting sometime in the seventeenth century, and developed rapidly in the eighteenth century. The notion of privacy is tied to the rise of the modern city, particularly the extension of its residential quarters and suburbs. Privacy is reflected, for instance, in domestic architecture, in the shift from the communal living, eating, and sleeping spaces of the medieval house to the well-demarcated private apartments, boudoirs, "closets," and alcoves of eighteenth-century upper- and middle-class housing. These private spaces supported the realization of new values attached to the individual and to the intimacy required for the individual's commerce with family, friends, and self. Inwardness, increasingly an ideal, required a realignment of modes of existence and practices of writing.[1]

Unlike literary forms that predominated in earlier periods—epic and lyric poetry, and the theater—the novel implies no ideal or tradition of oral recitation, and no communal participation of a live audience. It is indeed the genre for the breakdown of the communal audience, as

Stendhal was to note after he gave up his frustrated attempts to become a playwright because, as he put it, there was no longer the unified society, eager to celebrate its communal values, on which the theater of the Renaissance and the seventeenth century depended for its effects. Reading to oneself, silently, already implies a certain value attached to privacy, a practice of self-communion that may be connected to an ideal of spiritual meditation and pietism deriving from the Reformation, and that depends on the extension of literacy and the concepts of private space and leisure time for intimate experience.[2]

One reads a novel alone, typically in private. One can do so because it is printed in multiple copies which, whether bought or borrowed from the lending library, for the duration of the reading are in one's private possession. This privacy of consumption is made possible, of course, by the public distribution made possible by the modern printing press. Hence the fundamental paradox: the novel that provides this experience of private consumption depends for its manufacture and retailing on mass production, duplication, and the distribution made possible by nascent capitalism—including that most promiscuous of new businesses, advertising. This experience of privacy in reading is of course matched by the privacy of writing, in which one has no immediate live response from the audience of the sort given to the oral storyteller, the epic bard, and even the playwright, particularly when—as was so often the case in the Renaissance and the seventeenth century—the playwright was also an actor who could shape his words and gestures according to the audience's responses. We have learned from anthropologists and linguists that in oral cultures, verbal meaning depends in large measure on the context of the speech act. Writing, and especially writing reproduced in the anonymity of printing, creates instead an "autonomous discourse," detached from its author, belonging strictly to no one.[3] The novelist, like the reader of the novel, must deal with a decontextualized discourse in which the transmission of fact and emotion is not subject to control or verification (one cannot say to the novelist, "What did you mean by that?" and the novelist cannot say, "Do you see what I mean?"). For privacy is also solitude. As Walter Benjamin states, "The reader of a novel . . . is isolated, more so than any other reader."[4] This solitude and isolation make the reading of a novel the most intimate of literary experiences, a transaction without the mediation of actors or speakers, in which one typically feels an empathetic closeness to characters and events.

Private life, private experience, is also the subject of the novel from its very inception. Watt has persuasively argued the connection between the new interest in private experience and the rise of middle-class consciousness, including new values attached to individualism, to the domestic sphere and the private lives of women, and to the Protestant ethic, with its emphasis on the individual's right to a personal interpretation of life and value. Watt is of course talking about England, but one might want to add that even in Catholic countries (Spain, France), and even in literary traditions that remain more closely attached to aristocratic milieux of authorship and readership (France, especially), the matter of the novel typically concerns the private experience of an individual and the problematic relation between this experience and the requirements of the social realm. The emphasis varies, to be sure: an early Spanish picaresque novel, *Lazarillo de Tormes* (1554), shows the individual stripped to his bare essentials, engaged in a struggle to survive, to get food and drink; whereas the first great novel in the French tradition, Madame de Lafayette's *La Princesse de Clèves* (1678), presents an individual whose very being is defined by the demands of public sociability—in a court where everyone is under observation—and who must struggle to define a private realm. It bears noting that in France, virtually at the outset of the eighteenth century, Alain-René Lesage offers a kind of parable of the subject matter of the novel in *Le diable boîteux* (1702), in which the "devil" Asmodée removes the rooftops of a series of Parisian dwellings, in order to make us privy, precisely, to the private lives enacted under them.

The most typical manifestation of this overdetermined privacy of the novel, and no doubt the most important example for the future development of the genre, is of course the works of Samuel Richardson. As Francis Jeffrey commented in the *Edinburgh Review:* "With Richardson, we slip, invisible, into the domestic privacy of his characters, and hear and see every thing that is said and done among them, whether it be interesting or otherwise, and whether it gratify our curiosity or disappoint it."[5] Like Lesage's removal of the rooftops that normally protect privacy, Jeffrey's image of 'slipping invisible' into the domestic privacy of characters' lives suggests another element of the paradox that the novel's concern with privacy is necessarily constituted as an invasion of privacy.

Privacy and its invasion are very much thematized in Richardson's novels: *Pamela* and *Clarissa* dramatize the attempts to violate their heroines' privacy, and the heroines' acts of resistance to that violation are themselves violations of privacy, in that they entail the written revelation of the most inward matters. Scribbling from their "closets"—those most private of rooms—Pamela and Clarissa in their private correspondence lay bare their souls, and thus demonstrate that its readership can turn the most private correspondence into the most public. The dramatic potential of this paradox will be fully exploited later in the century by Choderlos de Laclos in *Les liaisons dangereuses,* an epistolary novel in which those characters who understand the nature of correspondence control the reading of letters; they make sure that certain private letters obtain a public reading, for instance, and write other letters as *double-entendres* that will be read in radically differing senses by different readers. The Marquise de Merteuil and the Vicomte de Valmont encode various readers' responses in the very writing of letters, in acts of linguistic proteanism. As the *Avertissement* to that novel tells us, almost all of the emotions recorded in the correspondence are "feigned or dissimulated," which means that the revelation of the private may not be immediately apparent—that every letter must be subject to a kind of double reading that must take into account more than anything else the intended effect of revelation of the letter. The familiar or intimate letter provided novelists with a model for recording private life and consciousness—Richardson began his career by writing epistolary models for a newly literate middle class; Marivaux in France defined the stylistic level of the novel in terms of the *style noble familier* used in correspondence—and they quickly learned to exploit both the intimacy of the letter and the violation of that intimacy that comes from making a story from the exchange of correspondence.

The thematics of privacy invaded and revealed are not confined to the epistolary novel, as *Le diable boîteux* demonstrates, and also *La Princesse de Clèves,* a novel which famously turns on a confession, the *aveu* of Madame de Clèves to her husband of her love for Monsieur de Nemours which she will resist revealing to its object throughout the novel. Nemours, in a central moment of the novel, steals the miniature portrait of his beloved, in a symbolic violation of privacy that prefigures Clarissa's rape by Lovelace. But Madame de Clèves is able to resist violation. Indeed, her whole existence becomes predicated on resistance to the prying demands of court life, its insistence on public enactment and its subjection of everyone's private life and feelings to the penetrating gaze, *le regard.* By the end of the novel, following her husband's death, she can assure her integrity only through retreat from the court, the choice of *le repos*—absence and quietude—over love. The novel dramatizes an agonized conflict between the invasion of privacy and the protection of privacy, which can be maintained finally only through silence and self-effacement—by definition unnarratable, which means the novel must end.

The novel, then, can make private life the object of its concern only through invading the private sphere by opening it up to the irrevocable publicity of writing—imaged so often in the eighteenth-century novel by the publication of a private correspondence.[6] Novelists demonstrate again and again that they are acutely conscious of this paradox through their thematizations of the struggle of privacy and its invasions. These struggles often take the form of an attempted male invasion of a female private sphere, with all the sexual imagery of unveiling, stripping bare, and penetration that accompanies it. Madame de Clèves' joint refusal of Nemours' suit and of the publicity of court life marks an exemplary understanding of the nature of the private sphere and that which violates it. The rape of Clarissa offers the other, more frequent scenario: the destruction of the woman's space, her very being, by the male's violent penetration. Pamela's successful negotiation of Mr. B's attempts to invade her private sphere of being, accomplished by convincing him to subscribe to a bourgeois ethic of marriage which redefines the private sphere in terms of a social institution—marriage not as simply the (feudal) alliance of genealogies and fortunes, but as a union of affection and regard—produces the happy or comedic outcome, which would have a durable life in the genre. The outcome of *Les liaisons dangereuses,* where the collected correspondence of the characters circulates among fashionable society and provokes a hypocritical rejection of everything that society has been shown to believe and to practice, marks a kind of limit-case of privacy become public, resulting in a confusion of realms revealing the moral chaos of the world represented.

The dynamic of privacy and its invasion may suggest why the novel, no doubt from its inception, and notoriously in the eighteenth century, gave a large place to the erotic and to the pornographic. For what is ultimately more private—in the dominant bourgeois ethic, at least—than the sexual life? The closets and boudoirs in which Richardson's and Laclos' characters indite their epistles are suggestive of the amorous alcove, and their epistles themselves assume or reabsorb that sexuality which the very situation of letter writing—the separation of the correspondents—makes it, for the moment, impossible for them to bring to action. What in Richardson and Laclos is invested in the letter becomes, in other novelists, the investment of the letter in sexual life.

Many of the erotic novels of the eighteenth century explicitly concern the opening up of the private life, indeed the hidden life, to writing. For instance, *Le sopha,* by Crébillon *fils,* uses as its central narrative device the spirit which serially inhabits several sofas and recounts the amorous transactions performed on them, like a pre-technological bugging device that invades people's privacy when they are least aware of being over- 33 heard or observed, and most anxious not to be. Still more to the point is Diderot's *Les bijoux indiscrets,* in which a magic ring has the power of making women's sexual parts speak despite themselves, and reveal those very stories that the women most would like to keep hidden. One might also evoke in this context the scene of Fanny Hill's initiation, in John Cleland's *Memoirs of a Woman of Pleasure,* where she watches a sexual encounter through an aperture from the "dark closet" in which she is concealed. These novels, and so many others of the time, constitute the class of texts that Jean-Jacques Rousseau described as "books that can only be read with one hand." Rousseau thus figures the ultimate privacy and intimacy, not only of the subject of such novels, but also of the scene of their reading.

What ultimately is to be revealed in the invasions of privacy that constitute the novel of private life may be what Henry James would call "the great relation" between men and women, but may be also—even beyond that—the body itself, typically in moments of sexual quickening, since in these moments it becomes most charged with meaning and narratable energy, but also in other forms of rebellion against the mind, in sickness, pain, hysteria, mortal combat. In other words, the novel of private life is not only about psychological subjectivity, the inner life of the soul, but as well about what was increasingly coming to be considered as the most private of affairs, the individual's body. For the body itself is subject to the process of privatization, becoming less a subject of public discourse and open display, more a hidden object coquettishly shown and the object of insatiable curiosity—a process that would evolve further in the next century, as the female body, in particular, became more and more heavily covered with layers of garments and social taboos.[7] In eighteenth-century France, the erotic tradition demonstrates the point most obviously, and its paroxysm in the works of the Marquis de Sade shows the naked body become the sole place on which significance can be inscribed: the only space of writing. But the more decorous middle-class tradition of Richardson also makes the body the ultimate place of the semiotic. As some of Richardson's best recent commentators have suggested, Clarissa's body becomes the site on which the aspirations, anxieties, and contradictions of a whole society are played out.[8]

1. Jean-Honoré Fragonard, *La chemise enlevée*. (Paris: Louvre. Photo © R.M.N.)

The eighteenth-century fascination with nudity, which extends, for instance, to its discourse on the "savage state" and the natives of the newly discovered Tahiti, suggests this concern with the body as the final integer of reality and meaning: that which you find when all the veils are stripped away. We may recall the contemporary memorialist and novelist Duclos' remark that truth is female, and naked, and that it is thus "from a secret love of Truth that we pursue women with such ardor; we seek to strip them of everything that we think hides the Truth." Furthermore, the rise of materialism as a philosophical position made the body, in the absence of any transcendent principle beyond nature, the substance to which any metaphysical speculation must ultimately return as the precondition of mind.

The visual arts in the eighteenth century offer many examples of unveiling, from the decorously allegorical to the intimate, such as Jean-Honoré Fragonard's *Le feu aux poudres* and *La chambre à coucher* and *La chemise enlevée* (ca. 1765), which self-consciously conceive representation as a moment of penetration into a situation of privacy (Figure 1).

The effect of these representations depends on the apparent security of the subjects, the women, seemingly protected by privacy at the very moment when, in the act of unveiling or of representation itself, that figured privacy is being stripped away. In *La chemise enlevée,* spectatorship is itself analogous to the act of pulling off the woman's shift, with the spectator's vision substituting for that of the obscured figure performing the act, which appears to be momentarily blocked by the shift itself. Spectatorship is made complicit with a violation of intimate space.[9] Still more interesting to consider are reactions to visual representations that do not explicitly unveil, but rather challenge the spectator—certain spectators, at least—to imagine what lies beneath the represented, to perform the unveiling. One finds some notable instances in Denis Diderot's reactions to the paintings of Jean-Baptiste Greuze—paintings ostensibly devoted to the new bourgeois ethic of privacy, domesticity, sensibility, and sentiment, but nonetheless charged by a certain ambivalent eroticism, especially in the representation of adolescent girls captured on what appears to be the verge of unconscious passage into adult sexuality. Diderot's method of reading such paintings, for instance Greuze's *Jeune fille qui pleure son oiseau mort* (Girl weeping for her dead bird), is to make explicit that passage into sexuality that the subject ostensibly denies, by unfolding a kind of fictive invasion of her privacy (Figure 2).

In his *Salon of 1765,* Diderot waxes rapturous over this painting: "The pretty elegy! The charming poem! . . . Delicious painting! The most agreeable and perhaps the most interesting of the Salon."[10] Following a few lines describing the pose of the figure, Diderot's prose seems to mimic the coyness, even cuteness, of Greuze's sentimental representation: "Oh, the pretty hand! The pretty hand! The beautiful arm! Notice the truthful details of these fingers; and these dimples, and this softness, and this blushing tint with which the pressure of the head has colored the tips of these delicate fingers, and the charm of all this." The praise of the painting slides into praise of its subject, becoming yet more animated, and perhaps more suspect: "One would move closer to this hand in order to kiss it, if one didn't respect this child and her pain." It then focuses on the kerchief that covers her bosom: "This kerchief is thrown on the neck in such a fashion! So supple and light! When one sees this detail, one says, *Delicious!* If one stops to look at it, or returns to it, one exclaims: *Delicious! delicious!* Soon one finds oneself conversing with this child, consoling her."

As in his reaction to Richardson's novels, Diderot has now written

2. Jean-Baptiste Greuze, *Jeune fille qui pleure son oiseau
   mort*. (Edinburgh: National Gallery of Scotland)

himself into the world represented in Greuze's painting, becoming a
participant rather than a mere observer.[11] There ensues a three-page
dialogue with the girl—in which the girl's part consists mainly of revelatory movements, glances, gestures—where Diderot postulates that the
real cause of her dreamy and melancholic attitude is not the simple death
of her pet bird, but a more intimate, and unavowable, drama. Her
weeping for the bird is a displacement of affect: she is really weeping
over a "fault," which has to do with the visit of a young lover during
her mother's absence. Diderot implies that she has ceded to the lover's
demands. Will he be true? And didn't your mother's tenderness to you,
when she returned, simply increase your sense of shame? As the scenario
continues, the bird is imagined to have died from lack of food and water
since the girl has been so preoccupied with her lover. Perhaps the lover
gave her the bird. Then the bird's death becomes an omen of the death
of love. So that by the end the dead bird has been reinvested with

symbolic affect, now of a more momentous sort, concerning the girl's passage into adult sexuality.

Diderot finds the girl "interesting," and notes: "I don't like to give distress; in spite of that, I would not be displeased to be the cause of her pain" (536). Here he has at last imagined himself into the role of the girl's lover, as part of the intimate prehistory and cause of the represented scene. The adjective *intéressante,* applied to young women, has a long history in both sentimental and erotic literature, and in both cases suggests that the signs of suffering, linked to erotic constraint, make the object of attention more appealing. Diderot, in dismissing the opinion of observers who think the girl is really weeping over the death of her canary, refers us to an earlier Greuze painting, *Le miroir cassé* (The broken mirror), which, like *La cruche cassée* (The broken pitcher) more overtly depicts the emotion caused by loss of innocence. Would a girl of her age weep for a dead canary? This leads Diderot to ask himself the question which any viewer of these Greuze paintings at some point inevitably raises: "But what age is she, then?" He notes that her head suggests fifteen or sixteen years old, her arm and hand eighteen or nineteen. Such ambiguities permeate Greuze's representations of his young women, who are in transition from the protected space of childhood to an adult privacy subject to violation.

As such, the young women lend themselves admirably to the creation of narrative on the part of the observer. Diderot exerts pressure on the painting's subject of a minor domestic episode in order to move beneath and beyond what is presented to the viewer; he opens up a yet more intimate sphere which he coyly but unremittingly violates, inventing a narrative of sexual initiation played out on the girl's body that the still image of the painting both conceals and suggests. The very privacy of the subject depicted in the painting appears to elicit a desire on the part of the observer to penetrate and violate that privacy, to make public that which the painting would keep reticent about. That the girl is represented as unconscious of the spectator's gaze may be an invitation for that gaze to penetrate and violate. One may ask how much the invitation to the violation of privacy is "in" Greuze's painting, and how much is the product of Diderot as observer. The question is unanswerable, but one may want to surmise, from this example as well as from the literary ones mentioned earlier, that the notion of privacy is consubstantial with the idea of its violation. Constituted against the prying gaze of the world, privacy necessarily recognizes—factors in, as it were—that gaze, as part of its need to be veiled. So we know privacy by way of its

THE BODY IN THE NOVEL

invasion, just as we know innocence by way of its loss, and indeed could not know it otherwise.

Rousseau's Private Bodies

The person who best understood this difficult dialectics of privacy and invasion, and who most clearly perceived that at stake is ultimately the place and the meaning of the body, was Jean-Jacques Rousseau. In gestures that are interdependent, Rousseau radically invades privacy—most notably his own—and gives the body an importance in the generation and inscription of meaning, thereby marking a profound turning point in the history of consciousness. The body itself, in its affects and arousals, becomes both a place where meaning is enacted and a creator of meanings—meanings of a kind that can be created nowhere else. The body is made semiotic: it becomes a sign, or the place for the inscription of multiple signs. (We may recall that semiotics was originally a branch of medical science, as old as Hippocrates, concerned with symptoms or signs that told the story of an illness.) In turn the body thus semioticized becomes a key element in narrative meanings; it carries the burden of significance of a story. Once again, semioticization of the body is accompanied by the somatization of story.

I shall begin not with Rousseau's novel *La nouvelle Héloïse,* though I'll come to that, but with his *Confessions,* which in many ways has more to do with the future history of the novel than does his epistolary novel. To confess, of course, is to promise the revelation of that which is most secret. Confession is a central act in the violation of privacy, and the notorious *aveu* of Madame de Clèves to her husband—the aspect of Madame de Lafayette's novel that contemporary critics most argued about—is emblematic of how important confession is to our sense of getting at the most private realm. Rousseau's notion of avowal, confession, self-revelation is intimately linked to his claims about the bodiliness of certain of his life's central meanings. Rousseau's first *aveu* concerning his own body comes early in Book 1 of the *Confessions,* and it is described, just after it has been made, as "the first step and the most painful in the obscure and slimy labyrinth of my confessions."[12] He goes on: "From now on I am sure of myself: after what I have just dared to say, nothing else can stop me."

The confession concerns his spanking by Mlle Lambercier, the sister of the minister Lambercier who had been charged with his education, at what he claims was the age of eight, though modern scholars think he must have been eleven. This punishment, which the young Jean-Jacques anticipates with terror, in fact brings other feelings: he found "in the pain, even in the shame, an admixture of sensuality that had left me more desire than fear to experience it again from the same hand" (15). He waits, then, without fear for a recurrence, and when it comes, "I profited from it." He continues: "This second time was also the last, for Mlle Lambercier, noticing no doubt from some sign that this punishment was not achieving its purpose, declared that she gave it up and that it tired her too much. We [his cousin Bernard and himself] had up till then slept in her room, and in winter sometimes even in her bed. Two days later we were made to sleep in another room. I henceforth had the honor, which I would gladly have passed up, to be treated by her as a big boy." The "sign" by which Mlle Lambercier perceives that her spanking is producing the wrong result never is specified. We may safely assume from the context that is the sign of sexual arousal.

Rousseau is describing, then, what we would now understand as the creation of an erogenous zone. His body has been signed by the spanking; it has had the place of the erotic signifier designated on it. Rousseau goes on, in a remarkable piece of self-analysis, to describe how this branding of his body by the erotic signifier determined his sexual orientation for the rest of his life. "Who would believe that this childhood punishment, received at the age of eight from the hand of a woman of thirty, determined my tastes, my desires, my passions, my self for the rest of my life?" When he reaches adolescence, he tells us, "Long tormented without knowing by what, I devoured pretty women with an ardent eye; my imagination recalled them to me ceaselessly, only to put them to work in my fashion, and to make of them so many Mademoiselles Lambercier." And when he reached adulthood, "My old childish taste, instead of vanishing, so associated itself with the other, that I could never disassociate it from the desires aroused by my senses" (17). Since he cannot bring himself to express what he wants, "I have thus passed my life in coveting and remaining silent with the persons I loved the most. Never daring to declare my craving, I entertained it at least by relations that preserved the idea for me. To be at the knees of an imperious mistress, to obey her orders, to ask her forgiveness, were for me sweet pleasures, and the more my lively imagination inflamed my blood, the more I had the look of a lover transfixed."

In other words, the marking of Rousseau's eight- or eleven-year-old body by the signifier of the erotic has a determining force in the narrative of the rest of his life. Freud would comment, rather sententiously, on this episode in 1905, in his *Three Essays on the Theory of Sexuality:* "Ever since Jean-Jacques Rousseau's *Confessions,* it has been well known to all educationalists that the painful stimulation of the skin of the buttocks is one of the erotogenic roots of the *passive* instinct of cruelty (masochism). The conclusion has rightly been drawn by them that corporal punishment, which is usually applied to this part of the body, should not be inflicted upon any children whose libido is liable to be forced into collateral channels by the later demands of cultural education" (*Standard Edition* 7:193). Freud's language here in fact recapitulates Rousseau's own statement, "How one would change one's method with children, if one saw better the far-removed effects of the method used always without discrimination, and often without discretion!" (14). Rousseau is clearly an example of someone whose libido has been forced into Freud's "collateral channels," a phrase which provides an image of the organizing lines (the "obscure and slimy labyrinth") of his narrative of his "deviant" private life. Freud moreover at the beginning of his chapter on "Infantile Sexuality"—which contains the comment on Rousseau—makes a general statement about narrative causality that stresses the importance of Rousseau's discovery about himself: "It is noticeable that writers who concern themselves with explaining the characteristics and reactions of the adult have devoted much more attention to the primaeval period which is comprised in the life of the individual's ancestors—have, that is, ascribed much more influence to heredity—than to the other primaeval period, which falls within the lifetime of the individual himself—that is, to childhood."

Rousseau, in a remarkable piece of archeological excavation (to use one of Freud's favorite analogies), finds in the primeval period of his own life an explanation for what he characterizes variously as a "strange taste," a "depravity," and a "madness," which gives a specific orientation to his sexuality for the rest of his life. Throughout the *Confessions,* there are repetitions and returns of this motif: in relation to a certain Mlle Goton, for instance, with whom he had "private meetings that were quite short, but quite animated, in which she deigned to play the role of the schoolmistress, and that was all, but that all, which in reality was all for me, seemed to me the supreme happiness" (27); or much later, in his unconsummated relation to Madame d'Houdetot. Not only his explicitly sexual life, but his character—his timidity, his incapacity to express his desires, even his revulsion at unjust punishment and his subsequent rejection of all forms of tyranny—are to be linked to his childhood punishment. In other words, the narrative of his life depends in an important way on the original marking of his body, on what he calls "the first traces of my sensible being" (18). Confession leads us to the marking of private parts of the body, and these are held to determine the whole future narrative.

The private parts of Rousseau's body—and especially his bottom— 41 are explicitly at issue in other episodes of the *Confessions* as well. At the start of Book 3, we find Rousseau, an adolescent in Turin, dreaming of a woman who would give him a quarter of an hour like the one with Mlle Goton. But the years have brought a sense of shame, and an increase in his timidity. Rousseau instead seeks dark alleyways where he can expose himself to women "in the state in which I would have wished to be in their company. What they saw was not the obscene object, I didn't even give that a thought; it was the ridiculous object" (89). The passage, in the coded language that Rousseau generally uses to talk of his erogenous zones, suggests that it is backside rather than penis that he exposes—the "object" specified by Mlle Lambercier's punishment, which is thus retrospectively confirmed in its determinative force. The desired punishment never comes, however. Instead, one day, he exposes himself in a courtyard where serving girls come to draw water from the well, having first ascertained that there are deep cellars leading off the courtyard in which to hide. Although he offers what he describes as "a spectacle more laughable than seductive," some of the girls are offended, and call for a man. Rousseau retreats into the labyrinthine cellars. He is pursued. Instead of reaching deeper darkness, he comes out in a lighted portion of the cellar, and is brought up short by a blank wall. The man— "a big man wearing a big moustache, a big hat, a big sword," escorted by a number of the women—seizes him and demands an explanation. Thus pushed to the wall, Rousseau has recourse to what he calls "un expédient romanesque": a novelistic invention, a fiction. He recounts that he is a young foreigner of high birth whose mind is deranged, that he has escaped from his father's house because he was going to be locked up, that he will be done for if his identity is made known, and that he can perhaps some day reward an act of grace. Contrary to his expectations, the fiction works: the man lets him go.

Rousseau's exposure of the erotically marked part of his body is here directly linked to the capacity (and the necessity) to create fictions, to tell stories about his life as it might have been. The whole scenario here—exposure in the corner of a courtyard surrounding a communal well, retreat into dark cellars which end in light and a blocked passage, discovery effaced by the creation of a fictive identity and history—

suggests a sexualized geography and an allegory of sexual self-discovery, which deviates into fiction, as indeed, Freud tells us, all sexuality does, since it inevitably reposes on unconscious, infantile-determined scenarios of fulfillment. According to Freud in the *Three Essays,* all sexuality can be considered "perverted" in that satisfaction is never a matter of simple genital utility, but always consubstantial with the imaginary and the phantasmatic. Rousseau in this passage tells us that self-exposure leads not to a simple or direct act of self-recognition, but rather to a deviated recognition of self in the fictional story. If self-exposure is an analogue of confession—and thus the whole of the *Confessions* a literary enactment of the scene in Turin—what one confesses is not direct or simple, but a fictionalization of experience in which phantasy plays a large part, as it does in the choice of that marked part of the body that is exposed.

Rousseau connects the erogenous body to fiction-making in a more classic way when he later describes his masturbatory reveries on his return from Italy, when he has learned "ce dangereux supplément qui trompe la nature" (109): "this dangerous supplement that cheats on nature." He notes that "this vice that shame and timidity find so convenient has moreover a great advantage for the intense imagination: that is, to dispose, as it were, at its will, of the whole female sex, and to make the beauty that tempts it serve its pleasure without having to obtain its consent"—its *aveu.* This recalls a passage from Book 1, where Rousseau describes how, having exhausted the stock of the local lending-library, his imagination appeased his nascent sensuality by "nourishing itself with the situations that had interested me in my readings, recalling them, varying them, combining them, and appropriating them to such an extent that I became one of the characters that I was imagining, and always saw myself in the positions most agreeable to my wishes" (41). Both auto-eroticism and fictive imagining are means of appropriating and disposing of women, and, especially, of putting oneself in the position of pleasure. As Jacques Derrida has demonstrated, for Rousseau the "dangerous supplement" characterizes writing as a whole, as the mediated state of language, the double substitution of words for things and signs for words, as the possibility of error and deceit.[13] Yet the written word is also the condition of Rousseau's first uninterrupted "consciousness of myself" (8), which comes in reading—as his consciousness of the connective "channels" of his life's narrative comes in the awakening of sexuality through punishment. The linguistic state of mediation, duplicity, and fictionality is directly connected to that original mark on Rousseau's backside. The need to narrate both his own life, including its scenarios of desire and fulfillment, and the fictions he invents—philosophical and novelistic—bring us back to the irreducible signifier inscribed on the body.

This is made clear once again when, in Book 9 of the *Confessions*, Rousseau describes the genesis of his novel *La nouvelle Héloïse*. Nearly forty-five years old, Rousseau has withdrawn from Paris to the isolation of the Ermitage. He falls into a kind of erotic revery, in which he evokes the women he knew during his youth (most never possessed) and pleasures himself from his memories. "I found myself surrounded by a harem of houris . . . My blood takes fire and boils, my head is turned despite its grey hairs" (427). Having no outlet in reality for the state of intense passion he works himself into, he throws himself instead into "le pays des chimères,"the world of fictions, imagining a correspondence among two charming young women and a young man, tutor to one of them, with whom he explicitly identifies. In the midst of his dreamlike composition of the novel, he will be visited by Sophie d'Houdetot, whom he promptly invests with all the erotic charge of his fiction, making her the object of a love which he arranges never to fulfill—since, he tells us, the mere thought of the kiss he would receive from her, upon visiting her, was enough to provoke a kind of hallucinatory revery ending in masturbation.[14] The erotic has been fully invested in the fictional.

The body in *La nouvelle Héloïse* is strongly marked by phantasmatic erotic investments. It is the place where scenarios of desire, fulfillment, censorship, and repression are played out. During the course of the novel, the body ostensibly progresses from an erotic to a political definition, as the society of Clarens is constituted under the watchful eye of the austere Wolmar, the husband Julie takes in an arranged marriage following her "fault" with her tutor, Saint-Preux. But the erotic is always just below the surface, and at the last it reasserts its claim on pleasure *(jouissance)* from beyond the grave, in Julie's testamentary letter, which confirms that the work of repression and sublimation has failed. I want to attend to a single passage of the novel, which I think tells in a complex way of the importance of the body in the discovery of privacy, and which prefigures much of the discourse of the body in the nineteenth-century novel.

My text is Letter 54 of Part 1, from Saint-Preux to Julie, written from her "cabinet" where he is awaiting their nighttime rendezvous, in which he will finally become her lover. The whole letter thus is animated by his desire, which supplies the very principle of organization of its descriptive rhetoric. The opening of the letter makes it clear that Saint-

Preux has reached the inner sanctum of Julie's privacy: "I come full of an emotion that grows on entering this retreat. Julie! Here I am in your closet, here I am in the sanctuary of everything my heart adores" (J'arrive plein d'une émotion qui s'accroît en entrant dans cet asile. Julie! me voici dans ton cabinet, me voici dans le sanctuaire de tout ce que mon coeur adore).[15] He goes on to describe the charm of this "mysterious dwelling place." It is full of Julie, her perfume, her "vestiges." Julie's presence is signaled most of all by the pieces of her clothing scattered about, each of which brings to mind the part of the body it normally hides: "All the pieces [literally: the parts] of your scattered clothing present to my ardent imagination the parts of yourself that they hide" (Toutes les parties de ton habillement éparses présentent à mon ardente imagination celles de toi-même qu'elles recèlent). This sentence suggests that the rhetoric of the passage relies on the metonymical naming typical of eighteenth-century erotic literature, which generally designates body parts in a language which remains elegant and "proper" while allowing for easy decoding. The pieces of Julie's clothing are, so to speak, literalized metonymies, metonymical *objects,* which give a particularly vivid presence to the bodily parts they do not name but do reveal, as that which they normally cover, and which—by the fact that they are not now *on* the body—they now uncover. This suggests, among other things, the extent to which Rousseau looks toward later novels in the "realist" tradition, which are typified by their use of metonymy and synecdoche, the use of concrete details in the creation of character traits and plot.[16] One could also say—especially as the letter continues—that Saint-Preux's approach to Julie's body is fetishistic, investing in accessory objects the source of pleasure, masking the absent phallus of the mother by the choice of an erotically signifying substitute. In fact (as I shall propose later) the principle of most narrative approaches to the body could be considered fetishistic, because they so often involve detours by way of accessory objects. What may be most remarkable in this passage is the way the absent body is reconstituted and animated through the present pieces of clothing.

Saint-Preux goes on to detail the "parts" of Julie's dress: her bonnet, which only "feigns" to cover her blond hair; "this happy kerchief" (*cet heureux fichu),* which hides the shoulders and bosom, "about which for once I won't have to complain"; "this elegant and simple négligé which marks so well the taste of the one who wears it; these darling slippers that a shapely foot fills so easily; this delicate corset that touches and embraces . . . such an enchanting figure! . . . in front two slight contours

. . . O voluptuous sight! . . . the whalebone has given way from the pressure . . . Delicious imprints, let me kiss you a thousand times! Ye gods, what will it be when . . . Ah! Already I feel this tender heart beat beneath a happy hand!" The passage is built on a series of words designating the mark of Julie's body on the articles of clothing. While the first use of "mark"—"marque si bien le goût de celle qui le porte"— is relatively abstract, it sets up the series composed of *remplit* (the foot that fills the slipper), *touche, embrasse, a cédé,* and finally, in summary, *empreintes délicieuses,* the mark of Julie's breasts on her corset.   45

Now, it so happens that the term used by Rousseau for corset (as was the usage of the time) is *le corps.* The corset is a body, one that "embraces" and gives form to the body, and in turn takes its shape from the body. Viewed from the inside, it gives the form of the body in its "imprint," as its mold or negative. Thus Saint-Preux perceives Julie's breasts in their "delicious imprints" on the corset, their volume marked by the fact that the structuring whalebone has given way under their pressure. (One could contrast this passage with Saint-Preux's later disparaging comment on Parisiennes, who by their tightly laced corsets attempt to make it appear that they have firmer bosoms than is in fact the case—using the corset to structure rather than having it structured by the body.) Julie's corset is like a sculptor's mold for the casting of a body—with the body itself, in this case, also the molding, creative force.

One might read in Saint-Preux's ecstasy over the corset a discreet trace of the story of Pygmalion and Galatea, a story dear to Rousseau's heart: he wrote a new species of opera he labeled "mélodrame" entitled *Pygmalion.* The key moment of that opera comes when Pygmalion, trembling with desire, unveils the statue in his studio, and decides that the sculpted draperies hide Galatea's bosom too much. It is when he takes his mallet and chisel to uncover Galatea's breasts that he feels under his hand "la chair palpitante": Galatea in her moment of metamorphosis into living flesh.[17] Like Pygmalion, Saint-Preux is the artist of desire who wants to give flesh to his erotic dream. But Saint-Preux doesn't have before him the "ivory maiden" of Ovid's tale; he has only the mold and impress from which to create the body itself.

"Le corps de Julie," the article of clothing, as metonymy enables us to read "le corps de Julie," the real thing, in its reversed image (as in the *camera obscura*), as an imprint. This serves as an effective image of language in relation to desire and to the body as object of desire: language captures only the imprint or impress of the body, its presence by way of its absence. One could read here a representation of representation itself, as the imprint of things by way of signs—as "reality" known by way of desire, with its ultimate integer, the desired body, signed as an absent presence and a present absence through language. Saint-Preux's writing can say not the body itself—the passage is notably full of ellipses, and the night of love that follows will not be directly described—but only its imprint, somewhat in the manner of the imprint Rousseau received on his own body from Mlle Lambercier's punishment. It is the mark on the body or the mark of the body signed by arousal and desire that mark the passage of the body from non-representationality into writing.

It is significant that at this point Saint-Preux feels the need explicitly to give a motivation for the fact that he is writing, in a situation where writing must seem quite out of place—although perhaps in a deeper sense it is profoundly motivated: according to the scenario of Rousseau's *Essai sur l'origine des langues,* not need but passion presides at the creation of language itself. Saint-Preux tells us that he has fortunately found ink and paper in Julie's closet, and that he is writing out his feelings in order to "cheat my emotions in describing them." This follows immediately on the last sentence of the paragraph from which I have quoted, in which he says that waiting for her in such a place is intolerable. "O come, fly to me, or I am lost." Saint-Preux seems on the point of succumbing to his own use of what Stendhal would very impolitely criticize as Rousseau's "style branlant," his masturbatory style, which may here appear as that manner of writing, and need for writing, which is the origin of writing itself. Julie then enters, to put her body in the place of its imprint, to supersede writing; and the letter comes to an end.

I have dwelt at some length on the mark applied to Rousseau's body, and on the mark left by Julie's body, because these markings appear to be key moments in the creation of a modern semiotics of the body that will have an important history in the nineteenth- and twentieth-century novel. It is as if the body could not take a place in narrative writing without first being "initialized" (to use a bit of jargon from computer technology) by way of a mark, to indicate that it has become capable of receiving the imprint of messages. It has been signed; it has become signifiable and indeed itself a signifier. In a tradition strongly marked by the Cartesian analysis of mind and body we tend to think of the body as that which is most recalcitrant to spirit, as the other of signifying practices. At the same time, we know that the body itself is a cultural construct, and indeed a phantasmatic construct, since our ways of conceiving it and its parts originate in infantile scenarios of want and gratification. To divide the somatic from the psychic, including the imaginary and the symbolic, is ultimately impossible. And yet, we are at the same time naive realists about the body, of necessity: need, pain, illness and mortality ever remind us of the limits of somatic compliance with the psychic. Bringing the body into the field of the signifiable, making it an actor in the process of semiosis, seems to require recognizable moments of marking.

47

The body, or a part of the body, becomes a place for the inscription of messages preeminently through scenarios of desire, which endow bodily parts with an erotic history and thus with narrative possibilities. In the *Confessions,* Rousseau's body is a key signifier in the narrative of his life because of its initialization by Mlle Lambercier's spanking. In *La nouvelle Héloïse*—in a more complex scenario—Julie's body becomes the obsessive object of a massive writing project originating from its presentation by way of its impress or imprint, so that it becomes a kind of allegory of the relation of representation to desire and its objects. The prime modern theoretician of the body as semiotic, Freud, would of course largely confirm such a view of the body. Starting from his work on hysteria as a problem in representation—where unconscious desire, unavailable to the conscious subject, plays out its stories through its imprint on the body—Freud insists on conceiving the body as a talking body. Jacques Lacan, rethinking Freud in the terms of modern linguistics, stresses the figural nature of desire and symptom, as different positions of the signifier in relation to the signified unavailable to the conscious mind.

But long before Freud comes on the scene, the body, made semiotic through its marking, becomes a key organizing element in narratives. This seems almost inevitable when one considers that in the modern novel desire provides the protagonist's motivating drive and the whole subtending dynamic of the narrative. One could find further examples from the late eighteenth century in Diderot's *La religieuse,* Laclos' *Les liaisons dangereuses,* and the texts of Sade—which give us marking in its paroxystic form. The whole point of "Philosophy in the Boudoir"— the title could be given to most of Sade's texts—is to make the body the scene of discourse. Sade's libertines must articulate fully the outrageous acts they perform on and with the body: logos and body must be shown to be inseparable. And yet, since in some sense they are not—the limits of the body resist the excessive ambitions of Sadean language—Sade's writing becomes interminable, an endlessly repetitive speaking of recombinations of the same thing. Sade's work stands in an interesting relation to contemporaneous discourses of the body created by the politics of the French Revolution, which conferred on the individual's body a new responsibility and held it accountable to the state in unprecedented ways.

This will be the topic of discussion in the next chapter, along with the novels of Balzac, which stage over and over again scenes where the body is marked in order to assure its function as narrative signifier. Balzac indeed attempted somewhat fumblingly to work out a semiotics of the personal and social body in the fragmentary texts that he intended to collect under the title *Pathologie de la vie sociale:* texts about how people reveal themselves through their clothing, accessories, and bodily movements. The enterprise prefigures Freud's *Psychopathology of Everyday Life,* which is his most comprehensive statement of the body's multiple signifying effects.

The historian Carlo Ginzburg has pointed out the enduring importance of a little-discussed form of knowing by way of traces, clues, and marks—following a track left by a criminal, for instance. Ginzburg derives this kind of knowing from the lore of the hunter, who tracks the passage of his prey through hoofprints, broken twigs, droppings, and other such traces. Following these metonymies—parts for wholes, results for the cause—the hunter follows a narrative path to his quarry. "Perhaps," writes Ginzburg, "the very idea of narrative (as distinct from the incantation, from conjuring or the invocation) was first born in a society of hunters, from the experience of deciphering traces."[18] This age-old kind of knowing takes on a renewed importance in the detective story, and in the work of Freud, who also follows a narrative path by way of traces left by infantile imprints and the history of unconscious desire. And I think it is characteristic of the nineteenth-century novel as a whole, with its plots of education and recognition and its presentation of reality as enigmatic, requiring an inquest into the nature of its signs in order to decipher them. These inquests often lead to discovery of the importance of a certain body that takes on special meaning, as goal, origin, or both: a body that becomes the signifier of signifiers. It is very often the body of the beloved, but not always. It can be the apparently deviant body of an assumed malefactor—Balzac's Collin, Dickens' Magwitch—or the sexually deviant body of the adulteress (Emma Bovary, Anna Karenina) or the prostitute (in Balzac, in Eugène Sue, in Dostoevsky), or the problematic body of the protagonist himself (Stendhal's impotent hero in *Armance,* Kafka's hero transformed into a monstrous vermin). We are led to believe—perhaps we do believe—that meaning lies deep within a veiled private realm, and that the most private part of that realm is simply the human body.

Privacy, the Law, and the Body

Our modern sense of the body and its private meanings has its proximate origins in the Enlightenment, whose definitions of the individual in society, as my examples have suggested and as the work of social historians confirms, are still current in Western societies. In good measure, their currency has to do with their shaping force in the creation of modern legal codes and the making of constitutions that are still, with whatever modifications, in effect. I mention this because my reflections on privacy may have some bearing on current debates in the United States about whether or not the Constitution implies a "right to privacy" that dictates that decisions concerning the body, particularly in its sexual and reproductive uses, should fall to the individual alone and not be subject to state regulation. The new and intense concern for privacy in the Enlightenment suggests that the concept of personhood elaborated by those whose thought provided the context for the framers of the Constitution included a private domain, an inviolable space opened only by an invasion of privacy, with the individual body very much at its center.

The abortion debate of course turns on the individual woman's right to control her own body. The formulas worked out in the 1972 Supreme Court decision in *Roe v. Wade* attempt to fix a period of time during which the body of a pregnant woman is not yet inhabited by a "person," and therefore not subject to any compelling state interest in the continuation of the pregnancy to term. Within this period of time, the "right of privacy . . . is broad enough to encompass a woman's decision whether or not to terminate her pregnancy" (*Roe v. Wade,* 410 US, at 153). This right of privacy is not absolute, however, since once a fetus reaches "viability"—the presumed capability of living outside the womb—the state may regulate and even proscribe abortion. Hence Justice Blackmun's well-known argument by "trimesters": the right of the woman (and her physician: *Roe* continually "medicalizes" the issue) to choose without restriction during the first trimester, the right of the state to regulate abortion "in ways that are reasonably related to maternal health" during the second trimester, and during the third trimester the right of the state "in promoting its interest in the potentiality of human life" to regulate and even proscribe abortion (164–65).

THE BODY IN THE NOVEL

The argument concerning the Constitutional right to privacy which stands behind the majority opinion is only summarily presented in *Roe*. It is given in more detail in one of *Roe*'s chief precedents, the 1964 case which invalidated the State of Connecticut's ban on the use of contra-

ceptives, *Griswold v. Connecticut*. Writing for the majority, Justice Douglas announced that "the First Amendment has a penumbra where privacy is protected from governmental intrusion" (*Griswold v. Connecticut*, 381 US, at 483). The sanctity of privacy is strikingly rendered by Douglas in an imagined scenario of its invasion: "Would we allow the police to search the sacred precincts of marital bedrooms for telltale signs of the use of contraceptives? The very idea is repulsive to the notions of privacy surrounding the marriage relationship" (485–86). Douglas continues: "We deal with a right of privacy older than the Bill of Rights—older than our political parties, older than our school system. Marriage is a coming together for better or for worse, hopefully enduring, and intimate to the degree of being sacred." That "penumbra" of the First Amendment, then, has to do with our deep-seated feelings about the sanctity of intimacy. Justice Goldberg, in his concurring opinion, sketches the background of the Ninth Amendment in order to claim that the framers believed "that fundamental rights exist that are not expressly enumerated in the first eight amendments" (492) and that "the right of privacy is a fundamental personal right emanating 'from the totality of the constitutional scheme under which we live'" (494; the quotation is from Justice Brandeis, dissenting in *Olmstead v. United States*).

Describing the "zones of privacy" created by various guarantees of the Bill of Rights, Douglas cites *Boyd v. United States* (1886), a case which itself reaches back to British law:

> The principles laid down in this opinion [by Lord Camden in *Entick v. Carrington* (1765), 19 How. St. Tr. 1029] affect the very essence of constitutional liberty and security. They reach farther than the concrete form of the case then before the court, with its adventitious circumstances; they apply to all invasions on the part of the government and its employees of the sanctity of a man's home and the privacies of life. It is not the breaking of his doors, and the rummaging of his drawers, that constitutes the essence of the offence; but it is the invasion of his indefeasible right of personal security, personal liberty, and private property, where that right has never

been forfeited by his conviction of some public offence,—it is the invasion of this sacred right which underlies and constitutes the essence of Lord Camden's judgment. (484)

The "privacies of life" have here become "this sacred right." In the examples I have cited from Rousseau and other eighteenth-century novelists, "privacies" were becoming "sacred," although they could be known as sacred, come to consciousness as inviolable rights, only by publication of images of their violation, including writing constituted as an invasion of privacy.

The cases of *Roe* and *Griswold* confirm, at two centuries' distance, that "privacies" evoke a "sacred right" most of all when the individual human body is at stake. Justice Douglas's image of the police invading "the sacred precincts of marital bedrooms" is a euphemistic evocation of what bodies do in bedrooms. It suggests that the realm of sexuality—in *Griswold*, limited to maritally legitimated sexuality—is the realm of ultimate privacy, and more generally, that what the individual does with his or her body within the "sacred precincts" of intimacy is a fundamental secret. Hence the urge to know this secret, to produce a detailed discourse of this secret, to match privacy with an invasion that opens up the private while at the same time insisting that it remains private. The private is an object of never-ending curiosity—of a basic "epistemophilic" drive—precisely because, whatever its violations, it remains the space to which we assign final secrets. Intimacy is of the body, and the body is private.

To bring this story up to date, I note that in the most recent Supreme Court ruling on abortion, *Planned Parenthood of Southeastern Pennsylvania v. Casey* (decided June 29, 1992), the opinion of the Court, delivered by Justices O'Connor, Kennedy, and Souter, attempts to recast the controversial "right to privacy" in terms of the Fourteenth Amendment protection of liberty, as "a realm of personal liberty which the government may not enter" (60 LW, at 4799). The right of personal liberty includes within it a right to "bodily integrity." Justice Stevens, in his separate opinion, speaks of a woman's constitutional interest in liberty, and states: "One aspect of this liberty is a right to bodily integrity, a right to control one's person" (60 LW, at 4818). There is in these arguments a no doubt comprehensible desire to find, in the Fourteenth Amendment, solider textual authority than what Douglas (in *Griswold*) located in the "penumbra" of the First Amendment. Nonetheless, the view of personhood, personal liberty, and bodily integrity evoked in *Casey* derives from the same intellectual and moral context as the notion of privacy.

52   In closing, I want to hark back to that "dark closet" from which Fanny Hill, in *Memoirs of a Woman of Pleasure,* first observes two naked bodies in action. In Cleland's novel, this scene is quickly succeeded by a second, in which the more experienced Phoebe takes Fanny back to the "dark closet" to observe, through "a long crevice in the partition," the tryst of Polly Philips and her handsome Genoese lover. What they observe is fully detailed, centering on the Genoese's "grand movement, which seem'd to rise out of a thicket of curling hair," and on Polly's "red-center'd cleft of flesh, whose lips, vermilioning inwards, exprest a small rubid line in sweet miniature, such as *Guido's* touch of colouring could never attain to the life or delicacy of."[19] We are at the core of the private body. The watching fulfills what is clearly Phoebe's intent, to arouse Fanny, leading to Phoebe's exploration of Fanny's body, now awakened to sexuality. In other words, the scene observed, and minutely described, between Polly and her lover takes effect in the dark closet, in the sexual quickening of the observer's body, a quickening which is then detailed and marked out by Phoebe's expert hands. There is here an analogue of the reading process, whereby experience described takes a toll on the reader: the arousal that matters is less that of Polly and her lover than that of the voyeurs—and, beyond that, the readers of Cleland's erotic novel. Somewhat in the manner of Saint-Preux's experience with Julie's corset, it is in the *camera obscura* that one has the imprint of the sexual body. And since the ultimate intent of the scene, as of the book as a whole, is to arouse its readers, the *camera obscura* figures both the experience of reading and the scene of writing, the place in which a phantasmatic body of desire is imprinted or figured, through the linguistic sign, as an absent presence or a present absence.

   Such a reading of the scene is both confirmed and complicated by what follows, when Phoebe takes Fanny to bed, and while caressing Fanny's body insists that Fanny caress hers: Phoebe forces Fanny's hand "half strivingly towards those parts where, now grown more knowing, I miss'd the main object of my wishes; and finding not even the shadow of what I wanted, where every thing was so flat, or so hollow, in the vexation I was in at it, I should have withdrawn my hand but for fear of disobliging her" (41). What Phoebe obtains Fanny describes as "rather the shadow than the substance of any pleasure." The passage reveals its phallic bias (as, we shall have ample occasion to see, does so much writing about the body), reminding us that Fanny's first-person narrative is really the invention of a man, and making the implicit claim that the writing instrument that produces substance rather than shadow is a male privilege. At the same time, it makes the "hollow" female body, as in the case of the imprint of Julie's body in the corset, the place where the male, and society as a whole, will inscribe its meanings. To the extent that we, as secondary voyeurs in these scenes, take pleasure in what we construct through the written word, we are ambiguously in the position of the phallus and the position of the hollow: in the realm of the imaginary we are invited to identify with the phallus, but in the realm of the symbolic—on the plane of writing itself—we are responding to the shadow, and to bodies that are not flesh but the construction of phantasies and desires.

I risk saying "we" here because these scenes, despite their evidently phallic perspective, suggest that the position of the reader is more ambivalent, mobile, even androgynous, than simply masculine. It may be possible to imagine oneself as both male and female in relation to Cleland's erotic scenarios. Such mobility in relation to desire would seem to be characteristic of the eighteenth-century novel. Many moments of *Les liaisons dangereuses*, for instance, suggest that an ideal reader would espouse the position not only of Valmont, or of Merteuil, but of both, making the viewing of sexualized bodies, and the reading of texts, a more "polymorphous" experience than it is often held to be.[20] The eighteenth-century novel often seems to take pleasure in creating a polymorphous sexuality, whereas the nineteenth-century novel will tend to enforce the law of gender, and its attendant repressions, with more censorious force.

One may in any event detect in such moments of Cleland's novel a further allegory of the efforts made and the problems encountered in knowing the body, in inscribing meanings on it, and in inscribing it within narrative. The rise of the novel is a major episode in the long history of curiosity. The novel takes this curiosity into the sphere of private life, invading the domain it claims to speak of and for. And within private life, it finds that what is most private, most difficult to speak of, most a problem to represent, is the private body. The body cannot be left in a nonsignifying somatic realm. It must mean. But it will do so only when made part of a web of signifying practices. These would be a central preoccupation of the nineteenth-century novel.

THE BODY IN THE NOVEL

3 Marking Out the Modern Body: The French Revolution and Balzac

TO TALK OF THE "modernity" of the body that emerges in the late eighteenth and early nineteenth centuries is not, of course, to claim that the body itself is different in substance from what it was before. What have changed are the conditions of its understanding and the ways in which it enters into systems of meaning. The notion of the modern body is first of all intertwined with the new notion of personal identity that is inaugurated by Rousseau, given political force in the wake of the French Revolution, and fully accepted by the self-conceiving, socially mobile protagonists of a novelist such as Honoré de Balzac. As Clarissa Harlowe and Rousseau suggested in their different ways, and as politics and culture will increasingly affirm, the material body, like the individual personality, is a final point of reference, an irreducible integer, in views of the world that are increasingly secularized. Whatever the continuing force of sacred history—the assumption of paltry human time into cosmic time, and the bodily resurrection following the end of time— predominant modes of thought see the body as a biological entity, doomed to destruction, existing only for a time, and therefore irreducibly important for that time. In a more traditional culture, the meaning of bodies was in large measure assigned by social structure and practice, by inherited conceptual systems, and by an enforced consensus on the place of bodies in a hierarchy assumed to be largely immutable and underwritten by divine law. With the decline of traditional systems of belief, the meanings of the body no longer are assigned; they must be achieved. This means that each body must in turn be made semiotic— receive the mark of meaning. Narratives often dramatize the making of that mark of meaning, the process by which a body becomes an intelligible sign. I shall explore these questions first in the founding political event of modernity, the French Revolution, and then in the particularly decisive example of the novels of Balzac.

The Revolutionary Body

The Revolution, according to Charles Baudelaire, was made by voluptuaries: "La Révolution a été faite par des voluptueux."[1] The remark occurs in his notes on *Les liaisons dangereuses,* whose sexual combat, revelatory of social chaos, he sees as preparatory to the Revolution. The "voluptueux" he has in mind are no doubt Choderlos de Laclos and his revolutionary protector, Philippe-Egalité, and probably such other aristocrat revolutionaries as Mirabeau and Talleyrand. The characterization clearly does not extend to Robespierre the incorruptible, nor to the citizens of the Jacobin Republic of Virtue, which increasingly revealed a puritanical determination to put an end to the libertine tradition, and finally created in the Fête de l'Etre Suprême a symbolic return of the censorious name of the father. But Baudelaire's remark may serve as a useful reminder of the extent to which the body, and its freedoms, capacities, pleasures, and responsibilities, became a central concern of the Revolution and the focal point of its expressionist aesthetics.

Reading the political oratory and cultural manifestations of the Revolution, and considering its symbolic political gestures, we are again and again forcibly impressed by the "bodiliness" of revolutionary language and representation, the need to conceive the revolutionary struggle in both a practice and a language which hold the body ultimately responsible and make its position within the scheme of things the necessary measure of success or failure. One can see in the Revolution the origins of an "aesthetics of embodiment," where the most important meanings have to be inscribed on and with the body. This is a relatively new phenomenon in the history of literature. In many ways its precursor is the very man so often held responsible for the Revolution, Rousseau, who in his *Confessions* gave a dramatically new role to the body—his own body—as a prime determinant of his life's meanings and of the construction of the narrative of that life. To be sure, during the *ancien régime* the body, be it the tortured body of the criminal or the sacred body of the king, is very much a part of everyday life and symbolism. But this body belongs to a traditional system, a product of both Christian and popular cultures, that is taken for granted. When this traditional system is voided of meaning by the Revolution, a new aesthetics of embodiment becomes necessary. The system of assigned meanings is

THE FRENCH REVOLUTION AND BALZAC

followed by one where meanings must be achieved through an active semiotic process in which the body is newly emblematized with meaning. The body in early Romantic literature, and thereafter, assumes a new centrality as a site of meaning. During the Revolution, the new popular genre of melodrama provides a literalistic realization of this new importance of the body as the site of signification.

Consider, in this context, the performative quality of revolutionary oratory.[2] Jacobin oratory is abstract, but it is also violent and excessive, and when its abstractions are translated into actions, people live or die as a consequence of rhetorical moves. The apparently disembodied language of Jacobin rhetoric in fact points to a new discipline of the body. During a revolution, with the collapse of the old order and its laws, its social orderings, and its very systems of meaning, language must attempt to work directly on the external world, including the physical bodies that ultimately compose the body politic. Thus a language that claims to be doing things with words—to be remaking reality by so ordering it—very often is placing bodies on one side or the other of the line that separates virtue from terror. Bodily punishment demonstrates that the discourse of law is not merely abstract, but reality itself: the idea embodied.[3] When Saint-Just, in his first speech before the Convention, concerning the judgment of Louis XVI, states "I can see no middle ground: this man must either reign or die," he gives us the essence of Jacobin rhetoric: the exclusion of the middle ground, the polarization of categories, and the assignment of persons exclusively to one of the categories in such a way that their bodies must bear witness to the result.[4] The king's body is of course an essential token in this rhetoric. As Saint-Just well understands, in traditional jurisprudence the body of the king is sacred, impersonal; its nature is to reign. This is why he believes it would be a mistake simply to judge Louis as an ordinary citizen, as some of his colleagues had proposed. Saint-Just in fact restores the special aura of the king's body, which is different from that of any other citizen's—restores the *ancien régime* sense of kingship in order to extirpate it. Louis must be judged as an enemy, as that very body that is contrary to the principle of popular sovereignty, and therefore must be expelled from the citizenry. If he is not to reign, he must die.

The king's body is merely the initial and foundational instance in a rhetoric of the demarcation of bodies. In his report that led to the perpetuation of Revolutionary Government until the time of peace, Saint-Just states: "There is no prosperity to be hoped for so long as the last enemy of liberty shall breathe. You have to punish not only the traitors, but even those who are indifferent; you have to punish whoever is passive within the Republic and does nothing for her: for, from the time that the people manifested its will, everything that is opposed to it is outside sovereignty; everything that is outside sovereignty is enemy."[5] One notes, with a certain chill, the process of differentiation: the rhetorical exclusion of any position in-between, the impossibility of indifference. Anyone who does not accept the will of the people as articulated by the Comité de Salut Public is outside the realm of sovereignty, and therefore is an enemy—a status that requires the sacrifice of one's body. The implacable logic continues in Saint-Just's "Rapport sur les suspects incarcérés," where he states: "What constitutes a Republic is the total destruction of everything opposed to it."[6] In the same report, he makes the definitions in terms of which this statement becomes self-evident: "Monarchy is not a king, it is crime; the republic is not a senate, it is virtue. Whoever is soft on crime wants to re-establish the monarchy and immolate liberty" (196–97). These propositions claim self-evident status. They allow no argument, no compromise, no middle position. Bodies are on the line, on either side of it—in the camp of virtue or that of crime; for those in the latter, the guillotine awaits. And the guillotine itself represents an abstract notion of judgment embodied in a machine for the exemplary punishment of bodies.

The grandiose rhetorical gestures of the Terror are thus immediately translated into *la prise de corps,* the seizing of bodies, and into their decapitation, in a grim realization of the traditional metaphor of amputation of the gangrened members of the social body. As the historian Dorinda Outram has argued—using the terms of Norbert Elias—the Revolution saw the development of a newly controlled, autonomous, impermeable, stoic body, which was "of vital importance to its users and its audience at a time when the first use in French history of state terror on a mass scale was demonstrating how, on the contrary, in reality the body was frail, vulnerable, ultimately disposable."[7] More so than in any prior political regime that I can think of, the individual must take public responsibility for his or her body, account for it, which is in part a consequence of the new emphasis on the individual brought by the Enlightenment and of the bodiliness given to this emphasis by Rousseau.[8] Saint-Just's "Rapport sur les suspects incarcérés" ends with a decree that reads in part: "The Committee of General Security is invested with the power to liberate patriots in prison. Any person who asks to be freed shall give an account of his conduct since May 1, 1789." This summons to individual responsibility for one's actions is the obverse of the ac-

THE FRENCH REVOLUTION AND BALZAC

countability of individuals to the power of the state. Its outcome is what Simon Schama has called "the body count": failure to produce a correct accounting of one's actions holds one responsible, in one's own body.[9]

This insistence on bodiliness is strikingly in evidence in one of the more bizarre and macabre episodes of the Revolution, the disinterment of the bodies of the kings of France from the Abbey of Saint-Denis. In the process of extirpating the criminal idea of monarchy, the Revolution discovered that it needed to get rid of what the journal *Les Révolutions de Paris* called the "impure remains" and the "vile bones" of past monarchs.[10] During October 1793, the desecration of kings reached its apogee. The bodies of those mythic figures from the past, including the monarch dear to every French heart, Henri IV, and the Sun King, Louis XIV, were exhumed and thrown into quicklime in the common pit—the fate also of Louis XVI after his execution in January of the same year. Even Saint Louis ended up in this grave of commoners. It may be a strange comment on the enduring charisma of the anointed body of the king that even when inanimate it had to be destroyed, effaced, reduced to nothingness. Regicide was somehow incomplete until the substantial body left behind at the passing of kings was wholly eliminated from the new regime of virtue. The positive gesture complementary to this act of eradication was the transport to the Panthéon of the bodily remains of those intellectual precursors of the Revolution: Voltaire in July 1791— shortly after the King's attempted flight ended at Varennes—and Rousseau, belatedly, in October 1794, following the demise of the Jacobin Republic for which later historians so often held him responsible.

October 1793 also saw the execution of Marie-Antoinette, following a trial in which her crimes against the Republic were made to appear inextricably linked to her sexual immorality. Accused of insatiable "uterine furors," of liaisons with both men and women, the *Autrichienne*'s alleged conspiracies with the enemy were matched by her supposed attempts to debauch and ruin the Bourbon males, not only her husband, but also her son, the Dauphin. The *enragé* Hébert managed to introduce into the prosecution the claim that she initiated the Dauphin into incestuous play and masturbation, thus seriously damaging his health. Along with the generalized need to read crimes as bodily, there seemed to be a specific need to place women's criminality squarely on their sexuality. They were aristocrats, thus libertines—both Agrippina and Messalina, in the classic rhetorical accusation—thus lacking in the modesty and fidelity characteristic of good petite-bourgeoise sans-culotte wives, thus out of their place, thus driven by ungoverned ambition finally attributable to ungovernable sexuality.

Excellent recent work on women in the Revolution—by Lynn Hunt, Joan Landes, Sarah Maza, and Dorinda Outram—has made us aware of the peculiarly relentless exclusion of women from the radical renovation that ought logically to have furthered their liberation. The Republic of Virtue did not conceive of women occupying public space; female virtue was domestic, private, unassuming. As Outram writes: "The same arena which created public man made woman into *fille publique*."[11] October 1793 also saw the defeat of revolutionary radical feminism, as the feminists were beaten, literally, by the proletarian *poissardes;* the Convention went on, early in November, to order the closure of the women's revolutionary clubs. Madame Roland went to the guillotine, and shortly before her, Olympe de Gouges, the author of *Les droits de la femme et de la citoyenne* (1791), as well as the anti-conventual play, *Le couvent, ou les voeux forcés* (1790). As Chantal Thomas has noted, Marie-Antoinette, Olympe de Gouges, and Madame Roland were grouped together by the *Moniteur Universel* as examples of unnatural women: "Marie-Antoinette . . . was a bad mother, a debauched wife, and she died under the curses of those she wanted to destroy . . . Olympe de Gouges, born with an exalted imagination, took her delirium for an inspiration of nature . . . The Roland woman, a fine mind for great plans, a philosopher on note paper, the queen of a moment . . . was a monster however you look at her . . . Even though she was a mother, she had sacrificed nature by trying to raise herself above it; the desire to be learned led her to forget the virtues of her sex."[12] Political women, scribbling women, debauched women: they all come together as examples of "the sex" out of control, needing the ultimate correction in order to conform to what Saint-Just calls the "mâle énergie" of the Republic.

Even more than by these three women, the danger of the sex in politics was represented by Charlotte Corday (as Chantal Thomas also has shown). Her act of stabbing Marat in his bathtub brought into the symbolic arena the hand-to-hand combat of denatured female aristocrats—indulgents, federalists—and male friends of the people. To her judges, she was simply a "monster" in female guise, something like an example of demonic possession, to which women traditionally were most susceptible. In the subsequent cult of Marat, Charlotte Corday is present only in that gash in Marat's breast, a kind of displaced representation

3. Jacques-Louis David, *Marat assassiné*. (Brussels: Musées
Royaux des Beaux-Arts. © A.C.L. Brussels)

of her woman's sex as a wound on the martyred man. David's painting,
Marat assassiné (Figure 3) says it all: the ecstatic face of the martyr, the
drops of blood on the immaculate sheet, the quill pen still grasped next
to the kitchen knife fallen on the floor, the bathwater become a pool of
blood—all these elements suggest the intrusion of ungoverned female
sexuality on a life dedicated to the higher cause. The male body has
been made to pay for the primal drives of the woman's body. At the
same time, Marat's apotheosized body has gained a realm to which the
woman's body has no access.

It is through David's painting that Charlotte Corday's letter, written in order to win an audience with the great man, has been immortalized. We can still decipher it today: "Il suffit que je sois bien malheureuse pour avoir droit à votre bienveillance" (The simple fact of my misfortune is my claim to your benevolence). The letter makes the Friend of the People a victim of his very benevolence, here ignobly practiced upon by 61 a consummate hypocrite. The letter is all the more perfidious in that its language of Rousseauian sensibility belongs to the repertoire of the good guys, not the villains. The sentence is typical of those spoken by the virtuous characters in melodrama—a genre that had not yet been so christened in 1793, but which had already seen its proto-examples on the stages of Paris: Boutet de Monvel's *Les victimes cloîtrées* of 1791 is often considered the first melodrama.

October 1793 also saw the staging of the representative melodrama of the Terror, Sylvain Maréchal's *Le jugement dernier des rois,* which opened to great acclaim at the Théâtre de la République—formerly the Théâtre-Français—two days after the execution of Marie-Antoinette. "There is a fit spectacle for republican eyes," gloated Hébert in his newspaper, *Le Père Duchesne.*[13] The Comité de Salut Public ordered three thousand copies of the printed text, and the Ministry of War then signed up for six thousand, to send to troops at the front in order to kindle their republican zeal. But the best measure of the success of the play may be that the Comité de Salut Public, at a moment when gunpowder was one of the most precious commodities in France, granted the petition of the Théâtre de la République for the "twenty pounds of saltpeter and twenty pounds of powder" needed to produce the volcanic eruption that ends the play, killing off all the monarchs of Europe—the "crowned villains"—that it has assembled on a desert island.

Le jugement dernier des rois, subtitled a "Prophecy in One Act," envisions a Europe in which the sans-culottes of all the nations have risen up against their monarchs, deposed them, and brought them, under the watchful eye of an international sans-culotte police force, to a desert island. On this island lives a virtuous old Frenchman, who was exiled because he dared to protest against the abduction of his virginal daughter by royal courtiers. On a boulder next to his hut he has inscribed the motto: "Better to have as neighbor / A volcano than a king. / Liberty . . . Equality." The castaway has made friends with the savages who paddle over in canoes from a neighboring island; they are naturally noble and, once instructed by the castaway—acting on the example of Rousseau's *vicaire savoyard*—come to join him in worship of the sunrise. The sans-culottes lead in the deposed monarchs one by one: George III of England, Francis II of the Austro-Hungarian Empire, William of Prussia, Ferdinand of Naples, Vittorio-Amedeo of Savoia, Charles of Spain, Stanislas Augustus of Poland, and Catherine, Empress of All the Russias, plus the Pope. Predictably, they fall into monarchical behavior. George tries to beg off on grounds of insanity; Charles of Spain implores the Pope to solve their difficulties by performing a miracle; Catherine tries to lure Stanislas into an amorous tryst in a cave. They fall to squabbling over a crust of bread, and the stage is littered with broken scepters and crushed crowns. Their dissension is ended by the eruption of the volcano, and they descend in flames into the open trap of the theater.

Maréchal's play, in any sober view, is pretty silly stuff, but it is animated by Jacobin rhetoric of sensibility and ferocity, virtue and terror, in a theatrical form. To say that melodrama was the genre of the Revolution—perhaps its only enduring cultural creation— is nearly a truism, since revolutionary public speech itself, as the examples from Saint-Just indicated, is already melodramatic. Charles Nodier would later claim that "melodrama was the morality of the Revolution," by which he meant that it is inherently a democratic form, in which the humble of the earth stand up to overbearing tyrants and express home truths about the value of the good heart, the sanctity of the domestic hearth, the essential moral equality of all, and the fraternity of the virtuous, and win through to see villainy punished and virtue rewarded in spectacular fashion in the last act.[14] Following Nodier, we might say that melodrama is the genre—and the rhetoric—of revolutionary moralism because it states, enacts, and imposes its moral messages in clear, unambiguous words and signs. Melodrama is a hyperbolic mode, of course, and preeminently the mode of the excluded middle, which one finds in Saint-Just's speeches and in all Jacobin rhetoric: those who are not with us are against us, there is no compromise possible between polarized moral positions, the world is defined by a vast Manichaean struggle of light and darkness. Saint-Just, in a famous line of his "Institutions républicaines," states: "The republican government has virtue as its principle; if not virtue, terror. What do they want who want neither virtue nor terror?"[15] Anything in between virtue and terror is simply unthinkable. As in melodrama, there is no place for moral indifference or nuance; there are only pure, unadulterated moral positions.

Subtlety is not the mode of *Le jugement dernier des rois,* nor of any other melodrama. Its world is the world-turned-upside-down of carnival. The kings are in chains and the sans-culottes reign supreme, handing

down sentences both just and inflexible with all the high moral senten-
tiousness of melodrama. There are all the sonorous clichés of Jacobin
rhetoric, both the denunciations of rulers for sexual immorality as well
as tyranny—"Was there ever a nation that at the same time had a king
and had decency?" asks the leader of the sans-culottes—and the fulsome
praise for the domestic as well as civic virtues of the sans-culottes, "who
earn their bread by the sweat of their brow, who love work, who are
good sons, good fathers, good husbands, good friends, good neighbors,
but who are jealous of their rights as they are jealous of their duties."[16]
As in all melodrama, people are characterized with unambiguous epi-
thets: "Venerable old man!" "Brave sans-culottes!" "Crowned monsters!" Home truths are emphatically announced: "these savages are our
elders in liberty, for they have never had a king. Born free, they live and
die as they were born." The presence of these somewhat superfluous
noble savages, who speak through gestures, attaches this play firmly to
the origins of melodrama in pantomime. Gestural speech is a constant
in melodrama because it permits the creation of visual messages, pure
signs that cannot lie—the undissimulated speech of the body.

The play also participates in what one might call the pathos of Jacobin
rhetoric, which is always trying to call into being a reality that does not
yet exist. It is subtitled "a prophecy," since it envisions the extension of
revolutionary reversal to the whole of Europe. It is the vision of the self-
styled "Orator of the Human Race," Anacharsis Cloots, who claimed
that he would not rest until there was a republic on the moon. Like the
oratory of the Convention, the rhetoric of the play—indeed, the play
itself—is performative, seeking by the power of ever more violent words
to impose the Jacobin republic on a recalcitrant world. *Le jugement
dernier des rois* in effect says: "Be it enacted that there are no more
kings." Between that rhetorical moment—the fictive moment of the play
itself—and its realization stand all the foreign armies and the internal
traitors (the hoarders, the federalists, the indulgents, and so on). As the
rhetoric of denunciation at the revolutionary tribunals needed not merely
to inculpate but to destroy—to create the rationale for elimination—so
here the leader of the sans-culottes draws up the bill of particulars against
the monarchs and calls upon "nature" to eliminate them: "Nature,
hasten to finish the work of the sans-culottes, breathe your fire on this
refuse of society, and plunge kings forever into that nothingness from
which they never should have emerged." In the world outside the stage,
the performative is enacted by the guillotine, purging those who cannot
understand that there is no middle ground between virtue and terror;

onstage, "Nature" is under the command of rhetoric, and the volcano promptly erupts to destroy the kings, consuming their very bodies.

The melodramatic body is a body seized by meaning. Since melodrama's simple, unadulterated messages must be made absolutely clear, visually present, to the audience, bodies of victims and villains must unambiguously signify their status. The bodies of the virtuous victims are typically subjected to physical restraint. Boutet de Monvel's *Les victimes cloîtrées* offers a final act in which the heroine and the hero are confined in the deepest cells of a convent and a monastery, respectively, representing the evil power of the monks who act at the behest of the aristocrats. They will be liberated by a republican mayor, draped in his tricolor sash, in a dramatic gesture of freeing the body from oppression. The *in-pace* (the solitary dungeon) of a convent is similarly used in the unfortunate Olympe de Gouges' drama *Le couvent, ou les voeux forcés*, among numerous other examples. The body sequestered and enchained, unable to assert its innocence and its right to freedom, becomes a dominant element of melodrama that endures long after the Revolution. Guilbert de Pixerécourt, the first undisputed master of the genre, returns again and again to the situation of imprisonment, in such plays as *Le château des Appenins, Les mines de Pologne, La forteresse du Danube*, and *Latude, ou trente-cinq ans de captivité;* the titles alone suggest the nightmarish Gothic spaces in which the virtuous are confined. None of these melodramas can reach its dénouement until the virtuous bodies have been freed and explicitly recognized as bearing the sign of innocence. This sign is often inscribed on the body itself, in the form of a birthmark or other stigmata, or is an emblem worn on the body since childhood: marks and emblems that eventually permit the public recognition of the virtuous identity. *La croix de ma mère*, the token that establishes identity, indeed has become the proverbial sign of the melodramatic recognition scene. And very often the final act of melodrama will stage a trial scene—as in some revisionary version of the revolutionary tribunal—in which the nature of innocence and virtue is publicly recognized through such signs, and publicly celebrated and rewarded, while the villain is bodily expelled from the social realm: driven out, branded as evil, and relegated to a space offstage and outside the civilized world.

It is in the context of melodrama's recourse to the body as the most important signifier of meanings that we can understand why nearly every melodrama has recourse to moments of pantomime, which are not simply decorative but often convey crucial messages. *Le jugement dernier des rois,* for instance, has that group of noble savages with whom the Europeans can communicate only in gestures—but without misunderstandings, since "the heart's the heart in all countries." In an important moment of the play, these savages instinctively express their horror and loathing of the kings of Europe in bodily language, representing before our eyes the correct, unprejudiced, nonverbal, visible reaction to tyranny. As the genre develops, one finds many more highly elaborated examples of the mute role, which is often the bearer of the most sublime messages in the play. A notable instance is the mute Eloi, in Pixerécourt's *Le chien de Montargis,* who faces the excruciating experience of standing trial, for a crime he did not commit, while unable to defend himself verbally. His gestures and postures constantly evoke a realm of higher law and truer judgment in which he will be vindicated. Much late eighteenth-century reflection on the nature of language and its origins tends to the view that gesture is the first and ultimately the most passionate form of communication, which comes to the fore when the code of verbal language lapses into inadequacy. As Marmontel put it, "It is especially for the most impassioned moments of the soul that pantomime is necessary."[17] Only the body can speak for the soul at those moments.

Melodrama constantly reminds us of the psychoanalytic concept of "acting out": the use of the body itself, its actions, gestures, and sites of irritation and excitation, to represent meanings that might otherwise be unavailable to representation because they are somehow under the bar of repression. Melodrama refuses repression, or rather, repeatedly strives toward moments that break through repression to the physical and verbal staging of the essential, when repressed content returns as recognition of the the deepest relations of life, as in the celebrated *voix du sang* ("You! my father!"), and of moral identities ("So you are the author of all my wrongs!"). Breaking with the decorum of classical theater, melodrama promotes an exaggerated style of acting, in which facial expression and body language speak. In the logic of melodramatic acting out the body itself must pay the stakes of the drama: the body of the villain is publicly branded with its identity, exposed in a formal judgment scene, and then, if not killed in hand-to-hand combat, driven from the stage and banished from human society; while the body of persecuted virtue is rewarded, fêted, married, and emblazoned with all the signs of the public recognition of its nature.

The aesthetics of embodiment is hence central to melodrama, and melodrama crucial to the Revolution. Indeed, the connection between melodrama and the Revolution was to the first writers on the subject, notably Charles Nodier, self-evident: melodrama simply enacted on the stage, in a heightened, excessive, Manichaean, hyperbolic form, the national drama being played out in the Convention, in the sections, in the tribunals, and on the scaffold. It was a genre that had to be invented to do justice to—to match, as it were—the excessive rhetoric and action in the streets. Beyond the specific genre of melodrama, and beyond the Revolution, the embodiment of meaning—the inscription of messages on the individual body—becomes a key new element in the aesthetics of modern narrative.

Balzac's Bodily Marks

The final section of Balzac's great novel *Illusions perdues,* in so many ways the archetypal novel of the nineteenth century, is interrupted by a long excursus on "la contrainte par corps." David Séchard, the inventor who has been bankrupted by the debts and forgeries of his brother-in-law Lucien de Rubempré, has fallen victim to the machinations of the Cointet brothers, who want to force him to reveal the secret formula he has discovered for the manufacture of cheap paper to feed the burgeoning newspaper industry. In contemporary jurisprudence, the body of the debtor was considered subject to seizure so long as an arrangement to pay his creditors was not secured. The *contrainte par corps* was designed to make the debtor relinquish any assets he might have. In other words, the body was considered a substitute for deficient material goods, and its constraint a way to produce restitution. David's *contrainte par corps*—which takes place in the most melodramatic circumstances— prefigures the more radical *prise de corps* undergone by Lucien himself in the sequel novel, *Splendeurs et misères des courtisanes,* where he is arrested on charges of extortion and detained in the Conciergerie prison. Here he commits suicide, hanging himself from the bars of the window in his cell. The body of Lucien—which throughout these central novels of *La comédie humaine* has been the object of desire by women from the highest as well as the lowest circles of Parisian society, by the master criminal Jacques Collin alias Vautrin, and by Lucien himself—pays the final price of its infractions.

Balzac's attention to the body as defined by the legal system offers a symbolic entry into a modern conception of the body as that by which and in which individuals are ultimately held responsible. If, as Oscar Wilde declared, "The nineteenth century, as we know it, is largely an invention of Balzac," the new importance Balzac attaches to the body as semiotic vehicle is very much a part of that invention, among the first comprehensive treatments of the body as an irreducibly important narrative signifier.[18] In the intrigue that immediately precedes David Séchard's *contrainte par corps*, Lucien de Rubempré, the poet and journalist whose meteoric Parisian career has ended in disaster and a return to his provincial point of departure in Angoulême, has undertaken to repair the misery caused to his sister Eve and her husband David by reconquering Angoulême's reigning society. Essentially, this has meant dressing his elegant and seductive body in borrowed Parisian clothes, produced at his urgent request by his old journalistic pals and their actress mistresses, in order to cut a figure with those he thinks can save David's desperate situation. He fails, once again, by assuming that his representation as the bedecked dandy is sufficient to embody that meaning. David is unwittingly lured from his hiding place by a forged letter (concocted by his enemies from a specimen of Lucien's handwriting) and arrested. He surrenders his valuable secret to the Cointet brothers moments before the arrival of a courier bringing fifteen thousand francs, restitution from Lucien, who has sold himself to the Reverend Carlos Herrera, a supposed Spanish priest who is really Jacques Collin, alias Vautrin, the archcriminal, demon of the underworld, and masterplotter of *La comédie humaine*. David's body thus pays for the failure of Lucien to impose himself—as he had so often managed to do during his brief but brilliant Parisian glory—through his body. The story of Lucien's life as the creature of Jacques Collin will be told in *Splendeurs et misères des courtisanes*, which reaches its climax with Lucien's *prise de corps*, his detention, and his suicide. As a consequence of losing Lucien, Collin gives up his lifelong protean combat against society, surrenders to the magistrate Camusot, and assumes his "last incarnation" as chief of the secret police.

67

Of all the remarkably significant bodies in Balzac, Lucien's bears special mention, both because of the central importance of the novels in which he figures, and also because of the great textual attention accorded his body. The first given is that Lucien is exceptionally beautiful, with the special beauty the text assigns to poets: "The poet was already poetry itself," in the eyes of his first protectress, Madame de Bargeton; and he is often referred to as a living poem.[19] This beauty, we are repeatedly told, has something feminine about it: the initial description of Lucien suggests that he might be taken for a girl in disguise, and mentions in particular that he has the hips of a woman, which, we are told, is "a clue that rarely misleads" to the character of Lucien's ambition, which will use any means to its ends (5:145–46). When Lucien has brought ruin on Eve and David, Eve will comment that "there is in the poet a pretty woman of the worst sort" (5:653), summing up Lucien's career as a prostitute of his talents and the kept man of prostitutes. In *Splendeurs et misères des courtisanes,* his giving in to the seductions of Collin, whom Rastignac had resisted, is attributed to his being "this man half woman" (6:505).

Lucien's body is a consistent clue to his inconsistent career. It has an absolute appeal, to women and to the homosexual Collin; loving and desiring Lucien never needs justification or textual motivation, but is simply the natural and unquestioned response to his beauty. Those enamored of Lucien come from the highest ranks of society and the lowest: a partial list includes Madame de Bargeton, the actress Coralie, the Duchesse de Maufrigneuse, the Comtesse de Sérisy, the prostitute Esther, and Clothilde de Grandlieu. On the other hand, Lucien's body, like a couturier's dummy, exists to be clothed and decorated; success in the Parisian world very much depends on the self-representations he can achieve. Upon his arrival in Paris, at the start of part two of *Illusions perdues,* a walk in the Tuileries garden permits him to compare his unfashionable provincial costume to the elegant toilettes of the dandies. As he observed the accessories of Parisian high life—the gloves, the buttons on the coats, the canes, the cufflinks, the riding crops, the pocket watches—"the world of necessary superfluities became apparent to him" (5:270). His provincial dress and his unauthorized use of the aristocratic name de Rubempré (his mother's family name) lead to his social excommunication by Madame d'Espard—the arbiter of the Faubourg Saint-Germain—when he appears in her box at the opera. Lucien immediately grasps the remedy: a visit to Staub, the most fashionable Paris tailor, who has the talent "to highlight his charming forms." When he has fitted out Lucien, Staub comments, "A young man dressed in this manner . . . can go promenade in the Tuileries; he'll marry a rich Englishwoman within two weeks" (5:289). When Lucien has achieved his rapid and short-lived success as a journalist and set up house with Coralie, he gains those necessary accessories: "Coralie, like all fanatics, loved to adorn her idol; she ruined herself to give her beloved poet those elegant furnishings of elegant men that he had so much desired during his first stroll in the Tuileries. Lucien thus had marvelous canes, a charming lorgnette, diamond buttons, clasps for his morning cravats, rings with precious settings, and splendid waistcoats in sufficient number to match the colors of his costume" (5:479). Thus adorned, his body has the same effect as his journalism: it imposes him on Parisian society, creating desire, jealousy, and a kind of irresistible force of success. But, again like his journalism, this self-representation is an insufficiently motivated sign. It does not have the backing in hard cash and true power that would make it durable.

Lucien's unpardonable lapse, we are told, is his failure to profit by his transformation by making Madame de Bargeton—who finds him irresistible in his metamorphosis—his mistress; this achievement would give carnal substance to his appearance. The problem is that Lucien "had, like an ogre, tasted fresh flesh" (5:487)—the body of Coralie—and is too satiated to respond to Madame de Bargeton's advances. Lucien has become a *viveur,* and in the Balzacian sexual economy this means that the satisfactions of his body deplete the resources of his mind. Lucien displays a certain languor because he is "heureux tous les jours" (5:471), a classical euphemism meaning that he has daily sexual satisfaction, with the result that he lives "in the dissipation in which he lost his energy"; thus "the spring of his will" is softened and offers no resistance (5:491–92). The subjacent metaphor here, as so often in Balzac, concerns sexual expenditure. As the parabolic story of *La peau de chagrin* makes most evident, a man has a limited resource of sexual energy, which he can spend in a brief orgiastic bodily existence, or conserve in a long life of intellectual mastery in the manner of the antiques dealer of that novel, who is one hundred and two years old, or of the emblematic Gobseck, the usurer who comes into so many of the novels of *La comédie humaine,* and who conserves himself as he capitalizes his money, living vicariously through others' drama, never expending the self. "To spend" continues even today to have a colloquial meaning of achieving orgasm. In the economy of Balzac's world, sexual expenditure is explicitly and consistently a loss of energy, and of life itself, and fully consonant with the spending of money. The body is an integral part of this early capitalist economy, and its sexuality represents the venture capital that Balzac's ambitious young men have to invest.

The counterpart to the male *viveur* is the courtesan, whether actress, prostitute, or other form of kept woman to whom the patriarchal sexual economy has assigned the role of arousing and satisfying male desire. The courtesan's life is a brief flare of glory. Coralie dies at the age of nineteen, after seeing all her rich furnishings seized by the bailiffs, and a number of others meet tragic ends. The courtesan makes remarkably frequent appearances in *La comédie humaine,* no doubt because, as Albert Béguin remarked, she is preeminently the creature with a destiny, whose parabolic social trajectory tellingly reveals the nature of the sociosexual economy.[20] As the journalist Etienne Lousteau puts it, describing Esther in the early pages of *Splendeurs et misères des courtisanes:* "At age eighteen, that girl has already known the highest opulence, the lowest misery, men on every social story. She has a kind of magic wand with which she unleashes the brutal appetites so violently suppressed in men who, while concerning themselves with politics or science, with literature or art, still are passionate at heart. There is no other woman in Paris who can say as well as she does to the Animal: 'Come out! . . .' And the Animal leaves its cage, and wallows in excess" (6:442). The prostitute's body is by definition a storied body, itself enacting and also creating narratives of passion, lust, and greed as it passes through the social economy.[21] Furthermore, its narratives directly involve the cash nexus, the exchange of money for bodies.

This exchange is the prime force of the plot in *Splendeurs et misères des courtisanes,* which turns on Collin's attempt to capitalize Esther's beauty in order to provide Lucien with the million francs he needs to buy up the estates formerly owned by his mother's family and establish himself as landed gentry, and thus to obtain the hand in marriage of the highly aristocratic Clothilde de Grandlieu. Lucien's gravest problem, following his return to Paris as the creature of "Carlos Herrera"—who remains a hidden presence within Lucien's social career—is the question repeatedly posed about him in society gossip: "De quoi vit-il?" (What does he live on?). His mentor's concern must be to make the system of sociosexual exchanges yield a more traditional and enduring precapitalist value: land. When he discovers that Lucien has taken Esther, alias "La Torpille" (the Torpedo) as his mistress, Collin quickly decides that her beauty constitutes a "capital" that can be exploited (6:569). The mechanism of exploitation lies to hand because the ultra-rich banker, the Baron de Nucingen, has caught a glimpse of her walking at night in the Bois de Boulogne and fallen hopelessly in love with her. Thus Collin's game will be to capitalize Esther's beauty through Nucingen's passion, creating sufficient obstacles to its realization to raise the ante so that Lucien may finally acquire the million he needs, while at the same time maneuvering Nucingen and Esther—who has been redeemed by her love of the poetic Lucien, and wants no part of her former life—toward an erotic dénouement. Part two of the novel, which bears the title "A combien l'amour revient aux vieillards" (The cost of love for old men), deploys prodigiously inventive plots and counterplots, as Nucingen's agents struggle against Collin's and we enter an underworld of private spies and counterspies, disguises, and dirty tricks. The plot quickly becomes as sordid as its motivating principles, notably when the virginal Lydie, daughter of Nucingen's principal undercover agent Peyrade, is abducted and raped by some of the felons under Collin's command. Lydie's body pays for the capitalization of Esther's.

As for Esther, she accepts the use devised for her by Collin since, sublime creature that she is, she chooses to sacrifice everything in order to establish Lucien in a high social position. Her self-sacrifice is accompanied by a remarkable lucidity, which seems often to belong to Balzac's courtesans: an acute awareness of their place in the social economy. When Nucingen presses Esther finally to take him into her bed, she responds in a letter: "You paid for me, I owe myself. There is nothing more sacred than the debts of dishonor. I don't have the right to *liquidate* myself by throwing myself in the Seine. One can always pay a debt in this frightful coin, which is good only on one side: thus you will find me at your orders. I want to pay in a single night all the sums that are mortgaged on that fatal moment, and I am certain that an hour of me is worth millions, all the more so in that it will be the only one, the last. Afterward, I will be paid up, and free to stop living" (6:603).

Esther understands the inflated exchange value that has been created on her body, and the inescapability of the system that has created that value: the "debts of dishonor" are, in a sexual-capitalist economy, the most sacred, her body the ultimate legal tender. Effacing that currency through a premature "liquidation" in the waters of the Seine would incur the worst of dishonors, the unpaid debt (a view incidentally confirmed in Balzac's epic of debt and repayment, *César Birotteau*). At the same time, she seems to claim an absolute value for her body, an hour of which is worth millions; once the debt is paid, the value is hers alone to dispose of. The contradictions of the capitalized body come clearly into view: it belongs to the economic system while it is at the same time regarded as one's own, last, and perhaps only possession. Esther is caught squarely in this contradiction. Does she or does she not have the right to dispose of her own body? Her "solution" is a compromise; she will satisfy the economy by one hour in bed with Nucingen, then kill herself.

The result, for Esther, is a lived irony, a doubling of her being, a splitting of body from consciousness:

She kept in her heart an image of herself which at once made her blush and made her proud; the hour of her abdication was always present to her consciousness; thus she lived as double, taking her role as an object of pity. Her sarcasms showed the internal deep contempt that the angel of love, contained within the courtesan, felt for the infamous and hateful role played by the body in the presence of the soul. At once spectator and actor, judge and prisoner at the bar, she realized the admirable fiction of the Arabian Tales, where one almost always finds a sublime being hidden under a degraded exterior, and whose type, under the name of Nebuchadnezzar, is in the book of books, the Bible.   (6:643–44)

Esther's then commits suicide, but in a final irony, her act becomes the occasion of the discovery, by the lawyer Derville, that she was the sole kin of the usurer Gobseck for whom he had been searching—and thus that she was the inheritor of seven million francs. Bequeathed by the terms of her will to Lucien, the seven million again arrives too late: Lucien himself has already committed suicide. This fortune—possibly the most considerable of *La comédie humaine*—eventually falls, in varying shares, to Collin and to Lucien's provincial relatives. The bodies disappear, the circulatory economic system remains.

Lucien dies because his body has been contaminated by the economy of which it has been a part—by living off the sale of the prostitute's body and, beyond that, living as the object and the product of Collin's eros. Even in death, Lucien's body continues to contaminate. The fourth and final part of *Splendeurs et misères des courtisanes* recounts the efforts of several Faubourg Saint-Germain great ladies, aided by Collin, to save their reputations from the taint of having loved Lucien. Letters are suppressed, witnesses suborned, history rewritten, in an ultimately successful effort to quarantine society from the sordid bodily exchanges that have taken place. Collin himself must change his body: the final section of the novel bears the title "La dernière incarnation de Vautrin," as if to mark the radical nature of his transformation when, following his collapse at the news of Lucien's death, he surrenders to the magistrate Camusot, and then enters the service of the police.

The prefiguration of Collin's conversion—what the text calls his "Dix-huit Brumaire," recalling the date of Napoleon's coup d'état—comes when he is stripped to the waist by Camusot and struck on the shoulder with the ebony *verge*, or bat, to see if there will be a reappearance of the letters *TF* (for *Travaux Forcés*, forced labor) branded in the flesh of criminals. The examination is inconclusive: instead of the letters, seventeen holes appear in the flesh. As the bailiff points out, one can read these holes as marking the place of the now absent letters. And as readers of *Le Père Goriot,* we know that Collin was indeed so branded; when he is drugged by Mlle Michonneau and slapped vigorously on the shoulder, the *marque infamante* reappears clearly. In *Splendeurs et misères* *des courtisanes,* what is left of the mark is "quite vague," according to Camusot, too vague to assure conviction (6:751). Collin maintains that the holes are the result of gunshot wounds. In fact, the self-inflicted wounds with which he has sought to efface what was known as *la marque* are sign of a death and rebirth. Although his denials are contradicted by Lucien, the effacement of his mark is the symbolic precondition of Collin's ability to achieve one final transformation: more than a disguise this time, a radical self-alteration.

The official *marque infamante* borne by Collin is an almost obsessive motif in *La comédie humaine,* possibly all the more fascinating to Balzac because the abolishment of branding criminals in 1832—before the bulk of his novels were written, but after the period represented in the novels—resulted in a new social anxiety about the recognition of habitual malefactors.[22] The "mark" constituted the sign of the outlaw whose excluded body puts the social body into question. As Collin states to the assembled denizens of the Pension Vauquer at the moment of his arrest, in *Le Père Goriot:* "We have a lesser infamy on the shoulder than you have in the heart, you flabby members of a gangrened society" (3:219). The mark is a version of *la croix de ma mère,* the melodramatic sign of recognition. But the sign branded on the body (like the cross incised on the body in Dumas' *La Tour de Nesle*) is a bit different from the mother's cross or other token most often worn by the hero or heroine of melodrama: the metonymy of identification has become incorporate, a part of the body, a metaphor of inner identity that can, at the appropriate crisis, reappear as embodied text. The branded sign becomes an indication of the implication of the body itself in a drama of hiding and revelation, the end of a process of tracking by way of clues—partially revelatory signs that need interpretation—which has been described by Terence Cave, following Carlo Ginzburg, as the "cynegetic" model of knowing: knowing according to the huntsman's lore, following the traces left by the quarry, constructing a narrative line of explanation ending in recognition.[23] The signed body points to the deep implication of the body in narrative: the body as the place where central narrative meanings are inscribed or branded, and the place of the body within the narrative dynamic, its role as key narrative signifier. That is, the body itself, its experiences and destinies, will be called upon to carry forward the narrative plot and to embody its meanings.

74   The mark on Collin's body points the way from the sociosexual economy of bodies in *Illusions perdues* and *Splendeurs et misères des courtisanes* to some of the strangest and most powerful scenarios in Balzac's oeuvre, which involve the body in extreme situations and scenes of its marking with hyperbolic meanings. They dramatize moments when the body is initialized and thus brought into meaning. Among many examples, two novellas demand attention here: *La Duchesse de Langeais* (one of the three tales included in the collection *Histoire des treize*), and *Une passion dans le désert*. In *La Duchesse de Langeais*, we have a clash of wills concerning the body of the Duchess. General Montriveau, who has returned from his explorations in the African desert with a naive and candid heart, and whose passion for the Duchess becomes an absolute in his life, demands to possess her; while the Duchess, a pure product of Faubourg Saint-Germain society, argues that the social laws and conventions have deprived her—in ways quite different from the courtesan—of "the right to dispose of my person" (5:961). She objects: "The gift of my heart wasn't enough for you, you brutally demanded my person" (5:996), and plays out a coquettish game of giving and withholding herself.

The tale spins out its narrative from the "person"—here a clear euphemism for body—of the Duchess. She originally belongs to a kind of restricted libidinal economy which never quite reaches the state of desire. She enlists all her charms to please Montriveau. "But all her conversation was only in some manner the body of the letter; there should have been a postscript in which the principal thought would be spoken" (5:948). If it is only in a postscript that one might find her bodily desire, the problem becomes one of access from letter to postscript, from the signifiers of her conversation to the signified of desire. In Lacanian terms, one could describe the "body of the letter" as the metonymical chain, the slippage of the signified from under the signifier, the textualization of a desire that cannot name its object; whereas the postscript might be that metaphor that would offer access to the occulted signifier pointing to the place of unconscious desire. Given these problematics, one might expect the Duchess's body itself to be "metonymized," to be presented only in parts that never cohere as the object of desire, since they are never assumed as its subject. This is in fact what the text presents.

Montriveau's absolute and exigent desire encounters the Duchess's game-playing, which turns aside and atomizes desire, so that it becomes fetishistically attached to parts of her body: to her feet, to her scarf, to accessories she has touched, to the curls of her hair, to her hand, "insatiable" for kisses, but always blocking access to more. Montriveau's courtship becomes "the work of a Penelope," constantly to be redone (5:959). One evening, we learn, "he kissed the hem of the Duchess's dress, her feet, her knees; but, for the honor of the Faubourg Saint-Germain, we cannot reveal the mysteries of these boudoirs, where one desired everything from love, except that which could prove love" (5:978). Whatever may exactly be underway in this scene, afterward Montriveau decides that the Duchess's caprices form "veils with which a celestial soul had covered itself, and which he had to lift one by one, like those in which she wrapped her adorable body" (5:979). His relation with the Duchess thus takes on the form of the striptease, the progressive but incomplete unveiling.[24]

It is in this context that Montriveau, counseled by his more experienced friend the Marquis de Ronquerolles, decides he must take action. He has the Duchesse abducted from a ball and brought blindfolded to his apartment, where, as punishment for having toyed with his absolute and candid love, he proposes to brand her on the forehead with a red-hot iron which his three masked confederates are at that moment preparing in the next room. "Thus will you wear on your forehead the shameful mark applied to the shoulder of our brothers the convicts" (5:998).

Rather than resisting the notion of her branding, the Duchess immediately accepts it, indeed calls for it. "Ah! my Armand, mark, mark quickly your creature as a poor little possession . . . When you thus have marked a woman as your own, when you have an enslaved soul wearing your red cipher, oh, then you can never give her up, you will be forever mine . . . But the woman who loves always marks herself. Come, gentlemen, come and mark, mark the Duchesse de Langeais. She belongs forever to Monsieur de Montriveau. Come quickly, all of you, my forehead burns hotter than your red brand" (5:998). The proposed mark brings the Duchess's instantaneous conversion from the coquette to the fully romantic woman, passionate and forever enslaved to Montriveau. The brand appears to be the signifier of what the title of part three calls "la femme vraie," the true woman who has been hidden under layers of social and psychic convention.[25] The touch of the red-hot signifier appears in this case to cross the bar of repression, to bring out what has

THE FRENCH REVOLUTION AND BALZAC

all along been latent in the Duchess, to unrepress, to give access to the hidden signifier of desire. One wonders what to make of the fact that the branding iron prepared by Montriveau represents a cross of Lorraine—a sign rich in traditional associations, including the virginal Jeanne d'Arc, but one that does not spell out any message. The absence of specific meaning in the cross may make it all the more effective as the sign of desire itself.

Although the brand is never applied (faced with the Duchess's conversion, Montriveau loses "faith" in the enterprise), the scene evokes a tradition running from the Marquis de Sade to *Histoire d'O,* in which the phallic mark is seen to correspond to, and to provoke, the woman's desire for the total gift of her body and herself—her realization of her own desire in enslavement to male desire. It is, in this sense, a thoroughly patriarchal scenario, a phantasmatic enactment of a male desire for domination which answers the question of what woman wants with the claim that she wants the phallus, and wants to be so positioned in regard to the phallus that she assumes its desire. The body of the woman, in this scenario, finds fulfillment and enters meaning only in the phallic mark: "You have just created me," the Duchess says to Montriveau (5:999).

Yet Balzac's text goes on to complicate this patriarchal scenario. Although the Duchess now insists on making a public display of her passion, thus compromising herself socially, Montriveau shows himself incapable of reading the mark he has himself created: he does not understand the Duchess's conversion, thinks that she is still engaged in coquettish games, and fails to respond to her ultimatum in timely fashion. Thus he loses her to the convent. When he realizes what he has done, he too understands that the game has ceased and that he is faced with an absolute desire, on his part as well as hers, that must be satisfied. He then undertakes his search of the convents to find her. When she refuses to return to him, he plans, with the aid of his twelve blood brothers (who along with him constitute the occult society of "Les Treize"), to abduct her from the convent. The assault on the convent, perched on the rocky island, becomes a substitute formation for taking possession of the body of the Duchess. The Thirteen must "open a path to the convent through the very places where access seemed impracticable" (5:1032); after eleven days of labor, they arrive "at the foot of a promontory rising some sixty meters above the sea, a rock face as hard for men to climb as it would be for a mouse to ascend the polished curves of the porcelain belly of a smooth vase. Fortunately this granite plateau was fissured. Its cleft, whose two lips were as rigid as straight lines, allowed them to attach, at one-foot intervals, wooden posts in which these bold workmen sank iron pitons" (5:1033). The bodily landscape stands for the Duchess in her absence, in fact in her ceasing to exist as desiring subject: when the Thirteen reach their goal, they find the Duchess has expired. All they abduct from the convent is her corpse. They carry it down to the waiting boat, and Ronquerolles proposes to Montriveau a quick sea burial: "This was a woman, now it is nothing. Let's attach a cannonball to each of her feet, throw her in the sea, and not think about her any more except as we think of a book read during childhood" (5:1037). To which Montriveau replies—and these are his final words in the text: "Yes . . . for it is nothing more than a poem." The Duchess's body, signed by the passion that eventually destroyed it, at the last becomes fully textualized, first as a book read in childhood, finally as a poem.

The story of the proposed marking of the Duchess's body, which then produces her own self-marking, is a remarkable example of both the semioticization of the body and the somatization of story. It is as if the body of the Duchess were in a state of latency until the threat of Montriveau's mark creates it, "initializes" it, so that it assumes its place in the sexual economy of exchange. As a result, the whole of the story becomes inscribed on that body: it attaches itself to the destinies of the body, from the opening scene in which Montriveau is seeking for clues to the hidden presence of the body, to the end where the body appears to invest itself in the very landscape while it is wasting away. The body of the Duchess is possessed entire only when dead. The whole narrative moves toward that impossible possession, playing out desire as metonymy: the body is atomized into its parts—and its parts are fetishized—according to the forward movement of desire that cannot seize its object until it is too late, until that end which records the death of desiring. Does the mark of the letter kill, or does it give life? Only when correctly interpreted, it would seem, can it give access to the meaning of desire, and that interpretation appears to come too late—not in the "body of the letter" but in the "postscript."

In *La Duchesse de Langeais* as in its companion novella, *La fille aux yeux d'or,* the woman's body is held in constraint and marked according to the dictates of male desire, and thus becomes the key term in the narrative action. In *La fille aux yeux d'or* even more than in *La Duchesse de Langeais,* the mark is explicitly phallic, the discovery on the part of the sequestered Paquita Valdès of the meaning of sexual difference. But

THE FRENCH REVOLUTION AND BALZAC

another tale from the wilder shores of love is perhaps even more subtle and interesting: *Une passion dans le désert*. Like a number of Balzac's most problematic and experimental narratives, *Une passion dans le désert* has a significant framing structure, which sets off the principal tale as a recounting, elicited by a particular situation and by the insistent questions of an interlocutor, as if to suggest that it is a tale forced into the telling. The first narrator of *Une passion dans le désert* has just left Monsieur Martin's menagerie with a woman friend, who remarks with astonishment at how Martin is able to tame wild beasts. The narrator replies that it is not all that astonishing, that beasts have "passions" and can be taught the vices of the civilized—a remark that has thematic implications if we know that Henri Martin was reputed to make his animals docile by satisfying them sexually before a performance.[26] The narrator goes on to recount that the first time he visited Martin's menagerie, he found himself next to a former soldier who had lost his right leg, a man on whose face "Napoleon's battles were written" (8:1219), who commented that all of Martin's art held no secrets for him, and then proceeded, after dinner and a bottle of champagne, to tell his story to the narrator. The woman accompanying the narrator then wheedles and coaxes him into writing out the soldier's story. The soldier's tale thus comes to us as told by himself to the narrator, who has served as its scribe or ghost writer, transmitting it as a third-person narrative to his woman friend.

The soldier's story tells of his capture by Arabs during General Desaix' campaign in upper Egypt, his escape from his captors, his wandering lost in the desert, and his discovery of a hillock with some palm trees, which turns out to have a spring and a cool grotto. His sleep in the grotto is interrupted by the sound of heavy breathing. When the moon rises, he perceives that the entrance to the grotto is blocked by a sleeping panther, its muzzle stained with gore from a recent kill. He at once thinks of shooting or stabbing the beast, but fears that to do so would result in his death in the embrace of its death throes. As he looks at the panther with fear and fascination, we learn "It was a female. The fur of the belly and the thighs was sparkling white" (8:1224). The gender of the panther is crucial to the narrative. Its indication initiates an extended analogy between panther and woman. At sunrise, the panther yawns, "thus showing the terrifying spectacle of her teeth and her forked tongue, as rough as a file. 'She's like a charming mistress! . . .' thought the Frenchman upon seeing her roll over and make the gentlest and most winning movements" (8:1225). As he begins to caress the panther, in order to pacify her but also from admiration for her beauty, the soldier discovers that she is "an imperious courtesan," insatiable for caresses and play. She is "demanding," she can display "the physiognomy of an artful woman," she is "coquettish" and "jealous."

The detailing of her beauty includes the rings on her tail, her "warm and silky flanks," her "soft and fine contours, the whiteness of her belly, the grace of her head," and "the grace and youth of her contours"; "The blond fur of her dress shaded with fine gradations into the matte white which distinguished her thighs. The light shed profusely by the sun gave a sheen to this living gold, these brown spots, so as to make them indefinably attractive." Above all, the panther's playful response to the soldier's touches suggests erotic foreplay. "He thought involuntarily of his first mistress, whom he had antiphrastically nicknamed *Mignonne,* because she was so fiercely jealous that all the time their passion lasted he had to fear the knife with which she always menaced him" (8:1228)—and he calls the panther Mignonne ("Darling"). This naming is important. The panther is named as a woman, which itself appears an *antiphrase,* a statement intentionally and ironically contrary to fact. But his first mistress was also called Mignonne *par antiphrase,* in ironic contradiction to her dangerous, one might say pantherish, behavior. The two contradictions of fact function as a kind of double negative, affirming the nature of the panther as in fact *mignonne,* the truly amiable mistress he has been looking for. The soldier imagines that he may be the panther's "first love," and it appears that she becomes his.

As the mutual seduction between the soldier and the panther unfolds, they enter a kind of prolonged courtship, filled with caresses, games, solicitations of pleasure, provocations, anxieties. He gently scratches her head and neck with his dagger until she purrs. When the soldier tries to escape one night, the panther tracks him down, just in time to rescue him from a patch of quicksand. From now on, they are companions till death, their caresses necessary to one another. As an amorous partner, the panther suggests that woman is both fascinating and dangerous, a body in need of constant attention, insatiable for touches and gestures because of a desire that never can be set to rest. The discourse repeatedly takes us back to the fascinating cavity of the panther's mouth, both alluring and terrifying, with its rows of sharp teeth: it appears as a representation of the *vagina dentata,* mythologically associated with male fears of castration by the woman's sex. And there is also the detail of the panther's tail, repeatedly evoked: "This powerful arm, round like a gourd, was almost three feet high" (8:1227). Described unfailingly as erect, the tail makes the panther something like the phantasmatic "phallic woman," and increases the sense of her potential danger as a woman. Janet L. Beizer astutely remarks the analogy-by-compensation of the panther's tail and the soldier's missing limb—missing, that is, by the time he tells his story: "The return of the tail represents a graft of repressed material onto the official form of the story."[27] In an extended analogy, then, we are invited to view the panther as a woman. But the insistence of the analogy also forces us to read it the other way round—to view woman as panther: graceful, feline, coquettish, and potentially dangerous. This vector of the analogy may be more important for understanding the story's real preoccupations. Like discourse of the courtesan, discourse of the female animal is a way in which patriarchal society permits talk of female sexuality. The extended analogy of panther and woman allows men to speak of female sexuality as alluring and dangerous, coquettish and insatiable, in ways that could not be articulated without the analogy. Direct discourse about female sexuality, at least as it would concern respectable women, is impermissible.

The panther Mignonne thus represents a particularly attractive and potentially dangerous sexuality, where danger and attraction are indissolubly linked. We are reminded of other Balzacian scenarios in which intense sexuality evokes the possibility of mutilation and castration: in *La fille aux yeux d'or* (where the alluring Paquita Valdès is described as a "tiger" [5:1064]), in *Sarrasine* (where castration is made literal, and negates the possibility of sexual love), and, in more attenuated form, in *La Duchesse de Langeais*, in *Illusions perdues* and *Splendeurs et misères des courtisanes*, where sexuality at a certain point maims or kills or becomes simply impossible. *La peau de chagrin* provides the allegory of sexuality as essentially self-destructive, a loss of self in the self-expenditure of orgasm. *Une passion dans le désert*, no doubt because it has transferred the discourse of female sexuality onto the animal, provides the most direct representation of love of a woman as potentially, perhaps inherently, mutilating, an experience in which the man's body receives the mark of the woman's wound.

Such appears to be the story encoded in the strangely mutilated ending of *Une passion dans le désert*. The narrator's written account breaks off at a moment of intense passion and understanding between the soldier and the panther. At this point, the narrator's interlocutor—she who has read the written account—comments, obtusely or sarcastically: "I've read your brief on behalf of animals" (8:1231). But she wants to know how the story ended. The narrator is now forced to supply the ending he has up to now suppressed (as if, like the narrator of *Sarrasine,* who is reluctant to tell his story, he knew it contained dangers for the teller in relation to the listener). The story ended, he says, as all great passions do: with a misunderstanding. He lets the soldier finish the story in his own words: "I don't know how I hurt her, but she turned against me as if enraged; and, with her sharp teeth, she bit into my thigh, only gently, no doubt. Thinking that she wanted to devour me, I plunged my dagger in her throat. She rolled over with a cry that froze my heart, I saw her in agony, looking at me without anger. I would have given anything in the world, even my cross [of the Legion of Honor] which I didn't yet have, to bring her back to life" (8:1232).

The text allows us to read their final misunderstanding as taking place during an actual sexual consummation of their relationship. Yet to do so is to force the extended metaphor of the text to yield a literal meaning that it tends to refuse. The drama is played out instead on the level of primal male phantasies about the seductive and devouring female. The panther's bite into the soldier's thigh is undecidably both a love caress and a wounding, and his destructive action in reply is a response to both—as well as an ironic comment on his claim to understand M. Martin's secrets for taming beasts.[28] Nothing in the text explicitly links the panther's bite to his amputated leg—French soldiers arrive to save him, and the text ends with his reflections on the spirituality of the desert—but it is impossible for the reader not to make the linkage, at least in the realm of the phantasmatic. If the panther represents female sexuality at its most intense, seductive, and devouring, it "follows"—in a certain infantile logic—that the man's body must pay the price of a surrender to the force of that sexuality. The price is represented by amputation, a displaced analogue of castration, and by the soldier's final reflections on his loneliness and his regret for his life in the desert. The very title of the tale, *Une passion dans le désert,* is oxymoronic: the desert is by definition depopulated, inimical to the exchange of mutual passion, confined to the autoerotic and narcissistic passions. In a sense, the soldier's narcissism comes to the fore at the end of the story, when he deals with the threat of Mignonne by destroying her, with that very dagger he has earlier used to scratch and caress her body—but not before the passion of and for the female has made its mark on his body.

His body at the end bears the mark of having engaged female sexuality. Or more accurately, his body at the beginning bears this mark: we learn of the soldier's amputated right leg at the outset of the story, and it is never referred to again. It is as if the man who has given a place to female passion is always already mutilated because he is marked by the sign of female mutilation. The only way to avoid that mutilation, in Balzac's world, seems to be in the manner of Gobseck or the antiques

dealer of *La peau de chagrin,* through living as "the neuter gender," refusing to enter the sexual economy at all. All of Balzac's passionate male lovers end up really or symbolically mutilated or deprived, if not dead. Sexual passion exacts this toll, on the body itself. In *Une passion dans le désert,* the narrative form of the tale itself bears the mark of mutilation, in the originally incomplete telling of the story, then the filling in of the dénouement in response to the woman listener's demand, followed by a breaking off that leaves us in doubt about how the story told has affected the relation of teller and listener. Has mutilation—as in *Sarrasine*—established itself in the very situation of narrating, in the process of narrative transmission?

The presence in *La comédie humaine* of such texts as *Une passion dans le désert, La Duchesse de Langeais, La fille aux yeux d'or*—and there are others in a similar vein—forces us to reflect on the destinies of the sexual body in Balzac's more overtly social and "realist" texts, and to perceive how much the body, there too, is marked by primitive scenarios which commingle intense desire with fear, and desire for the woman's body with dire results to the male body. Time and again, these novels reach moments when male desire for the woman's body unleashes a reaction in the realm of female sexuality that, by a circuit of return, marks the male body in a drastic manner. An example among many would be *La Cousine Bette,* where the devastating effects of Valérie Marneffe's sexual body are registered not only in the disintegration of the Baron Hulot and his family, but eventually also as a specifically sexual bodily pathology, in the exotic disease that destroys Madame Marneffe and her lovers. Another kind of example is provided by *Le lys dans la vallée,* in which Félix de Vandenesse's passion for the chaste Henriette de Mortsauf produces a self-negating sexual economy where repression eventually takes a fearsome toll. Madame de Mortsauf dies in agonies of unfulfilled desire, consumed by a thirst which, in her deathbed delirium, she explicitly identifies as the product of unconsummated passion: her final illness reads as a fully realized conversion hysteria, in which the body becomes the symbolic site of unconscious desire. As for Félix, her death, and her vengeful testamentary letter—in which she reveals that she desired him, and wanted him to break the economy of abnegation—leaves him mutilated: "I tried to detach myself from the force by which I lived: a torture comparable to that by which the Tartars punished adultery, fixing a member of the guilty person in a piece of wood, and leaving him a knife to cut it off with if he didn't wish to die of hunger" (9:1204). The image contains a clear displacement: for *a* member of the *guilty person,* one can read *the guilty member.* Félix finishes in symbolic castration, which is then repeated, doubled, in the framing structure of the novel when the new object of his affections, Natalie de Manerville, responds to a reading of his confession with a punishing refusal to be his mistress, perceiving that he is marked by a permanent "dryness of the heart" (9:1229). Once again, the desublimation of female desire strikes the male in his desire. The male's effort to mark the woman's body results in the unleashing of a sexuality that is wounding to the male. The project of making the body semiotic repeatedly appears to be as dangerous as it is necessary.

Balzac's persistent attention to the body—his "utopian" novel, *Le médecin de campagne,* is largely about the reform of the body—extends to a corpus of quasi-theoretical writings that he apparently intended to collect under the rubric *Pathologie de la vie sociale,* in close anticipation of Freud's title *The Psychopathology of Everyday Life.* In such fragmentary texts as "Etude de moeurs par les gants," "Physiologie de la toilette," "Physiologie du cigare," "Traité de la vie élégante," and "Théorie de la démarche," Balzac considers the bodily signs by which social man reveals his inner meaning. The enterprise is imperative, says Balzac, because in the platitudinous nineteenth century, when social distinctions have been effaced and people no longer reveal their social status and function through their dress and appearance, such small signs as the cut of a waistcoat or the knot of a cravat become revelatory when properly studied. One needs a semiotics of bodily adornment and personal accessory in order to know people: what Balzac calls "la vestignomie" has become "almost a branch of the art created by Gall and Lavater."[29] In his reference to the pseudo-sciences of phrenology and physiognomy, to which he gave loose allegiance, Balzac demonstrates again his concern to make the body constantly semiotic, a concern that extends to Madame de Mortsauf's conversion hysteria as much as to Lucien de Rubempré's acquisition of the accessory signs of the Parisian dandy. The *Pathologie* was to be a "complete anthropology" of social life.[30] As such, it was to establish the principles of legibility of the social animal, the sign-system by which every bodily adornment, movement, and gesture could be read.

THE FRENCH REVOLUTION AND BALZAC

The legibility of the body is indeed a central Balzacian obsession: he is intent on making all bodily signs, whether natural or artificial, yield their cultural meaning. The enterprise corresponds with the obsession of looking. Balzac's world is subtended and transversed by the gaze. People spy on one another, and disguise themselves in the attempt to avoid prying eyes, but rarely with success since the penetrating observer can always find the signs he needs to make meaning. The most insistent observer of all is the Balzacian narrator, who constantly scrutinizes and interrogates faces, surfaces, and appearances, in order to detect the meanings that they cannot help contain. As D. A. Miller has argued in *The Novel and the Police,* Balzac's narrative vision corresponds to the model of Jeremy Bentham's panopticon prison, in which a centrally posted surveillant can, himself unobserved, observe and interpret the appearances and the movements of all others.[31] Vision in Balzac—as in other realist writers I shall discuss later—almost always is "scopophilia," to use Freud's term: an investment of sexual desire in the gaze. The hidden observer deciphering others offers countless examples of Luce Irigaray's "phallic gaze." Yet Balzac's evident pleasure in vision and his repeated announcement of the triumphs of observation over the hidden (which will be codified in Sherlock Holmes's deductions from the minutest details) encounter limit-cases, which we have already touched upon in discussion of such texts as *La Duchesse de Langeais* and *Une passion dans le désert:* moments when looking produces not clarity and mastery but trouble, the inability to see, and the disempowerment of the observer. These moments characteristically concern looking at the female body as the object of desire while conceiving its potential as desiring subject.

"Woman and paper are two white [or blank] things that suffer everything," Balzac remarks.[32] This cryptic comment may indicate the affinity of marking the (female) body with marking paper. Both are considered to be blank before the marking, perhaps passive as well, since they "suffer" everything. They suffer, perhaps, because they receive the imposition of the phallic signifier, in the manner of the red-hot cross of Lorraine in *La Duchesse de Langeais* The effect of phallic vision, we have noted, seems so often to strike back at the observer, to make him suffer. Is it then in compensation that the writer or artist attempts to ply his phallic instrument—as when, for instance, Balzac, preparing to write *Le lys dans la vallée* as a riposte to Sainte-Beuve's novel *Volupté,* announced that he would impale Sainte-Beuve on his pen? Yet Balzacian writer and artist figures are themselves so often struck dumb, blind, impotent, as in *Gambara, Facino Cane,* and *Le chef d'oeuvre inconnu.*

Writing on and writing in the body are necessary to writing itself, but they inevitably bring compensatory punishments.

In concluding this exploration of the Balzacian body, I want to mention a scene in Balzac's first fully achieved novel, *La peau de chagrin*, which appears as a nexus of the problem of the female body made the object of the glance of the desiring male subject who is obsessed with the question of woman's desire. Raphaël de Valentin, the prototype of Balzac's young protagonists animated by a strong desire to possess women, riches, and glory, is stymied in his pursuit of Foedora, the "woman without a heart" whom he accuses of being an "atheist in love," since she appears entirely resistant to the demands of desire, incapable of entering at all into the sociosexual economy.[33] In an effort to understand "the enigma hidden in this beautiful semblance of woman" (10:185), he resolves to spend a night hidden in her bedroom, to "examine her corporeally as I had studied her intellectually, in order finally to know her entire" (10:179). In particular, he wonders whether she may not resemble a figure "in a book recently published by a poet, a true artist's conception chiseled in the statue of Polycles" (10:178–79). A variant reading from the first edition of *La peau de chagrin* clarifies this obscure allusion: it refers to the novel *Fragoletta*, by Henri de Latouche, which contains the story of a hermaphrodite; there is a statue of a hermaphrodite attributed to the sculptor Polycles. Thus the scene of corporeal curiosity is introduced by a doubt as to Foedora's sexual identity, the possibility that she might, as Balzac put it in his book review of *Fragoletta*, lack "a complete sex."[34]

The scene develops as a kind of striptease, as Foedora's chambermaid—curiously named Justine, as if in allusion to Sade—removes the articles of her clothing one by one. Thus we reach the awaited moment: "Justine unlaced her. I looked at her curiously at the moment when the last veil was lifted. She had the bosom of a virgin, which dazzled me; through her shift and by the light of the candles, her pink and white body sparkled like a statue of silver that shines under its gauze envelope. No, no imperfection should have made her fear the furtive eyes of love" (10:184). The lack of "imperfection" seems merely to contribute to Foedora's status as "enigma": her body is all-too-perfect, a "statue of silver," like the work of a sculptor. The lack of an imperfection suggests that the "woman without a heart" is also the "woman without a sex," who gives no hold to love because there is no entry into her. As a result, Raphaël is "dazzled": the male observer's glance is turned back on the subject, branding him with the impossibility of ever possessing Foedora.

THE FRENCH REVOLUTION AND BALZAC

Here and elsewhere, Balzac's regressive scenarios generate close analogies to Freud's narratives of the infantile perception of sexual difference, especially the boy's perception of the female body as presenting the threat of castration—represented here, as it often is, by the dazzling threat to the observer's eyes—and a denial of what has been seen. It is interesting to note that despite the announcement that Foedora's last veil has been lifted, her body remains lightly veiled by her shift, for the covering up or glossing over—*beschönigen*—of what he has seen is typical of the boy's reaction to his perception, according to Freud in "The Infantile Genital Organization" (*Standard Edition* 19:143–44). This moment in *La peau de chagrin* also evokes Freud's reflections on "Medusa's Head": Medusa's effect of turning the observer to stone is figured both in Foedora's statue-like quality, and in Raphaël's enforced immobility in the window-bay from which he watches. Just before the passage quoted above, Foedora discusses with Justine her dissatisfaction that her hair was excessively crimped that evening, which has an echo in Freud's remark that Medusa's snaky locks offer "a confirmation of the technical rule according to which a multiplication of penis symbols signifies castration" (*Standard Edition* 18:273). Noting that the Medusa symbol is worn by the virgin goddess Athene, Freud claims that Athene thus "becomes a woman who is unapproachable and repels all sexual desires—since she displays the terrifying genitals of the Mother." Without entering into the place of Raphaël's mother in *La peau de chagrin* we seem to detect here, as in the other Balzac texts, a scene of infantile curiosity, a looking at and unveiling of the woman's sex that presents a literalistic version of the castration complex, as an actual experience of menace rather than a law imposed upon desire—though of course Balzac's narrative itself will be governed by laws deriving from the scene, including the law that negates any narrative development for this particular object of desire. Foedora's body—suspended, like that of the hysteric, in an undecided gender identity—itself remains unmarked, non-semiotic, unavailable to narrative. Raphaël's passion will play itself out with the courtesans Aquilina and Euphrasie, and with the generous, self-sacrificing Pauline. Foedora remains the enigma of woman, and as such essentially non-narratable. Nothing happens to her because, unlike the Duchesse de Langeais or Paquita Valdès, her body never is marked.

La peau de chagrin thus provides an example in the negative of that process of semioticization of the body that appears so important throughout *La comédie humaine:* a process that results in an impressive somatization of stories because the destinies of the body so marked tend to play out the narrative plot. That is, in Balzac's work we are repeatedly made witness to the moment at which the narrative text stages the marking of a body in order to narrativize it, as if in an allegory of that semiotic operation that must occur if the body is to become a narrative signifier. The importance of this process is confirmed by Balzac's descriptive and "theoretical" texts, from the *Pathologie de la vie sociale* and elsewhere, which all insist upon finding those signs that will allow the body to be read as socially signifying, as the key player in a story played out according to social codes and determinants. This social body is a prime token of exchange value in the capitalist economy—the nexus of the exchange between money and desire, for instance. In fact, the social economy is always already a sociosexual economy, in which the underlying metaphors of investment, conservation, and expenditure refer as much to the economics of libido as to the circulation of money. If Balzac invents the nineteenth century, he also in many ways—in the wake of Rousseau, to whom he owes so much, and in the wake of the Revolution, which creates a necessary aesthetics of embodiment—invents the modern body.

The mark of meaning on the body, the process of its semioticization, is a central issue in all of the texts that I have looked at. When one moves from Rousseau to the French Revolution, the process of assigning meaning to the individual's body leaves the domain of the individual to become a pressing concern for the state—for those who are trying to define and to institute the new order. With Balzac, we enter an emergent capitalist economy which necessarily uses the body in certain ways. At the same time, that economy is part of the story of the body, undergirded by the economies of desire. Balzac seems a particularly important point of entry into the modern conception of the body because he so often takes us into the laboratory where meaning is invented, for and on the body: he repeatedly shows us the creation of the semiotic body in his strange scenarios of bodily marking. We are made to witness the creation of a necessary sign in modern narrative.

4 The Body in the Field of Vision

REPRESENTING THE BODY in modern narrative—as the examples looked at thus far suggest—seems always to involve viewing the body. The dominant nineteenth-century tradition, that of realism, insistently makes the visual the master relation to the world, for the very premise of realism is that one cannot understand human beings outside the context of the things that surround them, and knowing those things is a matter of viewing them, detailing them, and describing the concrete milieux in which men and women enact their destinies. To know, in realism, is to see, and to represent is to describe. To the extent that persons are the object of knowledge, they too must be described, not only in their psychological composition but also in their "objectal" form, as bodies. While the bodies viewed are both male and female, vision is typically a male prerogative, and its object of fascination the woman's body, in a cultural model so persuasive that many women novelists don't reverse its vectors.[1] Looking in the realist tradition seems in fact to be highly gendered, perhaps most of all because by the nineteenth century gender is assumed to be part of the essential definition of persons and bodies. The more fluid, androgynous potential of bodies that one finds in Renaissance romance—in Edmund Spenser, for instance—and still in latent form in some of the Romantics, whose erotic ideal suggests androgyny (one finds traces in both Balzac and Mary Shelley), seems to be fully repressed in realism, as in modern culture as a whole. While spectatorship and readership may in fact be more fluid and androgynous than is often assumed, the optical "laws" implicit in the narratives I shall discuss are predicated on apparently rigid understandings that social life and its actors are primordially structured and motivated by the law of sexual difference, which is considered indeed to be the prime source of life's dramas.

Emma Bovary's Body

In *Madame Bovary,* during the night following the famous ball at the Château de La Vaubyessard that will so stimulate her desires for a more glamorous life, Emma Bovary opens the window of the room assigned to her and Charles in the château and looks out: "She gazed for a long time at the windows of the château, trying to figure out which were the rooms of the people she had noticed during the evening. She would have liked to know their lives, to get into them, to become part of them."[2] The window, like the mirror, is a traditional metaphor of realist vision directed at the world. The window here works in both directions: Emma is looking out, and also attempting to look in, and to get in *(y pénétrer, s'y confondre),* to make her post of observation the means of access to the lives of others.[3] More than the traditional window through which one looks in one direction, this doubled window frame figures both the techniques and the ambitions of realist writing: it deploys a gaze sub-tended by the desire to know, a gaze that wants both to record the observable and to penetrate to the essential, to appropriate both ap pearances and their inner principles. This project, the passage suggests, is not necessarily realizable. Emma cannot see into the other lives behind the other windows; the gaze subtended by desire produces the work of the imagination, and with it the possibility of error, the illusions of desire.

Shortly before Emma's meditative vigil at the window, during the ball itself, a servant climbs up on a chair and breaks two window panes. "At the sound of the breaking glass, Madame Bovary turned her head and noticed in the garden the faces of the peasants pressed against the windows" (85). This momentary intrusion of the outside world—the world Emma hopes to have left behind her—starkly recalls the social coordinates of the novel and Emma's uneasy, never completed trajectory from the farm of her childhood to a small-town bourgeois existence which can never satisfy her real aspirations: to the city, the aristocracy, and a life of leisured romance. The breaking of the window panes revealing the gaze of the peasantry on the gentry also stands as another emblem of realism—the objectification of a class and a way of life examined from without, at a distance, and, especially, examined visually, subjected to a gaze both fascinated and hostile. The smashed window panes take us beyond the traditional post of observation at the window and the appropriating gaze directed toward others that it so often implies. The smashing of the panes—to reveal those watchers outside who are other, excluded, in a state of opposition—seems to abolish mediations (of appropriation or exchange) between observer and object, to make the gaze "naked," directed at the object in a particularly detached and scrutinizing manner. There is always a relation of desire between watcher and watched; here the desire suggests hostility, a standoff rather than interpenetration. Smashing window panes, it is worth noting, returns in one of Henry James's essays on Balzac as an image of the moment when strict observation releases something that he calls "vision": "one of those smashes of the window-pane of the real that reactions sometimes produce even in the stubborn."[4] In the smashed window pane we seem to have the excitement and the potential danger of vision—what makes the application of vision to the field of vision itself the stuff of drama.

Emma Bovary's body is very much held in a field of vision; it is in fact the object to which the narrative gaze, which takes in multiple details of life in Tostes and Yonville l'Abbaye, constantly returns. Emma's body in many ways defines our sense of the realist body: the body relentlessly presented by an invisible observer, who can be variously situated in the place of observing characters—through the play of *style indirect libre*—but in his very mobility and lack of identity is also panoptical. Emma's body is over and over again the object fixed and brought into focus by a subtending gaze that can be animated by fascination or hostility, by tenderness or irony, miming both Emma's own desiring gaze from the window of the château and the peasants' alienated gaze through the smashed window panes. *Madame Bovary* in this manner exemplifies the desires inherent in realist vision—to appropriate the world, to exchange places with others—as well as the hostilities implicit in the exercise of vision on an objectified other.

The reader's sense of the presence of Emma's body is so intense and so memorable that it comes as something of a surprise, upon rereading the novel, to find that there is really very little in the way of full-length portraiture of Emma. Even on her wedding day, a full page is devoted to the toilettes of the wedding guests, whereas we only glimpse Emma during the walk to the Town Hall: "Emma's dress, too long, dragged a bit on the ground; from time to time she stopped to lift its edge, and then, delicately, with her gloved fingers picked out the weeds and burrs"

(54). Observation of Emma often seems to dissipate in the mediocrity of her observers, for instance her lover Léon: "She was the beloved of all the novels, the heroine of all the plays, the vague *she* of all the volumes of poetry. He rediscovered on her shoulders the amber color of the 'Bathing Odalisque'; she had the deep bosom of feudal noblewomen; she looked like 'The Pale Lady of Barcelona'; but above all she was the Angel!" (342). Characteristically, when Charles Bovary attempts to study his wife's eyes in detail, he ends up seeing the observer, himself, reflected in them: "His own eye became lost in these depths, and he saw himself in miniature to the shoulders, with the kerchief tied around his head and the top of his nightshirt unbuttoned" (61). If eyes are traditionally the mirrors of the soul, that part of the body which gives access from the physical to the spiritual, here the mirrors instead reflect the observer, displaying his everyday banality. His gaze seems to have no grasp on the other's reality.

It is tempting to ascribe the lack of pictorial coherence of Emma's body to the insufficiency of her observers, but this may be too easy a solution, since the elusive narrator-observer rarely takes the opportunity to go beyond their limited visions. Although the panoptical observer doesn't, in the manner of Léon, reduce Emma to literary clichés—which are so much the inspiration of her self-conceptions and aspirations—and doesn't, like Charles, reflect his own inanity, he appears to make even less of an effort to see her entire. In fact, while we have many details, including her dark hair, her supple waist, her amber skin, her white fingernails, her dark eyes with their soft black eyelashes, we have rather little sense of what she looks like. Descriptions tend toward the metonymical, accumulating details of her body and especially of her dress and accessories. Emma tends to become a fetishized object, or rather, an object that is never seen whole because her accessory details become fetishes, arresting attention along the way. Charles, shortly after their marriage, offers a characteristic presentation of Emma by way of accessories: "He couldn't stop himself from continually touching her comb, her rings, her stole" (62). When Emma takes Rodolphe as her lover, we learn of her self-presentation to him: "It was for him that she filed her nails with the care of a metalsmith, and that there was never enough cold cream on her skin, or enough patchouli in her handkerchiefs. She loaded herself with bracelets, rings, necklaces" (249). When we see her in the perspective of her second lover, Léon, we are told: "He admired the exaltation of her soul and the lace of her petticoat" (342). This last example, linking the spiritual abstraction and the material detail in a zeugma worthy of Alexander Pope, suggests the procedure and the problem: Emma as an object of the gaze and of desire is repeatedly "metonymized," fragmented into a set of accessory details rather than achieving coherence as either object or subject.

It is not easy to know how to understand this incoherence of Emma's body. One could rationalize the incoherence on the thematic plane, noting that Emma's three men, Charles, Rodolphe, and Léon, all are limited agents of desire, with the result that the object of desire never can be wholly known. One could read in this light the famous passage describing Emma's beautification by adultery—"Never had Madame Bovary been so beautiful as at this time" (257)—which was cited as particularly shocking by Flaubert's prosecutor, Ernest Pinard, at the trial of *Madame Bovary*. The passage, once again, insists upon details: eyelids, nostrils, the fleshy corners of her lips shaded by a bit of down, and so on. Although her enhanced beauty is caused by her adulterous passion for Rodolphe, the descriptive paragraph leads us to another observer: "Charles, as in the first days of their marriage, found her delicious and completely irresistible." Closing the passage with the beguiled gaze of the deceived husband may indicate the problem of desire underlying the visual field: the general inadequacy of the libidinal economy to give a fully valued and persuasive image of its animating center, Emma. Furthermore, one could say that the failure to penetrate to the romantic core of Emma works as a demonstration that there is no such core; her romantic soul is inauthentic, a product of her readings in romance and her inability to achieve a mature relation to desire. Emma's body and her person never cohere, just as her passions never cohere into the romantic love she seeks, just as her very subjectivity never coheres into what an English novelist would have called "character."[5] The fragmentation of Emma's body into parts and accessories is, in this reading, part of Flaubert's theme, in a sense the very subject of his novel: the inauthenticity of desire that has come to be called "Bovarysme" results in, and results from, the metonymization of the body as both subject and object of desire. It is as if the celebrated Lacanian "mirror stage" failed, in this instance, to deliver a coherent external image as well as a coherent inner sense of self. In this particular mirror held up to the world, the body and the self are seen to be fragmented.

Yet the novel gives evidence of something more radical and disturbing than the thematics of fragmentation: a certain perturbation of the field of vision and the act of seeing. If the play of *style indirect libre* allows the authorial persona to hide behind the persons in the fiction, it also can permit a synthesizing vision, of the sort we are given for the contexts of Emma's passions—the Bovarys' house, the town of Yonville l' Abbaye —but never for her body, the focal point of the novel. The passage on Emma's beautification by adultery, for instance, begins as the narrator's presentation, only to dead-end in the limited vision of Charles. The pervasive limits to the vision of Emma's body appear to be themselves symbolized, given their *mise-en-abyme,* in the notorious scene of the cab with the lowered shades which perambulates aimlessly through Rouen while Léon seduces Emma within. If this episode appeared highly shocking to Flaubert's first readers—it was one of the passages censored by the *Revue de Paris* during the novel's serial publication—it is in part because of its denial of the transparency of bourgeois existence; its insistence upon veiling the body indicates that the body is in a state of infraction. The body denuded behind the lowered shades of the cab is not innocent—quite the contrary. But all one sees of it is the "naked hand" that emerges from behind the shade, to throw away the torn pieces of the letter Emma has written to announce her break from Léon. That naked hand bears the freight of what is denied to sight. And when Emma herself emerges from the cab, her veil is pulled down, hiding her face.

One can best grasp the problematics of description of Emma by contrast with novelists such as Balzac and Dickens, in whose worlds accessory details are always legible as a signs of the whole, as keys to such inward concepts as "character." Details for Balzac and Dickens are essentially synecdoches, parts that stand for a whole, indicial signs which, correctly deciphered, give access to meanings. In Flaubert's world, however, details often seem to resist behaving as proper synecdoches. Particularly when they concern the body, they lead to no coherent construction of the whole; the eye and the mind are pulled back to the object-detail itself.[6] For instance, at the moment when Emma gives in to Rodolphe's seduction, eye and mind are arrested by details of the fabric of the clothes the two of them are wearing: "The cloth of her dress caught on the velvet of his riding coat, she bent back her white throat, which filled with a sigh; and, giving way, all in tears, with a long shiver and hiding her face, she abandoned herself" (217). To take another sort of example, from the period when Emma and Léon's passion has waned and she is striving to mask the banality of their trysts: "This disappointment was quickly eclipsed by a new hope, and Emma returned to him more aroused, more avid. She undressed herself brutally, ripping out the fine cord of her corset, which hissed around her thighs like a slithering adder" (362). Scenes of undressing are particularly pertinent to narratives of the body—as moments of revelation and recognition—but here we are once again sidetracked by the accessory: the attention of the eye, and the ear, are drawn to the corset lacing, figured as a sinister snake.

Revelation and recognition are imprinted not directly on Emma's body, but in a gesture and a detail of an article of clothing that reveal the impossibility that undressing will result in the fullness of passion that she seeks—or in the full vision sought by the reader. The *mise-en-scène* of the erotic body does not lead to seeing that body.

A final example of the presentation of Emma's body is perhaps the most revealing of all. It comes during Emma's death agony—after she has poisoned herself with arsenic—when the priest administers extreme unction:

> Then he recited the *Misereatur* and the *Indulgentiam,* dipped his right thumb in the oil and began his unctions: first on the eyes, which had so coveted all worldly luxuries; then on the nostrils, avid for warm breezes and the smells of love; then on the mouth, which had opened to lie, which had groaned with pride and cried out in pleasure; then on the hands, which had taken delight in soft touches, and finally on the soles of the feet, once so quick when she ran to the satisfaction of her desires, and which now would walk no more. (410–11)

In this valedictory, Emma's dying body is extraordinarily alive as the site of sensual pleasures, but alive in its parts, in localized organs of sensory contact with the world. This final inventory again resists totalization of Emma's body. Only as a corpse does Emma's body seem to achieve coherence, a shape that can be grasped and modeled: "The sheet sloped downward from her breasts to her knees, rising up again to the point of her toes" (418).

The demise of Emma's erotic body is closely linked to its commodification, as the various accessories and articles of fashion purveyed to her by Lheureux turn into the debts that provoke her suicide. Commodification finds its ultimate expression in the repossession of her personal effects by the *huissier,* who makes out his inventory before two witnesses: "They examined her dresses, the linen, the bathroom; and her existence, even in its most intimate recesses, was, like a corpse being autopsied, wholly exposed to the gazes of these three men" (377). The estimating gaze of the bailiff, appraising the market value of those accessories that so define Emma's erotic body, recalls that her body also belongs to a market economy. It suggests that the gaze of the realist novelist is, almost by definition, part of the same economy, a gaze that partakes of commodity fetishism. One might reflect, in this context, on the importance of Hippolyte's clubfoot in the novel: Charles's surgery on the foot is supposed to bring him the glory that Emma so desires for him, and to restore her love for him. Its abject failure—followed by amputation of Hippolyte's leg—throws her back into "all the bad ironies of adultery triumphant" (246). Charles in remorse then buys Hippolyte a prosthetic leg so magnificent that Hippolyte can bring himself to wear it only on special occasions, preferring a wooden peg for everyday use. If the foot is the most common object of erotic fetishism, Hippolyte's club foot is both the fetish par excellence and its opposite: a fetish requiring amputation, and substituted for by a highly fetishized commercial simulacrum.

One could argue, in an apparent paradox, that the fragmentation of the object of the gaze makes *Madame Bovary* the very type of the realist novel. Roman Jakobson asserts that metonymy is the typical figure of realist fiction, which uses details, fragments assembled through contiguity, to achieve its effect of a furnished world where subjectivity and desire are always rubbing up against the hard edges of the world of things.[7] Jakobson's prime example is another suicide of another adulterous woman, Anna Karenina: her handbag becomes the telling, tragic detail when she throws herself before the oncoming train. Yet Anna Karenina is seen more fully than Emma Bovary; her descriptive fragments construct a more finished portrait. In another instance, Emile Zola's visual tableaux—his framed shots, often inspired by analogous moments in Flaubert—more thoroughly inventory and order the details selected by vision, working toward apparently exhaustive and static pictures rather than the elusive impressionism of Flaubert.[8] Flaubert's practice, here as elsewhere, offers a version of a realist strategy so radical that it at times (especially in the later novels, *L'éducation sentimentale* and *Bouvard et Pécuchet*) virtually "deconstructs" the realist enterprise. Particularly where the object of vision is a person—a person who is, visually speaking, first of all a body—Flaubert tends to suggest that there is no essence, no coherent substance, no real object of desire, behind or beyond the phenomenal surface. Another way to put this, in thematic terms, is that Emma Bovary has no body—of her own. Her body is the social and phantasmatic construction of the men who look at her. If the narrator is included among these men, the result of Flaubert's practice

THE BODY IN THE FIELD OF VISION

is nonetheless a kind of feminist response (as in the celebrated phrase, "Madame Bovary, c'est moi") in contrast to the essentialist otherness of Balzac's women-as-enigma, in that it denies authority to the observers' construction. If Flaubert is the realist par excellence, he also suggests the ultimate impossibility of realism insofar as it is subtended by the desire to know. There is something unsatisfactory about the field of vision: it can never quite see, in its entirety and its meaning, the body that is its central concern. To the extent that the body in realism is essentially gendered—because sexual difference is assumed to be definitional—the realist visual discourse is frustrated.

Scopophilia, Epistemophilia, and the Body

The intent of these too cursory remarks on the presentation of Emma Bovary's body is to raise some larger questions about the status of the body in the field of vision in those master nineteenth-century novels that define our sense of the realist tradition and its relation to the objective world. It is evident that sight has always been both a central faculty and a central metaphor in the search for truth. "Since the days of Greek philosophy sight has been hailed as the most excellent of the senses," writes Hans Jonas. "The noblest activity of the mind, *theoria*, is described in metaphors mostly taken from the visual sphere."[9] Sight is the sense that represents the whole epistemological project; it is conceived to be the most objective and objectivizing of the senses, that which best allows an inspection of reality that produces truth. "I see," in our common usage, is equivalent to "I know"—*voir* is *savoir*. But truth is not of easy access; it often is represented as veiled, latent, or covered, so that the discovery of truth becomes a process of unveiling, laying bare, or denuding. Jean-Paul Sartre's epistemology isolates what he labels "the Actaeon complex": "One pulls off the veils of nature, one unveils it . . . ; any research always involves the idea of a nudity that one exposes by putting aside the obstacles that cover it, as Actaeon pushes aside the branches the better to see Diana at her bath."[10] As Sartre's image so clearly indicates, the epistemic principle, and the point from which vision is directed at the world, have largely throughout the Western tradition been assumed to be male, perhaps especially within the history of philosophy. That which is to be looked at, denuded, unveiled, has been been repeatedly personified as female: Truth as goddess, as sphinx, or as woman herself.

"Supposing truth is a woman—what then?" asks Nietzsche at the start of *Beyond Good and Evil,* evoking a long tradition of philosophical thought, which he then brands clumsy in its approach to woman.[11] The reflection of the eighteenth-century *moraliste* Charles Pinot Duclos, connecting the pursuit of truth and the erotic pursuit of women, bears repetition here: "I don't know why men accuse women of falsity, and have made Truth [*la Vérité*] female. Problem to be solved. They also say she is naked, and that could well be so. It is no doubt from a love of Truth that we pursue women with such ardor; we seek to strip them of everything that we think hides the Truth; and, when we have satisfied our curiosity on one, we lose our illusions, we run to another, to be happier. Love, pleasure, and inconstancy are only a result of the desire to know Truth."[12] Duclos thus summarizes what I have called the metaphysical Don Juan tradition: the idea that the need to seduce and to know large numbers of women, and to move on constantly from one to another, is connected with a continually unsatisfied quest for knowledge. This tradition produces a semantic convergence of the erotic and the epistemic in the words *libertin* and *libertinage,* which in the seventeenth century refer both to free thinking and to free living: thought uncontrolled by the teachings of the Church (atheism or some variant thereof) and an erotic life uncontrolled by social and religious conventions. It is a durable tradition, explicitly recognized as a tradition from Théophile de Viau, whose *libertinage* led to his prosecution in the early seventeenth century, to Diderot, whose spokesman in *Le neveu de Rameau* announces: "My thoughts, they're like loose women."[13] It continues to our time as Sartre's "Actaeon complex," one of the categories in which the philosophical tradition—perhaps especially in phenomenology—conceives knowledge of, and appropriation of, the other.

Sight, knowledge, truth, and woman's body: such a nexus intertwines central and highly charged attitudes and gestures of our culture. Man as knowing subject postulates woman's body as the object to be known, by way of an act of visual inspection which claims to reveal the truth—or else makes that object into the ultimate enigma. Seeing woman as other is necessary to truth about the self. An absurdly literal instance of this tradition is the anonymous Victorian author of *My Secret Life,* who claimed intercourse with some twelve hundred women and was particularly intent on looking at the female genitals. In his study of *My Secret Life,* Steven Marcus has recourse to the classic psychoanalytic explanation for such a compulsive visual desire: it is the search for the missing phallus, motivated both by anxiety at its absence and by a need for

THE BODY IN THE FIELD OF VISION

reassurance that its absence in the other assures its presence in himself.[14] One could interpret many elements of the philosophical inspection of truth within the Freudian (and Lacanian) problematics of the male's confusion concerning the woman's genitals. For instance, when Descartes, in the second of his *Méditations métaphysiques,* places himself at the window and says that he sees men walking in the street, he is obliged to ask himself (on the principle of universal doubt) how he knows that they are men, and not simply "specters or feigned men who are only moved by springs."[15] Descartes resolves the problem by claiming that it is the power of judgment, not simply vision, that allows him to identify the men as men. But the problem is not so easily set to rest. The "feigned men who are only moved by springs" return in the form of the female automaton Olympia, in Hoffmann's *Der Sandmann*—and the ballet *Coppélia* that Léo Delibes derived from it—where the failure of Olympia to be a woman is closely linked to problems of vision and desire: Nathanaël's fear that Dr. Coppelius has plucked out his eyes; the empty eye sockets that replace Olympia's deep, mirroring eyes when her inhumanness is revealed; Nathanaël's final hallucination, in which he apparently decides that his flesh and blood beloved, Klara, is also a mechanical doll. Freud's study "The Uncanny" centers on his reading of *Der Sandmann,* and makes much of the equivalence of blinding and castration, which takes us back to the beginning—to the *Oedipus*—and forward to the work of feminist theorists on what Luce Irigaray calls "the phallic gaze."[16]

Does philosophy, at least when it is considering the phenomenal world, implicate a phallic gaze, hard and appropriative, denuding and violative, in the manner of Sartre's Actaeon? And does psychoanalysis simply repeat the visual trope of the philosophical tradition? Irigaray notes— and deplores—that Freud's scenarios of sexual difference are invariably visual: they have to do with the male (in the first instance, the little boy) looking at the female genitals. This valorization of the visual, as I suggested earlier, is by no means an arbitrary element in Freud's thought. Not only in his mythic scenario of mankind's first assuming erect posture and thus exposing the genitals to sight, but also in his model of intellectual inquiry, Freud argues for the primacy of an erotically invested visual relation to the world, and first of all to the body. Scopophilia—erotic pleasure in looking—is for Freud in *Three Essays on the Theory of Sexuality* one of the "component instincts" that make up human sexuality from earliest childhood, and one that takes as its particular object the genitals and their functioning. The instinct or drive for looking, the

Schautrieb, is closely related to the instinct or drive for knowledge, the *Wisstrieb.*[17] The erotic investment in seeing is from the outset inextricably bound to the erotic investment in knowing, in the individual's development as well as in the Western philosophical and literary traditions. And the value given to the visual in any realist tradition responds to the desire to know the world: it promotes the gaze as the *inspection* of reality.

I need here to develop in more detail the psychoanalytic visual model mentioned in Chapter 1. According to Freud, the drive to know originates in the child's perception of the anatomical distinction between the sexes, and in the overwhelming question addressed to the world, and to its parents: Where do babies come from? All of the child's curiosity, all its endless questioning, derive from these original issues. Traditionally the questions of origins and of sexual difference never received an adequate answer from the adult generation, but rather displaced answers which did not satisfy the child and produced further confusion; yet even the most detailed factual answer could not really satisfy the child, since the child's bodily experience is not adequate to allow it to understand the nature of adult sexuality and the meaning of sexual difference. That is, what Freud calls the "diphasic onset" of sexuality in humans—in which sexual curiosity and erotic investigation precede biological sexual maturity by many years—insures that the desire to know will from the beginning be frustrated, and will construct itself on a model of frustration: the desire is always in excess of the capacity of objects of knowledge to satisfy it. The child's curiosity addresses itself to the body (the child's own, and those of the parents) and particularly to the genitals as necessarily, but obscurely, keys to the riddle of the sphinx. For the male child (the focus of Freud's attention), interest in the penis—his own, then its presence or absence in others—creates "an urge to investigate" and an interest in "sexual research."[18]

Thus realist vision partakes of an erotic investment in knowing, or what Toril Moi, following one of James Strachey's translations of Freud's term *Wisstrieb,* has forcefully described as "epistemophilia."[19] The body held in the field of vision is par excellence the object of both knowing and desire, knowing as desire, desire as knowing. But since the epistemophilic project is always inherently frustrated, the body can never be wholly grasped as an understandable, representable object. Freud in *Leonardo da Vinci and a Memory of His Childhood* (1910) suggests that the investigatory gaze becomes fixated on an imaginary body, the phallic woman:

THE BODY IN THE FIELD OF VISION

Before the child comes under the dominance of the castration complex—at a time when he still holds women at full value—he begins to display an intense desire to look, as an erotic instinctual activity. He wants to see other people's genitals, at first in all probability to compare them with his own. The erotic attraction that comes from his mother soon culminates in a longing for her genital organ, which he takes to be a penis. With the discovery, which is not made till later, that women do not have a penis, this longing often turns into its opposite and gives place to a feeling of disgust which in the years of puberty can become the cause of psychical impotence, misogyny and permanent homosexuality. But the fixation on the object that was once strongly desired, the woman's penis, leaves indelible traces on the mental life of the child, who has pursued that portion of his infantile sexual researches with particular thoroughness. Fetishistic reverence for a woman's foot and shoe appears to take the foot merely as a substitutive symbol for the woman's penis which was once revered and later missed; without knowing it, 'coupeurs de nattes' play the part of people who carry out an act of castration on the female genital organ.   (Standard Edition 11:96)

Freud's description (posited exclusively on the putative experience of the male child—but one could say the same of much nineteenth-century fiction as well) suggests that the visual inspection of reality, as the core component of the epistemophilic project, is doomed never to grasp its "real" object, since that object is imaginary, impossible. This may offer some explanation of why those bodies that come within the field of vision can be known only partially, metonymically, and fetishistically. It may also suggest that the nature of desire that comes into being under the law of the castration complex assures that the object of desire can never yield to the project of knowing: it will always in some sense be an imaginary object. Thus it may be that looking at the body is inherently unsatisfactory; sight finally gives no access to that which would satisfy its demands by offering some version of "truth." Perhaps other senses, such as touch and smell, must take over from sight for a nearer approach to the body. But these senses—repressed, in their public use, by the progress of "civilization"—don't belong to our cultural definition of the epistemological project.

The consequences of constructing a field of vision in which looking is essentially an erotic activity associated with male sexuality, and the object of vision therefore an exhibited female, have been well elaborated in film theory, since film is preeminently the medium that constructs its techniques, its technology, aesthetics, and ideology, on the gaze. As Laura Mulvey writes, in a classic essay, "cinematic codes create a gaze, a world, and an object, thereby producing an illusion cut to the measure of desire."[20] More specifically, the cinema produces, as the counterpart to scopophilia, exhibitionism of the female body. As Mulvey also says: "In a world ordered by sexual imbalance, pleasure in looking has been split between active/male and passive/female. The determining male gaze projects its phantasy on to the female figure which is styled accordingly. In their traditional exhibitionist role women are simultaneously looked at and displayed, with their appearance coded for strong visual and erotic impact so that they can be said to connote *to-be-looked-at-ness*" (p. 19)—a phrase that applies to the display of the female body not only in the cinema, but in our culture as a whole. While scopophilia is pleasurable, it is also threatening, since the gaze is constructed on difference, and thus originally on the male's perception of the woman as castrated. To be sure, actual spectatorship may be more complex than this model allows; we may be far less rigidly gendered in our imaginative lives. (Mulvey proposes in a later essay that a woman can engage in phantasized, "transvestite" identification with the phallic gaze, and a man can no doubt fantasize himself in the exhibitionist role.)[21] Mulvey also argues that spectatorship activates the classic reaction to perception of woman as castrated: a deflection into fetishism, the investment of accessory objects or attributes with erotic significance as signs of the missing phallus.

It is tempting to generalize the notion of fetishism when talking about the field of vision and its objects in the realist novel, to move beyond a concept of fetishism as a specific sexual "perversion" and see it rather as an inevitable and important component of a certain aesthetic. What is of interest here is less the denial of castration and the fear of the woman's genitals that underlie the etiology of fetishism according to Freud than the perception of an unrationalizable sexual difference and, in the case of fetishism, the insistence that the missing object of the investigatory glance is present elsewhere. "Something else has taken its place, has been appointed its substitute, as it were, and now inherits the interest which was formerly directed to its predecessor," Freud writes in his essay, *Fetishism* (1927). He continues: "But this interest suffers an extraordinary increase as well, because the horror of castration has set up a memorial to itself in the creation of this substitute" (*Standard Edition* 21:154). That is, the object in itself undergoes a repression that

THE BODY IN THE FIELD OF VISION

then charges substitute objects with a greatly increased affect. Accessory details, metonymies of body, parts instead of wholes: these become the privileged objects of the realist gaze. The body itself does not entirely cohere as a descriptive object because of the plethora of "part objects" by way of which it is known. Flaubert's use of such a gaze is made clearer in retrospect by such later novelists as James Joyce and Alain Robbe-Grillet: the latter, for instance, gives an extreme version of how understanding—mental judgment, in Descartes' sense—is prevented, or interfered with, by an insistence on excessive detail that keeps the mind from grasping larger outlines and wholes within the descriptive field.

If such metonymization within the field of vision is inherent to vision itself, its production can also be described in terms of formal causes, or technologies: in the cinema, the movement of the camera and of bodies in and out of the space it frames; in literature, the linear nature of the signifier, which means that an image or idea cannot be presented at once, but must rather unfold in sentences. Descriptive prose is inherently metonymical, building the whole from parts; and even painting of the nude frequently narrativizes the body, dramatizing in its very brushwork the approach to the body rather than its capture. Still photography may be the one exercise of vision in which the body can be held as a whole, because it is held motionless: which may suggest why photography, almost from the moment of its invention, has been a privileged medium for the pornographic image, and also why, as Roland Barthes suggests, it has a peculiar kinship with death.[22] The photographic gaze can see the body whole only by killing it; we recall the ultimate coherence of Emma Bovary's body only when it has become inanimate. The scene in Zola's *Thérèse Raquin* where Laurent views the bodies of young women in the morgue, and views an elegant young woman viewing a male body, confirms a certain ambition of realist prose to immobilize the bodies in its field of vision. In a sense, in still photography the body in its entirety becomes the fetish, the substitute for that which is not there; whereas in descriptive prose, in the camera work of most cinema, and often in painting, one approaches the body, never allowing that it is not there, but never quite reaching it. One cannot indeed reach it without arresting the process of vision. The work of the realist gaze must remain rest-less, constructive, unsatisfied, ever engaged in foreplay.

What is true of the descriptive field applies as well to the narrative construction of Flaubert's novels, and in general to the dynamic structuring (the plot) of the realist novel. Freud describes the fixation of the fetishist on a certain object as comparable to "the stopping of memory in traumatic amnesia":

> As in this latter case, the subject's interest comes to a halt half-way, as it were; it is as though the last impression before the uncanny and traumatic one is retained as a fetish. Thus the foot or shoe owes its preference as a fetish—or a part of it—to the circumstance that the inquisitive boy peered at the woman's genitals from below, from her legs up; fur and velvet—as has long been suspected—are a fixation of the sight of the pubic hair, which should have been followed by the longed-for sight of the female member; pieces of underclothing, which are so often chosen as a fetish, crystallize the moment of undressing, the last moment in which the woman could still be regarded as phallic. (*Standard Edition* 21:155)

Narrative in the realist tradition, broadly defined, moves from detail to detail, incident to incident, creating plot, character, and ideological vision through the accumulation of details which the reader can arrest and hold in summary evaluation only once the end has been reached—though Flaubert tends to evacuate meaning even from the summing up, especially in his later, more radical, novels. The process of undressing, rather than the object finally undressed, represents and corresponds to the dynamic of plot, which moves toward the promise of an ending but delays and resists that ending—which will mark its end, a terminal quiescence.[23]

It is as if the frustrated attempt to fix the body in the field of vision set off the restless movement of narrative, telling the story of approach to, and swerve away from, that final object of sight that cannot be contemplated. Direct contemplation would be petrifying, producing a Medusa-body, as in some of Balzac's scenarios. Narrative is thus generated as both approach and avoidance, the story of desire that never can quite speak its name nor quite attain its object. As I mentioned earlier, Roland Barthes claims that "classical" (essentially, nineteenth-century) narrative tends to become a striptease, a progressive undressing or unveiling of meaning. In *Le plaisir du texte,* he introduces a specifically fetishistic model of narrative unveiling when he asks, "Isn't the most erotic place on the body *the place where clothing gaps?*"—the piece of skin seen in the interstices of clothing.[24] Returning to *Madame Bovary,* we find a classic instance at the moment Rodolphe is leading

Emma to the scene of their first lovemaking: "But her long riding dress got in her way, even though she held it up by the hem, and Rodolphe, walking behind her, fixed his eyes on the delicate white stocking exposed between the black fabric and the black boot, like a bit of nudity" (215). Barthes contrasts such "gapping" to the classical striptease narrative, in which

> all the excitement is concentrated in the *hope* of seeing the genitals (the schoolboy's dream) or of knowing the end of the story (the novelistic satisfaction). Paradoxically (since it belongs to mass consumption) this pleasure is more intellectual than the other: it is an Oedipal pleasure (to denude, to know, to learn the beginning and the end), if it is true that all narrative (all unveiling of the truth) is a staging of the Father (absent, hidden, or suspended)—which would explain the consubstantiality of narrative forms, family structures, and interdictions on nudity, all brought together in our culture in the myth of Noah's nakedness covered by his sons.

We may not want to make so sharp a distinction between the text of "striptease" and the text of "gapping"—Barthes tends to exaggerate the difference between "readable" and "writeable" texts—but rather to see both processes at work in the realist tradition of narrative: the promise of eventual uncovering, which may involve partial and even unexpected uncoverings along the way, is nonetheless consubstantial with an interdiction on total nudity, as a violation of the law of the father. The castration complex, I noted in Chapter 1, sets up, in the name of the father—internalized as the superego—a law of desire that is subject to basic prohibitions and therefore inherently problematic. This law presides as well in narrative, dictating that the object chosen as the target of desire can never be wholly reached, never possessed in a way that would satisfy the regressive scenarios of unconscious desire. It may be part of the curious logics and elaborate rituals of veiling and unveiling that the woman's body may at last operate as a kind of negation of the truly feared, and thus ultimately taboo, nudity: the paternal phallus, the symbol of the law. Whatever may stand in the place of the finally protected nudity—and perhaps there is nothing there, only a blank filled with our imaginary projections—the dynamic of realist narrative, and realist vision, has less to do with the ultimately denuded than with denuding, "the moment of undressing" in Freud's terms, as in Emma's unlacing of her corset. This traditional dynamic is effectively parodied in the Nausicaa episode of Joyce's *Ulysses,* when Leopold Bloom watches Gerty MacDowell exhibit ankle and leg on the beach, while—prepared by his memories of the novel *The Sweets of Sin*—he reaches orgasm as a voyeur. The narrative and visual mechanism is also well understood by traditional Hollywood cinema, in which the unbuttoning of a blouse and the first glimpse of hitherto covered flesh is followed by the significant fade-out.

"The progressive concealment of the body which goes along with civilization keeps sexual curiosity awake," Freud writes in *Three Essays on the Theory of Sexuality,* in the context of a discussion of scopophilia (*Standard Edition* 7:156). The work of recent social historians confirms the perception that the more the body, especially the female body, becomes covered with layers of clothing—as it famously did during the nineteenth-century—the more attention is directed to undressing it, and the more erotic investment is made in the accessory objects that need to be removed in the undressing.[25] This tradition leads to Georges Bataille's subversive insistence, in *L'érotisme,* that the erotic is a dangerous (and therefore affirmative) violation of interdictions, and that its "decisive action is making naked," *la mise à nu.*[26] Bataille's rather adolescent novel, *Histoire de l'oeil,* offers a definitive comment on vision and the sexual body: the eyeball of the slaughtered priest ends up in Simone's vagina. In the dominant novelistic tradition, however, vision rarely reaches so replete a conclusion. It never can quite see what it claims to want to see, since sight cannot give access to the living body, and since the body viewed may in any event ultimately be an imaginary object, the product of delusional infantile visual scenarios. Vision is inherently unsatisfactory, and in its exercise accessory objects tend to take over the field of vision in a form of perception that is fundamentally metonymic— always creating an approach to wholeness of vision of the body without ever quite providing it. The nineteenth-century realist novel is in this sense less "panoptical" than the work of Michel Foucault might lead us to believe: the guardian in his watchtower never can see everything; his vision is frustrated, always in the process of unveiling rather than in contemplation of the unveiled.[27] Looking is alluring and dangerous since the final object of the looking is taboo. Narrators are in fact more nearly voyeurs than watchmen; their post of observation is at the keyhole rather than in the tower, and what they see is partially obscured. Stories will very often, both in narrative structure and theme, concern curiosity directed at the concealed, clothed, hidden body, with the concomitant suggestion that the source and meaning of the story is somehow hidden on or in that body.

In the words of Toril Moi, "Freudian theory posits the drive for knowledge (epistemophilia) as crucially bound to the body and sexuality."[28] But since the epistemophilic drive is always inherently frustrated, the body that is its object can never wholly be known. The infantile concept of the phallic mother symbolizes the unavailability of any real knowledge of another's body by way of the scrutinizing gaze. We know the body in the erotically charged field of vision only partially or metonymically. In the dynamic of narrative, we are always approaching that body, circling it without grasping it. At one extreme, the body must be killed before it can be represented, and indeed Freud acknowledges the link of the instinct for knowledge with sadism, since the instinct for knowledge "is at bottom a sublimated off-shoot of the instinct of mastery exalted into something intellectual" (*Standard Edition* 12:324). Attempts at seeing and knowing are attempts at mastering, and our technologies of representation, including descriptive prose, always bear witness to that impossible enterprise of arresting and fixing the object of inspection. Such may be the very motive of representation. At another extreme, one that more and more comes to the fore as realism develops into its "modernist" phase, the frustrations of knowing produce a questioning of the epistemophilic project itself. The observer/knower is put into question, and the very principle of knowing—or of possessing—another body comes to appear hopeless.

Detecting the Bodily Narrative

Many—perhaps most?—novelistic texts speak conjointly of scopophilia and epistemophilia, and suggest that knowledge is ultimately to be sought in knowledge of the body put into erotic relation to the knower. If in the traditonal realist novel our attention is mainly directed to the objects of sight and knowledge, a certain line of work developing from this tradition shifts our inspection to the very process of seeing, particularly to its limits, and to the problematic place of the observer and the treacherousness of observing. Such works began to appear with some frequency around the turn of the century, beginning in the 1890s with Henry James, Joseph Conrad, and Ford Madox Ford, and continuing with Raymond Radiguet, André Gide, and Marcel Proust, to give a very partial list. In the visual arts, perhaps the most notable example is the later work of Degas, where people—especially women—are viewed in moments of intimacy as if through keyholes. It is work often characterized by a quasi-epistemological concern with the place and perspective of seeing and with the grounds of knowing.

Henry James in many ways offers the most challenging and most telling examples. While all his fiction is concerned with knowing, and especially the grounds for knowing the motives, desires, and needs of others, the series of texts stretching more or less from *The Aspern Papers* (1887) to *The Beast in the Jungle* (1903) and including *The Turn of the Screw, What Maisie Knew, The Figure in the Carpet, The Awkward Age,* and *The Sacred Fount* makes most explicit the passion and the anxiety of watching others from a given "post of observation." Indeed, the drama of these texts almost always turns on the uses and abuses of observation, on questions of what one can know, and what one can make of or do with what one knows. Observation can become an excessive prying into and manipulation of the lives of others, or else the basis of self-induced obsessions that undermine the very possibility of knowledge of the outside world. And in the most extreme cases—perhaps most of all *The Turn of the Screw* and *The Sacred Fount*—there is no basis for deciding whether the dark plots reported by the observer in fact belong to reality or only to private obsession. These texts record a radical standoff between world and mind, between perception and thought; they cast doubt on the very project of the realist novel, and open up intricate relations between fictions and their referents.

Most pertinent to the observation of the body is *The Sacred Fount,* since it concerns a narrator-observer's attempt to penetrate and to understand the sexual relationships among his fellow guests during a weekend at the English country house Newmarch—that is, in a closed field of observation. His narrative is elaborated from the approaches and frustrations of vision. *The Sacred Fount* is, to be sure, a somewhat "perverse" example of the body in the field of vision, since it is so highly cerebral. It tends to present the issue as a purely epistemological problem. But this problem derives from the narrator's evident epistemophilia, which is inseparable from his scopophilia: his drive to know expresses itself in, and is subtended by, his erotically invested gaze. That gaze is very much directed toward the "gapping" in the appearances put forth by his fellow guests at Newmarch; it searches for the indices that will allow him to figure them as naked, both as defenseless and as erotically engaged in a sphere of privacy that he would lay bare.

The premises of the observer-narrator's problem to be solved emerge first during the train ride to Newmarch. Two of his weekend companions, Gilbert Long and Grace Bissenden, appear to him rejuvenated, displaying more than their customary wit and intelligence. In the case of Gilbert Long, Grace Brissenden herself, in conversation with the narrator, suggests that the cause of the change is "a very clever woman"—Lady John.[29] When, at Newmarch, he discovers Guy Brissenden to be strangely aged and depleted, he begins to be "conscious, vaguely, of being on the track of a law" (23): in each couple, licit or undercover, one of the pair "pays" for the improvement of the other by a corresponding depletion. As he originally formulates the law to another guest, the painter Ford Obert, R.A.:

> "One of the pair," I said, "has to pay for the other. What ensues is a miracle and miracles are expensive . . . Mrs. Briss had to get her new blood, her extra allowance of time and bloom, somewhere; and from whom could she so conveniently extract them as from Guy himself? She *has*, by an extraordinary feat of legerdemain, extracted them; and he, on his side, to supply her, has had to tap the sacred fount. But the sacred fount is like the greedy man's description of the turkey as an 'awkward' dinner dish. It may be sometimes too much for a single share, but it's not enough to go round." (29)

The central metaphor of the sacred fount returns us to Balzacian views (not to mention the prevalent Victorian notions) of sexuality as a limited economy in which there is a finite amount of sexual substance, whose spending entails depletion. James's narrator develops the corollary, that expenditure of this capital inevitably enriches someone else. The economy is by definition a threatening one, since there is a scarcity of capital; there is not enough of the vital substance to go round. Because the economy is postulated on sexual relations—"intimacy of course had to be postulated," says the narrator (28–29)—we are given a Darwinian view of the struggle to drink at the sacred fount: sexual intimacy will produce winners and losers; "love" relationships feed what is ultimately a struggle to the death of isolated egos.

The closed sexual economy of Newmarch thus tends to express itself in a set of relations, in which one term has gained or benefited while the other has suffered loss or depletion. The first statement of the pertinent relations would look like this:

Grace Brissenden	+	Guy Brissenden	−
Gilbert Long	+	Lady John	−

But it quickly becomes apparent to the narrator that the second pair of names won't really do, since Lady John turns out to be "all there"— quite the contrary of depleted. By what Ford Obert calls the "torch of your analogy" provided by the narrator's law, one must use the matrix to find the person to fill that blank erroneously filled by Lady John. The working hypothesis, in the early stages of the novel, really looks like this:

Grace Brissenden	+	Guy Brissenden	−
Gilbert Long	+	?	−

An important corollary to the narrator's working hypothesis is that the missing person must be present at Newmarch, a corollary strictly derived from the original hypothesis, in that the hypothesis is based on relation, and the couple knows the relation to be necessary, and therefore the partners do not travel separately. It is a closed system, and the narrator finds a "special beauty in my scheme through which the whole depended so on each part and each part so guaranteed the whole" (223). Thus the narrator's task resembles that of Claude Lévi-Strauss's celebrated *bricoleur:* he must work only with the *moyens de bord,* with what is available to him on the spot, within the laboratory of Newmarch.[30] The narrator finds this structural patterning confirmed in the very architecture of the park at Newmarch, where the green paths meet in circles which open perspectives on new paths, which lead to symmetrical circles. "We were in a beautiful old picture, we were in a beautiful old tale, and it wouldn't be the fault of Newmarch if some other green *carrefour,* not far off, didn't balance with this one" (130). The *carrefour* becomes the emblem of the observer's field of vision, the perceptual grid that he finds in, or imposes on, the world in which he moves. What complicates his search, of course, is that the partners have every interest in avoiding detection, by screens such as overtly cultivating apparent relations with other "innocent" parties.

As Ford Obert puts it to the narrator, the game is "honourable" so long as the "investigator" plays by the rules, which means confining himself to "psychologic evidence." He elaborates: "Resting on the *kind* of signs that the game takes account of when fairly played—resting on psychologic signs alone, it's a high application of intelligence. What's ignoble is the detective and the keyhole" (66). Although this pays tribute to the narrator's avowed principles, it's not certain that the game is really played, or can be played, without some version of "the detective and the keyhole." There is no record of the narrator's literally peeping through keyholes, but he nonetheless as observer establishes voyeuristic relations with the objects of his vision: relations that create an affectively charged field between observer and observed, with the potential for dynamic interactions.

Observation returns us again and again to the body, and particularly to two bodies, in the relation of giver and taker, spender and getter, given its central expression in the metaphor of the sacred fount. Thus in conversation with Grace Brissenden about the search for the woman who must be in relation to Gilbert Long, the narrator brings her to a statement of the type of exchange he has postulated. Grace Brissenden says:

> "One of them always gets more out of it than the other. One of them—you know the saying—gives the lips, the other gives the cheek."
>
> "It's the deepest of all truths. Yet the cheek profits too," I more prudently argued.
>
> "It profits most. It takes and keeps and uses all the lips give. The cheek, accordingly," she continued to point out, "is Mr. Long's. The lips are what we began by looking for. We've found them. They're drained—they're dry, the lips. Mr. Long finds his improvement natural and beautiful. He revels in it. He takes it for granted. He's sublime."
>
> It kept me for a minute staring at her. "So—do you know?—are *you!*" (80–81)

The last moment of this exchange points to a particular complicating factor of the narrator's complicitous conversations with Grace Brissenden: while using her as a partner in his desire to penetrate the relations of others, in this case specifically Gilbert Long and the woman they now have designated as May Server, he is also scrutinizing her, in order to confirm his perception of her relation with the man he now most often refers to as "poor Briss," and particularly to find out whether she, as the gainer in that relation, has any awareness of her own implication in such a relation.[31] When he tells her she is "sublime," he as much as accuses her of drinking at the sacred fount. When she replies, "You've *made* me sublime. You found me dense. You've affected me quite as

Mrs. Server has affected Mr. Long," she either unwittingly admits of such a relation, or else outwits the narrator at his own game, specifically by putting him in the place of "poor Briss." This implication the narrator picks up when he in turn replies, "I do feel remarkably like that pair of lips. I feel drained—I feel dry!" This points to a further complicating factor, this one specifically a complication for the reader: the narrator, we realize, whatever his pose as objective observer, must himself be part of the field of observation, must to some extent participate in the relations he is observing and in the story he is reporting, and thus by his very presence must alter the observed, but in ways that are difficult to detect since he is our sole informant.

The lurid, intensely physical image of lips and cheek reminds us that, despite the "high application of intelligence" that the novel dramatizes and itself represents, the ultimate referent of all the narrative cerebrations is physical intimacy, of the sort that in this world must be hidden from literal sight. James's subject is ultimately what Josef Breuer described to Freud—on the threshold of the latter's discoveries about the sexual etiology of hysteria—as "secrets of the alcove."[32] That is, at the heart of the social relations that so preoccupied James is the relation of relations—the sexual—which cannot be observed directly and cannot be spoken, but which nonetheless determines all the others, since it is the locus of both power and meaning. The sexual relation is a true "primal scene" in Jamesian narrative, something that can never be directly recovered—as in Freud's case history of the Wolf Man—but that must be figured in the analyst's construction of his patient's biography in order to make sense of it.[33] Here we have the encrypted core of reality, known only in its effects. If James's characters and narrators seem repeatedly to operate by a kind of astronomical observation in which the presence of unseen planetary bodies is postulated by the pull of their gravitational fields on bodies in the field of vision—as when the narrator of *The Sacred Fount* sets out to look for Gilbert Long's lover in order to explain his appearance and behavior—they are responding to a world in which the ultimate source of power and meaning, in the passionate conjoining of two bodies, must remain hidden. What is directly observable is never what is most important, which is why vision lives in so intense and exacerbated a state, why it is always seeking to penetrate—why its metaphorical constructions inevitably lead to the evocation of bodies, and to stories told about them.

Vision in *The Sacred Fount* repeatedly leads back to a figuration of bodies in unseen relation, like the sinister image of the cheek and the lips. In particular, the narrator's pursuit of May Server, through the green alleys and *carrefours,* leads to an observation of her in which, according to him, "her exquisite weakness simply opened up the depths it would have closed" (135). He goes on to render a picture of the victim in which his prose heightens victimization to a melodramatic mode of representation:

> I saw as I had never seen before what consuming passion can make of the marked mortal on whom, with fixed beak and claws, it has settled as on a prey. She reminded me of a sponge wrung dry and with fine pores agape. Voided and scraped of everything, her shell was merely crushable. So it was brought home to me that the victim could be abased, and so it disengaged itself from these things that the abasement could be conscious. That was Mrs. Server's tragedy, that her consciousness survived—survived with a force that made it struggle and dissemble. This consciousness was all her secret—it was at any rate all mine. I promised myself roundly that I would henceforth keep clear of any other.   (135–36)

The passage concerns observation and consciousness, and especially his observation of her consciousness of her status as victim. But it does so in extraordinarily physical images: May Server as prey, as sponge wrung dry, as shell voided and scraped. The metaphors of expenditure of sexual substance are not far from the surface, and we see their enactment on the body itself. The result is not, as the narrator here seems to claim, a truce in his pursuit of knowledge of the victim; a few moments later, he presses her further for "confirmation" of what he has observed. "I was dazzled by my opportunity" (142). This "dazzlement" returns us to the primary faculty of sight that the narrator exercises on the field before him, and in context it suggests a moral cruelty in sight that the narrator, blinded by the very light he produces, can't see. Observation itself—including that of the novelist in the realist tradition—is an intellectual prerogative of dubious moral status. It is also epistemologically dubious, in that self-dazzling observation is unable to distinguish between the seen and the organizing categories of perception—for instance that "torch of analogy" which the narrator uses to illuminate his field of vision. As he reflects during an important dialogue with Ford Obert, "I struck myself as knowing again the joy of the intellectual mastery of things unamenable, that joy of determining, almost of creating results, which I have already mentioned as an exhilaration attached to some of my plunges of insight" (214). If "determining" results already implies the intrusion of the observer into the field of the observed, which contaminates observation, "creating" results suggests a possible radical severance of observation from its objects, and the constitution of a fiction in their place.

The conversation with Ford Obert is one of two decisive dramatic encounters in the latter part of the novel. Obert, a painter, has himself been using the narrator's "torch of analogy" to illuminate the field of vision. "I've blown on my torch, in other words, till, flaring and smoking, it has guided me, through a magnificent chiaroscuro of colour and shadow, out into the light of day" (222). Obert believes that he has moved out of the Platonic cave to see things as they are. Part of what he has seen is that May Server has "changed back": she is now "all there," she has changed from a minus to a plus. If this is the case, it allows the narrator to find a place for a perception he thinks he has had, that Gilbert Long has also returned to his original state, and is now a minus. This suggests a possible radical transformation of the matrix:

| Guy Brissenden | − | May Server | + |
| Gilbert Long | − | Grace Brissenden | + |

Obert, observing May Server's improvement, has been looking for her lover, but simply decides he is not present at Newmarch. But the narrator can postulate Guy Brissenden, originally associated with May Server because they were both victims, as occupying this place. If Gilbert Long has moved from plus to minus, it may not be as a result of May Server's opposite move, but because of a new liaison. This in turn sets the narrator on a new search: to see if Long and Grace Brissenden are associated as lovers. And yet, it might rather be that Gilbert Long and Grace Brissenden have come together as two plusses who sense that their use of their victims is threatened by the narrator's observation of them. Long's "change back" would thus represent "a represented, a fictive ineptitude" (294).

This is the kind of problem that faces the narrator in his climactic dialogue with Grace Brissenden. He begins to understand the possibility that his role of observer has begun to alter the observed by producing dissimulation and protection in those he observes, including his accomplices. He reflects that Grace Brissenden's request for a meeting with him may result from a consultation with Gilbert Long. "I had spoiled their unconsciousness, I had destroyed it, and it was consciousness alone that could make them effectively cruel. Therefore, if they were cruel, it

THE BODY IN THE FIELD OF VISION

was I who had determined it, inasmuch as, consciously, they could only want, they could only intend, to live" (295). "To live," here as in *The Ambassadors* and elsewhere in James's fiction, in essence means to live sexually, and the "cruelty" in question results from their fighting to

114   maintain their sexual relations: from their intention to continue drinking at the sacred fount, exploiting the bodies of their lovers. Thus Grace Brissenden's version of events is necessarily a smokescreen, and the very act of wanting to speak to him a principle of untruth in her narration. The narrator's observations have turned the field of observation against him, in a way for which he is responsible. His reflections now lead him to the conclusion that this is a necessary result of his role:

> And I could only say to myself that this was the price—the price of the secret success, the lonely liberty and the intellectual joy. There were things that for so private and splendid a revel—that of the exclusive king with his Wagner opera—I could only let go, and the special torment of my case was that the condition of light, of the satisfaction of curiosity and of the attestation of triumph, was in this direct way the sacrifice of feeling. There was no point at which my assurance could, by the scientific method, judge itself complete enough not to regard feeling as an interference and, in consequence, as a possible check. If it had to go I knew well who went with it, but I wasn't there to save *them*. I was there to save my priceless pearl of an inquiry and to harden, to that end, my heart.   (296)

The passage records a discovery made repeatedly in James's fiction, the discovery that the observing consciousness may be, by its very nature, manipulative, and that those who have seen much may, on these very grounds, act the role of villain. One thinks of Gilbert Osmond in *Portrait of a Lady,* of Lord Mark in *The Wings of the Dove,* of the narrator of *The Aspern Papers,* among many others. What is striking in *The Sacred Fount* is not only that it should be the narrator who so explicitly renounces fellow-feeling in order to preserve his "inquiry," but that this should be presented as a necessary consquence of his post of observation—as if to say that the very premises of fiction as an inquiry into the real are morally unjustified.

The image of the "exclusive king with his Wagner opera" may allude to mad King Ludwig of Bavaria, which then prepares what follows in the final chapter, where Grace Brissenden first of all completely revises the sets of relations, tells him that Gilbert Long's lover is Lady John, and that May Server has "made up" to Guy Brissenden, and, further, gives Brissenden as the authority for her certain knowledge of this. Not only does this change relations, it destroys their balance, since in her terms both Long and Lady John are minuses, both May Server and Brissenden pluses, and the metaphor of the sacred fount is superseded by banal liaisons. The principle of knowing through observation is also superseded by the banal revelation through her husband's tattling. Yet conceivably, the narrator makes out, this could all be a smokescreen to cover her own place in the matrix. But to determine that would entail the narrator's placing himself in relation to her. This he cannot quite succeed in doing, since by the end she appears to have wrested the very principle of observation and narration from him, to leave him with "a mere heap of disfigured fragments" (311). He attempts to make her collaborate once again in fitting the fragments together, but she refuses, and further, tells him his whole construction is unsubstantiated. "My poor dear, you *are* crazy, and I bid you good-night!" are her final words to him. He then can plan only to leave Newmarch on the earliest possible morning train: to renounce, that is, the field of his observational experimentation. We might say that the narrator has fallen victim to Sartre's "Actaeon complex," if we recall the punishment of Actaeon, dismembered for his insistence on seeing.

115

The narrator's construction, and thus the whole of *The Sacred Fount*, turns out to be a self-consuming artifact, an elaborate narrative assemblage which at the end is dismantled piece by piece, yet in such a way that it could be reassembled by some other narrative authority who had not, in the manner of this narrator, lost faith in the enterprise. For the reader, *The Sacred Fount* is something of a do-it-yourself narrative construction kit, but one that never yields clear interpretive results. The situation is given emblematic form early in the novel, when the guests at Newmarch view an old painting:

The figure represented is a young man in black—a quaint, tight black dress, fashioned in years long past; with a pale, lean, livid face and a stare, from eyes without eyebrows, like that of some whitened old-world clown. In his hand he holds an object that strikes the spectator at first simply as some obscure, some ambiguous work of art, but that on a second view becomes a representation of a human face, modelled and coloured, in wax, in enamelled metal, in some substance not human. The object thus appears a complete mask, such as might have been fantastically fitted and worn. (55)

As the narrator states, "It's the picture, of all pictures, that most needs an interpreter." May Server proposes that one could call it "the Mask of Death," to which the narrator replies that it's rather "the Mask of Life," since the man's own face is deathlike, whereas the mask is "blooming and beautiful." But to May Server, the mask has "an awful grimace," while the narrator finds it "charmingly pretty." There is also disagreement as to whether the man has just taken off the mask, or is about to put it on. Ford Obert thinks the mask looks like a "lovely lady," to which the narrator adds that it looks "remarkably like May Server." She in turn suggests that "the gentleman's own face is the image of a certain other gentleman's," in apparent reference to the narrator; Ford Obert denies this application, while claiming that the resemblance is to someone else at Newmarch. This sets off a search resolved by Gilbert Long's identification of this someone as "poor Briss"—and all present concur. The narrator is thus able to read the painting as an allegory of the sacred fount, but only with a relation of persons—May Server as plus conjoined to Guy Brissenden as minus—that he will postulate much later in his cerebrations. Although the painting cries out for interpretation, it offers no sure principle for interpretation. Interpretation of the artificial face, the mask, is as arbitrary as interpretation of the narrator's constructed fiction, and of the novel itself.

The narrator's construction of the world he has observed and scrutinized at Newmarch remains, as he characterizes it, in the realm of "the secret success, the lonely liberty and the intellectual joy": it is the private revel of "the exclusive king with his Wagner opera." Observation and the narration given of it appear, finally, as self-contained and narcissistic acts that cannot be held accountable either to their referents or to their narratees—Ford Obert, Grace Brissenden, the reader. It's not simply that the narrator is "unreliable," but that there is no possible test of what "reliability" might mean within the frame of the novel. In comparison to other Jamesian narratives where interpretation is fully undecidable, such as *The Figure in the Carpet* and *The Turn of the Screw*, *The Sacred Fount* appears yet more radical since there is no detectable motive for narration itself. The nature of the governess's experience in *The Turn of the Screw*, for example, motivates her need to tell it: indeed, narration at least intends to be self-justification. Narrative construction in *The Sacred Fount*, however, appears quite gratuitous, the exercise of pure sexual curiosity, of a principle of observation that tests itself against nothing—not even the narrator's own subjectivity, since we are given virtually no insight into this—other than the apparent assumption of a universal epistemophilia wanting to find the stuff of story in the observable bodies in its visual range.

The Sacred Fount comments on a long novelistic tradition of curiosity about the sexual conjoinings of other people; it belongs to the general tendency of the novel from its inception to invade privacy in order to open up the realm of private personal experience, and to find the body in its sexual relations at the core of privacy. Scopophilia and epistemophilia are inextricably conjoined. If the principle of investigation at work in *The Sacred Fount* ostensibly eschews the "ignoble" business of "the detective and the keyhole" in favor of a higher intellectual form of observation, this superior kind of vision proves no less invasive—only, perhaps, less effective. To the extent that the purification of observational narration is dramatized in the novel, it becomes a kind of allegory of a problem that fiction in the realist tradition generally fails (or refuses) to acknowledge directly: the radical problem of optics posed by an observation of the real, and most particularly by that part of the real that most claims to remain hidden. *The Sacred Fount* is in one sense a parody of the Victorian drapery of the body, reminding us that for some high-minded Victorians even piano legs had to be hidden, lest they produce impure thoughts.[34] The narrator of *The Sacred Fount* is thoroughly prurient, in exact proportion, one might say, to his inability to see beneath the draperies. For all its intellectual refinement, the novel is a pendant to the enumeration of sexual parts and positions in *My Secret Life*. *The Sacred Fount* at times verges on parody of the novelistic tradition centrally concerned with observation. At the same time, it dramatizes tellingly the issues raised by any observational fiction that begins to take seriously its epistemological problems: its focus becomes, of necessity, the observer, himself observed, not at the keyhole—as in Sartre's famous scenario—but in the process of doing without, and thus giving us a report that casts doubt on the whole project of observation. The bodies at Newmarch, supposedly conjoined in what James once called "the great relation," remain resolutely draped despite the nearly Sadean combinations the narrator has "seen" them in.

In the chronology of James's work, *The Sacred Fount* appears as something of an act of exorcism. While his later fiction, that of the "major phase," maintains an evident concern for problems of knowing and the epistemological uncertainties of any vantage point of observation, it nonetheless moves from the radical concern with the narcissism of observation to narratives in which the body can on occasion—on crucial occasions—be seen. One thinks of the climactic scene of *The Ambassadors*, where Lambert Strether, who has all day thought of himself as moving within the gilded frame of a Lambinet painting, sees just what is needed to complete the tableau: Chad and Madame de Vionnet together in their rowboat, in a visual revelation of their intimacy of a kind the narrator of *The Sacred Fount* never certainly has. Madame de Vionnet by the end of *The Ambassadors* is indeed remarkably present, as a sexual (and exploited) body, "afraid for [her] very life."[35] As in this novel, in *The Wings of the Dove* and *The Golden Bowl* sexuality and the body are absolutely central concerns, and for all the elaborate indirection of Jamesian prose, Kate Croy and Charlotte Stant, in particular, emerge as desirable and desiring bodies with vivid sexual presences. If the "high Modernism" that James in so many ways inaugurates always displays a high degree of epistemological awareness—in the work of such writers as Joseph Conrad, Ford Madox Ford, and André Gide—it also tends to work through epistemological complications to revelatory moments of looking, to moments of smashed windowpanes that call for revaluations, and reinvest significance in narratives of the body within the field of vision.

Looking at Albertine

Before concluding this discussion, we need to look briefly at an example from the novelist who, perhaps more than any other, both sums up the realist tradition and fully explores its epistemological issues, Marcel Proust. *A la recherche du temps perdu* explores—among other illusions—the illusory belief that meaning is to be found in bodily knowledge of the other. Epistemology is closely bound to the effort to see into the "secrets of the alcove," most tellingly in Swann's jealous attempt to know Odette's secret lives. Sexual jealousy in the *Recherche*, and indeed what is conventionally called love, repeatedly shows itself to be the very principle of epistemology, and the desire for possession of another's body—a possession that is inherently impossible—becomes a restless, unfulfillable quest for knowledge.[36] Given the erotic charge of the quest to know others, it is not surprising that the *Recherche* repeatedly stages moments of revelatory looking. One of the earliest of these is the revelation of sadism the young "Marcel" receives in the famous scene at

Montjouvain, when he watches Mlle Vinteuil and her friend through the open window—a scene that marks him indelibly, perhaps all the more so in that its erotic dénouement is masked when Mlle Vinteuil closes the shutters and blocks his view.[37] Another crucial moment of vision inaugurates the volume *Sodome et Gomorrhe*, as Marcel watches from a window on the landing of the stairway and sees simultaneously the pollination of a flower by an insect and the encounter of the Baron de Charlus with Jupien: his first revelation of homosexuality, which will induce a whole new reading of reality, a general revision of everything he has seen. Both these scenes are recalled when, during the war, in a disreputable hotel, Marcel watches through a peephole as Charlus is flogged by various hired hands. Vision is an essential motif of the *Recherche;* Marcel frequently seeks places, especially elevated places, from which he can observe, himself unobserved, including the "petit cabinet sentant l'iris" in which he makes his first autoerotic discoveries. The drama of the *Recherche* is often that of a sexually charged vision of the world that specifically informs the vocation of the novelist-to-be.

One passage explicitly concerning viewing of a woman's body deserves attention. It comes in *La prisonnière*, when Marcel has sequestered Albertine in his apartment, in a desperate gesture of possession that can never in fact arrest the movement of this "être de fuite." It is while Albertine is sleeping that he feels that he most nearly possesses her, though it is possession in the absence of her self, when she has become something like a plant, and then—when her sleep has become deepest—like "a whole landscape."[38] This landscape then evokes the seashore at Balbec (where he first met Albertine), and when he has undressed and taken his place next to the sleeper, he finds himself "embarked on Albertine's sleep." This sometimes leads, he tells us, to his reaching orgasm simply by lying against her. "It seemed to me in these moments that I had possessed her more completely, like something unconscious and without resistance in mute nature" (3:73). It is thus only when the woman's body has been reduced to unconsciousness, when it has been made part of the natural world, that Marcel is able to feel fully in possession of her—at the moment when the body becomes purely the body, no longer subject to the ever-changing expressions of personality. We are reminded of the narrator's earlier qualification of the act of lovemaking, in the case of Swann and Odette, as "the act of physical possession—in which moreover one possesses nothing" (1:234). One cannot possess another, and to the extent that possession is exercised on

THE BODY IN THE FIELD OF VISION

the body of another, one approaches that condition most fully when the body is looked at as an object of consciousness that is itself unconscious.

The descriptions of Albertine asleep lead to an evocation of his undressing her before going to bed: that moment of unbuttoning, the gapping of clothing that promises a revelation in the first full view of her naked body:

> Before Albertine had obeyed me and taken off her slippers, I opened her shirt. Her small breasts, mounted high, were so round they had less the air of being an integral part of her body than of having ripened there like two fruits; and her abdomen (hiding the place which on a man is made ugly as by an iron staple stuck in a broken statue) closed, at the meeting point of the thighs, by two shells of a curve as drowsy, as peaceful, as claustral as that of the horizon when the sun has disappeared. She took off her shoes, and lay down next to me.   (3:79)

This description of the woman's body contains a parenthetical comparison to the man's, where the penis is referred to as making his body ugly in the manner of the iron staple, or armature *(crampon)* used to reinforce a broken sculpture *(une statue descellée)*—one that has come apart or been taken from its socket. The penis is represented by an image that appears to imply its detachability, even its mutilation, as that which is there only to repair—in unaesthetic fashion—something that is broken. The contrast of the woman's body to the man's once again seems to produce anxiety about the status of the penis, a vision of it as not (necessarily) there. If it is the attribute that is supposed to define maleness, here it seems a precarious sign, and one that would be willingly exchanged for the woman's more beautiful sex. Yet it is there, as the principle of contrast—and hence as the very epistemological principle— that enables the vision of the woman's sex. Difference, if only temporarily assumed through the attachment of the penis, is what permits knowing.

What is known, by contrast, is very much in the realm of the unknowable: it is closure, recalling the closure of bivalves ("se refermait, à la jonction des cuisses, par deux valves")—we are still in the Balbec seascape—in a curve which is drowsy and full of repose. It is also "claustral," and its closure finally evokes the horizon after sunset. The woman's body, even when Albertine is awake—and they are about to make love—

reminds him of sleep, of a nature that appears to be beyond the pleasure principle, in a kind of cosmic quiescence. The anxiety created by the male gaze at the female sex here is directed at the male body alone. The female body is here no Medusa's head, but rather that landscape where desire finds peace, though a peace which has an almost deathlike stillness. If, as Freud argues in his essay "The Uncanny," the female genitals may appear uncanny (unheimlich) to the male, it is because they are in fact too familiar, too heimisch: they are, after all, his first home, or Heimat. The un of unheimlich, according to Freud, is the mark of repression of what is too familiar. In this passage from Proust, the observer seems to have moved through the conflictual dynamics of desire and repression to find the woman's sex as peaceful, and perhaps as a final home or resting place. The woman here combines all three figures of woman identified in Freud's essay "The Three Caskets": mother, lover, and goddess of death. The correct choice of woman—as in the choice of the lead casket in The Merchant of Venice—is simultaneously choice of love and death. "Choice stands in the place of necessity, of destiny," writes Freud. "In this way man overcomes death, which he has recognized intellectually."[39]

Albertine's body in Marcel's field of vision thus sets off a kind of cosmic scenario of love and repose. But in context it also denies the possibility of possession, even by knowing: the woman's body is conceived to be part of mysterious natural processes. In a gesture common to patriarchal thought, the woman's body is assigned to nature, and therefore becomes ultimately irretrievable for culture. This sequestered and reposeful Albertine will be succeeded by Albertine in flight, in La fugitive, which opens up Marcel's greatest epistemological anguish in the novel: the agony of retrospective jealousy, the mad desire to know another person's past, to fill in the gaps created by absences and lies, the need constantly to revise the narrative of one's life through discoveries about another's biography. In Albertine's ultimately unseizable and unknowable body Proust's novel reveals, among other things, the anxiety of the realist descriptive writing project. It is inherently interminable, since it never can reduce the bodies of others to final stasis and repose. Bodies do not always sleep, they are not always horizons following the setting of the sun. They can, in a sense, be known only in death—but perhaps less in their own deaths than in the death of the observing subject. We go on looking at bodies, attempting to detail them in order to fix them in the field of vision, but also attempting to conjure them away—as that anticipated point of rest, of arrest, that must be deferred as long as possible in the textual web.

The body in the field of vision—more precisely, in that field of vision which is so central to realist narrative—inevitably relates to scopophilia, the erotic investment of the gaze which is traditionally defined as masculine, its object the female body. All the technologies of the gaze—in writing as much as in filming—have been made complicit in this enterprise. An emblematic example from the cinema is Alfred Hitchcock's *Rear Window*, where the immobilized voyeur is a photographer, the object of his vision murder and bodily dismemberment, and the reward of the insistence of his prying gaze the rediscovery of erotic fulfillment with his woman friend. As the fictions most consciously concerned with the epistemology of observation demonstrate, scopophilia is inextricably linked with epistemophilia, the erotic investment in the desire to know. The inherently unsatisfiable desire resulting from the drive to know, as from the drive to see, tends to make the objects of knowledge graspable, and visible, only in parts, never in the wholeness of vision and understanding that would fulfill the observer-knower's quest. Another body never is wholly knowable; it is an imaginary object that returns us to questions about the meaning of difference, and to infantile investigations into origins. The kind of truth at issue here—the meaning in stories about the relations of men and women in a framework of observational attention to their bodies and movements—leads us back to the conjoined origin of knowing and the erotic, and the unfulfillable project of mastery of the object world. In a sense, that foundational narrative of our culture, the story of Oedipus, is about what happens when one pursues this desire to its bitter end. Fullness of knowledge strikes the knower blind. But this is only the ultimate mythic paradigm: in reality, we do not reach that fullness of knowledge; we are made to be content—and are not content—with parts, with revelatory moments, with undressings, with gaps in the veil.

5 Nana at Last Unveil'd?
Problems of the Modern Nude

THE BODY IN the realist field of vision is usually seen only in parts, or in fetishistically invested details. It is a desired object approached by way of an erotic dynamic of unveiling that impels the narrative forward while never quite giving access to that object. But suppose a narrative explicitly claims to break with the logics of romantic desire—to clear away ideological coverings in order to reveal the material body as determinate of meaning, as the physical "base" for which all the rest, including the social manifestations of passion, is merely a fragile superstructure. Suppose a novel centrally preoccupied with seeing the body naked, and making its nakedness the source of all meanings. Naturalism, as a species of realism that claimed a scientific framework for its presentations of life, and found in physiology its model for understanding human behavior, was bound to encounter the challenge, and the temptation, of a novel explicitly centered on the sexual body. Such is Emile Zola's *Nana,* a novel conceived (even more than Zola's other works) to address, openly and scandalously, a woman's body in its physicality, especially its sexuality, and to unfold the social meaning and narrative force of this body.

In choosing to address the body and sexuality by writing about a prostitute, Zola both opens the way to the frankest discussion of male desire and its object available in his time, and hedges his bets; as I noted in the case of Balzac, the courtesan was well established as a literary figure from early in the century. While Zola wants to strip the courtesan of the Romantic sublimity associated with a figure such as Balzac's Esther, and he largely succeeds in doing so, it is nonetheless easier for him to strip bare a prostitute than a "respectable" woman—and this may have a limiting effect on his general claim to denude. Zola's presentation of Nana displays much of the ambiguity surrounding the painted female nude, which had become, at the time of the novel, the most prized and commercially successful kind of art. Setting *Nana* in the context of the nudes painted for the annual art salons and the art market, we can

detect the contemporary canons of representation of the naked female body, and the problems that it posed. It should be evident that the problematics of the nude, painted or written, have to do with the looked-at female body and the male looker, in a discourse produced by a man for a presumptively masculinist audience—one that may well (and certainly did) include many women, but did not accord them a dissenting perspective.

The subject and its discourse inherently partake of what Eve Kosofsky Sedgwick accurately describes under the title *Between Men:* a male sharing of lore about the "dark continent."[1] To enter into the study of such a subject with critical sympathy may make one appear complicit in the attitudes of these men. Yet there is little to be gained in constant denunciations of their patent sexism. I believe it is possible to acknowledge certain repressions and hypocrisies of high bourgeois culture while at the same time analyzing a certain narrative dynamic.

Unveiling Nana

A major preoccupation of Zola's *Nana* is the undressing of its courtesan heroine. One could even say that a major dynamic of the novel is stripping Nana, and stripping away at her, making her progressively expose the secrets of this golden body that has Paris in thrall. The first chapter of the novel provides, quite literally, a *mise-en-scène* for Nana's body, in the operetta *La blonde Vénus*. When Nana comes on stage in the third act, a shiver passes through the audience, for, we are told, she is nude. Yet, we quickly discover, not quite nude: she is covered by a filmy shift under which her splendid body lets itself be glimpsed *(se devinait)*. "It was Venus born from the waves, with only her hair for a veil."[2] The denuding of Nana progresses in Chapter 5, when Comte Muffat and the Prince make their way backstage, to her dressing room (her undressing room), where they come upon her naked to the waist, and she covers herself with a bodice which only half-hides her breasts. Despite the repeated references to Nana as nude, it is only in Chapter 7, at the midpoint of the novel, that Nana is finally completely naked. In this scene she undresses before her mirror while Comte Muffat watches, looking at her looking at herself. Thus she is fully unveiled, frontally in the mirror, and from the back in Muffat's direct view. And yet, even the completely naked woman's body bears a troubling veil.

Let me return for now to Nana's stage nudity, in *La blonde Vénus*. The operetta in which she appears—something on the order of Meilhac, Halévy, and Offenbach's *La belle Hélène*—parodies Greek myths, principally the story of Venus caught in the act of adulterous coupling with Mars by her husband, Vulcan, who has constructed a clever wire net with which he traps her naked on the bed. It is a myth about unveiling, about the nude body displayed and made spectacle. The operetta begins on a "pasteboard Olympus"; by the second act the narrator of the novel sees it as the upside-down world of carnival: "Olympus dragged in the mud, a whole religion, a whole poetry stymied . . . Legend was trampled on, images of antiquity smashed" (3:200). This is the post-sacred world that Mircea Eliade has described as the realm of "degraded myths": Nana is a kitsch Venus. The post-sacred world is celebrating its new myths of industrial progress; the première of *La blonde Vénus* was scheduled to capitalize on the influx of visitors who have come to Paris for the opening of the Exposition Universelle of 1867, that display of manufactures, arts, and luxury articles that marked the apogee of Second Empire industrial and political power and secured Paris's reputation as the capital of luxury and pleasure.

The exposure of Nana's body very much belongs to the Exposition Universelle, and if one moves from the Théâtre des Variétés to the Champ de Mars, where the exhibitions of paintings were held, one finds bodies that bear a notable resemblance to her kitsch Venus, "Venus born from the waves, with only her hair for a veil." Most obviously—proudly displayed over a label that announced it had been purchased by His Majesty the Emperor—was Alexandre Cabanel's *La naissance de Vénus* of 1863 (Figure 4), which Zola described (in the journal *La Situation*) as an example of the academic art that pleases the public by adapting antiquity to the modern taste for the voluptuous. "The goddess, drowned in a river of milk, has the air of a delicious lorette, not made of flesh and bone—that would be indecent—but of a sort of rose and white marzipan."[3] The exhibition, which offered a retrospective of "the best" in French painting of the past ten years, also included similarly displayed nudes in Cabanel's *Nymphe enlevée par un faune* of 1861 and Félix-Henry Giacomotti's *L'enlèvement d'Amymoné* of 1865, both purchased by the Emperor as well, and in Jean-Léon Gérôme's *Phryné devant l'aréopage* of 1861 (Figure 5), which Zola characterized as a case of "aggravated nudity" because of Phryné's "modern" gesture of *pudeur*

4. Alexandre Cabanel, *La naissance de Vénus*. (Paris: Musée d'Orsay. Photo © R.M.N.)

5. Jean-Léon Gérôme, *Phryné devant l'aréopage*. (Hamburg: Hamburger Kunsthalle)

6. William-Adolphe Bouguereau, *Bacchante*. (Bordeaux: Musée des Beaux-Arts. Photo © Musée des Beaux-Arts de Bordeaux)

as her clothes are pulled off to demonstrate to the judges her irresistibility.[4] Also in the 1867 exhibition was a highly compromised *Bacchante* of 1863 by William Bouguereau (Figure 6), who was on his way to becoming the favorite painter of the new industrial and commercial bourgeoisie: for instance, Aristide Boucicault, the founder of the Bon Marché department store—the model for Zola's "Au Bonheur des Dames"—collected Bouguereau. To Zola, Cabanel and Bouguereau together represent "the triumph of cleanliness in painting, pictures as polished as mirrors, in which women can do their hair."[5]

If we move beyond the Exposition Universelle of 1867 to subsequent paintings of the same type that are closer to the date of publication of *Nana* (1880), we find Cabanel's *Vénus* of 1875 (Figure 7), which prompted Zola to write: "He is a genius of the classical who permits himself a pinch of face powder, something like Venus in the peignoir of a courtesan."[6] A few more examples: Bouguereau's famous *Nymphes et satyre* of 1873 (Figure 8), now in Williamstown, Massachusetts—Bouguereau became a favorite of newly wealthy American collectors—and his *La nymphée* of 1878 (now in Stockton, California), one of the twelve paintings he showed at the next Exposition Universelle, in 1878, where he was awarded the Medal of Honor; and, finally, Bouguereau's own version of *La naissance de Vénus* of 1879 (Figure 9), exhibited while

PROBLEMS OF THE MODERN NUDE

7. Alexandre Cabanel, *Vénus*. (Montpellier: Musée
Fabre. Photo: Frédéric Jaulmes)

Nana was appearing serially in *Le Voltaire*. Zola commented of Bouguereau that he was "the apotheosis of elegance; an enchanting painter
who draws celestial creatures, sugared bonbons that melt under the
gaze."[7]

Nana in her original presentation belongs to the prettified eroticism
of these popular salon paintings. She is not a figure from Toulouse-
Lautrec's (somewhat later) music-hall ladies and *cocottes*: she is too
pretty and healthy, too glamorous, for that. Nor is she one of Degas'
dancers or actresses, viewed from the wings or in the intimacy of the
toilette: she is too staged for that, a representation *of* a representation,
a consciously created and self-creating sex object. When we reflect that

8. William-Adolphe Bouguereau, *Nymphes et satyre.*
(Williamstown, Massachusetts: Sterling and Francine
Clark Art Institute)

the nudes of Cabanel and Bouguereau anticipate twentieth-century cal-
endar art, we realize that Nana is presented as a kind of Second Empire
pin-up. In other words, her aesthetic—or so it seems—is not Zola's.
Nana herself indeed explicitly disassociates herself from the aesthetic of
the novel in which she figures when she censures a novel she's read
about a whore; she displays "an indignant repugnance for this kind of
filthy literature, which had the pretension of rendering nature; as if one
could show everything! As if a novel shouldn't be written to give the
reader a pleasant experience! . . . Nana . . . wanted works that were
tender and noble" (339). Nana nude is a kitsch Venus, as the contem-

9. William-Adolphe Bouguereau, *La naissance de Vénus*.
(Paris: Musée d'Orsay. Photo © R.M.N.)

porary caricaturist Gill recognized in his drawing entitled *La naissance de Nana-Vénus* (Figure 10), which bears the caption: "Motif à tableau pour les BOUGUEREAU futurs" (Subject for a painting by future Bouguereaus).[8] Zola recognizes and stages her as a kitsch Venus, but without his endorsement; indeed, he does not in general endorse this created character, whom he deplores, but also finds troubling, less easily dismissed than the salon nudes whose eroticism he so vigorously denies.

As my quotations from his art criticism indicate, Zola consistently deplores this kind of painting, which cheats on nature by staging a glamorized nude body and motivating its narrative context with references to an irrelevant academicized classicism. Zola's art criticism—

10. Gill, *La naissance de Nana-Vénus. La Lune Rousse,* 19 October 1879. (Photo: David Richards)

reviews of exhibitions and salons, largely from the early stages of his career—militates in favor of a realism first pioneered by Gustave Courbet and illustrated for his own generation by Edouard Manet, the painter about whom he wrote at greatest length. (Manet's works were excluded from the Exposition Universelle of 1867; Zola publicly protested the exclusion, and Manet counteracted it by staging his own private exhibition.) The kind of nude that Zola applauded is best represented by Courbet's *Baigneuses* of 1853 (Figure 11), with its resolutely anti-classical body and its setting of the nude by a recognizably real, rural pond, next to a peasant woman. Courbet's painting contrasts sharply, indeed wilfully, with the usual treatment of the theme, for instance in the series of "Baigneuses" by Bouguereau. Indeed, it is still difficult today to read

11. Gustave Courbet, *Les baigneuses*. (Montpellier: Musée Fabre.
Photo: Frédéric Jaulmes)

Courbet's painting, with its heroic dimensions and domestic details—
such as the woman's stockings hanging from a branch—as other than a
denunciation of the convention it evokes. It prepares another, more
explosive denunciation of the academic tradition, ten years later, in the
painting Zola rightly saw as the major nude of his time, Manet's *Olympia* of 1863 (Figure 12). As Zola writes, "When our artists give us
Venuses, they correct nature, they lie. Edouard Manet asked himself why
lie, why not tell the truth; he introduced us to Olympia, this *fille* of our
own time, whom you meet on the sidewalks."[9]

Olympia, then, solves the problem of the realist modern nude—and
yet, not completely or definitively. Zola insisted upon seeing Manet and
also the Impressionists as *naturalistes* or *actualistes*—which explains why

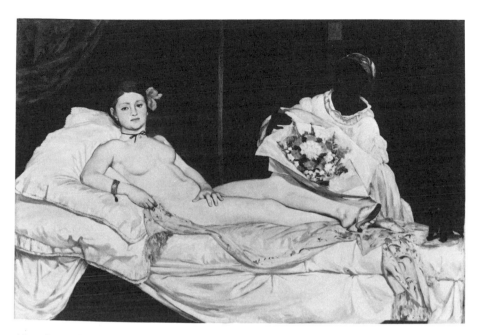

12. Edouard Manet, *Olympia*. (Paris: Musée d'Orsay. Photo © R.M.N.)

he eventually misunderstood and rejected the more daring experiments of Claude Monet and, especially, of his boyhood friend Paul Cézanne. The place of the nude in an aesthetic that is uncompromisingly dedicated to the real, the natural, and the actual poses problems that are not so easily resolved. One senses this in Zola's discussion of *Le déjeuner sur l'herbe,* shown at the Salon des Refusés of 1863, which he considered Manet's greatest painting. It realizes, he says, the dream of every painter: to put life-size figures in a landscape. And the scandal of this naked woman between two clothed men? First of all, says Zola, you can find more than fifty paintings in the Louvre that mix nude and clothed figures—an odd argument in favor of what he sees as a definitively modern painting—and second of all, one should not be concerned with the subject of the painting but rather with its treatment: another odd argument in the context of an "actualist" aesthetic. He goes on: "Thus, surely the nude woman of *Le déjeuner sur l'herbe* is there only to furnish the artist an occasion to paint a bit of flesh. What you should see in the painting isn't a picnic on the grass but the whole landscape, with its vigorous and fine elements . . .; it's finally this vast ensemble, full of air [*plein d'air*], this corner of nature rendered with such perfect simplicity."[10] If the nude of *Olympia* is self-justifying, by the very subject of

PROBLEMS OF THE MODERN NUDE

the painting, that of *Le déjeuner sur l'herbe* poses more perplexing problems. Zola wants his natural-sized nude in a natural setting, but he doesn't quite know how to go about finding a rationale for it. He falls back on formalist considerations and the argument that the motivation for the figure in the setting is conventional and traditional, rather than natural, and he is unwilling to reach the conclusion that the very success of the painting may depend on this irresolvable tension.

The problem of the modern nude resurfaces in *L'oeuvre*, Zola's novel of 1886 about a painter, who has traits of both Manet and Cézanne. The protagonist, Claude Lantier, is painting a composition entitled "Plein air." The title picks up one of Zola's key terms in the description of *Le déjeuner sur l'herbe*, which is indeed commonly applied to the modern movement in painting of his time: painting that wants to move from studio to street and countryside. In fact, Claude's tableau closely resembles *Le déjeuner sur l'herbe*, with a fully clothed male, two women wrestling in the background, and a reclining nude woman in the center foreground. The academic architect Dubuche views the work in progress in Claude's atelier and expresses perplexity at the clothed man and nude women. "On n'a jamais vu ça," he exclaims. "The public won't understand . . . They'll find it dirty . . . Yes, it is dirty" (5:43). Claude and his novelist friend Sandoz (in many ways Zola's self-portrait) exclaim that Dubuche is a *sale bourgeois,* and that there are a hundred paintings in the Louvre to justify the composition, but they don't really answer the questions he raises, which continue to return insistently in the novel. For instance, the sculptor Mahoudeau is constructing an immense nude, "with the breasts of a giant and thighs like towers," and Sandoz inquires if she's supposed to be a *baigneuse,* to which the sculptor replies that he's going to put in some grape leaves and make her a *bacchante*—a favorite academic way of doing an animated female nude. This response provokes Claude's outrage: "A *bacchante!* Are you trying to make fun of us? Does that exist, a *bacchante?* . . . A girl harvesting, maybe? And a modern harvester, for the love of God! I know, I know, there's the nude. A peasant girl who's taken off her clothes, then. You've got to feel that, it's got to live!" (5:55). Again, Claude rejects the traditional salon justification of the nude by allusion to types from antiquity, but his talk of a peasant girl who may have taken her clothes off (during her harvesting, perhaps?) does not propose a coherent motivation for the modern nude.

This problem won't go away in *L'oeuvre*. Claude's would-be masterpiece is a vast tableau of Paris seen from the banks of the Seine, a detailed realist cityscape which yet contains in the foreground a boat with three women, one of them standing at the prow of the boat, completely nude, shining like a sun. Sandoz, despite his sympathy for Claude's work, is taken aback, and wants to know what the women are doing. Claude proposes that they have been swimming: "that gives me a motive for the nude [*un motif de nu*]" (5:143). But Sandoz is not convinced. "It's not very plausible, that nude woman, in the very center of Paris." Sandoz returns to the charge repeatedly in the following days, pleading the cause of "logic":

135

> How could a modern painter, who prided himself on painting only realities, let himself bastardize a work by introducing such imaginings. It was so easy to choose other subjects, where the necessity of the nude was clear! But Claude became stubborn, gave poor explanations, and violent ones, since he didn't want to confess the true reason, an idea of his that was so unclear he couldn't have stated it coherently, the torment of a secret symbolism, the return of an old romanticism that made him incarnate in this nudity the very flesh of Paris, of the nude and impassioned city shining with a woman's beauty. And he added to this his own passion, his love of beautiful bellies, of fertile thighs and breasts. (5:143)

He persists, to the astonishment of all his friends, with "this Venus born from the foam of the Seine, triumphant among the omnibuses of the quais and the stevedores of the Port Saint-Nicolas."

The nude here, rather than being integrated into the modern landscape, becomes a sin against the modern in art, a secret return of romanticism, an illegitimate recourse to symbolism that eventually brings Claude's art full circle, to one more "Birth of Venus." By the end of the novel, Claude, disabused of his obsession, looks at his own painting with distressed astonishment: "Who, then, had painted this idol of an unknown religion? Who had made her of metals, of marble, of gems, unfolding the mystical rose of her sex, between the precious columns of her thighs, under the sacred vault of her belly? Was it he who, without knowing it, was the craftsman of this symbol of insatiable desire . . . ?" (5:199). His dream of the modern nude has turned into the nightmare of denuded desire, concentrated on the symbolism—which Sandoz, and the whole value system of the novel, judge to be illegitimate—of the "mystical rose" of the woman's genitals. Claude's moment of recognition is followed by his suicide.

PROBLEMS OF THE MODERN NUDE

Returning to *Nana*, one is tempted to argue that the novel is conceived to provide a *motif de nu,* a motivation for the denuding of Nana that the text so much insists upon. One could imagine an argument, in a parody of some of the analyses done by the Russian Formalists, that would show the entire theme and plot of the novel as motivating devices for stripping Nana bare, so that finally, by the midpoint of the novel, she can be looked at in a way that naturalizes her nudity. One could say that Zola's solution here is closer to that of *Olympia* than that of *Le déjeuner sur l'herbe: filles* and *courtisanes,* after all, strip by profession. Thus, if Zola wished—as he said in a letter—to write a *poème du cul,* he has found a better motivation than Claude's misdirected desire to paint the "mystical rose" of the woman's sex.

Still, given the original presentation of Nana as a kind of kitsch salon Venus, one may need to ask whether, despite the easy motivation achieved in painting the nude as prostitute, Nana's nudity is indeed so natural. Nana is stripped naked at an artistic moment characterized by a kind of crisis in representation of the nude, as T. J. Clark argues in *The Painting of Modern Life,* and as the debates in *L'oeuvre* suggest.[11] Clark and another art historian who has studied the iconography of the nude in the Second Empire, Beatrice Farwell, establish Ingres, and particularly his *Vénus anadyomène* of 1848 (Figure 13) as the point of reference from which to track this crisis. As Farwell writes, Ingres "created the formula: high erotic content embodied in austere form of classic beauty. By the time of Cabanel the formula had become debased, or at any rate abused; it is still an unanswered question whether the Cabanels and Bouguereaus did what they did with the nude innocently or cynically."[12] In the 1860s, a painter had to find "some plausible and picturable reason for nudity," says Farwell—echoing Sandoz—or else resort to the standard academic motifs, or, in a somewhat more coherent historicizing gesture, make use of the "antique genre"—representing a supposed scene from life in ancient Greece, for instance—made fashionable by Gérôme's *Combat de coqs* of 1847.[13] One might add that another genre permitting the nude was the exotic Orientalist painting, deriving from Delacroix as well as Ingres, for example Gérôme's *Un marché d'esclaves* (Figure 14) which excuses its own display of the nude through representation of a "foreign" (barbaric, deplorable, enticing) practice of display of the nude. In other words, in the second half of the nineteenth century classicizing references—*bacchantes,* births of Venus, and the rest—or else the exotic distancing of the body, in time or in space, give the ready-made *motif de nu,* providing standard narratives in support

13. Jean-Auguste-Dominique Ingres, *Vénus
anadyomène*. (Chantilly: Musée Condé.
Photo: Lauros-Giraudon)

of moments of nudity. Conversely, one can say that the desire to denude
leads to the deployment of the defense mechanisms of classical or exotic
reference. The idea of the "modern nude" is something of an oxymoron,
an issue that clearly worried Manet, who once proposed that the models
in Thomas Couture's studio—where he trained—put their clothes on to
provide realistic referents; and then, somewhat contradictorily, considered how natural settings might be used for posing a nude, since it
seemed that the nude was "the first and last word in art."[14]

The problem is further complicated if one considers Farwell's argument that the frequency of the nude in salon art from the 1860s onward

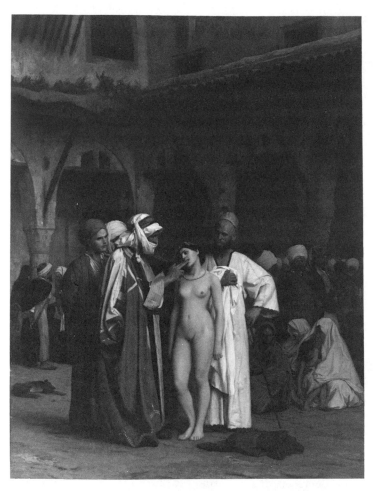

14. Jean-Léon Gérôme, *Un marché d'esclaves*. (Williamstown, Massachusetts: Sterling and Francine Clark Art Institute)

was linked to the increasing visibility of the courtesan as a social type, and to a new philistine public, headed by the Emperor, that considered the nude the apogee of art, worthy of gold medals and fetching good prices on the market.[15] This public—predominantly male, of course— also liked to recognize, or to claim to recognize, the courtesans who had served as models for the Venuses and *bacchantes:* a way of having your decorous classicistic reference while also decoding the contemporary erotic reality behind it. The stories being told by the nude body in this period were multiple and ambiguous. The "crisis" of the nude, Clark suggests, has much to do with the problem of negotiating between a

15. Henri Gervex, *Rolla*. (Bordeaux: Musée des Beaux-Arts. Photo © Musée des Beaux-Arts de Bordeaux)

particular, and sexed, body, and a generalized and idealized one. What happened when salon artists tried to reconcile the difference between the academic nude and the modern nude—rather than exposing the difference, as Manet did in "Olympia"—may be illustrated through the painting by Henri Gervex, *Rolla* (Figure 15), which was refused entry to the Salon of 1878 for indecency. The body here is still rendered in the idealizing manner of the salon artists, but its particularized, anecdotal context was considered shocking. If one knows Musset's poem "Rolla" of some fifty years earlier, one identifies the nude woman as Marion, on whom Rolla has spent his "last pistole," and he's at the window not simply to look out but to contemplate suicide. What may have shocked contemporary viewers even more than Marion's identity as a whore is her clearly marked passage from dressed to undressed: the pile of her discarded clothes on the floor that she has taken off to go to bed with Rolla.

The specific narrative context provided by the painting seems to make its nude display only more aggressive. As a contemporary commented, Marion is undressed rather than nude—though this is in blatant contradiction to the rendering of her body itself. The painting as a whole represents an uneasy compromise between the idealizing nude and the painting of modern life. Indeed, Zola accused Gervex of copying subjects and motifs from the Impressionists, whose studios he frequented, and then dressing them up and toning them down through the technical proficiency and finish he had learned during his apprenticeship in the atelier of Cabanel.[16] In *L'oeuvre*, Zola used Gervex as the model for the painter Fagerolles, who wins official recognition because he manages to adapt the painting of modern life he learns from Claude Lantier and his circle to acceptable salon taste. The issues posed by the oxymoronic concept of the modern nude remain largely unresolved in the paintings known to Zola. They are issues that would have to be reworked by Pierre-Auguste Renoir and Paul Gauguin, and then Henri Matisse.

It is in the context of crisis in the representation of the nude, in particular the difficult issues faced by the artist who wishes to represent the nude in modern life, that I now return to the scene where Nana undresses in front of the mirror, narcissistically admiring and caressing her own body while Muffat watches. As Nana undresses, Muffat reads an article in *Le Figaro*, entitled "La mouche d'or," which allegorizes Nana as an insect bred from the rot of the urban slums and come to infect the upper classes. She is a product of the proletariat, of four or five generations of alcoholics, who represents physical and social degeneracy in the "nervous disorder of her woman's sex." (*Sexe* here means both "the female sex" and "the woman's genitals.") Nana is a "germ of destruction . . . corrupting and disrupting Paris between her snowy thighs" (3:280). One notes the equation, typical in Zola, between female sexuality and the lower classes: the body as a source of class confusion, of potential revolution, as an object of fear.

When Muffat sets aside the newspaper article, he returns to looking at Nana. As his eyes follow her own glance detailing her own body, we reach the essentials of nudity:

> He thought of his former horror of woman, of the monster of the Bible, lubricious, smelling of the beast. Nana was covered with down, the down of a redhead made her body velvety; while, in her rear and her thighs like a wild mare's, in the swelling flesh carved with deep folds, which gave to her sex the troubling veil of their shadow, there was the beast. It was the golden beast, unconscious like a force, whose odor alone spoiled the world. Muffat looked and looked, obsessed, possessed, to the point where, having closed

his eyes in order to see her no more, the animal reappeared in the depths of the shadows, magnified, terrible, exaggerating its pose. Now it would be there, before his eyes, in his flesh, forever. (3:282)

When we reach Nana's sex, we reach a veil, which seems to be composed of both her pubic hair and the shadow thrown by her limbs. As in the staging of La blonde Vénus, unveiling ultimately encounters a veil, which is here the ultimate veil: the woman's sex as unknowable and unrepresentable. The male gaze, and the male imagination, can only swerve into the allegorical, to evocations of the Biblical monster and of the beast. Some of Zola's best critics—Jean Borie, Naomi Schor, Janet Beizer—have noted that this passage forcibly reminds us of scenarios sketched by Freud describing the boy's discovery of the female genitals, scenarios which both affirm and deny the absence of the phallus, and don't know what to see in its place.[17]

The problem of representing Nana's sex has its pictorial counterpart. Beatrice Farwell, in an essay on Courbet's Baigneuses, remarks that "neither Courbet nor Manet ever faced squarely the Realist's dilemma, in representing the nude, with respect to pubic hair versus the classical (or hairless) alternative, and that versus the true representation of the female anatomy."[18] Her comment points to a certain ambiguity, unease, hesitation, or loss of nerve in the break from the academic nude. The academic position was epitomized by the journalist Camille Lemonnier, reviewing the Salon of 1870, when he wrote that the nude "hides nothing because there is nothing to hide . . . It hides nothing and shows nothing."[19] Manet in Olympia solved the problem with an allusion to the classical expedient of a well-placed hand, but as Clark points out, the representation of this hand enraged contemporary critics. No doubt they were shocked because the hand so definitely suggests that there is something to conceal, whereas airbrushing the nude effaces the problem.[20] If one turns from the isolated case of Olympia to the series of nudes painted in the 1860s by the master realist, Courbet, one notes that the fully erotic Femme au perroquet of 1866 (Figure 16) uses the bedsheet in a academic gesture of classical draping. Zola himself expressed reservations about this picture, which he saw as a falling-off from the ambitions and the quality of the Baigneuses and the Enterrement à Ornans. Courbet, he comments, "has rounded off the too-hard angles of his genius."[21] There isn't much plein air here. One can surmise that Zola was not pleased with Courbet's other nudes of the 1860s, such as the Femme nue of 1868 (in the Philadelphia Museum of Art), which may have been

16. Gustave Courbet, *La femme au perroquet*. (New York: Metropolitan Museum of Art. Bequest of Mrs. H. O. Havemeyer. The H. O. Havemeyer Collection)

a reply to the academic painter Paul Baudry's *La perle et la vague* of 1863, or his *Femme nue à la vague* of 1868 (in the Metropolitan Museum of Art): they make too many concessions to official and commercial standards for the nude. The *Jeune baigneuse* of 1866 (in the Metropolitan) has some of the ambiguities of Nana, confounding the veil of hair and the veil of shadows. The infamous *Le sommeil* of 1866 (Figure 17) brings us close to the erotic games of Nana and Satin in Zola's novel, but its staging of these two sumptuous bodies may again glamorize too much to satisfy Zola's proclaimed aesthetic. Yet there are two paintings by Courbet that more directly address the problem of representing the female sex illustrated by Zola and commented on by Farwell: first the *Femme aux bas blancs* of 1866 (in the Barnes Foundation), which appears consciously to pick a somewhat "perverse" angle of vision; and then the truly infamous painting done, like *Le sommeil,* for the Turk Khalil-Bey, entitled *L'origine du monde,* of 1866 (Figure 18). Courbet's painting reads as a denunciation of the endless births of Venus, a decisive gesture toward hyper-realism in the representation of the nude, toward the achievement of a new visual language of the woman's body, but of course its elaborately maintained underground status in a sense removes it from the history of representation.

17. Gustave Courbet, *Le sommeil*. (Paris: Musée du Petit Palais. Photo: Lauros-Giraudon)

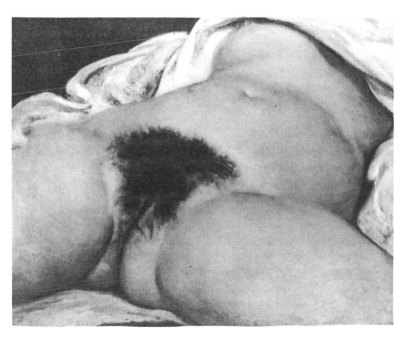

18. Gustave Courbet, *L'origine du monde*. (Paris: private collection. Reproduced with permission from Robert Fernier, *La vie et l'oeuvre de Gustave Courbet*, vol. 2. Lausanne: Bibliothèque des Arts, 1979)

L'origine du monde was in fact labeled the visual equivalent of Zola's "putrid literature" by the critic Ferragus (Louis Ulbach) in his review of *Thérèse Raquin,* but Zola himself, in reply, evaded mention of the painting—which he must have known—and indeed evaded the whole problem by suggesting that Ferragus' article should be consigned to the flames.[22] Ferragus' attack on "putrid literature" is echoed by Nana's own censure of the "filthy" novel in which she figures, but is not clear that Zola is willing, or able, to take the doctrine of "showing everything" as far as Courbet did. Courbet's painting in this instance may reveal too clearly for Zola's comfort the voyeuristic component of naturalist observation. And it may dislodge the viewer from his position of distanced spectatorship, bringing him into too close a confrontation of the desired object. It puts too decisive an end to the games of unveiling.

Yet Zola's ambiguous airbrushing of the nude Nana may not simply point to a loss of nerve on his part. The unrepresentability of her sex may actually be an essential part of Zola's story. Consider that Muffat's body, in a state of arousal, is never seen in the mirror in which Nana contemplates herself. He must, however—after the passage quoted—be standing behind her, since he will seize her from behind and throw her on the carpet, to possess her in an act in which he knows he possesses nothing. It is as if the mirror were tilted at some impossible angle which prevents us from seeing ourselves in the place of the male gaze directed at the female: something like—but different from—that famous mirror in Manet's *Un bar aux Folies-Bergère* of 1882 (in the Cortauld Institute), which does inscribe the male viewer, but displaces him from where we would expect him to be—the place where the viewer in fact stands.[23] If Muffat were reflected in the mirror, it would necessarily implicate the reader as a viewer of Nana self-reflected, which might risk revealing his possible arousal: something on the order of reading as erection—which the moralizing context of the scene provided by the allegory of "La mouche d'or" explicitly censors. The situation is given another type of representation in Manet's painting entitled *Nana* (Figure 19), which was refused entry to the Salon of 1877 as an "outrage to morality," perhaps because it clearly represented a well-known courtesan, Henriette Hauser, or perhaps, more pertinently and profoundly, because it overtly—and uneasily—inscribes the male spectator. The painting doesn't illustrate any specific scene in the novel—which hadn't yet been written, though Manet may have known from Zola of its subject—and certainly not the scene I am discussing, where the mirror is full-length. It is possible, though, that it suggested to Zola a certain problematic of the mirror in

19. Edouard Manet, *Nana*. (Hamburg: Hamburger
  Kunsthalle)

relation to the viewed and the viewer. This central scene in the novel
may be a narrative response to Manet's preoccupation with representation of the woman's body in the painting of modern life.

   The censorship of male sexual excitement in Zola's scene, which is of
course typical of virtually all artistic representation in the modern Western tradition, may correspond to the ambiguous representation of Nana's
body, which appears ever young, glamorous, untouched, and essentially
inaccessible. Moreover, her sexuality—as the mirror scene demonstrates—is essentially narcissistic. None of Nana's lovers, even those
who beat and otherwise abuse her, can really touch her or take possession of her. There is no way into her. In Freud's descriptions of infantile
male phantasies of the female genitals, if there is no phallus there, then
there is nothing there. Something is missing—but that conclusion is

20. William-Adolphe Bouguereau, *Jeune fille se défendant contre l'amour.* (Malibu, California: Collection of the J. Paul Getty Museum)

unacceptable. So there is something that is nothing, nothing that is something: an uncanny situation.[24] The narcissistic woman indeed most fully realizes the traditional male view of woman as an impenetrable enigma. At the risk of frivolity, I might illustrate Nana's narcissistic impenetrability through two more paintings by Bouguereau, first his *Jeune fille se défendant contre l'amour* of 1880 (Figure 20), with its voluptuous but thoroughly defended body, and then his *Le printemps* of 1886 (Figure 21), a strange portrayal of resistance to sexual solicitation. This painting, incidentally, has a curious history of male aggres-

21. William-Adolphe Bouguereau, *Le printemps*.
(Omaha, Nebraska: Joslyn Art Museum. Gift of
Francis T. B. Martin)

sion directed against it. When it was exhibited in 1891 in Omaha,
Nebraska, a viewer, one Carey Judson Warbington, threw a chair at it,
declaring: "I did it to protect the virtue of women." He was arrested,
tried, and found insane, and later committed suicide. Then in 1976,
again in Omaha—where the painting found its permanent home—a man
repeatedly threw a fifty-pound bronze statue at it, with the explanation
that "he thought the painting was filthy."[25] Thus it appears that ambi-

PROBLEMS OF THE MODERN NUDE

guities in sexual representation are not protection enough, at least when dealing with deranged interpreters.

If the unrepresentability of Nana's sex speaks of a deep thematic concern of the novel—Nana's inaccessibility to the male—this may in turn tell us something about the subtending dynamics of Zola's novel. Consider the explicit comment on the power of Nana's sex offered late in the novel by Mignon, one of the theatrical crowd, when he visits the sumptuous townhouse in which Muffat has established Nana, and where she has accumulated the offerings of scores of lovers. Mignon is impressed by this "magisterial monument" to Nana's force. He finds himself thinking, in comparison, of vast engineering projects he has seen: a "cyclopean" aqueduct near Marseille, the new port of Cherbourg, and the palace built by an industrialist who had created a monopoly in sugar refining. But all that pales in comparison to what Nana has accomplished, and how she has done it: "it was with something else, a dumb little thing that everyone laughed at, a bit of her delicate nudity, it was with this nothing, shameful and so powerful, whose force moved the world, that alone, without workers, without machines invented by engineers, she had shaken Paris and built this fortune under which dead men slept. 'Ah! in the name of heaven, what a tool!' exclaimed Mignon" (3:380).

This makes explicit, first of all, the male view of the female genitals as nothing, yet at the same time the object of anxiety resolved in pejoratives *(une petite bêtise)* and nervous laughter. Then, with the contradictory logic of the phantasmatic, the passage goes on to make this nothing everything, Nana's sex a lever whose force can lift the globe *(dont la force soulevait le monde):* an anti-phallus more powerful than the male member. Her sex is all the more powerful in that its mechanism remains hidden. More than a machine, it is a motor, a steam engine, as all the imagery of heat, hot vapors, and pressures associated with Nana suggests. We are given to understand that the whole dynamic of the narrative in *Nana* derives from, emanates from, her sex, which is perhaps ultimately why her sex cannot be directly represented. That is, the *puissance motrice* of the text is a *puissance occulte,* a hidden source of energy that can be known only in its effects, not in its generative principle. It is significant that by the end of this next-to-last chapter, Nana's sex becomes allegorized, very much in the manner of the "mystical rose" of Claude Lantier's painting: "her sex rose and shone upon its supine victims, like a sunrise lighting up a field of carnage" (3:381). This kind of allegorization will be severely criticized by the novelist Sandoz in

L'oeuvre, but the novelist Zola finds it the only way to represent the true, which is to say the dynamic, meaning of Nana's anatomy.

Doing Inventory on the Body

Most of Zola's novels are centered on a piece of social or industrial machinery, which almost always provides the energetic source of the narrative—often resulting, as Michel Serres demonstrates, in a thermo-dynamics of narrative.[26] The locomotive of *La bête humaine* is only the most obvious example of the combustion engine which, when it heats up, powers the plot forward, toward loss of control and, finally, crash and explosion. And the protagonist, Jacques Lantier, victim of his family's hereditary mental fissure, the *fêlure,* himself becomes an engine out of control, spewing forth murderous vapors. The simplest machine is the alcohol still of *L'assommoir,* with its constant heat and purring noise, producing a constant drip of distilled alcohol from its pipe that is quite literally the energy source for the novel, and for the destructive dynamic of its characters' lives. The coal mine of *Germinal,* the stock market of *L'argent,* the central food markets—les Halles—in *Le ventre de Paris* similarly serve as narrative machines or, better, narrative motors, in that they work by internal combustion. Such is the woman's body in *Nana,* the most carnal motor that Zola imagined.

Nana constitutes Zola's closest approach to the woman's sexual body as the dynamic principal of narrative. But other of his novels provide telling illustrations of the motor force of the woman's body, perhaps most of all *Au Bonheur des Dames* (1883). The central institution of this novel is the department store—represented in its moment of great capitalist expansion during the Second Empire—which itself is powered by the woman's body. That body is not so directly confronted in *Au Bonheur des Dames* as in *Nana;* it is represented rather in its clothes and accessories, and in the uncontrollable desire for bodily coverings and adornments created by modern publicity and display. *Au Bonheur des Dames* is preeminently the novel of commodity fetishism, and since the commodities fetishized by the market are articles of woman's clothing, the Marxist notion of fetishism converges with the Freudian, in an overheated economy that is both an erotic and a cash nexus.

The department store of *Au Bonheur des Dames*—modeled in large part on Aristide Boucicault's immensely successful Au Bon Marché—comes into its glory as part of the transformation of Paris by Baron Haussmann (who himself appears in the novel, thinly disguised as Baron

Hartmann) under the orders of Napoleon III. New avenues and boulevards are cut through the old labyrinth of Paris streets, making travel across the city much more practicable and bringing people out of their traditional fidelity to the *commerce du quartier* into a larger economy and the new pleasures of shopping in a palace of diversified goods. The new Parisian cityscape permits a theatricalization of commerce. As opposed to the old specialized commerce, where one entered a shop looking for a single type of goods, which were then laid out on the counter, the department store depends on display, on the *étalage*, which takes place in a new kind of space, the *vitrine*, or display window. We are at the birth of that most modern of social behaviors, shopping, and its distinctive form that we call "window shopping."[27] The traditional window of realist fiction here becomes the display window, abolishing the barrier between street and shop, outside and inside, inviting the spectator to come in and become a shopper with its spectacle of the goods for sale. And what is for sale, in Zola's view, always leads us back to the woman's body.

It is the window displays of Au Bonheur des Dames that first attract the attention of Denise Baudu, the young woman who is to be the novel's heroine, the morning she arrives from Normandy with her two brothers. Dazzled and seduced, they follow the series of windows along the street, from umbrellas, to silk stockings hung so as to show "the rounded profiles of calves," stockings with "the softness of a blonde's skin," then gloves, with the "narrow palm of a Byzantine virgin, that stiff and almost adolescent grace of women's clothes that haven't yet been worn," then silks, satins, and velvets, and finally the ready-made coats and dresses, "in this chapel raised for worship of the graces of woman." This initial encounter with the windows of Au Bonheur des Dames concludes with a picture of the *mannequins,* the dummies displaying the ready-made clothes: "The round breasts of the dummies swelled the material, the large hips exaggerated the narrowness of the waists, the missing head was replaced by a large card stuck with a pin in the red velvet of the collar; while the mirrors, on the two sides of the window, through a calculated play reflected and multiplied them endlessly, peopled the street with these beautiful women for sale, who wore their prices in large numerals in the place of their heads" (4:20). Zola's allegorizing tendency is already at work in these early pages of the novel: these exaggeratedly female bodies, endlessly reflected in the mirrors, displayed to the street, with a price tag in the place of their heads—the public display of prices was one of the decisive innovations of the department store over the old commerce—suggest the whole dynamic of commerce by seduction on which the novel, like the department store, is based. The first chapter ends, as rain and night descend on Au Bonheur des Dames—"the machine purred on, still active, spewing forth its steam in a last roar"— with an image of one of the dummies, dressed in a velvet coat trimmed with silver fox, showing "the profile of a woman without a head, who was running through the downpour to some evening party, in the mysterious shadows of Paris" (4:31).

The novel insistently returns us to the woman's body as the object of display and the energetic source of commercial transactions. Indeed, the operating principle of Au Bonheur des Dames is the seduction of woman, a principle which is constantly "theorized" by the store's owner and presiding genius, Octave Mouret. Mouret is a widower, and a womanizer who strenuously avoids any serious entanglements with women—the "love plot" of the novel tells how Denise overcomes this resistance by herself resisting his seductions—in order to perfect seduction on the grandest commercial scale ever conceived. Seduction according to Mouret consists in creating desire, so that shopping for necessities is superseded by the purchase of the useless, seductive item. The store display is designed to throw in the way of the shopper goods she didn't know she wanted, artfully presented as alluring spectacle. As Mouret explains to Baron Hartmann, department stores create new desires in woman's "flesh"; they are "an immense temptation, to which she fatally succumbed." Mouret, as a kind of modern Blue Beard, is the inventor of "this mechanism to eat women" (4:55). Or, as we learn when Mouret has transformed his store into "the cathedral of modern commerce"— by a vast expansion predicated on Baron Hartmann's influence in opening up new avenues for the store's new facades—"Mouret had a single passion to conquer woman. He wanted her to be queen in his house, he had built her this temple in order to hold her there at his mercy. That was his whole tactic, to intoxicate her with his gallant attentions and traffic in her desires, exploit her fever" (4:132). Shopping thus becomes a "new neurosis" (4:144), complete with a new species of pathology, shoplifting, which is considered to be especially characteristic of pregnant women.

The novel is structured on three big days of special sales—with another special day in the middle, when the store does inventory, spreading out on the counters and numbering all the unsold articles. The last of these days inaugurates the new monumental facade of Au Bonheur des Dames with a great white sale, in a chapter that brings to its demonstrative

PROBLEMS OF THE MODERN NUDE

conclusion the narrative dynamic generated by selling to women those articles that define and create their social and erotic bodies. The climax of Zola's descriptive inventories comes when we are led on a walk through the lingerie counters. The passage reads in part (I omit mainly the exhaustive lists of different undergarments in this two-page paragraph):

All of woman's linen, the white underthings that are hidden, were set out on display in a series of rooms, arranged in different departments. The corsets and bustles took up a counter . . . an army of dummies without head or feet, ranks of torsos, dolls' busts flattened under the silk, with the troubling lubricity of the infirm . . . But then the luxury déshabillé began, a déshabillé strewn across the vast galleries, as if a group of pretty girls had undressed themselves from counter to counter, down to the naked satin of their skin . . . And the underthings appeared, and fell one by one: white slips of all lengths, the slip that reins in the knees and the slip with a train that sweeps on the ground, a rising tide of slips in which legs were drowning; bloomers in percale, in toile, in piqué, wide white bloomers in which a man's hips would be lost; shifts, finally, buttoned to the neck for the night, uncovering the bust during the day, held up only by narrow straps, in simple calico, in Irish linen, in batiste, the last white veil that slipped from the breasts, down along the hips. In the trousseaus an indiscreet unpacking, woman turned over and seen from the bottom up, from the petite-bourgeoise with her basic cottons to the rich woman hidden in lace, an alcove publicly opened, whose hidden luxury, whose plissés, broderies, valenciennes, depraved the senses as it overflowed in costly fantasies. Woman dressed herself again, the white wave of this deluge of underthings returned to its place under the shivering mystery of skirts [which, along with shirts, etc.] were going to animate themselves with the life of the flesh, scented and warm with the odor of love . . . (4:212)[28]

Zola's inventory here takes on the contours of a male adolescent's fantasy of seeing under skirts, in a hallucinatory vision that never reaches the genitals, which remain strictly unknown and invisible, but rather invests its erotic longings in the articles of clothing that cover the body most intimately. The passage is a textbook example of fetishization, of the libidinal cathexis of the substitute, in which the woman's body is seen in a series of metonymies, as fragments of an erotic delirium.

Like Freud's boy fetishist, Zola's narrator sees woman here from below, somewhat in the manner in which Muffat at one point views Nana from the wings of the theater, foreshortened, making her rear appear enormous. That is, reversal of "normal" perspectives claims a certain epistemophilic privilege, a gain in knowledge from seeing woman off her guard, turned round or turned over, in a gesture of male dominance. Woman turned over and displayed from below in this passage evokes the image of "an alcove publicly opened." Au Bonheur des Dames includes a place that has already been referred to as an "alcove," which is, curiously, the reading room Mouret has installed for the repose of his shoppers and which becomes a place for discreet rendezvous of adulterous lovers. The reading room is thus the inner sanctum of the department store, the place where desires aroused in shopping reach their erotic dénouement: it is, we are told, "the hidden-away alcove of the fall, the place of perdition where the strongest gave in" (4:147). This alcove, as a room in the store, is repeated in the flesh, in the "alcove publicly opened" which is both the woman's boudoir, the place of her dressing and undressing, and, metonymically, her genitals.

"These things are always *secrets d'alcôve!*" said Josef Breuer to his disciple Sigmund Freud, apropos of the causes of hysteria, thereby putting Freud on to the etiology of hysteria in what Breuer primly glossed as "secrets of the marriage bed" (*Standard Edition* 14:13). That alcove, which is by definition a closed and secluded place, contains secrets that are detected outside the alcove only in their effects, in chains of metonymies that unfold from a hidden cause. The psychoanalyst attempts to penetrate into the alcove in search of initiatory scenes, primal or otherwise. When Zola claims to open the alcove publicly, he of course does so incompletely, giving us not the scene or the "thing" itself, but those objects in which its hidden presence has been invested by the inquisitive male. The opening of the alcove in *Nana*, in the scene before the mirror, goes further toward representing the thing itself, the ultimate object of desires and the source of the erotic dynamics in the novel. The public opening of the alcove in *Au Bonheur des Dames* may, however, be more tellingly characteristic of Zola's novels, and of narrative in the realist tradition in general. It claims opening while repressing or denying what is really to be opened, and focusing instead on the accessories by which the male voyeur phantasizes the ultimate object of vision.

Au Bonheur des Dames, we are told toward the end of this final chapter, has created a new cult of the woman's body. Mouret's creation "brought a new religion, the churches that a failing faith gradually deserted were replaced by his bazaar, in souls that had become unoccupied. Woman came to spend in his establishment the empty, shivering, and anxious hours that she once spent inside chapels: hours spent in a necessary expenditure of nervous passion, a constantly renewed struggle of god against husband, a ceaselessly renewed worship of the body, with the divine beyond of beauty" (4:219).

Zola perceives that the logic of his various projects of seeing and knowing the woman's body requires that this body should eventually become a cult object, like any truly sacred object unknowable but worshipped through its icons. He perceives also that in modern capitalist economies, these icons belong to the marketplace: they require expenditure. Commodities are invested with passion, and passion spends itself in purchasing commodities, acquired not from need or for their intrinsic worth or even for their social status function—as in Balzac's world—but to fill the void of erotic revery.

Furthermore, these things that speak of the woman's erotic body are offered for sale to women themselves: there are very few male shoppers in Au Bonheur des Dames. While this might seem to suggest a primal narcissism of women, or an invitation to them to possess their own bodies, there is rather an alienation of women from their bodies, which have been taken over by the (male-owned and -managed) market economy, defined and fetishized by that economy, and offered back to women in piecemeal form, through the cash nexus. I am reminded of a sentence from Jacques Lacan's analysis of the psychic problem of female frigidity, which for him is a dialectical problem between men and women: "Man here acts as the relay whereby the woman becomes this Other for herself as she is this Other for him."[29] Mouret's establishment figures a culture in which a woman, through the relay of the economy, commercial and erotic, established by man, is forced to accept herself as other; she is foreclosed from her own desire, never in full possession of her own body. Mouret's temple to the woman's body confirms the moment in *Nana* when the archpriestess of pleasure suddenly declares that she has had no pleasure at all in sex: "ça ne me faisait pas plaisir, mais pas plaisir du tout. Ça m'embêtait, parole d'honneur!" (3:381). If this absence of pleasure on the part of the woman of pleasure was a cliché of Zola's culture, Nana's outburst also figures the enigma, for the male, of the pleasure taken by the woman's body. That Nana's, and in general the woman's, sex is unknowable, and therefore the source of narrative dynamics, is, after all, a story told by male narrators.

Zola's apparent preoccupation with a sexualized female body that he cannot fully strip, see, or know, but which he makes the source of social, commercial, and narrative dynamics in his novel, partakes of the logic of naturalism, with its intense visuality and its concern with the body. The obsessive nature of Zola's interest in the female body is perhaps both idiosyncratic and typical of the late nineteenth century, when writing about the body seems to take particularly exacerbated forms, with a particular concern for the ravages of sexuality—syphilis and the specter of racial degeneracy aroused keen public anxieties—and the power of the prostitute in society.[30] Further examples could be found in the work of Jules and Edmond de Goncourt, Joris-Karl Huysmans, Rachilde, and Jules Barbey d'Aurevilly. I want to note briefly one of Barbey's tales from *Les diaboliques* (1874), *A un dîner d'athées*, since it presents the issues under discussion in hyperbolic fashion, at once compelling and repulsive. The "atheists' dinner" of the title is an all-male affair, in which men exchange lore about women. The novella works through the narrative complications typical of Barbey—stories within stories within stories—finally bringing us to the tale of La Rosalba, mistress of Major Ydow and, it seems, of almost all the other officers of the regiment to which Mesnilgrand, the narrator, belongs. La Rosalba, also known as La Pudica, is a living oxymoron, since her *pudeur* is as real as her libertinage. La Rosalba becomes the riddle of woman, "impenetrable like the sphinx. Only the sphinx was cold, and she wasn't."[31] The hyperbolic dénouement of the story turns on a letter which Mesnilgrand—no longer her lover—finds her sealing with wax. The two appear to be on the point of renewing their liaison when Major Ydow is heard coming up the stairs, and Mesnilgrand must hide in the clothes closet. The Major wants to know to whom Rosalba's letter is to be addressed (something we'll never learn), then turns to insults, and to the question of who was the father of Rosalba's child—who did not survive infancy and whose heart they have preserved in a crystal vase. Rosalba tortures the Major on the subject of paternity, then declares that the father was not he but rather Mesnilgrand, whereupon the Major smashes the crystal vase and throws the embalmed infant heart at her—and she throws it back. Things get even worse. In a moment, Mesnilgrand hears a hideous cry from Rosalba, and breaks out of the closet:

155

La Pudica had been knocked down and had fallen on the table where she had been writing, and the Major was holding her there with a grasp of iron, all her veils lifted, her beautiful body denuded, twisted in his grasp like a snake that has been cut. But what do you

think he was doing with his other hand, gentlemen? . . . This writing table, the candle lighted, the sealing wax next to it, all these circumstances had given the Major an infernal idea—the idea to seal this woman, as she had sealed her letter—and he was laboring on this monstrous sealing, this frightful vengeance of a perversely jealous lover!

"Be punished where you have sinned, infamous whore!" he cried.

He didn't see me. He was bent over his victim, who was no longer crying out, and it was the hilt of his sword that he pushed into the boiling wax, using it as his signet! (276)

Hereupon Mesnilgrand plunges his own sword into the Major's back, calls for the doctor, is himself summoned by the bugle to a skirmish, and leaves without learning whether Rosalba has survived her atrocious punishment. (Félicien Rops, an artist of "decadent" subjects, chose this scene for one of the series of illustrations he did for *Les diaboliques* [Figure 22].) Mesnilgrand takes the infant's heart with him and, though a self-declared hardened atheist, he brings it to a priest for burial. Indeed his visit to the church, witnessed by one of his atheist comrades, provokes the demand for the story he has to tell—a story that may be intended to bring us to the threshold of belief.

The outrageous scene of Rosalba's punishment furnishes an allegory of the cultural story I have been delineating. In sealing Rosalba's sex and applying his sword hilt as his signet, his identifying mark, Major Ydow signs the woman's body on its very sex with the identity of the male—he who claims to be its possessor, but whose authority has been contested at the very roots of patriarchy, in the infant's paternity, in the name of the father. One of Mesnilgrand's listeners comments that the story sounds like "the adventure of Abelard, transposed to Eloise" (277), which would give us the impossible, phantasmatic scene of the woman's castration. Yet more significant is the juxtaposition of the sealed love letter and the sealed sex of the woman, a juxtaposition in which we must read the letter of the woman's sex. Rosalba's sex, the whole tale makes clear, is the source of all stories. Her body is storied throughout the regiment. By sealing her sex, Major Ydow attempts to put an end to these stories—to silence her sex. From this we may understand that

22. Félicien Rops, *A un dîner d'athées,* illustration to Barbey
    d'Aurevilly, *Les diaboliques* (Paris: Editions Lemerre, 1882).
    Photo: David Richards

stories, in the view of the male, are written with the woman's sex. That
may be the true secret of the sphinx. It is a troubling secret, to Zola as
to Ydow, because the command of patriarchy over the woman's sex is
always dubious: *pater semper incertus est,* paternity is a legal fiction,
and all the systems of control of the woman's body deployed in *Nana,*
in *Au Bonheur des Dames,* and in *A un dîner d'athées* may be menaced
by this essential uncertainty. Male narrators ultimately have no control
over the source of the tales they simply pass on. If stories are written by

PROBLEMS OF THE MODERN NUDE

23. Jean-Baptiste Greuze, *La cruche cassée*. (Paris: Louvre.
   Photo © R.M.N.)

the interior, hidden, mysterious woman's sex—rather than by the more
obviously instrumental phallus—then they are all by definition secret
stories whose dynamic and force can be known, and felt in their effects,
but never their hidden source.

I want to conclude by allegorizing at Zola's expense about his ideal
woman. In a letter written to his friend Paul Cézanne when he was
twenty years old, Zola declared that he had fallen in love with the girl
in an etching of a Greuze painting, promising himself "to love the
original, if such a portrait—doubtless an artist's dream—can have one."
The painting has been plausibly identified as Greuze's famous *La cruche
cassée* (Figure 23), whose subject has won many hearts over the years.[32]
The motif of the broken vase suggests the ambiguities of this innocent
but seductive figure: it metonymically introduces the idea of broken

maidenhead, loss of innocence, and evokes the evanescence of a moment of passage from childhood into the fallen world. Zola in his late forties, following years of an unhappy and sterile marriage, became the lover of his wife's maid, Jeanne Rozerot, and established a second and happy ménage with her, complete with children. In Jeanne Rozerot he seems to have found the original of the Greuze girl in *La cruche cassée*. He then transposed this idyll of the older man saved from despair by the radiant young girl into fiction in the last novel of the Rougon-Macquart cycle, *Le docteur Pascal,* published in 1893. Shortly before that, in 1891, Bouguereau exhibited his own version of *La cruche cassée* (Figure 24). It is a perfect reinvention of Greuze's painting for bourgeois taste of the late nineteenth century, and comes perilously close, for Zola's comfort, to Zola's aesthetic of the woman.

159

There is a conflict between Zola's artistic aesthetic, which is predicated on the need to strip bare, to denude, to break the academic mold and let in *plein air,* and his ideal aesthetic of the woman, which is more sentimentalized and reassuring, conceiving the feminine as something essentially innocent that is barely, not quite willingly or quite consciously, entering the world of adult sexuality. In his representations of women, this conflict takes a certain toll, charging his denuding of Nana, for instance, with images of fear, bestiality, and subversion of society by a sexually ungoverned proletariat, and promoting as the successful man-tamer the virginal, modest, self-controlled Denise Baudu. Between claiming to strip bare the prostitute who strips by profession and maintaining the veils of respectable women lies a zone of hesitation not unlike that revealed in some of the salon art Zola had the wit to deplore.

A woman's nudity is never completely representable for Zola because her final denuding is part of a scenario that brings fear and uncertainty. But these are accompanied by fascination, and by the implication that what is finally unrepresentable and unknowable is also the source of stories, the origin of the narrative dynamic. Zola's narratives of unveiling the female body sooner or later reach the problem of unveiling the female sex, which they find to be itself a veil—perhaps from the anxiety that its final unveiling would reveal there is nothing to unveil, or rather, that that apparent nothing is indeed something. *Je sais bien mais quand même,* runs the infantile response to the perception of anatomical difference. That is, the little boy knows that the woman is not simply a castrated male but is unable to rationalize the difference other than through the absence of the thing.[33] The narratives I have discussed turn on more or less infantile scenarios of the male perception of the woman's

24. William-Adolphe Bouguereau, *La cruche cassée*. (San Francisco: Fine Arts Museums of San Francisco. Gift of M. H. de Young)

body. At the same time, there appears to be a recognition that hidden within absence is that which really makes the difference: the source of narratives, both in the male's desire to penetrate, to possess, and to master, and in its own generative capacities, which can never be known but only reacted to by attempted mastery. As *A un dîner d'athées* suggests, the woman's sex writes stories whose address is undetermined. As *Nana* makes clear, the woman's sex is the most powerful of occult narrative motors.

The ambivalences of Zola's undressings may suggest some of the limits of the visual field centered on the body. Sight may be inadequate to account for another's body—may in particular be inadequate to describe that inwardness of the woman's body that the male viewer and narrator feel to be essential, both the sign of difference and the essence of the otherness that he would like to understand. Is there another representational system in which that otherness would make a difference other than the familiar evocation of difference? Can the woman's body be made to speak for itself, without the kind of more or less fearful relay by narrators concerned with controlling its force? There are such "contrarian" narratives, as we shall see.

6 Gauguin's Tahitian Body

I relived then the experience of the early voyagers, and through it that crucial moment of modern thought when, thanks to the great discoveries, humanity, which had considered itself complete, thoroughly finished, suddenly received, as a counter-revelation, the news that it was not alone, that it formed a piece of a vaster whole, and that to know itself it must first contemplate its unrecognizable image in this mirror of which a fragment forgotten by time was, for me alone, about to flash forth its first and last gleam.

Claude Lévi-Strauss, *Tristes Tropiques*

ANY ACCOUNT of the nineteenth-century preoccupation with seeing and narrating the body needs to think about a long tradition of European fascination with the bodies of other cultures—particularly, women's bodies from cultures considered exotic or primitive, which are used to define an alluring or menacing other of Western "civilized" sexuality. The trip to the Orient, to the Middle East or North Africa, became something of a standard gesture for writers and artists in search of a more colorful and apparently more indulgent alternative to gray, banal, repressed European civilization. Later, travel to islands of the Caribbean and the Pacific would offer sites of fantasy. The allure of the exotic is of course in the nineteenth century bound up with the extension of European colonialism. If "trade follows the flag," so do tourists, artists, and writers. The colonial network of transportation and communication gives them the means to make good on the fantasy. In his journey to Tahiti, Paul Gauguin offers a particularly interesting case, since his response to the myth of the exotic has itself become "mythic": he is the very archetype of the artist who abandons wife, family, and European culture for a "savage state" in which he will "go native." Gauguin enacts in a particularly literal way a century-long fascination with the exotic, and particularly makes clear its erotic content, its fixation on women's bodies thought to be innocent of the constraints of Western sexual mores. In his cultural confusions, his nativist and sexist assumptions, his mythmaking—in his writing as well as his painting—

and his painterly inventions, Gauguin offers a commentary on the exotic dream as it intersects with the history of representation of the body.

Gauguin's arrival in Tahiti on June 9, 1891, was something of a chance occurrence. To be sure, he had repeatedly proposed flight from Europe in order to found the "Atelier of the Tropics" with a few kindred souls. But his place of refuge might just as well have been Martinique (which he had discovered some years earlier, on an ill-fated trip to Panama), or Madagascar, or Tonkin, or Java. In 1887, he was talking of a commercial position in Madagascar; in 1890, of one in Tonkin. In between, he had visited the Exposition Universelle of 1889, where he was especially impressed by the exhibits of the French colonies, which occupied the whole of the Esplanade des Invalides. There he saw, surrounded by a magnificent reconstruction of a Tunisian palace—next to which was a Tunisian café with authentic bellydancers—and a Hindu pavilion and a reconstructed Malagasy village, a Tahitian hut, complete with Tahitians making and selling native crafts (the women, however, were all old, expressly chosen to avoid scandal). More impressive was the Javanese Village, which the illustrated guide published by the *Bulletin Officiel* tells us was one of the great hits of the Exposition—a sentiment which Gauguin echoes in a letter to Emile Bernard, in which he explains that he has managed to arrange a rendezvous with a mulatto woman there.[1] In fact, Gauguin's dream of flight seems to have been made concrete and specific through these colonial exhibits in the Exposition Universelle, in what we might think of as early versions of those simulacra spaces best represented in our time by Walt Disney World: reconstructed décors of distant civilizations, peopled with a few indigenous inhabitants to create the requisite atmosphere. In these much-commented-upon native settings of the Exposition of 1889, the nineteenth century's longing for the exotic is given a local habitation and a name, and Gauguin, like so many other visitors to this splendid world's fair, fell for it, whatever its inauthenticity.

In fact, the inauthenticity of the exotic is part and parcel of Gauguin's longing and his decision to depart. He is under the spell of a cultural version of exoticism created by European, and especially French, writers and artists from the eighteenth century onward. As he hesitates among Madagascar, Tonkin, Java, and Tahiti, one hears through his words a constant echo of the Baudelairean "anywhere out of this world." Yet not quite anywhere: Gauguin's reveries turn around certain constants— a warm climate, an easy life without the need for much money, tranquility, beauty, and the body of a woman. Tahiti becomes more and more the object of his fantasies from reading Pierre Loti's overblown Tahitian romance *Le mariage de Loti*—about his life with the beautiful young Rarahu—and also from reading a popular guidebook, which told him that for the Tahitians, "to live is to sing and to love."[2] As his desires came more and more to focus on Tahiti, he expressed the whole nexus of the exotic longing in a letter to, of all people, his wife: "May the day come (perhaps it will be soon) when I will run away to the woods in an island of Oceania, to live there on ecstasy, calm, and art. Surrounded by a new family, far from this European struggle for money. There in Tahiti, in the silence of the beautiful tropical nights, I can listen to the soft murmuring music of my heart in loving harmony with the mysterious creatures surrounding me. Free at last, without the worry of money, I will be able to love, sing, and die."[3] The prose of the guidebook has been incorporated in Gauguin's own. In another letter, he writes: "While in Europe men and women obtain the satisfaction of their needs only after ceaseless labor, while they struggle in the convulsions of cold and hunger, a prey to misery, the Tahitians, on the contrary, happy inhabitants of the forgotten paradises of Oceania, know of life only its sweetness. For them, to live is to sing and to love."[4]

It all sounds rather like a Club Med travel brochure: life on a beach, clad only in a *pareu,* in a primitive economy of precapitalist barter. We might as well recognize that Gauguin's Tahiti has the same inauthenticity as the reconstructed native villages on the Esplanade des Invalides, and that he is just one more pawn in the long cultural history of nineteenth-century exoticism, itself closely allied to colonialism, that is, to the domestication, exploitation, and commodification of the exotic. In this sense, Gauguin's trip to Tahiti stands directly in the lineage of all those journeys to the Orient undertaken by writers and artists earlier in the century—Chateaubriand, Nerval, Maxime du Camp, Flaubert, Delacroix, Gérôme—in search of an exciting other of European civilization, one that in particular promises a more free sexuality.[5]

Delacroix and Flaubert seem especially appropriate precursors of Gauguin's exotic dream since so much of their preoccupation with the Orient focuses on the erotic female body: the sensual, receptive, enslaved body of the harem in Delacroix (as also in Ingres and Gérôme), or the impassive yet infinitely usable body of the prostitute in Flaubert, which sometimes makes his trip to Egypt appear a journey from one bordello to another. Gauguin's guidebook to Tahiti was rapturous on the subject of Tahitian women, who were not only ideal models for an artist, but loving, sweet, and easy to possess.[6] Gauguin's letters never fail to include a mention of his projected native mistress as something "almost obligatory."[7] The Club Med vision of paradise of course includes a warm brown body, without much in the way of clothing. The primitivist version of exoticism that so attracted Gauguin differs from orientalism in preferring simplicity, including a sensuality that is not alluringly hidden within seraglios but, with another kind of allure, placed out in the open and naturalized. Charles Baudelaire imagined it:

165

> Une île paresseuse où la nature donne
> Des arbres singuliers et des fruits savoureux;
> Des hommes dont le corps est mince et vigoureux,
> Et des femmes dont l'oeil par sa franchise étonne.[8]

Gauguin's version of the myth of Tahiti does not differ in essence from that which exercised a certain fascination for the European imagination from the discovery of the island in the eighteenth century. Especially in France, from the moment Louis-Antoine de Bougainville returned in 1769 from his voyage around the world to report his discoveries, Tahiti was "L'Ile de Cythère," the new abode of Venus. If Tahiti appeared to many in France as the realization of Rousseau's speculations about the earliest forms of social organization—a primitive utopia which had instituted harmony and order but not succumbed to the division of property and the twin despotisms of church and state—it was foremost a sexual paradise, where the surplus repression that had created the discontents of European civilization simply had no currency, and the pleasure principle dominated without censorship. Freud's *Civilization and Its Discontents* (1930) makes a good counterpoint to Gauguin's letters and *Noa Noa*—his book about his first stay in Tahiti, to which I shall come presently—and the relevant chapters of Bougainville's *Voyage autour du monde* (1771).

Upon Bougainville's arrival in Tahiti, his two ships, *Boudeuse* and *Etoile,* were surrounded by native canoes, filled with men and, especially, women. "Most of these nymphs were naked, for the men and the old women who accompanied them had stripped them of the loincloth that they normally wear."[9] It was quickly evident that the men were offering these nymphs—*why* they were doing so is a question that will need some attention—and indeed they demonstrated with "unequivocal gestures" how the sailors were to make the nymphs' acquaintance. One of the girls even managed to reach the deck, "where she negligently let fall the wrap that covered her, and appeared to the eyes of all in the manner that Venus showed herself to the Phrygian shepherd: she had the same celestial form." Thus are the French sailors convoked to a reenactment of the Judgment of Paris.

The moment, and the style, are quintessential Bougainville. In the following chapter, he recounts his first visit on shore, and how, on his return to his launch, he was invited to sit down with a handsome islander who, accompanied by a flutist, "slowly sang for us what was no doubt an Anacreontic song: a charming scene, worthy of the paintbrush of Boucher" (191). *Et in Arcadia ego.* Bougainville—a man who can cite his Virgil from memory—consistently chooses a tropological frame of reference that situates Tahiti in a classical golden age, as reinvented by eighteenth-century artists such as Watteau and Fragonard: he and his men have wandered into a *fête galante* in which they have embarked for the Isle of Cythera. Despite the minor inconvenience created by the Tahitians' thievery—toward which Bougainville is far more indulgent than his English precursor, Captain Wallis, and his English successor, Captain Cook—life for the French crew develops into an Arcadian dream:

> Every day our men wandered in the country unarmed, alone or in small bands. They were invited to enter the houses, they were given refreshment; but here the civility of the hosts did not limit itself to a light collation; they offered us young women; the hut at once filled with a crowd of curious men and women who made a circle around the guest and the young victim of the laws of hospitality; the ground was covered with leaves and flowers, and musicians sang in harmony with the flute a hymn to pleasure. Venus is here the goddess of hospitality, her worship admits of no mysteries, and every moment of bliss is a national festival. They were surprised at the embarrassment that we displayed; our manners have proscribed such public behavior. I cannot guarantee, however, that none of the Frenchmen was able to overcome his repugnance in order to conform to the local customs. (194–95)

Bougainville has discovered not the anarchic "state of nature," but what Rousseau in his *Discours de l'inégalité parmi les hommes* (1754) called "la société naissante": a people who have emerged from barbarism and entered into a social compact which has not yet been adulterated—"the happiest and most enduring state." Here, as Rousseau puts it, is "the true youth of the world."[10] Diderot will epigrammatically make the application to Tahiti in his *Supplément au voyage de Bougainville:* "The Tahitian borders on the origin of the world, and the European on its old age."[11] Tahitian primitivism is conceived to be consubstantial with primal innocence, an admirable naiveté and openness about the body and its pleasures and freedom from the dissimulation inevitable in corrupted old civilizations. This version of the exotic is both spatially and temporally removed from contemporary Europe: the voyage out to the South Pacific is also a voyage back, to an earlier time.

Even the thievery of the Tahitians is merely a sign of their innocence of the notion of private property, which is of course for Rousseau the beginning of the end, an usurpation that leads inevitably to a society of masters and slaves and to the destruction of human felicity. The most patent disciple of Rousseau on board the *Boudeuse,* its physician and naturalist, Philibert de Commerson, at once equated Tahiti with Thomas More's *Utopia* and claimed that the Tahitians lived in a kind of harmonious communism, without any sense of exclusive property rights, either for things or for persons—a misinterpretation of Tahitian social structure which is revealing of certain Enlightenment requirements for utopia that will continue to play themselves out in various nineteenth-century European versions of socialism. Above all, this primitive Arcadia is a sexual paradise, where the prohibitions and inhibitions of civilization are shown to be artificial creations, demands for what Freud would call "instinctual renunciation" imposed upon mankind without any justification in nature herself. "They know no other god than Love," writes Commerson; for the Tahitians,

> Every day is sacred to him, the whole island is his temple, all the women are his altars, all the men his priests . . . There, neither shame nor false modesty exercises its tyranny . . . the act of creating another being is an act of religion . . . A hypocritical censor might see in all this only the lack of civilized manners, a horrible prostitution, the most open cynicism; but he would be wholly mistaken in failing to recognize the state of natural man, born essentially good, exempt from all prejudice, and following, equally without fear or remorse, the sweet impulses of an instinct which is always right because it hasn't yet degenerated into reason. (392)

Bougainville himself tries to puzzle out the system of Tahitian sexuality, noting that polygamy seems generalized among the ruling classes,

GAUGUIN'S TAHITIAN BODY

that lovemaking is honored, that a wife owes entire obedience to her husband, but that jealousy seems not to exist and a husband is often the first to offer his wife to another man. An unmarried woman appears to enjoy complete sexual license: "Everything invites her to follow the penchant of her heart or the law of her senses, and public applause honors her defeat. It doesn't appear that the large number of passing lovers she may have prevents her from later finding a husband. Why then should she resist the influence of the climate, the seduction of example? The air that one breathes, the songs, the dances, almost always accompanied by lascivious postures, everything recalls at every moment the sweetness of love, everything calls out to enjoy it" (216). Certain of Commerson's and Bougainville's terms—woman as sacrificial "altar" and "victim," her "defeat," men as "priests"—indicate their incapacity to think beyond the metaphors of their own culture, though the terms may have another kind of appropriateness within the patriarchal rules of Tahitian sexuality: it generally appears to be men who are offering their women to the visitors. Nonetheless, Commerson and Bougainville both overtly insist on the freedom of the Tahitian woman, as opposed to the European, which means her freedom to be true to woman's natural sensuality—which in turn increases her appeal to the male. This version of sexuality is consonant with an Enlightenment desire to cast off prejudice in order to discover the uncontaminated natural order of things. Tahiti appears a nearly miraculous realization of "good primitivism," and as such it offers excellent matter for reflection to a *philosophe* such as Diderot—who, without leaving Paris, can paint in his *Supplément* a portrait of Tahiti as the realization of those natural virtues and virtuous pleasures poisoned and distorted in Europe by centuries of morality preached by church and state.

For Diderot, as for Commerson, the free sexuality of the Tahitians is based on their understanding that the production of children is a an ultimate natural good; and the moral restrictions paraded by Diderot's imagined chaplain—including prohibitions on fornication, incest, adultery, and prescriptions of monogamy and eternal fidelity—only pervert and inhibit the realization of this good. Jealousy, coquetry, infidelity, false modesty—all these attributes of European sexuality derive from a history which has turned women into men's property. Sexual liberty in Tahiti is for Diderot more than anything else a powerful illumination of European sexual servitude. The discovery of Tahiti thus confirms Rousseau's *Discours* (which Diderot here seems to endorse despite his enmity for Rousseau), and serves as a source of Choderlos de Laclos' argument, in *Des femmes et de leur éducation,* that there is no way of perfecting the nature of women in the present state of European society since their natural wants and needs have been thoroughly adulterated by their enslavement to men. Diderot's disdainful Tahitian Old Man, whose speech begins "Weep, unfortunate Tahitians!" goes on to predict with quite chilling accuracy the consequences of the European discovery of this paradise: its contamination and eventual demise, through the introduction of the notion of private property, the creation of new unnatural desires in its women, the spread of venereal disease, and the imposition of European ideologies. Tahiti is a laboratory of philosophical primitivism, but one which, Diderot has the wits to realize, is doomed by the very arrival of the observer who would study it.

Bougainville's presentation of Tahiti under the aegis of the Judgment of Paris from amongst the naked Graces contrasts markedly with the account given by his predecessor, the first European to discover the island, Captain Samuel Wallis of H.M.S. *Dolphin.* Wallis's arrival in Tahiti apparently produced not boatloads of naked nymphs, but rather some tense trading encounters, the firing of warning rounds of cannon, and then a full-fledged combat, with Tahitian stone-throwing quickly overmastered by English cannonades and grapeshot. Several Tahitians had been slaughtered, probably without much provocation, before the English established their beachhead. And when the English did come ashore, it was to establish a trading post, under the watchful eye and the sole authority of the Gunner, alongside a river which served as a closely guarded frontier between the natives and the English. With the English, it was not the gift of sex but its barter that characterized the relations of female natives to male visitors. Wallis reports: "While our people were on shore, several young women were permitted to cross the river, who, though they were not averse to the granting of personal favours, knew the value of them too well not to stipulate for a consideration."[12] Or as George Robertson, Master of the *Dolphin,* puts it in his journal for 7 July 1767: "I was told by one of the Young Gentlemen that a new sort of trade took up most of their attention this day, but it might be more properly called the old trade."[13] The currency of the trading was quickly established as nails. Wallis claims that the "fathers and brothers" who brought young women to the trading area were "conscious of the value of beauty, and the size of the nail that was demanded for the enjoyment of the lady, was always in proportion to her charms" (Hawkesworth, 1:181). Yet Wallis's neat economy may be faulty, since in fact he spent much of the Tahitian stay sick in his cabin.

GAUGUIN'S TAHITIAN BODY

Robertson reports a simpler and perhaps more accurate progressive inflation of prices: on 21 July he notes "some of the Young Gentlemen told me, that all the Liberty men carried on a trade with the Young Girls, who had now raised their price for some Days past, from a twenty or thirty-penny nail, to a forty-penny, and some was so Extravagant as to demand a Seven or nine Inch Spike" (Robertson, 104). In fact, the *Dolphin* had by this point been rendered almost unseaworthy by the carnal trade: Robertson discovered that the seamen had been pulling nails and spikes from the ship's cleats, and that two-thirds of the hammock nails had disappeared, with the result that the men were sleeping on the deck—but no doubt finding themselves well compensated for it. Thus it became necessary for Wallis and Robertson to impose draconian regulations on trade.

The nails of the *Dolphin* represent a version of sexual commerce between Europeans and Tahitians somberly at odds with the Arcadian tropes of Bougainville. The Tahitians seem to have responded eagerly to the introduction of iron into their society—they had none before the arrival of the Europeans, and it must have appeared an exotic and marvelous substance, immediately suitable for making fishhooks and other tools and weapons. Bougainville reports that the Tahitians already have knowledge of the European metal and a word for it, *aouri,* which puzzles him until he eventually learns of Wallis's visit, about ten months before his own, and reasonably surmises that *aouri* is a Tahitian rendition of the English *iron*. It may then be that the apparent facility of sexual commerce with the Tahitians derived from their immediate, and intelligent, perception of the utility of this new substance introduced among them—as if their granting of sexual favors really meant: iron at any price.[14] If this were the case, they would be behaving in the manner imposed upon many colonized peoples, offering their natural resources in exchange for modernization. Gauguin will regularly describe the bodies of Tahitians as "golden"—*Et l'or de leur corps* (And the gold of their bodies), he lyrically entitled one of his paintings. In the commerce of the *Dolphin,* the golden body of pleasure is the natural resource exchanged—at bargain rates—for grim, utilitarian English iron. Complicit with the commercial exchange is a tropology: the precious but primitive "found" resource, belonging to an economy of abundance, enjoyment, and waste, set against the manufactured commodity, belonging to an economy of scarcity, capitalization, and repression. The Golden Age perceived by the French captain and crew was already, thanks to the English, on the way to its degradation into an Iron Age.

Thus Bougainville's belief that he and the Tahitians are freely offering gifts to one another marks an ideological blindness that prevents him from seeing the underlying terms of exchange. But the history of the *Dolphin's* stay in Tahiti, the armed encounter and the slaughter of a undetermined number of islanders by the mysterious and potent firearm, suggests still another interpretation of the facility with which women were offered up to the British sailors—and, ten months later, even more rapidly to the French. The women may have been offered in propitiation to outsiders who, the Tahitians recognized, had the power to destroy them all. I have not seen this interpretation suggested in the literature on the discovery of Tahiti, but it has a certain force of logic: once you discover that your stones are no match for their cannon and musket balls, you try to seduce them. Make love, not war. If this were the case, the myth of Tahitian sexual freedom would be the direct product of the European armed intrusion, and rather than an indication of a Golden Age, a tactical reaction to superior force.

But even if there was a measure of calculation in the presentation of those naked nymphs to sexually deprived sailors, one cannot wholly dismiss Bougainville's Arcadian vision, at least the notion that Tahitian sexuality is not subject to conventional European constraints—which in fact appears to be substantiated by modern ethnological work on Polynesian cultures, particularly that by Douglas Oliver and Marshall Sahlins.[15] Sahlins in particular—who is discussing Hawaii, which had much in common with Tahiti—makes the point that sexual relations were to a large extent creative of social relationships in Polynesian culture: that sex was pragmatic and performative, creating structure and patterning kinship. That is, sexual relations between a man and a woman were the foundation for other relations, rather than vice-versa. Sahlins further suggests that Diderot got it right in his *Supplément* when he had the wise Tahitian Orou say to the French chaplain: "More robust and healthy than you, we perceived at first glance that you surpassed us in intelligence, and on the spot we selected several of our most beautiful women and girls to receive the seed of a race better than our own. This is a trial we have made, and that could work out to our advantage. We have taken from you and yours the only asset we could take, and believe me, however savage we may be, we too know how to calculate" (Diderot, 484–85).

Le calcul sauvage, then, would be the use of a relatively unrestricted sexuality to gain some of the advantages that the invading foreigners possessed—using a traditional form or practice of Polynesian society to capture something that would be needed for that society to survive when its isolation had been broken down. From the Tahitian point of view, in this interpretation, sexual commerce involves using the body to provide for a stronger posterity.

Bougainville, Wallis, and Cook are all in agreement on the remarkable physical beauty of the Tahitians and the great care exercised by both men and women in maintenance and grooming. The Tahitians appear to have perfect teeth; they seem to live long lives in good health. The women's bodies, in particular, have not suffered the confining restrictions of the corset. And all Tahitians bathe at least twice a day, which to an eighteenth-century European who might not bathe that often in a month, clearly makes them connoisseurs of the body. Another form of the Tahitians' attention to the body is stressed in the first published account of the first voyage of Captain James Cook, who landed in Tahiti in 1769—as Bougainville was returning to France—in order, appropriately enough, to observe the transit of Venus across the sun. One of Cook's crew noted: "Both sexes indent or prick the flesh about and below the hips in a multitude of places, with the points of sharp bones, and these indentures they fill with a dark blue or blackish paint, which ever after continues, and discolours the skin in those places, rendering it black. This practice is universal among them, and is called tat-tow, a term which they afterwards applied to letters when they saw us write, being themselves perfectly illiterate."[16]

Tattooing makes the body itself a scene of writing, the place for the inscription of significant symbolic material. As Bougainville noted, women in Europe paint their faces, whereas those in Tahiti paint their hips and buttocks, as "an embellishment and at the same time a mark of distinction" (212). As a signifying practice, the tattoo calls into question facile polarities of the natural and primitive as opposed to the civilized and corrupt: the Tahitian body is subject to cultural processes impenetrable to the Europeans; it is the ground of a social semiotics that they cannot decode, but which they vaguely understand to be expressive of social structure and ideology. Like the practice of human sacrifice—of which an apparent instance was observed by Cook—"writing" on the body complicates the encounter of civilization and primitive utopia, without, however, giving the Europeans a sure basis for rethinking their tropologies.

The body in Tahiti demands interpretation from the moment of the discovery onward. On the one hand, we have the view, sententiously summarized in Hawkesworth's *Account,* that in Tahiti "there is a scale in dissolute sensuality, which these people have ascended, wholly un-known to every other nation whose manners have been recorded from the beginning of the world to the present hour, and which no imagination could possibly conceive" (Hawkesworth, 2:207). On the other hand, there is Diderot's attempt to reconstruct Tahitian sexuality on the model of utility, as the most basic of natural laws: "There is almost nothing in common between the Venus of Athens and that of Tahiti; the first is a gallant Venus, the second a fecund Venus" (Diderot, 470). The debate is still with us today, even if its ethnological terms have changed; we still are not entirely sure what to make of the apparently free circulation of sexual bodies in the Tahitian social economy, and we will never quite be sure, since the observed phenomena were irretrievably altered by the introduction of the first observers.[17]

One may ask what this early history of the image of Tahitian sexuality has to do with Gauguin's journey to Tahiti. I am not, of course, sug-gesting that Gauguin read Wallis and Bougainville and Cook and Did-erot, or that he puzzled overmuch about the structure of the Tahitian sexual economy. Nonetheless, the first experiences of Tahiti directly underlie the myth which Gauguin absorbed, from guidebooks, Loti's romance, the colonial exhibits, and the commonplaces of his culture. And the same problems of interpretation would arise in his discovery of Tahiti. He went there in large part because of the attraction of a sexuality ostensibly free of European conventions and repressions, and this meant that he, too, would eventually have to ask questions about the meaning of the sexual body in Tahiti. Like Diderot, he would be impelled to attempt to reach back beyond what that body had become, to try to postulate what it was before. In the absence of clear ethnographic evi-dence, he would have to make his own calculus—create his own *Sup-plément* in which he would reinvent the body of the Tahitian woman.

What Gauguin found in the Tahitian capital, Papeete, was not the Golden Age, or even the nascent Iron Age, but the grim results of a century of efforts by Protestant, Catholic, and Mormon missionaries, and the disintegration of traditional social structure at the hands of the colonial powers. Papeete was an ugly town of concrete houses with tin roofs, and the women were fully covered by shapeless sack dresses. Arriving on the eve of the death of King Pomaré V—after which, by prior agreement, rule passed directly to France, which in reality had been in control for decades—Gauguin chose in *Noa Noa* to see the passing of this monarch as the final extinction of Maori culture: "with

GAUGUIN'S TAHITIAN BODY

him disappeared the last traces of Maori customs. It was completely finished; nothing left but civilized people."[18] This is inaccurate, in that Polynesian culture had been pretty well eradicated long before the death of the decadent and drunken Pomaré V—in fact, there had been no kings in Tahiti until the Europeans set up one family of chiefs in this role—but the event is useful for Gauguin's mythological narrative. He continues: "Will I succeed in finding a trace of this so distant and so mysterious past? And the present didn't say anything worthwhile to me. To rediscover the ancient hearth, to revive the fire in the midst of all these ashes."

Like a number of other travel books, including Claude Lévi-Strauss's *Tristes Tropiques,* from the outset *Noa Noa* establishes itself as a quest, a journey back from a rotten civilization toward the savage state, which is also the place of a lost Maori culture.[19] In this quest, the Tahitian woman will naturally—as if predetermined by the history of European contact with Tahiti—play a central role, as the literal point of entry into the Polynesian soul. Gauguin's first woman, in Papeete, is the half-caste Titi, the only one he can find for the moment but clearly unsuitable for his larger purposes: "I was aware that this half-white woman, varnished through her contact with all these Europeans, wouldn't suit the goal that I had set for myself" (39). In search of a more authentic Tahiti, he moves on to the village of Mataiea, forty-five kilometers from Papeete. Finding his solitude unbearable, he sends for Titi, and she comes to him. "But, already civilized, accustomed to the luxury of the bureaucrats, she didn't suit me long. I separated from her. Alone again . . . Each day I became a little more the savage" (51)—yet still not savage enough. In both his life and his art, there is hesitation. "In the streams, golden forms enchanted me. Why did I hesitate to pour onto my canvas all that gold and all this rejoicing of sun? Probably old habits brought from Europe, that timidity of expression of our bastardized races" (47). In the terms that Gauguin has set for himself, only the body of a woman untouched by European civilization will answer to the needs of the primitivist myth. Ridding himself of the inhibiting vestiges of civilization must wait upon his discovery of Tehamana, the golden body inhabited by the Maori soul.

To understand the importance of this body for Gauguin, we need to consider briefly his earlier artistic versions of the woman's body, especially his nudes (of which there are relatively few before his Tahitian stay). The early *Etude de nu* of 1880 (also known as "Suzanne Sewing") which was highly praised by J.-K. Huysmans for breaking with the

25. Paul Gauguin, *Eve bretonne*. (San Antonio, Texas:
Marion Koogler McNay Art Museum. Bequest of
Marion Koogler McNay)

tradition of the academic nude and renewing the practice of Rembrandt,
shows an attempt to create a realism of the flesh that may in some
measure be a reaction against Gustave Courbet's turn toward eroticized
and glamorized nudes in the 1860s. In 1889, he paints the *Breton Eve*
(Figure 25), whose posture is based on a Peruvian mummy preserved in
the Musée de l'Homme, and who constitutes a repeated, agonizing motif
in Gauguin's painting of this period—she reappears, for instance, in *Life
and Death* (1889), where she is juxtaposed with a red-haired bather
who both looks back to "Suzanne" and looks forward to the Tahitian
paintings. Then, in 1890, he paints the enigmatic and troubling *La perte
du pucelage* (The loss of virginity; Figure 26). Gauguin tells us that the
fox is an "Indian symbol of perversity," but even without this gloss we
are aware that the narrative implied by the painting is not a happy one.
The expression on the girl's face is not decipherable, and the posing of
her body in the stark Breton landscape, with its straggling procession of

26. Paul Gauguin, *La perte du pucelage*. (Norfolk, Virginia: Chrysler Museum)

peasants, seems raw and provocative. If the loss of virginity has brought maturity and consciousness, surely it is not a consciousness of harmony. The traditional polarities of loss and gain, innocence and knowledge, Virgin and Eve, are inherent in the painting. Just before his departure for Tahiti, Gauguin attempted something rather different, a *Primitive Eve,* a tentative kind of painting in which he gave the body—derived, art historians tell us, from an Indian temple sculpture—the face of his mother, Aline Chazal.[20] The figure will be realized later, in Tahiti, in the well-known *Te nave nave fenua* (Delightful land; Figure 27). Here, Eve has become frankly "native," her setting exotically and fantastically paradisiacal and sensuous, and her nudity is presented boldly, without coyness, to the viewer.

The figure of Eve is the focal point for many of Gauguin's reflections on art, woman, and civilization. The most important statement to consider here is the letter he wrote to August Strindberg, during the year he spent in France between his two trips to Tahiti. He had asked Strindberg to contribute a preface to the catalogue of the sale of his paintings held at the Hôtel Drouot on 18 February 1895 to raise money for the second Tahitian voyage. Strindberg refused, admitting that he did not understand the paintings Gauguin had brought back from the Pacific. Gauguin

27. Paul Gauguin, *Te nave nave fenua*. (Chuo Kurashiki, Japan: Ohara Art Museum)

then wrote a reply to Strindberg's letter, and used that as his catalogue preface. After opposing Strindberg's "civilization" and his own "barbarousness," the letter focuses on Eve:

Before the Eve of my choice, whom I have painted in the forms and the harmonies of another world, your chosen memories perhaps evoked a painful past. The Eve of your civilized conception makes you, and makes almost all of us, into misogynists; the ancient Eve, who frightens you in my studio, might some day smile on you less bitterly. This world, which neither a Cuvier nor a botanist could possibly ever find again, could be a paradise that I have only sketched. And how far it is from the sketch to the realization of the

GAUGUIN'S TAHITIAN BODY

dream! No matter. To glimpse happiness, isn't that a foretaste of *nirvana?* The Eve I have painted (she alone) logically can remain nude before our eyes. Yours in this simple state couldn't walk without shame, and, too beautiful (perhaps) would be the evocation of an evil and a pain.[21]

Most interesting here is what Gauguin says about *looking* at the two Eves naked. He evokes a problem that, as we have seen, posed itself acutely to late nineteenth-century painters: how to look at nudity (which essentially meant female nudity) in a naturalizing way.

As I noted in Chapter 5, the classical tradition as embodied in Beaux-Arts practice and the innumerable nudes exhibited at the Paris salons had clearly become decadent; the nudes themselves were both erotic and prettified, a kind of Second Empire and Third Republic pin-up art that excused what it was doing through worn-out references to classical motifs—endless births of Venus, *bacchantes,* and bathing scenes. Following the revolutionary gesture of his *Baigneuses* in 1853, Courbet in the 1860s had produced a series of nudes that for the most part seemed to make considerable concessions to commercial taste. The Impressionists, with their desire to render modern life, and to place their paintings outdoors—*en plein air*—faced the difficulty of finding plausible and picturable settings for the nude—and in fact, there are not many nudes in Impressionist painting, with the exception of the later Renoir. The triumphant nude of Gauguin's time was Manet's *Olympia* (see Figure 12), a painting that Gauguin worshiped; he took the trouble to paint a copy of it, and he had a photograph of it with him in Tahiti. But *Olympia,* and the scandal it provoked, points to the problem: the naturalization of nudity in this case takes the form of showing up the artificiality of the neoclassical nude by displaying the nude as prostitute, as a clearly sexualized body offered to the spectator's glance in the same manner she is offered to paying customers. Gauguin wants instead something that would remain fully erotic but without the connotations of shame, scandal, and exposure. That he repeatedly insists on the figure of Eve—rather than, in the manner of Bougainville and nineteenth-century salon painters, evoking the Venus of classical mythology—indicates a stubborn and no doubt accurate perception that Venus is no longer the point, no longer what nakedness is all about in the Western imagination. Instead the figure of Eve, with all the connotations of sin and shame, and the complex entry into knowledge of good and evil, is central to his culture's perception of nudity, and thus must be reconceived. As Gauguin stated in an interview in 1895, in response to the question why he had gone to Tahiti: "To do something new, you have to go back to the beginning, to the childhood of humanity. [Note the unconscious echo of Diderot and the repeated association of the exotic, the primitive, and the childlike.] My chosen Eve is almost an animal; that's why she is chaste, although naked. All those Venuses exhibited at the salon are indecent, odiously lubricious."[22]

Thus Gauguin takes on the impossible challenge of revising Eve by creating a nude in paradise whose nakedness is meant to be looked at with joy and erotic pleasure but without connecting her evident sexuality to evil and pain. He claims to want to abolish the virgin/whore, angel/demon polarities that haunt much nineteenth-century art and literature—Baudelaire is a prime example—by postulating an "innocent" sexuality in a primitive Eden where European conceptions of good and evil are irrelevant. His success in this revision depends on a certain depersonalization of Eve. In praising her "animality," and giving her body a form that breaks with contemporary canons of grace and allure, while making her face somewhat expressionless, he severs her from traditional cultural constraints. It is a gesture that can be read as a challenge to Western canons of the female nude, though a gesture that may be tainted by colonialist assumptions.

One can in fact argue, as Abigail Solomon-Godeau has forcefully done, that Gauguin's primitivism is a "gendered discourse" that inscribes itself directly in a colonialist "dynamic of knowledge/power relations which admits of no reciprocity."[23] Solomon-Godeau goes on to say: "On one level, what is enacted [in the colonial encounter] is a violent history of colonial possession and cultural dispossession—real power over real bodies. On another level, this encounter will be endlessly elaborated within a shadow world of representations—a question of imaginary power over imaginary bodies." There is a general truth here, but its specific applications require more nuanced discussion. Solomon-Godeau distorts the original discursive framework of the European encounter with Tahiti, which was not a simple act of colonial possession—that came later—but rather a problem in Enlightenment philosophy and ethnology. Gauguin participates in this discourse in his attempt to imagine a version of Tahiti earlier than the one he found in the 1890s. He perforce participates as well in the later colonialist appropriation, but he also denounces it: he kept up a more or less constant critique of colonial officialdom in Tahiti and, later, in the Marquesas, and at one point wrote and published a bitterly satirical journal called *Le Sourire*.

GAUGUIN'S TAHITIAN BODY

Solomon-Godeau's argument does not do justice to the disruptive, interrogative force of Tahitian sexuality in Western discourse, and to the figuration of that force in Gauguin's Tahitian painting. To be sure, Gauguin's talk about Eve is shot through with masculinist assumptions, and his views of Tahiti with European conceptions of primitivism. Yet although his thinking is limited by the persistent polarities of his culture—including culture and nature, civilized and primitive, innocent and corrupt—he makes an attempt to reverse their values and subvert traditional European assumptions. While his thought is clearly constrained by the polarities, his consciously transgressive attitude toward their usual acceptance animates his painting.

I would argue that the painting marks a decisive break from contemporary European representations of the nude, and that Gauguin produces new and compelling art from within a discourse that remains hostage to primitivist myths because he turns this discourse to other uses. His objects of representation call into question traditional kinds of looking. His construction of the natural, in *Te nave nave fenua* for instance, is a matter of the utmost artifice, aimed at disarming our traditional view of the nude, and of the primitive, revising the space of our observation and the context of our looking. (Gérôme's smoothed and displayed Oriental bodies offer a good contrast here; see Figure 14.) Gauguin's presentation of the exotic continually refers us back—and is meant to refer us back—to the problem of the nude in Western art. In this sense, his flight to Oceania is less escapist than it might at first appear, and the art he created there is constantly antithetical, using the Tahitian body as a commentary on the civilization that produced Eve. Simply to dismiss the Tahitian paintings as images of naked brown girls sprung from the erotic fantasies of a sometime French stockbroker gone native is to reproduce his cultural blindness. Gauguin implicitly reaches back beyond the simpler forms of colonial domination, to participate, at a distance, in the earlier debate—that of Bougainville and Cook—about how the sexual body in Tahiti problematizes standard European versions of the body.

One should in this context note that Gauguin's Tahitian painting is full of references to traditional Christian scenes and iconography, most famously in *Ia orana Maria* (Ave Maria) of 1891 (in the Metropolitan Museum, New York) and *Te temari no atua* (The child of god) of 1896 (Figure 28)—the latter, especially, an extraordinarily complex interplay between Christian references (not only the title, but the stable and manger seen in the background) and resolutely Tahitian revision. I do not think it is accurate to see Gauguin as wishing to infuse his primitives

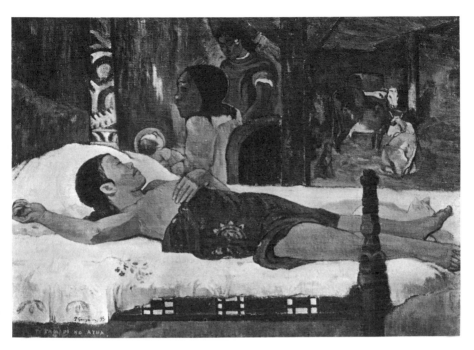

28. Paul Gauguin, *Te temari no atua*. (Munich: Neue Pinakothek)

with Christianity. Certainly everything he wrote about the Church and Christian morality is highly negative: religion is in his view a principal cause of the malaise of Western civilization. Rather, he seems to be attempting to rethink key elements of Christian mythology in terms of Tahitian primitivism, producing a revised version in which spirituality is reinvested in an unselfconscious dailiness. This is not to say that it is reinterpreted in a realist context, even within the reality of Tahiti: one has only to note that Tahitians did not use beds to see what an artificial construction this painting gives us. Clearly, Gauguin's paradise is a constructed one. He did not find what he wanted in Papeete—nor did he find it in Mataiea, or anywhere else on the island. In the absence of paradise found, he had to invent it.

Noa Noa is very much the record of that invention; indeed it is itself part of the invention, conceived as a kind of *vademecum* for Gauguin's Tahitian paintings, attempting to control the way in which they are to be read through a narrative of shedding civilization, progressing back to primitivism, and becoming savage. As autobiography, *Noa Noa* is misleading We know, particularly from Bengt Danielsson's demythologizing account, that Gauguin remained in many respects the baffled outsider: if food grew on the trees, he didn't know how to gather it; he was reduced to buying expensive tinned goods from the Chinese merchant; he never really mastered the language; syphilis and other diseases sent him frequently to the hospital; money—constantly expected from sales of his paintings in Europe, but never coming in time or in sufficient amounts—was an incessant worry.[24] *Noa Noa* is a record of Gauguin's self-conception, of the invented figure he chose to perpetuate. Thus he writes: "Each day is better for me; I come to understand the language quite well; my neighbors—three next doors, others scattered farther off—look on me almost as one of theirs; my bare feet from their daily contact with pebbles have become familiar with the soil; my almost naked body no longer fears the sun; civilization leaves me gradually and I begin to think simply, to have little hatred for my fellow man, and I function as an animal, freely." (53). As this passage suggests, becoming primitive for Gauguin has to do with learning to live in his body, in what he rather simplistically conceives as an uninhibited and guilt-free animality. As he would later write in a letter to Daniel de Monfried: "the animality that is in us is not so much to be despised as people say—Those damned Greeks who understood it all imagined Antaeus, who regained his force in touching the earth—The earth, it's our animality, believe me."[25] Becoming a savage, in Gauguin's conception, implicates one's own body and its relation to other bodies; the body of the other is a source of knowing, the means of access to the savage state. Two passages from *Noa Noa*, revelatory of both Gauguin's project and his confusions, deserve our consideration, and will lead us back to the place of the body in the Tahitian paintings, where he achieves more convincing solutions to the problems he sets for himself.

The first passage is one of the most curious episodes in *Noa Noa*. Needing a rosewood tree for a carving he wants to make, Gauguin undertakes a trip into the mountainous interior with one of his new friends, a handsome young man. As he follows his guide, who seems to know the invisible paths by smell—the primal sense of *Noa Noa*, whose title means "perfumed"—Gauguin notes the young man's graceful form, which seems to lack sex-specificity. Gauguin remarks in the margin of his manuscript that the Tahitians' bodies have an androgynous appearance, and he elsewhere returns to the theme: part of primitive bodiliness is a less sharply demarcated difference between the sexes. In the present episode, this situation leads to temptation, and to a confusion of sexual roles: "I had something like a presentiment of crime, the awakening of evil. Then a weariness at the role of the male who ought always to be the stronger, a protector; heavy shoulders with which to bear. To be for a moment the weaker being who loves and obeys. I drew nearer, without fear of the laws, trouble beating in my temples" (57). At this point, his guide turns around; seen from the front, he once more becomes clearly male—and Gauguin's trouble passes. They find and cut down a magnif- icent rosewood tree, and the cutting becomes a final destruction of the evil thoughts of the civilized man. "Well destroyed, in fact, all my old stock of the civilized. I came back calm, feeling myself henceforth another man, a Maori."

One could analyze this passage at some length, perhaps especially for the ambivalence of passivity and aggressivity it displays, and the confused conception of the homoerotic temptation as alternately domination and submission. In the margin of the manuscript of *Noa Noa*, Gauguin noted:

1 The androgynous side of the savage, the little difference between the sexes in animals.
2 The purity entailed by seeing nakedness and by the easy commerce between the sexes.
The lack of knowledge of vice among the savages.
The desire to be for a moment weak, woman.

Gauguin is attracted to androgyny, which is part of the animal purity of primitivism, while also part of its sensual appeal: it appears to liberate him from European categories of difference.[26] Yet that attraction leads to an interior experience of his own body as bisexual, to a homoerotic temptation that places him in the role of woman, and thus must be repudiated. His slide away from androgyny resolves itself in a feeling of guilt dispersed and innocence achieved. The incident might have given Gauguin an occasion to cast doubt on his unproblematic opposition of civilization and the primitive, and to reflect on the ways he needs to use Tahitian bodies for his critique of the European tradition of lubriciousness. But he doesn't in *Noa Noa* achieve this kind of self-reflexiveness, instead resolving the incident in a moment of male bonding with his Tahitian friend, and the claim that he has recovered radical innocence.

Gauguin is interested in a polymorphous bodiliness, but when it comes to foregrounding, touching, and representing a body, it must be clearly gendered as female—albeit a female body that breaks from the traditional Western sense of female gracefulness by being more powerful and compact, and less distinct from the male. (There are some male nudes from Gauguin's Breton period, but they are all young boys.) The passage from *Noa Noa* becomes virtually an allegory of a larger cultural need to maintain the "laws" of sexual difference. If contemplation of the male body can evoke the temptation of androgyny and a slide toward homo-eroticism, it is too dangerous to handle. Rather than exploring fully the polymorphous possibilities he has uncovered, Gauguin feels obliged to reassert sexual polarities, and to center cultural discourse firmly on the female body, where male artist and male viewers can inscribe and read without ambiguity messages of desire and revisions of a cultural tradition of representation. The placement of the passage also is important, for it precedes by a couple of pages Gauguin's most significant experience of a Tahitian's body, with Tehamana. The passage thus appears to record a preparation of his body for more direct intimacy with the savage state, for another move into communion with the primitive.

The discovery of Tehamana (in more accurate Tahitian, Teha'amana) occurs during the trip around the island that Gauguin undertakes to put still greater distance between himself and civilization. In the village of Faone, he is addressed by an islander as "the man who makes men"—that is, who paints them—and invited to lunch. Asked why he is traveling, Gauguin replies that he is looking for a wife, whereupon one of his hosts—a woman—offers him her thirteen-year-old daughter. Bougainville's Arcadian Tahiti has suddenly come alive again. Tehamana is first to stay with Gauguin for a one-week trial period. He brings this girl—whom he describes as simultaneously "melancholy and mocking"—back to his house in a largely silent journey. "Each of us observed the other; she was impenetrable; I was quickly beaten in this contest" (73). Once again, as in the letter to Strindberg, Gauguin's relation to the female body is presented within a problematics of looking, where the male attempt to penetrate an impassive exterior reaches an impasse that can be resolved only by physical penetration. Gauguin sums up their first week together in a phrase that anticipates the title of his late painting, *Et l'or de leur corps* (And the gold of their bodies): "Sometimes, during the night, *flashes of light . . . played over the gold of Tehamana's skin*" (ellipsis and emphasis are Gauguin's). The body is a decorated surface. But after Tehamana has gone to visit her mother, and then returned few days later, her cultural impenetrability is progressively breached by physical intimacy. Now, according to Gauguin's narrative, the true Tahitian idyll begins:

Each day at sunrise the light was radiant in my hut. The gold of Tehamana's face inundated everything around it and the two of us went to refresh ourselves in a nearby stream, naturally, simply, as in Paradise.

Everyday life.—Tehamana gives herself, more and more docile, loving; the Tahitian noa noa perfumes everything. Myself, I am no longer aware of the days and the hours, of Evil and Good: every- 185 thing is beautiful, everything is right . . .

Conversations on what goes on in Europe, on God, on the Gods. I teach her, she teaches me . . .

Everyday life.—In bed, at night: conversations. The stars inter- est her greatly; she asks me the name in French of the morning star, the evening star. She has trouble understanding that the earth turns around the sun. In her turn she tells me the names of the stars in her language. (75)

At this point, Gauguin inserts a passage on Maori cosmology, not only the names of the stars but the myths of creation associated with them. The passage is lifted from Gauguin's notebook entitled *Ancien culte mahorie,* which itself, scholars have discovered, is essentially a transcrip- tion of parts of a book which Gauguin had discovered in Papeete called *Voyages aux îles du grand océan,* by J. A. Moerenhout, a Belgian who was the American consul in Oceania and one of the first serious ethnog- raphers of the region.[27] It is unlikely, to say the least, that Gauguin could have learned this cosmology from the thirteen-year-old Tehamana, since a century of Christian missionary work had virtually extirpated traditional Polynesian customs, beliefs, and mythology. By the time Gau- guin reached Tahiti, at most a few Tahitian elders could recollect native traditions. The lore survived only in books written by Europeans, and what Gauguin attributes to his child bride is demonstrably book learn- ing. Her wisdom is bookish, as she is herself the cultural construction of Gauguin's need and desire to embody the primitive in a woman.

At this central moment of *Noa Noa,* then, Gauguin's search for the savage state leads him to the gift of the body of a Tahitian girl, who at first appears to be impenetrable golden surface; in bed with her he finally discovers the long-gone and mysterious Maori past, and indeed the key to Tahitian beliefs and ways. Or so he would have us believe. He wants us to understand that the golden body of this silent girl holds the key to what he has been looking for, that entering her body opens his way to primitivism as a coherent and totalized worldview, and to its symbols which—reformulated with the fictional revision that characterizes this moment of *Noa Noa*—would become part of his art. He depicted Te-

29. Paul Gauguin, *Merahi metua no Tehamana*. (Chicago:
Art Institute of Chicago. Gift of Mr. and Mrs. Charles
Deering McCormick. Photo © 1988, The Art Institute
of Chicago. All rights reserved)

hamana's relation to primitive cosmology in the painting *Merahi metua
no Tehamana* (The ancestors of Tehamana; 1893), which figures the
recaptured past against the wall in front of which his child bride, now
dressed in missionary clothing, is formally posed (Figure 29). We do not
need to read Gauguin's art in terms of the symbolism drawn from Maori
religion—I think it constitutes neither an occult key to the work nor a
coherent and legible iconographic system; it is more a decorative emblem
of primitiveness. Rather, Gauguin wants to invest the Tahitian body
itself with a spirituality that is in no way separate from the body but is

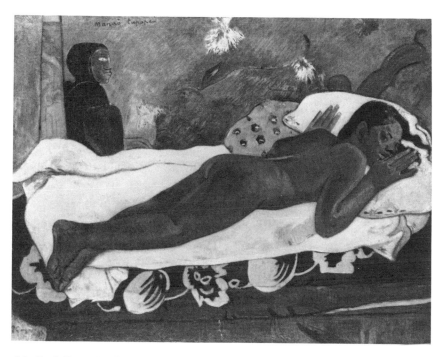

30. Paul Gauguin, *Manao tupapau*. (Buffalo, New York: Albright-Knox Art
Gallery. A. Conger Goodyear Collection)

instead an integral part of bodily knowledge and bodily meaning. The
Tahitian body would then be one that can and must be looked on naked,
not only without evocations of shame and evil, but with positive evocations of spirituality inscribed in the body itself.

An indispensable painting in this context is *Manao tupapau* (The spirit
of the dead watches; Figure 30), from late 1892, which illustrates the
next episode of *Noa Noa*. Gauguin, delayed on a trip to town, comes
home late at night to find the lamp in the hut gone out from lack of fuel
and Tehamana lying awake on the bed, staring in wide-eyed terror of
the legendary evil spirits of the night, the *tupapau*. Gauguin described
the scene and the painting several times: in a letter to his wife, in the
notebook dedicated to his daughter, *Cahier pour Aline*, and in later
versions of *Noa Noa*, insisting alternately on its Tahitian symbolism and
on its pictorial qualities, on its nature as a vision of Polynesian super-
stitions, and on its generic nature as a nude study in which the Tahitian
elements are simply a context for displaying Tehamana's body. He thus
thoroughly covers his tracks and eludes any single interpretive intention.
For our purposes, we may note that Gauguin says of Tehamana at the

moment he discovers her in the dark, "I had never seen her so lovely; above all, I had never seen her beauty so moving."[28] Alfred Jarry in a poem of 1894 described the nude in this painting as a "brown Olympia," and a number of art critics have noted Gauguin's evident ambition to rephrase Manet's painting—a photograph of which, we recall, was tacked on the wall of Gauguin's hut—in Tahitian terms. Like the body of *Olympia,* the body in *Manao Tupapau* is offered to the spectator's gaze, though in a pose that refuses to be a "pose"—refuses the self-display that one finds in *Olympia,* and the distinct impression that Manet's girl is available, for a price. Gauguin's nude is also available, but in a more unselfconscious way, and without connotations of venality. As an *Olympia* turned over, the nude of *Manao Tupapau* may suggest a comment on the problematics of penetrability and impenetrability posed by Gauguin—may suggest, to use his term, a greater "animality" than that evoked by the classic poses of the nude.

The naked female form, slipping toward the frontal plane of the canvas, challenges the traditional space—and dominance—of the spectator. It is offered to the gaze in a way that tries to make its nakedness, conceived as natural to the woman herself, a natural, inevitable, open object of vision, without sly overtones of sin or commerce. (Compare François Boucher's rear views of naked women, for example his *Mademoiselle O'Murphy* [Figure 31], which Gauguin would no doubt have included in his category of the "lubricious.") In contrast to the attributes of *Olympia* that betoken her exchange value—the pose, the bold gaze, the black servant bearing flowers sent by an admirer or a keeper—those of *Manao tupapau* suggest an economy of the gift, as it would be defined by Marcel Mauss: the free and generous offering, which must be responded to by a corresponding gift—which may here be the painting itself. The gift of the potlatch, as Georges Bataille points out, is related to the creation of sacred objects, which have no use value and belong not to an economy of exchange and accumulation but to an economy of waste and glorious expenditure.[29] Gauguin, one might say, is attempting to reach back beyond the economy of exchange to that of the gift—as it were, denying Wallis's version of Tahiti in order to resurrect Bougainville's vision.

This result is achieved in part by Gauguin's decorative treatment of the setting and the vaguely symbolic elements. The body of *Manao tupapau* calls to and is complemented by its background, the *tupapau* who is made to appear more decorative than truly frightening, the flowers—or are they bursts of light?—that play above her, in some

31. François Boucher, *Mademoiselle O'Murphy (L'odalisque).* (Paris: Louvre. Photo © R.M.N.)

representation of access to "Tahitianness" or "the Maori soul" or simply "the savage state" by way of the body itself, which, in its sculptural weight and volume, grounds the fantastic in bodiliness. A glance at another painting from the same year, 1892, entitled *Aha oe feii?* (Are you jealous?) may help to make the point (Figure 32). As Richard Field has observed, the pose of the seated figure is derived from a photograph that Gauguin owned of a frieze from the theater of Dionysos in Athens.[30] The heavy volume of the sculpted body—and also the accompanying reclining body, whose torso is thrust forward—is set against a flattened, decorative, luminous landscape. The spectator is invited to respond to these bodies as simply gorgeous, as part of the rich, unselfconscious abundance of a paradisal place which the bodies appear to create themselves, as their necessary context. We are reminded that Gauguin over and over in his letters to Daniel de Monfried refers to the irrealizing elements of these paintings, whose decor is "my invention" and "not painted according to nature."[31] In his painting, as in *Noa Noa,* Gauguin reaches back through a present Tahiti which has been irrevocably con-

32. Paul Gauguin, *Aha oe feii?* (Moscow: Pushkin Museum. Photo
  © Scala/Art Resource)

taminated to a primitive world largely of his own invention. It is a world
which foregrounds the body as something to be displayed, in a context
at once natural and unreal, as the ultimate integer of both pleasure and
meaning. Although Tahiti is always already in a process of loss—from
the very first European visitors onward—the response that Gauguin
offers is analogous to that of Diderot: imagine it, recreate it, not as it is
or even as it necessarily was, but as it might be. And like Diderot's
invention, Gauguin's gives pride of place to the body as at once sexual
and innocent, as an Eve that can be fully looked at.

I want to pursue these reflections by way of two more of Gauguin's
paintings, both from his second and final stay in Tahiti. The first is *Te
arii vahine* (The noble woman) of 1896 (Figure 33), which clearly alludes
to a long tradition of Western nudes, very much including Manet's
Olympia and that painting's prototype, Titian's *Venus of Urbino*
(Figure 34). (Another source mentioned is Cranach's *Diana Reclining,*
of which Gauguin may also have owned a photograph.)[32] *Te arii vahine*
evidently wants one to think of the nymphs and Dianas and Venuses of
Western art—perhaps even Eve, since the vine wrapped around the tree
trunk evokes the serpent wrapped around the tree of knowledge in a
number of Renaissance paintings, the pieces of mango evoke the forbid-

33. Paul Gauguin, *Te arii vahine*. (Moscow: Pushkin Museum. Photo
© Scala/Art Resource)

34. Titian, *Venus of Urbino*. (Florence: Galleria degli Uffizi. Photo © 1990,
Alinari/Art Resource)

den fruit, and the fan held behind her head by the Tahitian woman almost suggests a halo, triggering allusions to the Biblical tradition. But these allusions must almost be seen as comic, as citations from a tradition that has been made irrelevant by a place and a person so clearly uncon-

cerned with Western allegories of the *locus amoenus* and its loss. Especially when one considers the somewhat absurd cloth covering the figure's loins—held almost as if she didn't know its purpose—one has the sense of a Tahitian figure consciously posed by the artist within a Western iconographical tradition of which she is unaware and which doesn't concern her. She appears simply content to display her body, and all the elements of the fantasy landscape concur in its display.

The other painting is *Nevermore,* of 1897 (Figure 35), another canvas that has often been compared to *Olympia,* and whose model was the mistress of Gauguin's second Tahitian stay, Panhura (Tehamana, like so many colonial "wives," was left behind when he traveled back to France). In a letter to Monfried, Gauguin noted: "I wanted to suggest with a simple nude a certain barbaric luxury of long ago. The whole is drowned in colors that are deliberately somber and sad; it is neither silk nor velvet nor muslin nor gold that creates this luxury but purely matter made rich by the hand of the artist. No trickery . . . man's imagination

35. Paul Gauguin, *Nevermore.* (London: Cortauld Institute Galleries)

alone has enriched with fantasy this dwelling."[33] The comments suggest Gauguin's desire, once again, to replace the representation of reality, or even the impression of reality, with a consciously invented creation, something that not only is nevermore but never was, and that, at the same time, makes this nude body an object of contemplation and admiration that excludes traditional Western interpretations. As in *Manao tupapau,* the body is pushed up against the frontal plane of the canvas, thus challenging the traditional distanced and dominating place of the spectator, as if to provoke a kind of intimacy with the body, a demand that one respond to its intense presence.

All these Tahitian nudes—and there are of course many others— confirm a comment by Victor Segalen in one of his many evocative texts on Gauguin: "What did these child-beings give of themselves to Gauguin? Splendid *forms,* which he 'dared to deform'; *motifs* also, to ring out across the humid blue vibrations of the atmosphere, warm ambered notes, unctuous flesh with mirrored reflections, dusted with gold specks in the bright sunlight; *attitudes,* finally, in which he schematized the Maori physiology, which may contain their whole philosophy. He didn't look for an improbable Indian soul beneath the beautiful exterior: painting the natives, he learned to be an animal."[34] Segalen's romantic ethnology perpetuates the identification of the primitive and the childlike; he admits to seeing Tahiti through Gauguin's painting, and his prose here is rather too "artistic." Nonetheless, his basic perception is sound: the essence of Tahiti for Gauguin is a body that he "deforms" for his own purposes, in an effort to remove it from the duality of body and soul inherent in the tradition of the European nude as it was understood by his contemporaries. The body alone appears to open the way to that "nevermore," a richly textured world of pseudo-mythological reference which has the effect of further enhancing the emblematic resonance of the body itself.

One can take the measure of Gauguin's achievement in revising the nude in these paintings and a number of others, especially from his final years in Tahiti and in Hivaoa, in the Marquesas Islands. He had moved from Tahiti in 1901, in search of a world he imagined to be yet more primitive—he had heard there might still be cannibals there—and a fuller range of models. Take, for instance, the *Deux femmes tahitiennes* of 1899 (Figure 36), with the almost classical ease it has achieved in the presentation of the central figure's full, strong body that emerges into the sunlight to confront the viewer in full erotic beauty. Her face is impassive, neither soliciting nor refusing our gaze. The body itself is full

36. Paul Gauguin, *Deux femmes tahitiennes*. (New York: Metropolitan Museum of Art. Gift of William Church Osborn)

of both strength and repose. The unidentified flowers or fruits offered on the tray become a simple metonymy of the offered body. We can, to be sure, simply stigmatize the painting as one more example of a male gaze taking a depersonalized woman as its sexual object. But we may also find it moving and persuasive as a painting *about* looking: about the positive, guilt-free, invitation to take pleasure in the gaze directed at the body. The painting entitled *Et l'or de leur corps* (And the gold of their bodies) sums up in the simplest terms what Gauguin sought in Oceania. In the bodies of these paintings, Gauguin transcends what Segalen qualifies as "la fadeur du nu européen," where *fadeur* I think means both the washed-out coloring of the Caucasian body compared to the Polynesian body, and the moral and spiritual pallor of nudity in civilizations where it is unnatural, associated with undress, and castigated as impure.[35] Whereas Stéphane Mallarmé and W. B. Yeats were, at virtually this moment, worrying about how the body—of a dancer, for instance—might symbolize spiritual abstractions, Gauguin wants to invite us to contemplate the body itself, as itself significant. If his golden body has a long history of colonial exploitation and mystification—a history in which he necessarily participates—Gauguin also strives to create a context of looking in which this body recovers its dignity, self-sufficiency, and mystery.

One more painting needs to be considered, one of Gauguin's last, painted in Hivaoa in 1902: *Contes barbares* (Primitive tales; Figure 37). The painting has elicited much contradictory commentary. Yet the enigmatic trio and the provocative title call for an interpretive response. For me, it is tempting to see the male figure—who can easily be identified as Gauguin's friend the Belgian painter Meyer de Haan, but who here has been given supernatural claws instead of normal feet—as the figure of the European *conteur*. He would thus be the teller of the primitive tales, the inventor of the lush Edenic scene. He himself, however, remains indelibly marked by his slight remove from the scene; his position in the background and his posture and expression may betoken exclusion, jealousy, or the impossibility ever of entering the world he has imagined. In contrast to his anguished and indeed somewhat diabolical figure, the two women are full of repose. The figure facing us suggests a kind of nirvanic absolute calm. The red-haired woman in three-quarter profile forcibly reminds us of Botticelli's famous Venus, born, this time, from the creative powers of the artist. The women are offered for our contemplation, but the artist himself appears to be excluded from his creation. It is interesting to note that in an earlier portrait of Meyer de Haan, from 1889 (Figure 38), he is shown with two books before him on the table: Carlyle's *Sartor Resartus* and Milton's *Paradis perdu,* as in a prefiguration of his later production of a paradise which for him remains fictional. In *Contes barbares,* he is figured into the canvas somewhat in the manner of a patron represented in a traditional altarpiece: a giver, but not a partaker.

Gauguin's quest for his "Tahitian Eve," for a body that could be naked and sexual without sin, fear, or loathing, led him to an island that had taken its place in the European imagination from the moment of its

37. Paul Gauguin, *Contes barbares*. (Essen: Volkwang Museum)

discovery as paradise regained, but which, by the very fact of that discovery, was already in a state of loss. Gauguin's initial experience of Tahiti was that loss—and he ended his days in Hivaoa quarreling with the local clergy and being harassed by the representatives of the colonial government. His dream of a generous, primitive gift economy, as imaged in Bougainville's *Voyage,* is always necessarily undermined by Wallis's earlier version, which, whatever the reality of pre-discovery Tahiti may have been, ineluctably brought the exchange economy. Gauguin's life in

38. Paul Gauguin, *Meyer de Haan*. (New York: private
   collection)

Tahiti was, on the whole, far from primitive romance. But by acts of
will and imagination, in his art he made do with paradise lost, reimag-
ining the "nevermore," inventing what never was but should be.

   Although Gauguin begins as a deluded participant in the myth of
Tahiti—on the very banal level of the Colonial Exhibition and the travel
brochure—he manages to supplant, or perhaps more accurately to supplement, that myth with one of his own (which thereafter becomes part
of our myth of Tahiti).[36] While his thought is limited by colonialist
polarities—civilized and primitive, culture and nature—his attempt to

GAUGUIN'S TAHITIAN BODY

reverse the values usually assigned to them animate his art. I would argue that he does achieve a kind of "solution" to the persistent problem of the body in nineteenth-century art and culture: he effectively supplants an outworn cultural construction of the nude with a vision that radically reshapes our viewing of the body and sets a challenging standard for those twentieth-century artists who will go on to rethink the tradition of the nude. In its claim of mythological access to ancient Maori culture, Gauguin's solution stands within an old tradition of allegorization of the woman's body. Nonetheless, everything in Gauguin's performance of this body leads us back to contemplation of the body itself, as the site of beauty, pleasure, and value.

I find myself thinking back to that anonymous chronicler of Cook's first voyage who, after describing the Tahitian practice of tattooing their bodies, noted that upon first seeing the Europeans write, the Tahitians dubbed the practice tattoo. Gauguin's effort is a kind of tattoo: not so much writing on the body—though there certainly are messages inscribed on his nudes—but writing of and with the body. Inevitably, given Gauguin's cultural limitations, it is a gendered body; the male writer/painter produces his meaning on the woman's body. Within these constraints, Gauguin may succeed in making the body not so much a transcendent signified as a powerful signifier, a revised version of a traditional Western signifying practice. The Tahitian nudes take us out of the world of salon Venuses and engage us in a new form of bodily representation that will take the most innovative art of the twentieth century—beginning with the work of Henri Matisse—into new expressive uses of the nude. Although the problems posed by the body in the field of vision remain, the painterly language about it changes utterly.

7 What Is a Monster?
(According to *Frankenstein*)

monstrum horrendum informe ingens cui lumen ademptum
Virgil, *Aeneid*, 3:658

VIEWING WOMAN'S BODY in a phallic field of vision predominates in the nineteenth-century realist tradition, but there are examples of attempts to subvert this model and move beyond its epistemological implications to other kinds of knowing of the body. I shall
argue in the next chapter that George Eliot provides the best instance
of dissent from within the dominant tradition—a dissent that Freud,
attempting to supplant seeing by listening to the body, may also be
struggling toward. The present chapter returns to an earlier example of
the dissenting perspective, by another woman novelist, written before
the realist novel has established its hegemony—Mary Shelley's *Frankenstein*. Hence I propose here to violate chronology, and to interrupt the
general trend of my argument, to look closely at a text which is too
complex, peculiar, and interesting to be neglected.

Frankenstein, first published in 1818, concerns an exotic body with a
difference, a distinct perversion from the tradition of desirable objects.
The story of this ugly, larger-than-life, monstrous body raises complex
questions of motherhood, fatherhood, gender, and narrative. The afterlife of the novel in the popular imagination has been intensely focused
on that monstrous body, to the extent that the name "Frankenstein"
tends to evoke not the unfortunate overreaching young scientist Victor
Frankenstein but his hideous creation. This is both faithful and unfaithful
to Mary Shelley's original: faithful, in that a monster indeed, even
etymologically, exists to be looked at, shown off, viewed as in a circus
sideshow; unfaithful, in that Shelley's novel with equal insistence directs
us to issues of language in the story of the monster and his creator. In
fact, the central issues of the novel are joined in the opposition of sight

and speech, and it unfolds its complex narrative structure from this nexus.

That narrative structure involves framed or imbedded tales, a tale within a tale within a tale: in the outer frame, explorer Robert Walton writes to his sister Mrs. Saville, and tells of meeting Frankenstein in the Arctic; in the next frame, Frankenstein recounts his life story to Walton; in the innermost tale, the monster at a crucial moment tells his tale to Frankenstein. When the monster has finished, Frankenstein resumes speaking in his own right; when he has done, Walton resumes.[1] The nested narrative structure calls attention to the presence of a listener for each speaker—of a narratee for each narrator—and to the interlocutionary relations thus established. Each act of narration in the novel implies a certain bond or contract: listen to me because . . . The structure calls attention to the motives of telling; it makes each listener—and the reader—ask: Why are you telling me this? What am I supposed to do with it? As in the psychoanalytic context of storytelling, the listener is placed in a transferential relation to the narrative. As a "subject supposed to know," the listener is called upon to "supplement" the story (to anticipate the phrase Freud will use in the case history of Dora), to articulate and even enact the meaning of the desire it expresses in ways that may be foreclosed to the speaker. Storytelling in *Frankenstein* is far from an innocent act: narratives have designs on their narratees that must be unraveled. The issues posed by such a narrative structure may most of all concern relation, or how narrative relation relates to inter-subjective relation, and the relation of relation, in both these senses, to language as the medium of telling and listening, as the medium of transmission, transaction, and transference.

These issues take on their full import only in the context of the visual. I shall start with the opening of the innermost tale—which strikingly poses the issues of the visual— and then work out to the framing structures. Following the first murders committed by the Monster—Frankenstein's brother William strangled, the family servant Justine Moritz executed as his killer through maliciously planted evidence—Frankenstein seeks solace in the Alps above Chamonix. He penetrates the "glorious presence-chamber of imperial Nature," climbing to Montanvert and the Mer de Glace, hoping to recapture a remembered "sublime ecstasy that gave wings to the soul and allowed it to soar from the obscure world to light and joy."[2] His ascension takes him to a "wonderful and stupendous scene," overlooking the Mer de Glace and facing the "awful majesty" of Mont Blanc; his heart once again opens to joy, and he exclaims, in the tones of the Ossianic bard, "Wandering spirits, if indeed ye wander, and do not rest in your narrow beds, allow me this faint happiness, or take me, as your companion, away from the joys of life." At this point, the vision of sublimity is both fulfilled and undone by the sight of a superhuman shape that comes bounding toward Frankenstein over the ice. The Monster appears to be—as in his original creation—both born of nature and supernatural, and as such he puts normal measurements and classifications into question. In particular, he puts into question the meaning of looking, of optics, as the faculty and the science most commonly used to judge meanings in the phenomenal world.

Frankenstein's immediate reaction to the appearance of the Monster is to tell it to go away. When the Monster persists in his claim that he has the right to a hearing from his creator, Frankenstein curses the day of the Monster's creation, and reiterates: "Begone! Relieve me from the sight of your detested form" (97). To this the Monster, in a touching gesture, responds by placing his huge hands over Frankenstein's eyes: "Thus I relieve thee, my creator . . . thus I take from thee a sight which you abhor. Still thou canst listen to me, and grant me thy compassion." The Monster clearly understands that it is not visual relation that favors him—indeed, as we will discover when he tells his own story, his only favorable reception from a human being thus far has come from the blind de Lacey—but rather the auditory or interlocutionary, the relation of language. Thus, this first meeting of Frankenstein and his Monster since the day of his creation presents a crucial issue of the novel in the opposition of sight and language, of the hideous body and the persuasive tongue.

For the Monster is eloquent. From the first words he speaks, he shows himself to be a supreme rhetorician, who controls the antitheses and oxymorons that express the pathos of his existence: "Remember that I am thy creature; I ought to be thy Adam, but I am rather the fallen angel, whom thou drivest from joy for no misdeed. Everywhere I see bliss, from which I alone am irrevocably excluded. I was benevolent and good; misery made me a fiend. Make me happy, and I shall again be virtuous" (95–96). When we learn of the Monster's self-education—and particularly his three master-texts, Milton's *Paradise Lost,* Plutarch's *Lives,* and Goethe's *Werther*—we will understand the prime sources of his eloquence and of the conception of the just order of things that animates his plea to his creator. But beyond the motives of his eloquence, it is important to register the simple fact of Shelley's decision to make

WHAT IS A MONSTER?

the Monster the most eloquent creature in the novel. This hideous and deformed creature, far from expressing himself in grunts and gestures, speaks and reasons with the highest elegance, logic, and persuasiveness. As a verbal creation, he is the very opposite of the monstrous: he is a sympathetic and persuasive participant in Western culture. All of the Monster's interlocutors—including, finally, the reader—must come to terms with this contradiction between the verbal and the visual.[3]

By persuading Frankenstein to give his creature a hearing, thus opening the innermost frame of the novel, the Monster has adumbrated what Roland Barthes would call a "narrative contract" between narrator and narratee.[4] The narrative contract, like the psychoanalytic transference, is based on and implies the intersubjective, transindividual, cultural order of language. Language by its very nature transcends and preexists the individual locutor; it implies, depends on, and necessitates that network of intersubjective relations from which the Monster protests he has been excluded. That is, in becoming the narrator of his story, the Monster both dramatizes his problem and provides a model for its solution, the solution implicit in the discursive interdependence of an "I" and a "thou" in any interlocutionary situation.[5] The Monster's words assign to Frankenstein a parental role for the first time in the novel: "For the first time . . . I felt what the duties of a creator towards his creature were" (97)—a role all the more glaring in its neglect in that Frankenstein has dwelt at length on the parental love and concern lavished on him in his early years, the way he was guided by a "silken cord" toward happiness and goodness (33). By the time the Monster has completed his narrative, Frankenstein still feels horror and hatred when he looks upon this "filthy mass that moved and talked," but he also avows: "His words had a strange effect upon me. I compassionated him" (140). After establishing this tenuous link with his creator through narrative, the Monster takes the decisive step in his argument: "My vices are the children of a forced solitude that I abhor, and my virtues will necessarily arise when I live in communion with an equal. I shall feel the affections of a sensitive being and become linked to the chain of existence and events from which I am now excluded" (140–41).

The metaphor of the chain is one that will reappear in various guises throughout the novel. It represents relation itself, including affective interpersonal relations (see the "silken cord" of Frankenstein's childhood) and the relations between tellers and listeners—relations established through language and as language. The chain here closely resembles what Jacques Lacan calls the "signifying chain" of language, especially language as the vehicle of desire. In the Monster's confrontation of and narrative to Frankenstein, we have a representation of the Lacanian distinction between the imaginary and the symbolic orders. The imaginary is the order of the specular, of the mirror stage, and arises from the subject's perception of itself as other; it is thus the order of deceptive relations, of ideology and fascination. The symbolic order ultimately is language itself, the systematic and transindividual order of the signifier, the cultural system or law into which individual subjects are inserted.[6] In the specular or imaginary order, the Monster will never cease to be the "filthy mass." In the symbolic order, on the other hand, he can produce and project his desire in language, in relation to an interlocutor. It is, however, in the logic of Lacanian desire and the "signifying chain" that such desire should be unappeasable, a metonymical movement that extends desire forward without reaching a goal: a goal which cannot be named, since the object of desire is unconscious. The Monster's stated object of desire is for a mate, a female creature like himself, which Frankenstein must create. But we will have occasion to ask whether this demand truly corresponds to the needs stipulated by the Monster's desire.

Before considering the Monster's demand for—and Frankenstein's temporary acquiescence to—the creation of a female monster, it is important to register the Monster's narrative of his discovery of language, its contexts and its effects. His first experience with humanity, he tells us, already demonstrated the hopelessness of the specular relation: the shepherd he discovered in a hut fled shrieking from his sight, the villagers pelted him with stones. Retreating into a hovel adjoining the de Lacey cottage, he commences his education as voyeur, observing the family through an "almost imperceptible chink through which the eye could penetrate," seeing and himself unseen. His most important discovery is that of human language, which is presented in the context of human interaction and affect:

> "I found that these people possessed a method of communicating their experience and feelings to one another by articulate sounds. I perceived that the words they spoke sometimes produced pleasure or pain, smiles or sadness, in the minds and countenances of the hearers. This was indeed a godlike science, and I ardently desired to become acquainted with it. But I was baffled in every attempt I made for this purpose. Their pronunciation was quick, and the words they uttered, not having any apparent connection with visible

objects, I was unable to discover any clue by which I could unravel the mystery of their reference. By great application, however, and after having remained during the space of several revolutions of the moon in my hovel, I discovered the names that were given to some of the most familiar objects of discourse; I learned and applied the words, 'fire,' 'milk,' 'bread,' and 'wood.' I learned also the names of the cottagers themselves. The youth and his companion had each of them several names, but the old man had only one, which was 'father.' The girl was called 'sister' or 'Agatha,' and the youth 'Felix,' 'brother,' or 'son.' I cannot describe the delight I felt when I learned the ideas appropriated to each of these sounds and was able to pronounce them. I distinguished several other words without being able as yet to understand or apply them, such as 'good,' 'dearest,' 'unhappy.'" (106–107)

Like so much else in the story of the Monster's education through sensation, experience, and the association of ideas, his discovery of language stands within Enlightenment debates about origins, coming in this instance close to the scenarios of Rousseau's *Essai sur l'origine des langues,* which sees language as originating not in need but in emotion.[7] As the Monster encounters it, language is tied to human love and patterns of kinship and relation, as if in confirmation of the views of an anthropologist such as Claude Lévi-Strauss, for whom the structures of kinship are the first "writing" of a society. The Monster also discovers the proto-Saussurian notion that the linguistic sign is arbitrary, that there is no intuitable connection of a sign to its referent, and indeed that some signs ("good," "dearest," "unhappy") have no apparent referent. As a consequence, the Monster grasps the nature of language as a system, wherein meaning is created not as a simple movement from sign to referent but in context, dependent on the rule-governed relation of signs one to another.

Hence language presents itself as both the tool he needs to enter into relation with others, and a model of relation itself: it implies—it both depends on and makes possible—that "chain of existence and events" from which he feels himself excluded. The "godlike science" of language is thus explicitly a cultural compensation for a deficient nature; it offers the possibility of escape from "monsterism," which is precisely lack of relation, apartness. Language is what he must use to experience human love. In Rousseau's terms, it is a "supplement" to nature. The Monster tells Frankenstein: "I easily perceived that, although I eagerly longed to discover myself to the cottagers, I ought not to make the attempt until I had first become master of their language, which knowledge might enable me to make them overlook the deformity of my figure, for with this also the contrast perpetually presented to my eyes had made me acquainted" (108).

Language is richly thematized at this moment of the novel. With the arrival of Safie, we have lessons in French offered to an Arab, in the context of what we know to be a German-speaking region, the whole rendered for us in English. This well-ordered Babel calls attention to issues of communication and transmission, in somewhat the same manner as the narrative frames of the novel. The Monster learns language through overhearing, and observing, the instruction of Safie by Felix and Agatha. He learns to read—that is, he masters language in what is for Rousseau its mediate form, supplementary to the spoken word: the form in which it is most transmissible, since it does not demand presence, the specular relation, for its exchange, yet also the form in which it is potentially most deceitful, freed from immediate expressivity. The three texts which the Monster now discovers and reads—Plutarch's *Lives,* Goethe's *Werther,* and Milton's *Paradise Lost*—cover the public, the private, and the cosmic realms, and three modes of love. They constitute a kind of minimal Romantic *cyclopedia universalis.* Of the three, it is *Paradise Lost*—in the literalist reading the Monster gives it—that excites the profoundest reactions, and poses in emblematic terms the enigma of the Monster's nature. In the manner of Adam, he appears to be a unique creation, "united by no link to any other being in existence" (124). Yet, "wretched, helpless, and alone," he is unlike Adam. "Many times I considered Satan as the fitter emblem of my condition, for often, like him, when I viewed the bliss of my protectors, the bitter gall of envy rose within me." In particular, the intertextual presence of *Paradise Lost* insistently poses the relation of language to the specular, especially in the implicit comparison of the Monster to Eve, in two passages in which he views himself in a mirroring pool. "I had admired the perfect forms of my cottagers—their grace, beauty, and delicate complexions; but how was I terrified when I viewed myself in a transparent pool! At first I started back, unable to believe that it was indeed I who was reflected in the mirror; and when I became fully convinced that I was in reality the monster that I am, I was filled with the bitterest sensations of despondence and mortification" (108). This echoes Eve's report of the day of her creation, in Book 4 (460–76) of *Paradise Lost.* After first awakening to life, she finds a mirroring lake:

WHAT IS A MONSTER?

As I bent down to look, just opposite,
A Shape within the wat'ry gleam appear'd
Bending to look on me, I started back,
It started back, but pleas'd I soon return'd,
Pleas'd it return'd as soon with answering looks
Of sympathy and love; there I had fixt
Mine eyes till now, and pin'd with vain desire,
Had not a voice thus warn'd me, What thou seest,
What there thou seest fair Creature is thyself,
With thee it came and goes; but follow me,
And I will bring thee where no shadow stays
Thy coming, and thy soft imbraces, hee
Whose image thou art, him thou shalt enjoy
Inseparably thine, to him shalt bear
Multitudes like thyself, and thence be call'd
Mother of human Race: what could I do,
But follow straight, invisibly thus led?

The passage of course recalls Ovid's Narcissus, and anticipates Lacan's scenario of the infant's discovery of his reflected self—both same and other—at the mirror stage. Narcissism is here a temptation to which Eve, immediately enamored of her own image, would succumb, pining "with vain desire," were it not for the intervention of a divine voice that commands her to set aside this moment of primary narcissism in favor of sexual difference. The place "where no shadow stays" is almost explicitly the place of the phallus, as opposed to the insubstantiality of the female's sex and the love of two female bodies. As the Miltonic scenario unfolds, Eve's first perception of Adam is not itself sufficient to move her beyond primary narcissism: Adam is "fair indeed and tall," she says, "yet methought less fair, / Less winning soft, less amiably mild, / Than that smooth wat'ry image; back I turn'd" (4:478–80). She would return to the "answering looks" of the lake were it not that Adam at this point seizes her hand, and she yields to what is for Milton, in his thoroughly misogynist scenario, the explicit hegemony of the male.

Milton's story is thus about Eve's discovery of the law, which is variously the command of God, the law of sexual difference, and the rule of the phallus. In her submission to the law, she gives up desire for her own image, and for indifferentiation, with reluctance, in a prefiguration of her subsequent disobedience. The Monster, on the other hand, discovers himself as different, as violation of the law, in a scenario that mirrors and reverses Lacan's; the outer image—that in the mirror—presents the body in its lack of wholeness (at least in human terms) while the inner apprehension of the body had up until then held it to be hypothetically whole: "At first I started back, unable to believe that it was indeed I who was reflected in the mirror." The experience is anti-narcissistic, convincing the Monster that he is, indeed, a monster, thus in no conceivable system an object of desire. As the Monster will put it in the second passage of self-reflection, "Increase of knowledge only discovered to me more clearly what a wretched outcast I was. I cherished hope, it is true, but it vanished when I beheld my person reflected in water or my shadow in the moonshine, even as that frail image and that inconstant shade" (125). The mirror image becomes the negation of hope, severing the Monster from desire. He is simply outside the law, and thus will require a separate creation—his own Eve—in order to come under its sway. Thus his narrative plea to his creator concludes by focusing the discourse of desire on a new object to be desired, the monster woman.

The Monster's self-reflections in relation to *Paradise Lost* are succeeded by his discovery of the literal story of his creation, in Frankenstein's laboratory journal, which he finds in the pocket of the coat he has worn since the day of his creation. Here, he discovers that he is the anti-image of Adam: "God, in pity, made man beautiful and alluring, after his own image; but my form is a filthy type of yours, more horrid even from the very resemblance" (125). Self-recognition as "filthy type" completes the mirror stage of the Monster's development. He now knows he must trust wholly in the symbolic order. Having mastered language, he goes to confront the patriarch de Lacey. The "godlike science" at first appears to achieve the desired effects: "I am blind," de Lacey responds to the Monster's plea, "and cannot judge of your countenance, but there is something in your words which persuades me that you are sincere" (128). Sympathy is on the point of creating the Monster's first entry into the social chain, when Felix, Agatha, and Safie enter the cottage, and the Monster is brutally returned to the specular order: Agatha faints, Safie flees, and Felix violently separates the interlocutors. The Monster in consequence becomes explicitly Satanic: "I, like the arch-fiend, bore a hell within me" (130); he sets fire to what had late been his happy seat, and sets forth into the world in search of the hidden face of his creator, the *deus absconditus* who alone, now, has the power to bring him into social relation, through a second monstrous creation.

Along the way to his meeting with Frankenstein, the Monster—after being shot and wounded by a rustic whose daughter he has saved from drowning—commits his first murder, that of Frankenstein's brother William, in a scene that evokes the question of relation in the most acute ways. The Monster's first idea is to take the boy as a companion; in a common Enlightenment thought experiment, he conceives that a child is probably too young "to have imbibed a horror of deformity" (136). His error is immediately apparent: to his address of "Child," William in return calls him "monster! Ugly wretch! . . . ogre." But what provokes the murder is William's exclamation that his father is "M. Frankenstein"—Victor's father also, of course, and by extrapolation the Monster's "grandfather"—whom the Monster here calls "my enemy." When William lies dead at his feet, the Monster notices a miniature portrait worn around his neck: "I took it; it was a portrait of a most lovely woman. In spite of my malignity, it softened and attracted me. For a few moments I gazed with delight on her dark eyes, fringed by deep lashes, and her lovely lips; but presently my rage returned; I remembered that I was forever deprived of the delights that such beautiful creatures could bestow and that she whose resemblance I contemplated would, in regarding me, have changed that air of divine benignity to one expressive of disgust and affright" (136). This moment of scopophilic fixation, of the gaze erotically medused by its (painted) object, has a special resonance because we know (as the Monster does not) that the portrait is of William and Victor's dead mother. The novel is notable for the absence of living mothers: Felix and Agatha's mother is dead (and the word "mother" nowhere figures in the language lesson observed by the Monster), so is Safie's, Madame Frankenstein dies after contracting scarlet fever from her adopted daughter, Elizabeth—Frankenstein's intended bride—and the Monster of course has no mother, only a "father." The portrait of the dead mother thus represents an essential lack or gap in existence, most particularly for the Monster, whose primal erotic experience here is directly Oedipal, but censored from the outset: the father's interdiction of the mother as erotic object to the son has never been so radical as in the case of Frankenstein and his created Monster.[8]

The Oedipal overtones of the scene become richer and more complex as we read on. Having taken the portrait, the Monster enters a barn, where he finds a sleeping woman—Justine Moritz—whom he describes as "young, not indeed so beautiful as her whose portrait I held, but of an agreeable aspect and blooming in the loveliness of youth and health" (137). In imitation of Satan whispering into the ear of the sleeping Eve in *Paradise Lost,* the Monster whispers to Justine: "Awake, fairest, thy lover is near—he who would give his life but to obtain one look of affection from thine eyes; my beloved, awake!" But this first attempt at seduction on the Monster's part is self-censoring: when the sleeper stirs, the Monster reflects that if she awakes, she will denounce him as a murderer. As a consequence, he decides to pin the murder on her. 209 "Thanks to the lessons of Felix and the sanguinary laws of man, I had learned how to work mischief." He plants the mother's portrait in the folds of her dress and flees, with the reflection: "The crime had its source in her; be hers the punishment!" The claim is curious and excessive, since Justine is in no manner the "source" of William's murder, which takes place before the Monster has discovered her sleeping form. In the logic of desire, if not in syntax, we must find the referent of "her" in the mother herself. Under the (paternal) interdiction of the mother, the monster-child turns to a substitute woman, in a clear example of what Freud calls an "anaclitic" object choice.[9] When it becomes apparent that this object choice, too, is forbidden, censored at the root, the erotic drives turn to death drives, to sadism. The stolen portrait becomes, in the manner of Rousseau's famous stolen ribbon, a token of the reversibility of drives and the inversion of love offerings into poisoned gifts.

The story of this double crime terminates the Monster's narrative. He has now only to sum up the demand to which all his story has tended: "I am alone and miserable; man will not associate with me; but one as deformed and horrible as myself would not deny herself to me. My companion must be of the same species and have the same defects. This being you must create" (137). The Monster thus attempts to state the object of his desire. In constructing his narrative appeal, he has contextualized desire, made it, or shown it to be, the very principle of narrative, in its metonymical forward movement. This movement, in Lacanian terms, corresponds to the slippage of the inaccessible signified—the object of unconscious desire—under the signifier in the signifying chain. The movement now, as so often when stories are told to a narratee, passes on the desire to the interlocutor, who is charged explicitly with finding the object of desire: of crossing the "bar" of repression between signifier and that other occulted signifier that stands in the place of the signified of desire, in this instance by the creation of that which is supposed to signify desire. And yet, the Monster's call for a female companion, however sincere, may be only in the realm of conscious desire, may not have access—as how could it?—to what lies under the bar.

If one considers that desire (again in Lacanian terms) is born in the split between need and demand, where demand is always in excess of need (for nourishment from the breast, essentially) and is always an absolute demand for recognition, and thus desire is essentially unappeasable since it is driven by infantile scenarios of fulfillment, one wonders whether Frankenstein's provision of a female companion would really satisfy the Monster. Love depends on demand—it is the creation of speaking beings—and is in essence the demand to be heard by the other. What matters is not so much the content of the demand as the fact that it is unconditional; it expresses "not the desire of this or that, but desire *tout court*," writes Lacan. What is finally desired by the speaker is "the desirer in the other," that is, that the speaking subject himself be "called to as desirable."[10] The Monster's unconscious desire may most of all be for unconditional hearing, recognition, love from his parent. Its absolute requital could only take the form of handing over the mother, which in this case is barred not only by the law of castration but more radically still, since this mother does not exist and has never existed.

It appears that the Monster's artful activation of the symbolic order, in his narrative plea, results in a demand to his listener that, in its consciously stated desire, brings us back into the order of the imaginary—to the desire for phantasmatic satisfactions, impossible to fulfill. How can you create a mother substitute, or a relationship of the "anaclitic" type, when there is no mother to substitute for? The radically absent body of the mother more and more appears to be the "problem" that cannot be solved in the novel. The female monster, furthermore, is conceived quite simply as the mirror image of the Monster, with solely the sexual difference: she has no other definition than "a female me," which suggests her place in a primal narcissism which the Monster needs to, and cannot, go beyond, however "filthy" his mirror image. This inability to escape primal narcissism is suggested by other near-incestuous relations in the novel, particularly the marriage of Frankenstein and Elizabeth.

The female monster will never fully come into being. Frankenstein tears her nearly completed body to pieces, in another scopic scene: the Monster is watching at the window of the laboratory with a "ghastly grin" which turns to a "howl of devilish despair and revenge" when his promised body is denied him (159). It is as if the Monster's phallic gaze at the female monster's body makes Frankenstein aware of the bodily potential of a sexed pair of monsters. Ostensibly, Frankenstein abrogates the contract he has made at the end of the Monster's narrative appeal through his reflection on the "Eve problem": that procreation by the monsters will be simply a "propagated curse," and that the female monster, as a secondary creation, "might refuse to comply with a compact made before her creation" (158)—she might, like Eve, disobey the paternal injunction, which in this case stipulates exile from the inhabited parts of the globe. To allow the couple to create a race of monsters would be to create a new and wholly uncontrollable signifying chain from their desire, one whose eventual outcomes "might make the very existence of the species of man a condition precarious and full of terror." Rather than accepting a nurturing role toward the Monster, offering him "the small portion of happiness which was yet in my power to bestow" (140)—as he has decided to do at the close of the Monster's narrative—Frankenstein performs the ultimate gesture of castration on the desiring Monster.

211

The destruction of the female monster negates any hope that the Monster might gain access to a "chain of existence and events" that would offer him relation and the possibility—even the phantasmatic possibility—of satisfaction for his desire. The godlike science of language has proved deceptive: it has contextualized desire as lack, as metonymic movement in search of the meaning of desire, but it has not provided a way to overcome lack and satisfy desire—as, indeed, language never can. The Monster's error is to believe that signs in artful rhetorical patterns can produce the desired referent from one's interlocutor. His definition as monster leads him to an overvaluation of language, as that which could take him out of that specular position. Yet he is required, by the logic of desire, to attempt to make language produce another body, to return to the imaginary, the specular, and the drama of sexual difference.

The result is an exacerbated agon of desire between the Monster and Frankenstein, whereby the Monster strikes at Frankenstein, not directly, but through elements in Frankenstein's own "chain of existence and events": after William and Justine Moritz, Frankenstein's bosom friend Henry Clerval and his bride (and also adoptive sister) Elizabeth. "I will be with thee on thy wedding-night," the Monster tells Frankenstein after the destruction of the female monster (161), a remark that Frankenstein interprets as a direct menace to his person, thus repressing what the reader at once grasps: that the threat is to Elizabeth. On the wedding night he sends Elizabeth to the nuptial chamber alone, while he prowls about, armed with pistols, looking to engage in combat with the Monster. "Peace, peace, my love," he says to Elizabeth; "this night, and all will be safe; but this night is dreadful, very dreadful" (185). We may read this dread as related to the quasi-incestuous nature of his union with Elizabeth. As his father has said, in sounding Frankenstein's intentions: "You, perhaps, regard her as your sister, without any wish that she might become your wife" (144). Frankenstein denies this sentiment, but we cannot help but be struck by the complication and overlapping of kinship relations in the novel (as in the family in which Mary Shelley grew up), especially because they are thrown in high relief by the Monster's own lack of relation. As the Monster once again watches from the window, the wedding night ends in a necrophilic embrace, which may be in the logic of incestuous desire: "I rushed towards her and embraced her with ardour, but the deadly languor and coldness of the limbs told me that what I now held in my arms had ceased to be the Elizabeth whom I had loved and cherished. The murderous mark of the fiend's grasp was on her neck, and the breath had ceased to issue from her lips" (186). The Monster has marked the body of Frankenstein's bride at the moment when Frankenstein's desire is on the point of consummation, in dialectical response to the destruction of his monstrous bride. The Monster has put his body in the way of Frankenstein's desire.[11]

Frankenstein's narrative from this point on tells of the struggle of his nearly transferential relation with the Monster, where each represents the lack or gap in the other. "You are my creator, but I am your master;—obey!" (160) the Monster has said to Frankenstein, in a phrase that represents the impossibility of the situation in which each becomes for the other the "subject supposed to know" but neither can furnish satisfaction of the other's lack. Like the Monster, Frankenstein becomes explicitly Satanic: "like the archangel who aspired to omnipotence, I am chained in an eternal hell" (200). The Monster leads a chase that will take them to the lifeless polar regions, maintaining the willpower and the strength of his pursuer by leaving inscribed indications of his route and caches of food. "Come on, my enemy; we have yet to wrestle for our lives" (195) reads one inscription, nicely balancing enmity and affection.

The Monster, Frankenstein states following William's murder, is "my own vampire, my own spirit set loose from the grave and forced to destroy all that was dear to me" (74). The statement is as excessive and curious as it is accurate. It turns the Monster into a symptom, in Lacan's sense of the term—that is, a metaphor, a signifier standing for the indecipherable signifier of unconscious desire. It may ultimately speak of the sadism inherent in all intersubjective and especially familial orders of relation. In particular, it may in this novel suggest the destructive affect that inhabits the relational order of language, and particularly narrative language, in the transferential situation of telling and listening. The Monster's narrative of unrequited desire and unappeasable lack cannot produce access to the referent of desire. Instead, it passes on desire and lack, through the signifying chain of language and through the interlocutionary relation established in language, with the result that lack and desire come to inhabit the listener. As listener or narratee, once you have entered into a narrative transaction with the Monster, you are yourself tainted with monsterism: you cannot break out of the relation established by the pronouns "I" and "thou" once they are seen as complementary, each elusively representing the answer to the lack within oneself. The interlocutionary relation, like the transferential relation in psychoanalysis, could be dissolved only by the production of that which would answer the Monster's lack. Because this is impossible, lack is passed on through the narrative frames—which is indeed what the framing structure of the novel is all about.

Frankenstein, once he has become interlocutor to the Monster, is marked by the taint of monsterism, which he can never appease or dispel. When in turn, in the next frame (working out from the inside), Walton becomes Frankenstein's interlocutor, he, too, is marked by this taint. Walton, we note, is at the outset of the novel in a position analogous to Frankenstein's when he sets about his act of creation: he, too, is seeking for Promethean knowledge, dominion over the unknown, which in his case means exploration of the unknown polar regions. And like both Frankenstein and the Monster, he is searching for relation; he complains to his sister, Margaret Saville, that he has no one "to participate my joy" or to "sustain me in dejection" (18). Frankenstein speaks for both of them when he says: "I agree with you . . . we are unfashioned creatures, but half made up, if one wiser, better, dearer than ourselves— such a friend ought to be—do not lend his aid to perfectionate our weak and faulty natures" (27). Friendship, relation, interlocution, suggest an ideal model of the androgyne, which, as in the Platonic myth, has been split in half and now desires the missing half. But by the end Walton's hopes for both Promethean conquest and friendship lie "blasted," as his mutinous sailors vote to turn southward and Frankenstein sinks into death (204). All that remains to Walton is his epistolary narratee, his sister; and as he explains to her, being reduced to writing is no substitute for the living interlocutionary relation: writing is "a poor medium for the communication of feeling" (18). Moreover, his sister may never even receive these letters written from beyond the social world. In any event, for the reader of the novel, Mrs. Saville has no more existence than a postal address, or even a dead-letter office—the place where messages end up when they have nowhere else to go. Her lack of characterized personality makes her all the more effectively stand for the reader, as the ultimate receiver of all the nested messages of the novel.

Thus it is that the taint of monsterism, as the product of the unarrestable metonymic movement of desire through the narrative signifying chain, may ultimately come to rest with the reader of the text. Like Frankenstein at the close of the Monster's act of narration, like Walton at the end of Frankenstein's narrative, we have a residue of desire and meaning left over, which we must somehow process. Perhaps it would be most accurate to say that we are left with a residue of desire *for* meaning, which we alone can realize. One could no doubt say something similar about any narrative text, especially any narrative that dramatizes the fact and the process of its transmission, as "framed tales" always do. In *Frankenstein,* the thematization of the passing on of unresolved desire for meaning is particularly evident because the key question, the vital enigma, concerns the nature of monsterism itself. What is a monster? Reading inward from the outermost frame, the reader is led to believe that he or she is making a nearer approach to the solution to this problem; when the Monster speaks in his own person, assumes the pronoun "I," we enter the subjectivity of monsterism. But that solves nothing, and as we read outward from the innermost frame, we come to realize that we are following the process of the passing on of this unresolved question, in an unarrestable metonymy of desire.

In closing his narrative to Walton, Frankenstein warns his interlocutor against listening to the Monster's voice: "He is eloquent and persuasive, and once his words had even power over my heart; but trust him not . . . Hear him not" (198–99). Yet when the Monster does finally appear to Walton, saying farewell to Frankenstein's corpse, Walton bids him stay, and soon his impulses to destroy the destroyer of his friend are "suspended by a mixture of curiosity and compassion" (208)—the very elements required to seal again the interlocutionary relation, to produce a new narrative transaction. It is the Monster who unknots this relation—and its possible production of a new narrative frame, a new nested box containing the Monster and Walton—when he announces that he has resolved to destroy himself. Once the other of his transferential desire has ceased to be, the only choice that remains for the Monster is self-immolation. He announces to Walton: "Neither yours nor any man's death is needed to consummate the series of my being and accomplish that which must be done, but it requires my own" (210). A moment before, he has stated that with Frankenstein's death, "the miserable series of my being is wound to its close" (207). "Series" is here used in the sense of "sequence" or "order." Conceptually, this phrase is related to the "chain" which figures the Monster's understanding of human inter-relation, and its counterparts in language and narration. Failing to enter the "chain of existence and events," his narrative sequence has wound down to self-destruction. But the order in which he signifies cannot so easily be brought to a close, as the passing on of narrative messages, and narrative desire, may suggest.

In his peroration over Frankenstein's corpse, the Monster also claims: "Blasted as thou wert, my agony was still superior to thine" (211). While the context assigns the cause of this superior agony to the Monster's remorse, we may want to read it, more absolutely, as a statement about the fact of being a monster. That is the supreme agony, which no other problem in desire can efface. The phrase, like so much else in the novel, returns us to the question, What is a monster? The novel addresses this question in different registers. Initially, there is the creation of the Monster, which is a result of Frankenstein's illicit curiosity. He takes, in his youth, to reading such alchemical literature as Cornelius Agrippa, Paracelsus, Albertus Magnus. When his father censures such work as "trash," he—like Dora with her volume of Mantegazza—seems to be only the more convinced that they will enable him to "penetrate the secrets of nature" (38–39). He finds that philosophy has only partially "unveiled the face of Nature." "I had gazed upon the fortifications and impediments that seemed to keep human beings from entering the citadel of nature, and rashly and ignorantly I had repined" (39). Frankenstein recapitulates here the traditional imagery of nature as a woman, and proposes that truth is a difficult penetration into her body. As in the case of Dora, epistemophilia finally centers on the woman's body as the key to forbidden knowledge.

When he reaches the university at Ingolstadt, he falls under the spell of the chemistry professor Waldman, who tells him that modern scientists "penetrate into the recesses of nature and show how she works in her hiding-places" (47). This increases his desire to discover the hidden principle of life itself, to be able to bestow animation on inanimate matter—the Promethean revelation at the center of the text, which it of course censors. He then learns how to proceed backward from death to a new life, using the "loathsome" robbing of graves to create a new living species. "Life and death," he recalls, "appeared to me ideal bounds, which I should first break through, and pour a torrent of light into our dark world" (52). Yet when, after two years of intense labor, he stands over his created body and sees "the dull yellow eye of the creature open," his heart is filled with "disgust" and he flees from his progeny.

Frankenstein's intense curiosity for forbidden knowledge, coupled with his hysterical reaction to witnessing its realization, suggest, as the imagery of unveiling and penetration already indicated, that his epistemophilia centers on the arcana of the woman's body, specifically the mother's body in its reproductive function. The novel, as the psychoanalyst Marc A. Rubenstein has so well observed, is full of "primal scene imagery," to the extent that "the spirit of primal scene observation penetrates into the very structure of the novel and becomes part of a more deeply hidden search for the mother."[12] The Freudian primal scene is an intense object of infantile curiosity which, even without actual observation by the infant, can have the status of a "primal phantasy." Parental copulation is of course for any individual the origin of origins, the very "citadel of nature." The novel suggests a fixation on the primal scene in the conjoined obsession with origins on the part of both Frankenstein and his Monster—who are both deprived of a literal mother on whom to exercise their curiosity, with the result that they must strive to create the scene—and in the intensely visual nature of the scenes created. Most pertinent here are the scenes of the Monster's creation (the moment when the Monster opens his eye produces Frankenstein's hysterical reaction, very much in the manner of the traumatic dream of Freud's "Wolf Man"); the aborted creation of the female monster as the Monster watches at the window; and the wedding night, which recapitulates the Monster at the window, watching the nuptial bed become a bier.[13] Every time we reach one of the novel's manufactured primal scenes, something monstrous happens, and the observer is stricken, punished.[14] The very structure of the novel, as Rubenstein argues, suggests the pervasive effects of primal scene curiosity, a need to witness the forbidden moment of origin, which produces the inextinguishable taint of monsterism that gets passed on through the narrative chain.

It is significant, too, that the creation of the Monster from Frankenstein's studies in physics and chemistry, which are always on the verge of becoming metaphysics and alchemy, takes place on the borderline of nature and culture. The Monster is a product of nature—his ingredients are 100 percent natural—yet by the process and the very fact of his creation, he is unnatural, the product of philosophical overreaching. Since he is a unique creation, without precedence or replication, he lacks cultural as well as natural context. He radicalizes the situation of Eve, who also has no "model"—Adam is created in God's image, God is male; thus in whose image is Eve created?—and is hence a unique creation, but one that will then be replicated by half the human race. The Monster is, so to speak, postnatural and precultural. That a monster can be created within nature may stand as something of an indictment of nature itself, especially when one considers the generally ambiguous conceptual position of nature in the novel. An important thematic focus of this ambiguity is the figure of Henry Clerval, a being formed "in the very poetry of nature," Frankenstein tells us (quoting Leigh Hunt), who is described through the citation of lines from Wordsworth's "Tintern Abbey":

> The sounding cataract
> Haunted *him* like a passion: the tall rock,
> The mountain, and the deep and gloomy wood,
> Their colours and their forms, were then to him
> An appetite; a feeling, and a love,
> That had no need of a remoter charm,
> By thought supplied, or any interest
> Unborrow'd from the eye.

The italicized "him" replaces the "me" of the original. The lines are traditionally taken to represent the speaker's first, immediate, unreflective relation to nature, now lost to him but operative still in his sister Dorothy, to whom he can say that "Nature never did betray / The heart that loved her." Clerval loves and trusts nature, but he falls victim to the monstrous creation of his best friend and explicitly pays for Frankenstein's destruction of the Monster's mate. There is more to nature than sounding cataracts and sublime mountains: there is also one's friend's accursed curiosity, creating monsters demanding sexual satisfaction. It is in the awesome natural sublimity of the Alps, where Frankenstein has gone to seek consolation, that the Monster appears to his creator. One senses in Mary Shelley's novel a profound dissent from some of the more optimistic Romantic views of the moral principles embodied in nature—a dissent which recent readings of Wordsworth and P. B. Shelley find figured in some of their most problematic moments.

WHAT IS A MONSTER?

Nature in *Frankenstein* appears not to be a principle at all: it is rigorously amoral, it is absence of principle.

What, then, in unprincipled nature, is a monster? A monster is that outcome or product of curiosity or epistemophilia pushed to an extreme that results—as in the story of Oedipus—in confusion, blindness, and exile. A monster is that which cannot be placed in any of the taxonomic schemes devised by the human mind to understand and to order nature. It exceeds the very basis of classification, language itself: it is an excess of signification, a strange byproduct or leftover of the process of making meaning. It is an imaginary being who comes to life in language and, once having done so, cannot be eliminated from language. Even if we want to claim that "monster," like some of the words used by Felix and Agatha—"dearest," "unhappy"—has no referent, it has a signified, a conceptual meaning, a place in our knowledge of ourselves. The novel insistently thematizes issues of language and rhetoric because the symbolic order of language appears to offer the Monster his only escape from the order of visual, specular, and imaginary relations, in which he is demonstrably the monster. The symbolic order compensates for a deficient nature: it promises escape from a condition of "to-be-looked-at-ness."

That, we recall, is the term that Laura Mulvey applies to the "traditional exhibitionist role" given to women in the cinema.[15] When one considers the Monster's creation in the place of the absent mother, his role and very definition as the insistent object of visual inspection, with the inevitable hysterical reaction, and his equally insistent attempt to redefine his person within the medium of language, especially narrative language as the vehicle of interpersonal relation, one may ask if the Monster is not in fact a woman who is seeking to escape from the feminine condition into recognition by the fraternity.[16] The very peculiarity of a novel about the monstrous that insistently stages its central issues in terms of language, rather than in sheerly visual terms—characteristic, for instance, of Gothic novels—would thus become doubly determined: on the thematic level, by the Monster's attempts to escape the imaginary order; and in the creative process itself, by Mary Shelley's attempts to escape the generic and cultural codes that make heroines into objects to be looked at—a fate that such heroines as Jane Eyre or Gwendolen Harleth never entirely escape. If, as Mulvey and other feminist film theoreticians have argued, the male gaze defines both the place of the female and the codes for looking at and defining her—and also the very genres that stage that looking—we may want to understand the persistent counter-visual emphasis of the Monster himself, and the contexts created around him, as an effort to deconstruct the defining and classifying power of the gaze, and to assert in its place the potential of affect created in interlocutory language—as used, notably, in the relation of love.

The Monster would thus be a woman, but a woman who would answer Freud's infamous question "What does a woman want?" with the ostensible reply: to be a male, with a female to love. In the failure of that project, the Monster is forced to play the role of the castrating Medusa woman.[17] The novel of course never for a moment suggests that the Monster is anything but a male, and both Frankenstein and his creature assume that he is sexually functional as a male (there would otherwise be no need for Frankenstein to destroy the female monster). Yet the Monster never is given the chance to function sexually, and we are never given a glimpse of those parts of the body that would assure us that he is male. Of course we aren't: such is not part of the discourse of the novel (setting aside pornography) at the time. But this necessary cultural reticence, subjected to our retrospective critical pressure, may add a further ambiguity to the problems of definition of monster—may indeed add another dimension to that question "What is a monster?" A monster may also be that which eludes gender definition. In this sense, *Frankenstein* would be a more radical version of that considerable body of Romantic and "Decadent" literature—such as Théophile Gautier's *Mademoiselle de Maupin*, Henri de Latouche's *Fragoletta*, Balzac's *Sarrasine*, Rachilde's *Monsieur Vénus*—that uses cross-dressing and hermaphroditism to create situations of sexual ambiguity that call into question socially defined gender roles and transgress the law of castration that defines sexual difference. The Monster's demand for recognition by his father could then be read not only as desire for the absent mother but as a wish to be a sexual object for the father, in the manner of Freud's Senatspräsident Schreber.[18] Because a monster is that which calls into question all our cultural codes, including language itself, we can understand the persistent afterlife of Mary Shelley's creation, which shows us that, quite literally, once you have created a monster, whatever the ambiguities of the order of its existence, you can never get rid of it.

In this context, one might reflect on the moment when Frankenstein perceives the Monster for the first time following his flight from the scene of its creation. It comes when Frankenstein is on his way home after receiving news of William's murder. It is another of those scenes that bring into play the sublime power of nature. A storm breaks out in the Alps, a tempest "so beautiful yet terrific" (73). "This noble war in the sky elevated my spirits; I clasped my hands and exclaimed aloud, 'William, dear angel! This is thy funeral, this thy dirge!'" No sooner has he uttered these words than a flash of lightning reveals the presence of the Monster: natural sublimity once again produces the monstrous. With this revelation swiftly comes the thought that the Monster must be William's murderer. "*He* was the murderer! I could not doubt it. The mere presence of the idea was an irresistible proof of the fact" (73–74). The logic of the "mere presence of the idea" becoming an "irresistible proof of the fact" does not stand the test of reason. It is an excessive conclusion. Yet it is also true. The statement in fact mimes the process of creation of the Monster, who from a scientific idea becomes a bodily fact: an idea embodied.

We are always led back, in *Frankenstein*, to the peculiarity that this cultural creation, this epistemophilic product, has become part of nature—that the idea or concept of the monster, which at first has no referent in the natural world, gains one. It gains this referential status as a body. On a basic level, it is nothing but body: that which exists to be looked at, pointed to, and nothing more. You can't do anything with a monster except look at it. Like Virgil's Cyclops, it blocks out the light, including the light of reason, if reason be a matter of mental classification and rationalization. In this manner, the Monster offers an inversion of the many scenarios we have noted, in Balzac and other novelists, in which the human body is marked or signed in order to bring it into the field of signification, so that it can be a narrative signifier. In *Frankenstein*, language is marked by the body, by the process of embodiment. We have not so much a mark on the body as the mark of the body: the capacity of language to create a body, one that in turn calls into question the language we use to classify and control bodies. In the plot of the novel, that body cannot be touched by any of the human bodies; apparently indestructible, it can be eliminated only when the Monster himself chooses to burn himself up. "I shall ascend my funeral pile triumphantly and exult in the agony of the torturing flames" (211). Note that his words are in the future tense. The Monster's death never is recorded within the novel; it never becomes matter for retrospective narration. We know it is not so easy to get rid of the monstrous body linguistically created. Mary Shelley's monster is still out there. It has taken a permanent place in our imaginary.

8 Talking Bodies, Delicate Vessels

What in the midst of that mighty drama are girls and their blind visions?
They are the Yea and the Nay of that good for which men are enduring
and fighting. In these delicate vessels is borne onward through the ages
the treasure of human affections.

George Eliot, *Daniel Deronda*

H O W   D O E S   T H E body mean? The body in the nineteenth century,
we noted, is predominantly a body scrutinized, and not only in literary
discourse. At a time when the positivist sciences were vastly extending
their mastery over nature, there was necessarily a greatly increased
attempt to master the body in systematic discourses principally founded
on its visual inspection. In medicine, as Michel Foucault has shown, the
medical gaze—the evidence of the eyes—becomes newly dominant starting in the last years of the eighteenth century. The clinic becomes a space
for examining, comparing, and classifying diseases, and the opening of
the body—the dissection of cadavers—becomes the focus of medical
training.[1] A number of popular pseudo-scientific discourses claim authority in "reading" the body: the physiognomy of Johann Caspar Lavater, the animal magnetism of Franz Mesmer, the enduringly popular
phrenology invented by Franz Joseph Gall, the attempted establishment
of criminal typologies on the basis of physical characteristics by Cesare
Lombroso, the measurement of cranial capacities in the "anthropome-
trics" of Alphonse Bertillon. "Victorian scientists harbored an intense
somatic bias," writes Cynthia Eagle Russett in her study of nineteenth-
century biological and medical thinking; and their attention to the body
was directed through sight.[2] The century's most triumphant piece of
deduction from observation, and its most persuasive systematization of
how human bodies came to be what they are, were no doubt realized in
Charles Darwin's theories of evolution and natural selection, including
sexual selection. Various social Darwinisms then charted all sorts of
theories for future management of the body.

The psychiatric profession emerges in the nineteenth century as a discipline of those bodies that are improperly governed by their minds. During much of the century, psychiatry, in the manner of other branches of medical science, is intent on establishing the organic bases of its object of study. It seeks to find lesions on the brain to account for hysteria and other classified disorders. But the meaning of mental illness, and the way it reveals and dramatizes itself on the body, presents perplexities not so easily resolved. The search for their solution is in part responsible for new understandings of what and how the body signifies, leading by the end of the century to the revolution worked by Freud and to the establishment, in psychoanalysis, of one relatively coherent discourse of the body: a discourse founded in study of a certain pathological body—that of the hysteric—but then generalized to all bodies and the psychic conditions they signify. The way Freud comes to understand the language of the body, and to claim a necessarily narrative interpretation of it, is one of the subjects of this chapter. The other is how a novelist, George Eliot, in her extraordinary last novel, *Daniel Deronda,* attempts to understand the woman's body, to make it something other than an object of vision, and to supplant the visual with another kind of narrative model.

The Hysterical Body

It is useful to touch on some episodes in the history leading up to Freud's narrative constructions of bodily meaning. Medicine appears to enter its modern phase in the last years of the eighteenth century, and psychiatry assumes recognizably modern form at the politically, socially, and symbolically crucial time of the French Revolution, notably in the work of Philippe Pinel, which was influential well beyond France.[3] Concerned essentially with what was then known as "monomania," Pinel developed what he called the "moral treatment" (*traitement moral,* where the French *moral* connotes the English "psychological" as well as "moral"), meaning a therapy that, rather than attempting to deal with symptoms by direct action on the body (purging, bleeding, and so forth), sought to deal with those obsessive ideas that, Pinel believed, underlay the symptoms. Pinel thus anticipates Freud in understanding that mental illness, and its treatment, may have nothing to do with organic factors.

Most striking about the *traitement moral,* in our post-Freudian retrospect, is the dramaturgical and narrative nature of its therapies. Pinel arranged situations in which his patients' obsessional ideas, the bases of their "melancholy," could be acted out. For instance, in the case of a tailor who had uttered unpatriotic sentiments during the Reign of Terror, and had fallen into a morbid fear of the guillotine in which he could not eat or sleep, Pinel arranged to have three young physicians dress in the black robes of magistrates and present themselves at the asylum as a special tribunal. After interrogation of the tailor, they solemnly pronounced him to have "only the sentiments of the purest patriotism."[4] The mock trial worked—though the cure apparently did not prove lasting. The staged event constitutes an acting out of psychic conflict that one occasionally finds in the imaginative literature of the time— notably in the work of Balzac—and then in Freud's mature conception of transference, a dramaturgical space created between patient and analyst in which the patient's past affective life is replayed as if it were in the present tense.[5] One can perhaps fault Pinel's dramas only for being too much concerted by the doctor alone, rather than being the "dialogic" creation of patient and doctor.

Pinel's therapies also anticipate Freud's in some of the ways in which the body is made to signify, ways in which commonsense uses and meanings of bodily parts are supplanted by other charges of significance. For instance, there is the case of one of the most famous clockmakers in Paris, who is obsessed by the idea of building a perpetual motion machine. Overwork, combined with the alarms of the Revolution, finally lead to insanity, in the form of the belief that he has been decapitated on the guillotine and then, in a reversal of his sentence, given back a head—but the wrong one. To combat the notion that the clockmaker is wearing the wrong head, Pinel enlists the aid of another inmate at Bicêtre, who undertakes to discuss with the clockmaker the miracle of Saint Denis, who after decapitation is said to have walked with his head in his hands while covering it with kisses. The clockmaker argues that the legend is wholly plausible, citing his own decapitation as proof. To which the other inmate queries, with mocking laughter, what Saint Denis could in the situation kiss his head with—perhaps his ass? We are told that this question covered the clockmaker with confusion, that he ceased to speak of his decapitation, and that he returned to work and eventually to his family and never had a relapse.[6] This farcical recombination of the body, with its bodily pun on ass-kissing, looks forward to some of the obsessional symptoms which will call forth Freud's ingenious bodily hermeneutics.

Pinel was appointed chief physician for the insane at Bicêtre in 1793, as the result of a decision to "medicalize" treatment in what had prior to the Revolution been a nonmedical operation. In 1795, he was transferred to the Salpêtrière, the asylum for insane women, which in 1802 received a number of madwomen who were considered curable from the Hôtel-Dieu, in order to further his research. His brilliant career was thus a direct product of the French Revolution which, in treatment of the insane as in so many other social domains, marked a new attempt to rationalize institutions. The imagery of Pinel is very much linked to the Revolution, notably in the painting by Tony Robert-Fleury (dating from 1883), which depicts Pinel ordering the chains and manacles removed from the insane. This liberating gesture was in fact performed by Pinel when he took over the direction of the insane at Bicêtre. In Robert-Fleury's painting, we have the impression that the scene takes place at the Salpêtrière: it is notably women who are being unchained. Their dazed faces and contorted bodies strikingly represent the later nineteenth-century history of the cultural construction of insanity, which concentrated on women and on the woman's body as the place where insanity enacts its indecipherable messages.

Robert-Fleury's painting hung in the lecture hall of the Salpêtrière where, in the 1880s and 1890s, the celebrated J.-M. Charcot gave his weekly lectures. The connection between the two physicians is made by Freud in his obituary of Charcot (1893): "Charcot had repeated on a small scale the act of liberation in memory of which Pinel's portrait hung in the lecture hall of the Salpêtrière" (*Standard Edition* 3:19). Charcot's important contributions to the study of hysteria derived from his decision to take the condition seriously—not, for instance, to see it as malingering—and to describe with precision its various manifestations, to distinguish and label its stages and kinds, and particularly to classify the contractures and seizures associated with what he called "hystero-epilepsy." Hysteria of course has a long history, reaching back even earlier than Hippocrates, who named it after the *hystera* or uterus.[7] In the case of hysteria, nomenclature was destiny: it was conceived to be a female malady, and for centuries held to be the result of a wandering womb, whose displacement had to be corrected to effect a cure. Even when this view was discredited, the uterine theory took diverse other forms, ascribing hysterical manifestations to various troubles of the female reproductive system, including disorders of the ovaries. Charcot repeatedly protested against the etymological definition of hysteria, and indeed produced numbers of male hysterics to prove his point. But if he absolved the uterus, he tended nonetheless to see the hysterical constitution and disposition as feminized—in men as well as women—and he produced his most spectacular demonstrations with women.

In his work with hypnosis, Charcot was able to show that in many instances hysteria was not organically determined, but somehow the result of ideas that had dominated in the hysteric's psychic life at the time of a traumatic experience. It would be Pierre Janet, Josef Breuer, and Freud himself who would draw the consequences from this discovery and seek the etiology of hysteria in the patient's psychic life history, particularly in what had been repressed from consciousness. Charcot remained limited by his observational and descriptive context. Freud tells us that Charcot described himself as "un visuel," and indeed all the work of the Salpêtrière was remarkably oriented toward visual observation. Charcot's famous "leçons du mardi," in which he would examine a patient, supposedly without prior preparation, before an audience of disciples, were notoriously theatrical—and led to the accusation that his zealous assistants in fact prepared the women to be examined through suggestions, given under hypnosis, that would make them produce the symptoms the master wanted to find. The famous painting of Charcot at work—*La leçon clinique du Dr. Charcot* (1887), by André Brouillet, very much a pendant to the Pinel painting—shows him lecturing his disciples next to a woman whose torso is thrown back in a melodramatic posture, one that incidentally bares her shoulders, thrusts her bosom forward, and makes her, in this company of men, an object in which mental illness and female sexuality are visually linked. The young science of photography was given an important role in the Salpêtrière, to record the various stages of hysteria; a photographic studio and darkroom were installed, and from 1876 onward, an annual *Iconographie photographique de la Salpêtrière* was published.[8] A male viewer of those photographs, especially those of the "attitudes passionnelles" supposed to be characteristic of the "third period" of a hysterical attack, finds himself in the position of the voyeur summoned to look at the female body fixed and inspected by a new technology at the service of medical discourse. Charcot's treatment of hysteria very much belongs to the history of the nineteenth century's concern to capture the mysterious, rebellious female body in the field of vision.

The movement from Charcot to Freud can be aptly summarized— Stephen Heath has effectively done so—as a shift from seeing to listening.[9] Rather than viewing symptoms (or indeed, what one might describe in Charcot's case as "spectacularizing" them) Freud took his clue from the suggestions offered by his mentor Breuer's famous case of Anna O., who herself named the therapy she in large measure invented, with Breuer's intelligent collaboration, as "the talking cure."[10] If therapy can

225

TALKING BODIES, DELICATE VESSELS

take the form of verbalizing the histories and the associations surrounding the formation of hysterical symptoms—tracing back their ideational content—it is because symptoms themselves are the somatic result of psychic processes. The famous formula, "hysterics suffer mainly from reminiscences," does not mean that those reminiscences are abstract, that they are memories in intellectual form. They become so only through the work of therapy. To begin with—when the patient suffering from hysterical symptoms comes to the analyst—memories are unavailable to consciousness. They are rather written on the body. A large part of "the talking cure" is learning to listen to and interpret the body. And this can occur only when one has learned to understand the body as a writing and talking body. Freud takes a decisive forward step in the long history of reclaiming the somatic for meaning. In doing so, he creates our most thorough and convincing semiotics of the body.

Perhaps the most striking examples of Freud's efforts to make the body talk come when he discovers, or postulates, what are essentially bodily puns: moments in which the body is seen as directly though covertly enacting, as in a rebus, a word or verbal phrase. The case of Fraülein Elizabeth von R., Freud's first full-length case history—in *Studies on Hysteria* (1895)—offers some notable instances. She is suffering from violent pains in the legs, which, in the course of analysis, she associates with a series of unhappy family events that "had made the fact of her 'standing alone' painful to her" (*Standard Edition* 2:152). The hopelessness of ever moving out from the nexus of family unhappiness is further glossed as giving her "the feeling that she could not 'take a single step forward.'" In technical terms, Freud is describing the process of conversion, whereby the affect displaced from a repressed memory attaches itself to a bodily symptom which represents its hidden presence. But Freud also describes the process as "symbolization," by which his patient creates in her pain and difficulty in standing and walking "a somatic expression for her lack of an independent position and her inability to make any alteration in her circumstances" (2:176). In other words, a psychic state is written directly on the body, though in a covert form that the subject does not consciously understand. Freud supplements these examples from the case of Fraülein Elizabeth von R. with some others produced by Frau Cäcilie M., who is suffering from a severe facial neuralgia and who eventually is able to recall a scene of argument with her husband in which he speaks what she takes to be a bitter insult. "Suddenly she put her hand to her cheek, gave a loud cry of pain and said: 'It was like a slap in the face'" (2:178).

One cannot overestimate the radical nature of Freud's shift in interpretive paradigms here. Prior to her therapy with Freud, Frau Cäcilie M. has been treated by "the electric brush, alkaline water, purges"; seven of her teeth have been extracted, on the assumption that they were causing the neuralgia; and since some of the roots were left behind, further dentistry has been performed. To move from the assumption of an organic cause for the neuralgia to the hypothesis that it symbolizes the effect of a verbal insult, interpreted as a slap in the face, is to reorient definitively our understanding of the body and how it signifies. What is inscribed in Frau Cäcilie M.'s bodily pain is the symbolization of a mental affect. This particularly clear and simple example allows us to understand Jacques Lacan's insistence that symptom is metaphor, in his terms the substitution of one signifier, inscribed in the body's pain, for another, which is unavailable to consciousness since it lies under the "bar" of repression. In fact, in this instance there is a possible contaminating effect of metonymy on metaphor, as is so often the case in purely verbal, including literary, uses of metaphor.[11] When Freud makes his way back to what he believes to be Cäcilie's first attack of neuralgia, at age fifteen, he finds that there was, rather than symbolization, "a conversion through simultaneity": a painful sight, accompanied by feelings of self-reproach and repression, a "case of conflict and defense," that may have coincided with a "slight toothache or pains in the face" caused by her first pregnancy. This first type of conversion then was reactivated in her symptom in a process of direct symbolization.

Frau Cäcilie produces another symptom: "a violent pain in her right heel—a shooting pain at every step she took, which made walking impossible" (2:179). Analysis traces this pain's onset back to a stay in a sanatorium, to the moment when she is to leave her bed for the first time and go down to the dining room. The pain is created from her fear that she might not "find herself on the right footing" with the strangers with whom she was to dine—an instance that looks forward to the more sensational example of Dora's "faux pas," the phantasized misstep which leads to her hysterical reproduction of pregnancy. With Frau Cäcilie, the examples continue to accumulate, including "a stabbing sensation in the region of the heart (meaning 'it stabbed me to the heart')" (180). Freud is led, in the final paragraph of the case history, to a general speculation on the relation of language to physical sensation:

How has it come about that we speak of someone who has been slighted as being "stabbed to the heart" unless the slight had in fact been accompanied by a precordial sensation which could suitably be described in that phrase and unless it was identifiable by that sensation? What could be more probable than that the figure of speech "swallowing something," which we use in talking of an insult to which no rejoinder has been made, did in fact originate from the innervatory sensations which arise in the pharynx when we refrain from speaking and prevent ourselves from reacting to the insult? (2:181)

Freud refers us here to Darwin's *The Expression of the Emotions in Man and Animals* (1872), which argues that such expressions originally were actions, serving purposes. Sensations and innervations, Freud continues,

> may now for the most part have become so much weakened that the expression of them in words seems to us only to be a figurative picture of them, whereas in all probability the description was once meant literally; and hysteria is right in restoring the original meaning of the words in depicting its unusually strong innervations. Indeed, it is perhaps wrong to say that hysteria creates these sensations by symbolization. It may be that it does not take linguistic usage as its model at all, but that both hysteria and linguistic usage alike draw their material from a common source.

One senses an unresolved hesitation in Freud's thought here. The appeal to Darwin's *Expression of the Emotions* seeks to ground bodily expression in physical reactions, in external stimuli and the corresponding inner emotions, which over the course of evolution have attenuated into "mere" verbal representations. Darwin writes, for example: "My object is to show that certain movements were originally performed for a definite end, and that, under nearly the same circumstances, they are still pertinaciously performed through habit when not of the least use."[12] Darwin moves among the lower and the higher animals, establishing, for instance, that the expression of anger or affection in dogs and apes can be explained according to his three principles: the principle of serviceable associated habits, the principle of antithesis, and the principle of actions due to the constitution of the nervous system. Some emotional manifestations are susceptible of only rather hypothetical treatment, notably blushing, which has the peculiarity that it cannot be induced by physical means but must rather be produced by the mind. "Blushing" is one of the most instructive chapters in Darwin's work from a post-Freudian perspective, but it remains resolutely attached to physiology. In citing Darwin, and in closing his case history with the concession that hysterical symptoms may not involve symbolism at all, but may rather reach back to a common physical source of hysteria and linguistic usage, Freud comes close to renouncing the radical nature of his discovery.

Yet this is only one tendency of Freud's argument here, and the sanction of Darwin may cover another line of thought, which may well have influenced Darwin too. In arguing the origin of "figures of speech" in physical sensation, Freud inscribes his thought in a long Romantic tradition of reflection about the origins of language: a tradition that includes Rousseau (though his reflections are, as always, complex and difficult), Johann Gottfried Herder, the Grimm brothers, Johann Georg Hamann, and many others. This tradition wants to see language, and especially poetic language, as rooted in the imitation of natural actions and sounds. As Ralph Waldo Emerson put it, "Words are signs of natural facts . . . Every word which is used to express a moral or intellectual fact, if traced to its root, is found to be borrowed from some material appearance." And Herder claimed: "Every family of words is a tangled underbrush around a sensuous central idea, around a sacred oak, still bearing traces of the impression received by the inventor from this dryad . . . what was this first language of ours other than a collection of elements of poetry? Imitation it was of sounding, acting, stirring nature!"[13] Language in this tradition is considered radically and naturally metaphorical, and thus originally "poetic." The evolution of languages marks a necessary decline into greater abstraction, and into logical prose. Metaphors become "dead metaphors," figures of speech "mere figures." It then becomes the role of the poet to revive the latent metaphoric substratum of language, to make it speak afresh of bodily sensation and natural phenomena—as, for instance, in the relatively trivial but much-debated instance of onomatopoeia. It is not surprising that Freud attaches himself to this tradition, which after all was very much part of his formation as a late nineteenth-century humanist. He suggests his place in the tradition when, in one of his letters to Wilhelm Fliess, he reflects on the possible evolution of the verb *machen* (to make or to do) from an original reference to excretion, with connotations of work and accomplishment. He comments: "An old phantasy of mine, which I should like to recommend to your linguistic penetration, deals with the derivation of our verbs from originally copro-erotic terms like this" (*Standard Edition* 1:273). Many of Freud's later linguistic meditations,

TALKING BODIES, DELICATE VESSELS

such as the essay "The Antithetical Meaning of Primal Words" (1910), reflect this concern to trace words and verbal figures back to bodily experience, in a way that evokes both the Darwinian view of expressivity as an attenuated action, and the Romantic view of language as an imitation of natural phenomena.

The two traditions indeed are not wholly distinguishable or separate, however different the discourses that convey them. If language is originally borrowed from nature, its expressivity is like that analyzed by Darwin in the various signs by which emotion is expressed. But if language incorporates a notion of physical sensation—as in "a stab in the heart"—there is really no need to reach back through language to its supposed origins in sensory innervations. One can, as it were, act on the implications of the linguistic sign itself, act out its metaphor. In this sense, Freud's hysterics are behaving like poets, restoring life to dead metaphors. (They are, one could say, poets of primitivism, restoring meanings that are archaic, both in terms of their own lives and in the life of humanity.) Freud himself, in his case-histories of hysteria, in a sense gives new life to a novelistic tradition of the deciphering of bodily signs. If one reflects, for instance, on the long history of blushing in the novel, it is apparent that it is used as a sign in a highly coded psychological system, which makes of a blush, in certain specific contexts, a sure avowal of emotions that the actor might wish to conceal. At its most fully codified, the system of expression permits the creation of such a figure as Choderlos de Laclos' Madame de Merteuil, in *Les liaisons dangereuses,* who has learned perfectly to control her own verbal and facial expressions—to dissimulate thoroughly—while becoming the perfectly "penetrating" observer of the signs displayed by all other members of society. Freud, more in the spirit of a Romantic than an eighteenth-century novelist, remotivates conventional signs, showing the drama that can lie in the expression that one has been "slapped in the face." In his mature thinking, he implicitly moves beyond the Romantic tradition to suggest a view of language closer to that of structural linguistics: an understanding of symptom as metaphor, as part of a signifying operation that does not need to pass through the intermediate hypothesis of sensations. A well-known example occurs in the essay "Fetishism," where he reports the case of a young man "who had exalted a certain sort of 'shine on the nose' into a fetishistic precondition" (*Standard Edition* 21:152). The young man had been brought up "in an English nursery," but later had forgotten his English. His phrase is *Glanz auf der Nase* (shine on the nose), which in analysis turned out to be a bilingual pun in which *Glanz* stood for "glance." "Shine on the nose" thus translated into "glance at the nose," where the nose stood for the missing phallus in a typically scopophilic scenario. Here, one recognizes the determining power of the linguistic signifier itself in the establishment of a symptom-atology: as well as the capacity of the body to enact language, the power 231 of language to write the body. In Freud's mature thought, symptom is metaphor, in the rigorously linguistic sense defined by Lacan.

The specific bodily metaphors discovered in the cases of Fraülein Elizabeth and Frau Cäcilie need of course to be set in a larger story, the whole life story of the patient, which has caused psychic conflicts, through the work of desire and repression, to become inscribed as symbols in somatic form. Symptoms make sense, they speak, only as part of a narrative. In a celebrated comment in his discussion of the case of Fraülein Elizabeth von R., Freud remarks with bemusement:

> I have not always been a psychotherapist. Like other neuropathol-ogists, I was trained to employ local diagnoses and electro-prog-nosis, and it still strikes me myself as strange that the case histories I write should read like short stories and that, as one might say, they lack the serious stamp of science. I must console myself with the reflection that the nature of the subject is evidently responsible for this, rather than any preference of my own. The fact is that local diagnosis and electrical reactions lead nowhere in the study of hysteria, whereas a detailed description of mental processes such as we are accustomed to find in the works of imaginative writers enables me, with the use of a few psychological formulas, to obtain at least some kind of insight into the course of that affection. Case histories of this kind are intended to be judged like psychiatric ones; they have, however, one advantage over the latter, namely an inti-mate connection between the story of the patient's sufferings and the symptoms of his illness—a connection for which we still search in vain in the biographies of other psychoses. (2:160–61)

Psychoanalysis is necessarily narrative, and indeed, in its theoretical formulations, necessarily a "narratology": a study of how narrative works. The psychoanalyst is ever concerned with the stories told by his patients, who are patients precisely because of the weakness of the narrative discourses that they present—the incoherence, inconsistency, and lack of explanatory force in the way they tell their lives. The narrative account given by the patient is riddled with gaps, with memory lapses, with inexplicable contradictions in chronology, with screen memories concealing repressed material. Its narrative syntax is faulty and its rhetoric unconvincing. The work of the analyst must in large measure be a recomposition of the narrative discourse to give a more coherent—and thus more therapeutic—representation of the patient's story, to reorder its events, to foreground its dominant themes, to understand the force of desire that speaks in and through it.

While Breuer's report of the case of Anna O. displays the aridity of the psychiatric case history—composed of accumulated examples of symptoms and reasoned analysis of them—Freud's often read as dramatic narratives whose literary models are perhaps more than anything else the adventures of Sherlock Holmes. Take, for instance, the case of Miss Lucy R., which begins: "At the end of the year 1892, a colleague of my acquaintance referred a young lady to me who was being treated for chronically recurrent suppurative rhinitis . . . Latterly she had complained of some new symptoms which the well-informed physician was no longer able to attribute to a local affection. She had entirely lost her sense of smell and was almost continuously pursued by one or two subjective olfactory sensations. She found these most distressing. She was, moreover, in low spirits and fatigued, and she complained of heaviness in the head, diminished appetite and loss of efficiency" (2:106). With the appropriate transpositions, it sounds like the start of a number of Sherlock Holmes's cases in which a young lady in fear and distress comes to the Baker Street consulting room: "She raised her veil as she spoke, and we could see that she was indeed in a pitiable state of agitation, her face all drawn and gray, with restless, frightened eyes, like those of some hunted animal. Her features and figure were those of a woman of thirty, but her hair was shot with premature gray, and her expression was weary and haggard."[14]

As the case of Miss Lucy R. develops, patient and analyst pursue the meaning of a persistent smell of burnt pudding. Freud, like the detective, starts from "the assumption that my patients knew everything that was of any pathogenic significance and that it was only a question of obliging them to communicate it" (2:110). Under Freud's questioning—no hypnosis is used in this case, only the application of his hand to the patient's forehead—a scene emerges in which Miss Lucy's harassment by other servants in the household where she is governess is connected with the burning of a neglected pudding. But this situation seems inadequate to explain the strength and persistence of the symptom. Freud offers the hypothesis that she is in love with her employer. This will lead to the production of a replacement symptom: a persistent smell of cigar smoke, which allows the recovery of another, earlier scene, in which her employer behaved badly to his chief accountant. We have come closer, but still the scene doesn't explain its symptomatic result. Freud continues: "And now, under the pressure of my hand, the memory of a third and still earlier scene emerged, which was the really operative trauma and which had given the scene with the chief accountant its traumatic effectiveness" (2:120). This was the scene that "had crushed her hopes" of becoming the object of her employer's affections. With high drama, the originary, the true, the explanatory scene emerges, to solve the case and justify the analyst's hypothesis. What the body is trying to say in its symptoms is detectable only by way of a narrative account, one that takes us back into the past, to reorder the patient's original story in terms of causes and effects whose linkage has been lost from consciousness.

"It is interesting to notice," writes Freud toward the end of his "Discussion" of the case, "that the second symptom to develop masked the first, so that the first was not clearly perceived until the second had been cleared out of the way" (2:124). One seems to hear an echo here: "'The principal difficulty in your case,' remarked Holmes in his didactic fashion, 'lay in the fact of there being too much evidence. What was vital was overlaid and hidden by what was irrelevant. Of all the facts which were presented to us we had to pick just those which we deemed to be essential, and then piece them together in order, so as to reconstruct this very remarkable chain of events.'"[15] Freud continues: "It also seems to me worth while remarking upon the reversed course which had to be followed by the analysis as well. I have had the same experience in a whole number of cases; the symptoms that had arisen later masked the earlier ones, and the key to the whole situation lay only in the last symptom to be reached by the analysis." Like the detective story, the analysis is an inquest, moving back from present symptoms, clues presented to the analyst, to the signs left by earlier events, and eventually back to the beginning in order to construct the chain of events leading up to the scene of suffering. The narrative chain, with each event connected to the next by reasoned causal links, marks the victory of reason over chaos, of society and sanity over crime and neurosis, and restitutes a world in which etiological histories offer the best solution to the apparently unexplainable.

We know that Freud was a reader of Sherlock Holmes and that he himself perceived the close analogies between psychoanalysis and detective work.[16] It is perhaps not surprising that Freud's early case histories closely resemble the adventures of the London detective. He is on the track of what Breuer has mysteriously told him were always ultimately "secrets d'alcôve": secrets of erotic origin that must be constructed out of the present symptoms by way of a coherent narrative.[17] In these early versions of psychoanalysis, Freud at least implicitly claims that moving back from present symptoms, and the incoherent narrative offered in explanation of them, to the earlier symptoms covered by the later ones, and to their traumatic content, and then linking the events in an uninterrupted causal series, provides a narrative that is itself curative. Things soon become less straightforward and more difficult in Freud's understanding and practice of narrative. The constitution of a present narrative in relation to the story of the past becomes more complex and uncertain, the notion of causality more problematic; chronology itself is put into question by the workings of deferred action and retroaction; the parts played by event and by phantasm become more difficult to unravel. Already in the *Studies on Hysteria*—particularly in the case of Katharina—Freud discovers that a first traumatic experience can often become so only by way of a later experience, typically following puberty, that retrospectively sexualizes the first one and thus produces an affect that can become a hysterical symptom. Later—especially in the case of the Wolf Man—chronology and causality come to entertain even more complex relations, and the simple "chain" of the Sherlock Holmes story becomes an inadequate image. Still further complicating the writing of the narrative of the past that is to explain the present symptoms is Freud's progressive discovery of transference, which brings into play the dynamic interaction of the teller and listener, the dialogic relation of narrative production and interpretation. The observer/analyst discovers that he is implicated in the story which he is attempting to detect.

Dora's Case

Freud gives the psychoanalytic problem of narrative an extended discussion in his first book-length case history, the *Fragment of an Analysis of a Case of Hysteria* (written in 1900–1901, published in 1905), better known by the name of its subject, Dora. He begins a treatment, Freud notes, by asking the patient for "the whole story of his life and illness," but that is never what he receives. On the contrary: "This first account may be compared to an unnavigable river whose stream is at one moment choked by masses of rock and at another divided and lost among shallows and sandbanks." Freud's description of the patient's narrative continues: "The connections—even the ostensible ones—are for the most part incoherent, and the sequence of different events is uncertain . . . The patients' inability to give an ordered history of their life in so far as it coincides with the history of their illness is not merely characteristic of the neurosis. It also possesses great theoretical significance." The story of the life and the story of the illness must coincide *(zusammenfalten)*, and when they don't the story will have to be reworked by the analyst through other material, including bodily symptoms. After explaining that amnesias and paramnesias in the narrative serve the needs of repression, Freud concludes his preliminary discussion: "In the further course of the treatment the patient supplies the facts which, though he had known them all along, had been kept back by him or had not occurred to his mind. The paramnesias prove untenable, and the gaps in his memory are filled in. It is only towards the end of the treatment that we have before us an intelligible, consistent, and unbroken case history" *(Standard Edition* 7:16–18).

Mens sana in fabula sana: mental health is a coherent life story, neurosis is a faulty narrative. But Dora's is the case that decisively complicates Freud's understanding and practice of narrative, since in it he stumbles, as it were, upon the importance of transference as a crucial context in his effort to understand what his patient means, in word and body. Dora's case history is the key text of transition in Freud's understanding of narrative.[18] As the history of an aborted analysis, it reads like a failed Edwardian novel, one that can never reach a satisfactory dénouement, and that can never quite decide what the relations among its cast of characters truly are: as if Freud were one of Henry James's baffled yet inventive narrators (for instance, in *The Sacred Fount*), but one who must finally give it all up as a bad business.

Dora, we may briefly recall, insists that her father—who has brought her to Freud in order for Freud to "bring her to reason"—is having an affair with Frau K, despite his disclaimers, and, further, that she has been handed over to Herr K as payment for his tolerating the liaison between her father and his wife. This much Freud accepts as accurate, while insisting that she fails to recognize—represses—that she is in love with Herr K. His detective work, and his intellectual duel with the "sharp-witted" Dora, are mainly aimed at establishing this unavowed desire. Most readers of the case history will probably judge that Freud is on the wrong track: even if Dora may in some sense be "in love" with Herr K, the sordid mating game in which she is a pawn offers more than enough reasons to reject such a love.[19] One can nonetheless give a kind of abstract and perhaps grudging admiration to Freud's detective work in uncovering the attachment to Herr K that she denies. He finds, for instance, that Dora's governess has provided her with the kind of intimacy and affection she has given to the K's children—substituting, in both cases, for a lack of maternal concern. Since Dora herself analyzes the motive of the governess's attentions to herself as love for her father, Freud can, by a kind of structural homology, claim that her attention to the K children suggests her own love for Herr K. Then come the "proofs": her aphonia (loss of voice), matched with a fluency in writing letters, during Herr K's absences; her nervous cough, the pressure she feels on the thorax as a deferred result of Herr K's kiss. Further, Freud finds that Dora identifies both with her mother (previously loved by her father) and with Frau K (currently loved by her father), which allows him to establish her erotic feelings for her father, and indeed her revival of her feelings for her father as a "reactive symptom" used to suppress her love for Herr K. And yet, behind these feelings for the two male figures lies an erotic investment that is more deeply unconscious: her love for Frau K, the woman who "betrayed" her (by revealing her readings in sexology), who rivals with her for the men's love, and who curiously stands as the mysterious ultimate object of desire for everyone in the narrative. According to Freud, Dora is thus caught in a more complicated web of relations than even she at first believed—a complex of relations which Freud claims is necessary to make sense of her symptoms. One is reminded again of James's nearly contemporaneous novel, *The Sacred Fount,* where relations ramify in response to the narrator's "torch of analogy." What is at this point of Freud's case history inadequately factored in is the role of the detective-narrator, who himself may appear to be complicit with the men, Herr K and her father, who manipulate Dora.

Keeping in mind this factor of transference (including counter-transference) as a context of the relation between analyst and patient that will need further attention, we can turn first to the story—or stories, since they appear to be plural—that Freud detects in Dora's bodily symptoms. Plenty of these are present: her dyspnoea (shortness of breath), migraine, nervous cough, occasional aphonia; she develops a false attack of appendicitis, as earlier she underwent a false pregnancy. A symptom, Freud here announces, "signifies the representation—the realization—of a phantasy with a sexual content" (7:47). He is, then, more positive than in the *Studies on Hysteria* that the bodily represen-

236

tations of symptoms result from phantasies with sexual content. Let us take a first (and famous) instance. Dora breaks short her vacation with Herr and Frau K at an Alpine lake, later explaining to her mother that Herr K "had had the audacity to make her a proposal while they were on a walk after a trip upon the lake" (7:25). This incident in itself doesn't seem to Freud sufficiently traumatic. Then he discovers an earlier episode, when Dora was fourteen, in which Herr K, alone with Dora in his office, "suddenly clasped the girl to him and pressed a kiss upon her lips." Dora's reaction is a violent feeling of disgust, which Freud—with a phallocentric obtuseness that has been much criticized by commentators on the case—interprets as hysterical, a reversal of affect from pleasure to unpleasure. More interesting is Freud's interpretation of the displacement of sensation: Dora's disgust—a sensation in the mouth—and her statement that she can still feel upon the upper part of her body the pressure of Herr K's embrace lead Freud to reconstruct the scene. "I believe that during the man's passionate embrace she felt not merely his kiss upon her lips but also the pressure of his erect member against her body. This perception was revolting to her; it was dismissed from her memory, repressed, and replaced by the innocent sensation of pressure upon her thorax" (7:30). This migration of a sensation as it becomes a symptom—metaphor displaced, thus doubled by metonymy—leads to a whole "mapping" of Dora's body as Freud tries to explain how a single experience, Herr K's kiss, produces three symptoms (the disgust, the sensation of pressure on the upper body, and the avoidance of men "engaged in affectionate conversation"):

237

> The disgust is the symptom of repression in the erotogenic oral zone, which, as we shall hear, had been overindulged in Dora's infancy by the habit of sensual sucking. The pressure of the erect member probably led to an analogous change in the corresponding female organ, the clitoris; and the excitation of this second erotogenic zone was referred by a process of displacement to the simultaneous pressure against the thorax and became fixed there. Her avoidance of men who might possibly be in a state of sexual excitement follows the mechanism of a phobia, its purpose being to safeguard her against any revival of the repressed perception.

Here we have elements of what we might consider Freud's revisionary *carte du tendre:* the zones of the body as they can be erogenously activated to provide symbols that convey meaning.

Freud calls this reconstruction of the meanings derived from Herr K's kiss a "supplement" to Dora's story. Throughout this analysis—and his others—he seeks to supplement an original story that is essentially incomplete, full of gaps and implausibilities, incoherent links among events: a story that does not explain, and therefore is not therapeutic. Much of the supplementation takes the form of filling in the gaps in the story proffered by Dora with other material furnished by the interpretation of her bodily symptoms, and then by the interpretation of her two dreams, which in turn extend and supplement those symptoms. For instance, Freud claims to discover that Dora's aphonia corresponds to Herr K's absences, when she cannot speak to him—and in compensation manages to write letters with special ease. Freud then approaches the nervous cough by way of Dora's insistence that Frau K is having an affair with her father only because he is "a man of means" *(ein vermögender Mann)*. The way in which she says this phrase suggests to Freud that behind it lies concealed its opposite, *ein unvermögender Mann*, which could mean an impotent man (7:47). Dora, Freud claims, confirms this interpretation, and to his rejoinder that she contradicts herself in simultaneously maintaining that her father is carrying on an affair with Frau K and that he is impotent, she contends that she is aware that there is more than one way to obtain sexual gratification. This allows Freud to propose that she has been phantasizing a scene of fellatio between her father and Frau K, which explains the irritation of her own throat and mouth. Freud's logic hardly seems unimpeachable here, and his interpretation has been much criticized by commentators—led, in this instance, by Jacques Lacan.[20] But we may be interested, again, in how he uses his interpretation, even if it be erroneous, to map the erotic body. He finds a "somatic compliance" to be created from early experiences of sucking. "It then needs very little creative power to substitute the sexual object of the moment (the penis) for the original object (the nipple) or for the finger which does duty for it, and to place the current sexual object in the situation in which gratification was originally obtained" (7:52). Both aphonia and the nervous cough come to be symptoms that express several meanings, both simultaneously and in succession; it is part of the psychic economy of neurosis to reuse symptoms for different symbolic purposes once they have been formed.

Dora's body, in its production of symptoms, provides Freud with a generic script with which to supplement the incomplete story she has produced verbally. At a later moment in the analysis, when he has interpreted Dora's playing with her reticule as a "symptomatic act" signifying her desire to masturbate, Freud makes a general statement of his attitude toward such everyday symbolism, which most often goes unheeded:

> When I set myself the task of bringing to light what human beings   239
> keep hidden within them, not by the compelling power of hypnosis,
> but by observing what they say and what they show, I thought the
> task was a harder one than it really is. He that has eyes to see and
> ears to hear may convince himself that no mortal can keep a secret.
> If his lips are silent, he chatters with his finger-tips; betrayal oozes
> out of him at every pore. And thus the task of making conscious
> the most hidden recesses of the mind is one which it is quite possible
> to accomplish.   (7:77–78)

Freud here evokes the readings of ordinary speech and gesture that he performed, at nearly the same time as the Dora analysis, in *The Psychopathology of Everyday Life* (1901). The body's unintended speech enables him to plot that more complex narrative which, he claims, lies behind Dora's ostensible account.

Freud tells us that his first title for the case history was "Dreams and Hysteria," since the case seemed particularly well suited to demonstrating the role of the interpretation of dreams in an analysis. Dora's two dreams in fact occupy a large part of the case history, and both of them lead us back, through their verbal representations and Freud's interpretations of them, to the body again, as both the material of symbolism, the source of signifiers, and as ultimate signified. The first dream, in which Dora is awakened by her father because the house is on fire, turns on the "jewel-case": her mother wants to stop to save it, but her father refuses to let himself and the two children be burnt for the sake of the jewel-case. *Schmuckkästchen* (jewel-case) is, says Freud, a word "admirably calculated both to betray and to conceal the sexual thoughts that lie behind the dream" (7:91). In addition to its "innocent" meaning, it can refer to the female genitals, particularly if they are "immaculate and intact." The various trains of association in the dream—fire leading to bedwetting leading to masturbation leading to Dora's vaginal "catarrh"—all bring us back to the jewel-case. Not only does psychic life use the body to write its messages, as symptoms; but these messages eventually refer us back to the body once again, particularly to the site of sexual arousal and anxiety, as the place of desire and thus the source of story.

In the second dream, Dora is in a strange town, finds a letter from her mother announcing her father's death, looks for the station *(Bahnhof)*, sees a thick wood, finds herself back at home, and is told by the maid that the rest of the family has already gone to the cemetery *(Friedhof)*. In the course of interpretation of the dream, Freud begins to uncover "a symbolic geography of sex" (7:99). Dora's use of *Bahnhof* and *Friedhof* evokes *Vorhof*—"an anatomical term for a particular region of the female genitals." When to these are added the thick wood, and Dora's association with a painting she has recently seen that showed nymphs in a thick wood—"nymphae" being a name for the labia minora—Freud detects a representation of the female genitals. This representation, I note, is much like the sexual topography to be found in the final episode of Balzac's *La Duchesse de Langeais,* and also like the Renaissance "bower of bliss," and any number of eighteenth-century representations of the woman's sex in terms of bowers and thickets; Cleland's *Memoirs of a Woman of Pleasure* furnishes several examples. Dora's dream generates the most literary of metaphors for the woman's sex. In fact, anatomical representation in Dora's dream leads us to a book: Dora's "knowledge" of such technical terms as *Vorhof* and *nymphae* implies that her sexual curiosity led her to medical encyclopedias and to Mantegazza's *Physiology of Sex,* forbidden reading carried on with Frau K. Behind the dream lies the epistemophilic urge, curiosity about concealed knowledge of the woman's sexual body.

The most spectacular piece of interpretation of the second dream emerges from the conjunction of symptom and reading. Dora admits to having consulted a medical encyclopedia, but only in connection with an attack of appendicitis suffered by a cousin. Freud then remembers that she had reported an attack of appendicitis at some point in her past. She now states that "she had felt the pain in her abdomen that she had read about in the encyclopaedia" (7:101). The seeming appendicitis is then resolved by the onset of menstruation. Now, Dora connects this past symptom with a moment in the dream where she sees herself climbing stairs to her apartment, and relates that after her "appendicitis" she dragged her right foot, and had therefore tried to avoid stairs. Thus she has "used" her right foot as sign of the aftereffects of an illness read about in an encyclopedia, which, according to Freud, is really a displacement of "more guilty reading"—research into sexuality. The sexual nature of the causative factors of symptom formation is further elucidated when Freud asks about the time elapsed between the start of the foot-dragging symptom and the scene of Herr K's kiss by the lake, to receive the reply: nine months. Freud comments: "The period of time is sufficiently characteristic. Her supposed attack of appendicitis had thus enabled the patient with the modest means at her disposal (the pains and the menstrual flow) to realize a phantasy of *childbirth*" (7:103). Now an interpretation of the foot-dragging occurs to Freud: Dora senses   241 she has made a *faux pas* with Herr K, a "false step" resulting in a "childbirth" nine months later. In order to establish more solid grounding for this bodily pun, Freud searches for an infantile prototype of the symptom; and promptly finds it, when Dora confirms that as a child she had twisted the same foot—going downstairs—and had been unable to walk on it for some time.

Dora's "false step," inscribed on her body as Oedipus' casting out by his parents is inscribed in the wounded foot that names him, gives to Freud's text a note of triumph. He demonstrates to Dora that the childbirth phantasy points to her emendation of the scene by the lake—an emendation in which, rather than rejecting Herr K, she gives in to him—and thus that her love for Herr K has persisted, albeit in unconscious form, down to the present day. Here he tells us: "And Dora disputed the fact no longer" (7:104). This is the moment at which Freud's text makes the reader most uncomfortable, indeed sends the reader into revolt. Freud, we feel, has simply hammered Dora into submission, and forced her story into a shape which doesn't seem to take full account of the various binds and impossibilities of her situation. The best that can be said for Freud at this point is that he is not entirely unaware that he fails in Dora's case. She abruptly breaks off the treatment (having given an oblique warning in the business of the "two-weeks notice" produced by the governess whom Herr K also tried to seduce), an act of vengeance which forcibly brings Freud himself into the cast of characters with which Dora must contend—and perhaps also produces an act of retaliation by Freud, in the publication of Dora's case history. It turns out that all sorts of affects concerning Herr K and Dora's father have been playing off against the person of the analyst. Freud is not only the retrospective analyst of Dora's story, a privileged storyteller after the fact; he is part of it.

What comes to complicate Freud's relation with his patient is the workings of transference, by which the observer/analyst/detective loses his status outside the story and becomes part of it, in a "modernist" twist on the classical tale of detection. The transferential relation in turn complicates the case history he writes, since the relation of teller to listener becomes as important as the content and structure of the tale itself. Freud implicitly reveals that the relation of teller to listener inherently is part of the structure and meaning of any narrative text, in that the person who listens to a story and retransmits it inevitably becomes part of the interpretation and even the creation of that story. Following the failure in the case of Dora, any narrative account will have to give a place to transference, factor it in as part of the narrative situation.

Freud turns to the subject of transference in the case history precisely when it is too late to factor it into his writing, in the postscript. What are transferences? Freud asks:

> They are new editions or facsimiles of the tendencies and phantasies which are aroused and made conscious during the progress of the analysis; but they have this peculiarity, which is characteristic for their species, that they replace some earlier person by the person of the physician. To put it another way: a whole series of psychological experiences are revived, not as belonging to the past, but as applying to the person of the physician at the present moment. Some of these transferences have a content which differs from their model in no respect whatever except for the substitution. These, then—to keep to the same metaphor—are merely new impressions or reprints. Others are more ingeniously constructed . . . These, then, will no longer be new impressions, but revised editions. (7:116)

One is struck here by Freud's use of a textual metaphor to describe the transference. The transference is textual, we might say, because it presents the past in symbolic form, in signs, thus as something that is "really" absent but textually present, and which, furthermore, must be shaped by the work of interpretation carried on by both teller and listener. In other words, the way the narrative constructed from Dora's incomplete and fragmentary story, including the "supplementation" provided by her bodily symptoms, with their associations and interpretations, are put together—in a more successful analysis—must implicate the interaction of patient and analyst in an interactive and dialogic process. The way the body talks in psychoanalysis is reproductive and imitative, and takes as its interlocutor the other of the analytic situation. Such a complicating factor may be especially problematic when the patient is a woman, the analyst a man limited by the culture of patriarchy. Freud's flawed relation to Dora's story may betray most of all an insensitive relation to her body, ultimately to that "jewel-case" which he treats in rather cavalier fashion, with little sense for what George Eliot calls the "delicate vessels" of a young women's consciousness.

At the origin of psychoanalysis, Anna O. greatly distressed the respectable Breuer by producing a phantasy labor in which she was to give birth to his child—which led to his renouncing the treatment, and also to his suppression of this first evidence of the transference in the first case history of the *Studies on Hysteria.* In the *Studies,* Freud, in his first mention of the transference, calls such an involvement of the person of the analyst in the story a "false connection" (2:302). It is only in Dora's case that he comes to the realization that the false connection is also a necessary one, that "transference cannot be evaded," and that "it is only after the transference has been resolved that a patient arrives at a sense of conviction of the validity of the connections which have been constructed during the analysis" (7:116–17). The complexities encountered in the interpretation of Dora's symptoms—their overdetermination, the successive use of the same symptom to represent various affects, the displacement in time and site of the symptoms, the retroactive creation of somatic effects, the invention of complex verbal messages (such as puns) in condensed, compacted form—move Freud toward the more complex view of narrative that he would continue to develop in the case history of the Wolf Man and in such late essays as "Analysis Terminable and Interminable" and "Constructions in Analysis" (both from 1937). In many respects, it is the body of his patients (perhaps most of all the male body of the Wolf Man) that leads Freud to this more complex understanding of narrative, for these bodies insist, by way of signs, that they represent a past history of desire that can be made known and mastered in the present. In Freud's mature work, the body of the patient tells its story in a close corporeal relation to the analyst's body. The two bodies both are real, with their present physicality very much at stake, and are surrogates for other affective bodies from the past.

Dora's suffering body remains enigmatic to Freud, and one may be forced to the conclusion that the enigma of her body is very much what her story is about, for both patient and analyst. Lacan makes the point that Dora's homosexual attraction to Frau K—which Freud in a footnote considers to be "the strongest unconscious current in her mental life"— represents "a mystery, the mystery of her own femininity, we mean her bodily femininity—as it appears without veils in the second of the two dreams."[21] That dream, as interpreted by the analyst, centered on veiled representations of the woman's body as landscape. Freud concedes that he did not in the course of the analysis pay enough attention to Dora's love for Frau K, whose "adorable white body" she repeatedly praised "in accents more appropriate to a lover than to a defeated rival" (7:61). Freud notes: "These masculine or, more properly speaking, *gynaeco-philic* currents of feeling are to be regarded as typical of the unconscious erotic life of hysterical girls" (7:63). Indeed, the question posed by the hysterical body can be stated, according to Serge Leclaire, as: *Am I a man or a woman?*[22] Dora's curiosity about sexuality, her readings in Mantegazza and the encyclopedia—an epistemophilic drive very much oriented toward her own body—suggest a search for self-definition as a sexual body.

Hysteria, that is, always has to do with eros (while obsessional neurosis is connected to the death instinct or drive), and manifests a basic confusion about the identity of one's sexual body. Dora's homosexual desire, constructed on the original bisexuality of all human eros, puts into question the very gender distinction on which social life and expected comportment are based. The hysterical body in this manner threatens a violation of basic antitheses and laws, including the law of castration and the conditions of meaning. While the psychoanalyst interrogates the hysteric's body, the hysteric is also interrogating her own body. To read the hysterical body the analyst must renounce mastery and law-enforcing discourse in a way that Freud, at the time of Dora, cannot do. The hysterical body challenges the interpreter not only to find its story, but to revise conventional stories, to recognize that bodies exceed and infringe the social constructions of gender and desire.

These Delicate Vessels

A number of feminist critics have recently brought to our attention the high incidence of hysterical female bodies in fiction, especially in the novels of the later nineteenth century.[23] Charles Baudelaire promptly identified Emma Bovary as a hysteric (though one might now reclassify her as manic-depressive); Balzac's Foedora, the sexually ambiguous object of desire in *La peau de chagrin*, is an earlier example.[24] Zola seized on current medical representations of hysteria to present several of his women in crisis as subject to hysterical attacks. Edmond and Jules de Goncourt explicitly undertook study of the hysterical woman in *Germinie Lacerteux*. Barbey d'Aurevilly's women often reach moments of hysterical crisis—in *Le plus bel amour de Don Juan*, for instance, and *La vengeance d'une femme*—in which their bodies express what is repressed from consciousness, something always sexual in content. But these examples, which all concern male understandings and representations of the female body, interest me less than the attempt by a woman writer to make the hysterical woman's body the place of a special knowledge, the locus of a meaning that is not directly articulable but which, like Dora's resistance to Freud's "facts," revises our understanding of meaning, the kind of truth to be sought in narrative. The knowledge associated with the woman's body may belong to the story of women's curiosity, which so often—as in the case of Dora—brings both trouble and the affirmation that there is another narrative to the woman's life which the male gaze has failed to register.

245

Gwendolen Harleth, the heroine of George Eliot's *Daniel Deronda* (1876), seems by now to be well established in criticism as a hysteric. In particular, critics have dwelt on two scenes of hysterical conversion, in which Gwendolen goes rigid and white. First, the scene of charades and tableaux at Offendene, where she is to play Hermione in the moment from Shakespeare's *The Winter's Tale* in which the statue comes to life at the stroke of music; Herr Klesmer's "thunderous chord" on the piano apparently triggers the latch on the secret panel, which flies open to disclose "the picture of the dead face and the fleeing figure," provoking a "piercing cry" from Gwendolen. All eyes are drawn to her: "She looked like a statue into which a soul of Fear had entered: her pallid lips were parted; her eyes, usually narrowed under their long lashes, were dilated and fixed."[25] Herr Klesmer calls her reaction "a magnificent bit of *plastik*," attempting to allow her to pass it off as an effective piece of acting. But the acting is involuntary, produced on and by Gwendolen's body without her intention or her understanding of its meaning. It responds to what she obscurely recognizes as "that liability of hers to fits of spiritual dread," unmastered moments of "susceptibility to terror" (94). This scene of disclosure of what lies beneath the panel—"the picture of an upturned dead face, from which an obscure figure seemed to be fleeing"—prepares the moral climax of Gwendolen's story, with the drowning of her detested but feared husband, Grandcourt, an experience from which she emerges "pale as one of the sheeted dead" (750). She recapitulates over and over again to Deronda the scene of the drowning, and her conviction that, although it was accidental, it was also intentional since she wished him dead. It becomes a moment on which her psychic life will remain forever fixed: "a dead face—I shall never get away from it" (753); "But now—his dead face is there, and I cannot bear it" (758).[26] Thus the deepest ethical questions Gwendolen must pose to herself—about the nature of her motives and the definition of her character—take form as moments of hysterical conversion that must be unpacked in a language of moral and psychic analysis. And yet, these questions never can be wholly brought into language, even into that persistently probing language, familiar with scientific as well as poetic sources, that characterizes George Eliot's narratorial style. The language of the body at moments of crisis exceeds articulated speech and resists conceptual translation.

It is less the label of hysteria applicable to these two moments in *Daniel Deronda* that interests me than the questions of bodily knowledge and its meaning that they suggest. Even more interesting, in this context, is a third episode, which—between the charades at Offendene and Grandcourt's drowning—occurs on the verge of Gwendolen's wedding night, following her marriage to Grandcourt.[27] Brought to her husband's house at Ryelands, Gwendolen is "led by Grandcourt along a subtly-scented corridor, then into an ante-room where she saw an open doorway sending out a rich glow of light and colour" (405). It is in this "den" (as Grandcourt calls it), on the threshold of the nuptial chamber, that Gwendolen, reflected by mirrors—she "saw herself repeated in glass panels"—enters into a "moment of confused feelings and creeping luxurious langour" (406), the ambiguous prelude to the wedding night itself. A diversion is created by the arrival of a packet, which contains the family diamonds Grandcourt has promised her—diamonds which he had earlier given to his mistress, Lydia Glasher, and which she now, as promised, transmits to Gwendolen, but with a letter of irreparable vengeance:

> Within all the sealed paper coverings was a box, but within the box there *was* a jewel-case; and now she felt no doubt that she had the diamonds. But on opening the case, in the same instant she saw their gleam she saw a letter lying above them. She knew the handwriting of the address. It was as if an adder had lain on them. Her heart gave a leap which seemed to have spent all her strength; and as she opened the thin bit of paper, it shook with the trembling of her hands. But it was legible as print, and thrust its words upon her. (406)

Reading the letter produces in Gwendolen a "spasm of terror" which leads her to throw it in the fire; in her movement the casket falls to the floor and the diamonds roll out. "She took no notice, but fell back in her chair again helpless. She could not see the reflections of herself then:

they were like so many women petrified white; but coming near herself you might have seen the tremor in her lips and hands" (407). The scene, and the chapter—and all we ever learn about the wedding night—come to an end when Grandcourt, dressed for dinner, enters the room: "The sight of him brought a new nervous shock, and Gwendolen screamed again and again with hysterical violence. He had expected to see her dressed and smiling, ready to be led down. He saw her pallid, shrieking as it seemed with terror, the jewels scattered around her on the floor. Was it a fit of madness? In some form or other the Furies had crossed his threshold" (407).

It is no doubt stating the obvious to say that the scene plays out in symbolic form an unhappy Victorian wedding night, complete with the "adder" lying across the diamonds in the jewel-case, prepared for by "creeping luxurious langour" but resulting in multiplied images of "so many women petrified white," screams, hysterical violence—and the presence of the Furies. It is significant that Eliot can convey a sense of violation and the ensuing petrification of the woman without direct statement, using vocabulary and syntax all the more effective in that they mime the non-articulated quality of the woman's response, its very bodiliness.

The symbolic topography of George Eliot's scene makes it clear enough that the jewel-case that must be opened to assume ownership of the Grandcourt hereditary diamonds (they belonged to his mother) evokes the woman's genitals, even if we did not have the iteration provided by Freud's discussion of Dora's *Schmuckkästchen*. In the jewel-case in *Daniel Deronda*—which Grandcourt imprudently gave Lydia Glasher during his youthful passion for her, and which he makes a special journey to recover, although he has to be satisfied with Lydia's assurance that she will have them delivered to his bride—patriarchal possession and sexual transgression come together, as in the ultimate secret figured by the text. We recall that the very first pages of the novel also stage a drama of jewels, when Gwendolen pawns the necklace with turquoises that once belonged to her father in order to try her luck once more at the roulette table. The necklace is redeemed, anonymously, by Daniel Deronda, not yet introduced to Gwendolen but the fascinated observer of her at roulette, asking himself the famous questions that open the book: "Was she beautiful or not beautiful? and what was the secret of form or expression which gave the dynamic quality to her glance? Was the good or the evil genius dominant in those beams?" (35). One can read Deronda's return of the necklace as a critique of Gwendolen's insistence upon playing roulette. Playing, where jewels and jewel-cases are involved, may well represent masturbation. There is indeed a quality of narcissistic display to Gwendolen's behavior in the casino, and throughout the earlier part of her career as "The Spoiled Child," as the title of the first section of the novel has it. She enjoys being looked at by others, and repeatedly looks at herself in mirrors; she even at one point kisses her reflected image (47). Grandcourt's taking possession of the jewel-case whose contents represent his inheritance (although contaminated by the previous ownership of Lydia) puts an end to the play—and turns Gwendolen into the suffering woman who will be part of Deronda's learning experience.

Yet the scene of suffering on the threshold of Gwendolen's wedding night is not only about sexual violation and the male's taking possession of the woman's body. The diamonds have been sent by Lydia Glasher (whose very name suggests her melodramatic role in the novel) in a gesture whereby one woman strikes at another—strikes at her by way of her sex. The diamonds accompanied by the death-dealing letter—"I am the grave in which your chance of happiness is buried as well as mine"—suggests the transmission of poisonous knowledge from one woman to another. "It's a sort of Medea and Creüsa business," one of the characters will later comment (487), evoking Medea's revenge on the princess for whom Jason deserted her. The "poisoned gems" (407) specifically evoke sexual knowledge, like that passed from Frau K to Dora, used in vengeance to assure that the moment of Gwendolen's apparent worldly triumph in fact will seal her unhappiness. If Grandcourt can exercise control over the disposition of the jewel-case, the secret it contains finally is beyond the command of patriarchy.

Gwendolen's jewel-case, Dora's *Schmuckkästchen:* if these are representations of the woman's body in its private parts, and of a specifically feminine knowledge, how are they related to George Eliot's celebrated image of women as "delicate vessels"? The image comes at the conclusion of a passage which emphasizes the limited sphere of the young woman's experience, her confinement to private life (Deronda will in contrast have the world-historical itinerary): "Could there be a slenderer, more insignificant thread in human history than this consciousness of a girl, busy with her small inferences of the way in which she could make her life pleasant?" (159). The passage is in part an *ars poetica,* since the very premise of the Victorian novel—perhaps of the novel as a genre—is the unexpected significance of private life, the importance of the private individual and her consciousness amidst the stuff of dailiness.

Eliot by the end of the passage has reworked such a traditional justification into a melodramatic affirmation: "What in the midst of that mighty drama are girls and their blind visions? They are the Yea or Nay of that good for which men are enduring and fighting. In these delicate vessels is borne onward through the ages the treasure of human affections" (160). This affirmation of woman's role as carrier of human affection activates a traditional, even patriarchal, image of woman as womb, as a vessel of containment for the essence of humanity, which she transmits from generation to generation through acts of parturition and nurture. To the extent that the delicate vessel is the womb, it necessarily implicates the jewel-case, the woman's sex, her sexuality, and the social contracts transacted on her sex—transactions that have to do with ownership and transmission, which both figure as very important themes in the novel, the first in particular reference to the Grandcourt-Mallinger world, the second especially for Deronda and his relatives.

The womb is in fact the key to Deronda's story, since Jewish identity is traditionally transmitted through the mother. The momentous revelation of his parentage concerns not his father—who in many nineteenth-century novels is the occulted source of identity—but his mother, and the story of Mordecai and his sister Mirah turns on their dead mother. When Deronda reveals to Mordecai that Mirah has been found, he prepares his announcement by way of what might call a matronymic: she is introduced as "one who is closely related to your departed mother" (631). Then Deronda states: "Your sister is worthy of the mother you honored" (632). He refers, of course, to Mirah's preservation of her chastity, despite her father's attempt to sell her into prostitution. Mirah is a worthy vessel, and her womb, the last pages of the novel suggest, will be fertile, the vessel of transmission of a line that seemed in danger of extinction; whereas Gwendolen has no children by Grandcourt, and his estate passes to the son he had with Lydia Glasher, in a legitimation of bastardy. If Mirah's womb offers a future resolution of Deronda's story, the violation that gives access to Gwendolen's delicate vessel when she marries Grandcourt may make us question further woman's role as a vehicle of cultural transmission, the kind of culture she bears forward, and the role of woman's sexuality in relation to knowledge.

Both the delicate vessels and the jewel-case—and the locked panel over the terrifying picture that prefigures them—recall an ancient image associated with woman's knowledge: Pandora's box. Perhaps it is the most obvious pop psychology to point to the equivalence of Pandora's box and the female genitals, but it is worth noting that originally, in

Hesiod's *Theogony,* it was not a box but rather a jar that Pandora opened, so that the story of Pandora covers nicely both the jewel-case and the delicate vessels. As the archetypal story of female curiosity, it underlines those moments of Dora's history that involve curiosity, especially curiosity about the "forbidden" subject of sexuality (Dora's readings in Mantegazza, and so on), and about her own genitals and how they are to be used in a system of male-ordained exchange. Pandora and Dora together (did Freud give his patient a belittled version of the mythological character's name?) suggest a possible reading of Gwendolen with her jewel-case and as a delicate vessel. In the business of jewels (including that paternal necklace pawned in order to gamble), Eliot suggests that Gwendolen, like Dora, is interested in her own genitals, full of curiosity about their power to attract—as in her "dynamic gaze" that so intrigues Deronda at the start of the novel—and to create social transactions.

Gwendolen's story may be one more version of what Laura Mulvey has recently described as stories of female curiosity, emblematized by Pandora.[28] Mulvey mentions as an example Angela Carter's rewrite of the story of Bluebeard in her short story "The Bloody Chamber," which wittily and explicitly points to the myth in the titles of books the young bride finds in the library of her husband's castle—*The Initiation, The Key of Mysteries, The Secret of Pandora's Box*—and in the book illustration captioned "Reproof of Curiosity."[29] Left alone following her wedding night, she uses the one key on her husband's key ring that she has been forbidden to use, the one that opens the door to his "den" (the Marquis curiously uses the same word as Grandcourt, its animalistic overtone somewhat louder here), to find the remains of his three previous wives on the torture machines that ended their lives. The twist Carter gives to the tales of Bluebeard and Pandora comes in her heroine's understanding that the scenario of her curiosity has all along been controlled by the male: "The secret of Pandora's box; but he had given me the box, himself, knowing I must learn the secret. I had played a game in which every move was governed by a destiny as oppressive and omnipotent as himself, since that destiny was himself; and I had lost. Lost at that charade of innocence and vice in which he had engaged me. Lost, as the victim loses to the executioner" (34).

A "charade of innocence and vice": the phrase could also be used to characterize Gwendolen's wedding night which, like the earlier charade at Offendene, belongs to a patriarchal ritual in which "innocence" and "vice" are valuations set by the nuptial marketplace. (The charade at

Offendene staged a scene from *The Winter's Tale,* a play about the male's misprisions of female innocence and vice, and the ravages entailed by Leontes' insane jealousy.) A further twist of Carter's tale of course overthrows all this with the *dea ex machina* of the end, as the heroine's mother arrives on horseback to save her daughter from decapitation by the Marquis with a well-aimed bullet to his head.

Carter's version of Bluebeard makes us think of other traditional tales that also stage female curiosity. One that seems particularly pertinent is the tale of Sleeping Beauty, in the Grimm Brothers' version "Hawthorn Blossom" ("Dornroschen"). Because of her parents' failure to invite a thirteenth fairy, or old wise woman, to the feast in honor of her birth, Hawthorn Blossom is placed under a curse that she will die of a wound produced by a spindle—a fate commuted by one of the other fairies to a hundred years' sleep. Her father therefore undertakes to rid his kingdom of all spindles. But one day when Hawthorn Blossom—now sixteen years old—is alone in the castle, she finds a small closed room in a tower. She enters to find an old woman spinning, sees her spindle, asks its name, then touches it—and immediately falls into sleep, which envelopes the whole castle. A thick hawthorn hedge grows up round the castle. Would-be suitors who attempt to penetrate the hedge remain impaled on its thorns. Then, when the one hundred years' sleep has been accomplished, the Prince comes to the hedge, it parts of its own accord, he makes his way to Hawthorn Blossom, kisses her, she awakes—and life begins again throughout the castle. They are married, and live happily ever after.

Like so many of the Grimms' tales, "Hawthorn Blossom" seems to stage the mysterious processes of human maturation—processes that we can't really explain through logic, that must be given in narrative form, as a process. As in a number of other stories, particularly about young women, the natural processes of maturation go awry here: the girl is kept from all spindles, and when she does encounter this phallic object, she is plunged into an unnatural sleep. Her curiosity leads to "reproof." But temporal process will set things right. If the spindle suggests the male genitals, the hawthorn hedge evokes the female. When the time is ripe, it parts easily for the chosen lover. The tale seems to register curiosity about the sexual parts of both men and women. In the absence of analysis and ratiocination—which the folktale, in its "chaste compactness," always eschews, according to Walter Benjamin—we have a narrative about how we reach the right, inevitable terminus, through a process of deviation and correction.[30]

TALKING BODIES, DELICATE VESSELS

The plot of woman's curiosity, given various forms in "The Bloody Chamber," in "Hawthorn Blossom," in Dora's case history, and in *Daniel Deronda,* is quite similar to the plot of male curiosity (in Balzac and Zola, and so many others) in its orientation toward the markers of sexual identity. But the plot of woman's curiosity seems to have a special concern with what is contained within closed spaces: locked dens, tower rooms, jewel-cases, delicate vessels. Whereas the nature of the container is evident, and implies an interest in self-exploration, a kind of auto-epistemophilic drive, the nature of the contained is more difficult to articulate. What is the relation between a woman's sexuality, as implicated in the jewel-box, and the "treasure of human affections" transmitted through the ages by women? The difficulty of articulating more precisely what belongs to "woman's knowledge," and how we know it, is in large part the manner and the substance of *Daniel Deronda,* as of Eliot's other novels. Especially in the long, tortuous conversations between Gwendolen and Deronda about her moral and social dilemmas, about the problem of how she should live her life, Eliot reaches toward expression of moral subtleties rarely attempted in the novel. Only Henry James in his late fiction—particularly *The Wings of the Dove* and *The Golden Bowl*—can offer anything like Eliot's exploration of moral consciousness struggling in a world where moral imperatives are uncertain, and the scope for action is narrow—narrow precisely because it is a woman's life.[31]

Gwendolen's dilemmas can be articulated only in language which is inadequate—"in broken allusive speech—wishing to convey but not express all her need," as the narrator puts it (672). "Words were no better than chips," we are told at another point (662). If language can speak the specific question of whether or not she is guilty for wishing Grandcourt's death in thought, and abstaining from saving him in deed, it can never directly articulate the realm of moral consciousness to which this question refers us: a realm where the real issue is what does it mean, as a woman, to live a moral life? Eliot suggests the kind of problem she is dealing with early in the novel, after referring to the "iridescence" of Gwendolen's character: "For Macbeth's rhetoric about the impossibility of being many opposite things in the same moment, referred to the clumsy necessities of action and not to the subtler possibilities of feeling. We cannot speak a loyal word and be meanly silent, we cannot kill and not kill in the same moment; but a moment is room wide enough for the loyal and mean desire, for the outlash of a murderous thought and the sharp backward stroke of repentance" (72). Even this characterization of the problem falls short, as the denial in the phrase "we cannot kill and not kill in the same moment"—precisely what Gwendolen will accuse herself of doing—suggests.

The solution to the problem of what is contained in those "delicate vessels" is not direct. It is indicated by the words "borne onward through the ages," which direct us to Gwendolen as a person in a narrative, to future temporal unfolding, to the narrative potential of the delicate vessels, and indeed to the necessity of narrative as the form of discourse that allows one to approach the problem. When Gwendolen first meets Lydia Glasher by the Whispering Stones, in what she will later think of as "that scene of disclosure" (337), we read: "Gwendolen, watching Mrs Glasher's face while she spoke, felt a sort of terror: it was as if some ghastly vision had come to her in a dream and said, 'I am a woman's life'" (189–90). The ghastly vision returns when she sees Lydia Glasher while riding with Grandcourt in Hyde Park: to Gwendolen, it is a "Medusa-apparition" (668). Lydia Glasher as Medusa evokes, as Evelyne Ender effectively shows, the Freudian scenario of fear before the woman's genitals—as if, in Lydia Glasher, Gwendolen encountered fear of her own woman's sex. This has been prefigured in her original, "presexual" scene of hysterical reaction to disclosure, that of the "up-turned dead face, from which an obscure figure seemed to be fleeing with outstretched arms" hidden behind the panel at Offendene. But reading in Lydia's face the phrase "I am a woman's life" takes us beyond the atropopaic veiling of one's face before the woman's vulva. It poses the question of woman's narrative, of how to live it, write it, read it.

"I will try—try to live," Gwendolen tells Deronda in their final conversation; then she reiterates to her mother: "I am going to live" (878–79). It is a weak and tentative kind of conclusion, which stands in striking contrast to the restless questions that initiate the novel: "Was she beautiful or not beautiful? and what was the secret of form or expression which gave the dynamic quality to her glance? Was the good or the evil genius dominant in those beams? Probably the evil; else why was the effect that of unrest rather than of undisturbed charm? Why was the wish to look again felt as coercion and not as a longing in which the whole being consents? She who raised these questions in Daniel Deronda's mind was occupied in gambling . . ." (35). Gwendolen begins her novelistic existence in the manner of so many women in nineteenth-century fiction, subject to the male gaze, indeed defining her very position and nature as the coercive, magnetic object of that gaze: someone whose destiny will be determined by how she plays to the eyes of men. Gwendolen is always being looked at, whether on stage in charades, during the archery meeting at Brackenshaw Park (where Grandcourt first sees her), or in the Grosvenor Square townhouse. She is first displayed as a maiden to be married, then "on the scene as Mrs. Grandcourt . . .

watched in that part by the exacting eyes of a husband" (608). The novel's repeated insistence on various jewels that Gwendolen is to wear, from the original paternal turquoises to the Grandcourt family diamonds, becomes a leitmotif of woman as object of sociosexual display.

But in the second half of this extremely long novel, the reader senses a paradigm shift, comparable to that worked by Freud, from seeing to listening. In the difficult dialogues between Gwendolen and Deronda, marked by pauses and silences which indicate meanings that cannot be precisely defined, Deronda assumes a nearly transferential relation to Gwendolen—"Without the aid of sacred ceremony or costume, her feelings had turned this man, only a few years older than herself, into a priest" (485)—and constructs her moral itinerary for her, disallowing her characterizations of herself as a "guilty woman" while refusing any easy absolution, and insisting that she take charge of her future destiny. Indeed, the whole of the Deronda plot strikingly emphasizes voice, in Mirah's singing and especially in Mordecai's prophetic utterances, in distinction to sight. Voice and listening characterize a religious tradition that prohibits graven images, rejecting icons in favor of truth revealed by way of voice, which must be heard, interpreted, and then acted upon. The paradigm shift affects Gwendolen's story as much as Deronda's: by the end of the novel, her presentation as a visual object has been superseded by her flat and tentative choice to live, and—as she puts it in the note she sends Deronda on the morning of his marriage to Mirah—to "live to be one of the best of women, who make others glad they were born" (882). This is banal enough, but it does register her move from display to enactment of a more inward story. It appears to place her in the tradition of the delicate vessels, bearing forward some more inward kind of value—"the treasure of human affections"—through the ages.

The life Gwendolen is to live is left unspecified, as, indeed, is the definition of that "treasure." But it is important to register the way in which the novel moves her at the end from a specular to a biographical or narrative mode. It is as if she had ceased to be an object of spectacle to become identified with the innerness of the delicate vessels, and to trust to the unfolding of life in time to bring meaning to her life. The novel as a whole may thus propose a change in paradigm for the recording of a woman's life, away from the field of vision that originally defines—and entraps—Gwendolen, as it turns Lydia Glasher into the Medusa apparition, and toward a temporal unfolding that refuses a definitive meaning and instead argues that meaning can accrue only through narrative temporality. The narrator embeds this temporal paradigm in the novel, preparing us for changes in Gwendolen yet to come: "Sir Joshua would have been glad to take her portrait; and he would have had an easier task than the historian at least in this, that he would not have had to represent the truth of change—only to give stability to one beautiful moment" (151). This comment, among others, makes us realize that the first half of the novel—up to Grandcourt's drowning—is really an elaborate preparation, a motivation (as the Russian Formalists called it) for Gwendolen's entry into processes of change, where she is "dislodged" from the static world of narcissism (876) and forced into revisions of her being. Such a dependency of meaning on biographical process is a central effect created by Eliot's most accomplished fiction—certainly in *Middlemarch* as well as *Daniel Deronda*—and indeed an effect of most of the great nineteenth-century novels, which are long because their meanings unfold through time.[32] In the case of Gwendolen Harleth, Eliot seems to equate the necessity of narrative, of biographical meaning, with the woman's life—with private life, with the sphere of inwardness—affirming in this manner a fundamental tradition of the novel.

"The universe forcing itself with a slow, inexorable pressure into a narrow, complacent, and yet after all extremely sensitive mind, and making it ache with the pain of the process—that is Gwendolen's story," wrote Henry James.[33] James's emphasis on "process" stresses once again the inescapability of the narrative account for the unfolding of moral and psychological complexities, something that Freud also discovered in reporting his cases of hysteria. Eliot's account of a woman's life bears affinities with Freud's narrative ambitions at their best. It is not only that, as a number of critics have noted, Eliot in her own indirect language is capable of describing the "secrets of the alcove" with virtually as much fullness and frankness as Freud.[34] It is more that both Eliot and Freud insist that the account get beyond the spectacularization of symptoms, that it become a listening to the body rather than simply a viewing of it, and that it take the risk of putting the listener/narrator's own person into play in transferential relation to the subject of analysis. The transferential model of listening to the body's talk recognizes both the involvement of the listener and the final otherness of others' bodies and stories, both the capacities and the limits of knowing. It marks a partial subversion of the nineteenth-century model of the body held as an object of scrutiny in a detached and objective scientific gaze. Bodies do not yield their secrets in this manner. They must be listened to for their betrayals, read in their complex rhetoric, by a listener-reader whose position of mastery and authority is at issue. The content of the delicate vessels cannot fully be specified, only their narrative trajectory.

9 Transgressive Bodies

SEVERAL LAYERS of Victorian clothing have been removed since the nineteenth century; we are more used to the near-nakedness of others' bodies in certain specified situations. Literary representation of the body has generally evolved toward a greater explicitness in seeing and naming, toward the constitution of the body as a more open, public cultural construct. Visual representation of the body, in the cinema, in video, and particularly in advertising, has achieved a state of near nudity and an eroticized presentation that curiously seem to be in advance of what most sectors of the society really accept as permissible outside the confines of intimacy. But here we encounter one of the paradoxical aspects of representation in "the age of mechanical reproduction" (as Walter Benjamin famously called it): it invades that sphere of privacy which, in modern bourgeois societies, is supposed to be inviolable, and displays for mass public consumption public images of that which is supposed to be most private.[1] Privacy and intimacy more and more appear to exist only by way of the violations and exploitations that define them as special spaces. Our consciousness of a reserved space of intimacy strangely, perhaps pathetically, depends on relentless intrusion into it.

As I noted in Chapter 2, invasion of privacy characterizes the modern novelistic tradition from its very inception. With the rise of photography, visual representation achieves the same kind of reproducibility as the printed word. When inexpensive photographic reproduction becomes the preferred vehicle of the modern advertising industry, the body becomes the object of a particularly insistent barrage of representations that exploit what was thought to be private. Advertising has achieved what no artistic or literary genre could: making the private body a subject of everyday public discourse, especially visual discourse. Consider such banal instances as advertisement for underwear and deodorants, which have served, in somewhat different ways, to make the private body utterly public. The marketing of deodorant has worked by exploiting and creating anxiety about smells associated with bodily recesses, parts of the body not normally acknowledged in public. Thus its advertising has created a highly coded public discourse of the private, all along implying that the discourse aims to make the private remain so: a kind of general mentioning of the unmentionable. Underwear of course has a traditional erotic association, and a traditional role as fetish. Contemporary exploitation of this tradition may be best emblematized by the chain of stores called Victoria's Secret, which precisely achieves its success by designating as secret, and associated with Victorian concealment, that which it is publicly promoting. Still another accomplishment of contemporary advertising is the eroticization of male underwear, a process which had to contend with heavier layers of social repression and perhaps indifference. To fetishize the male anatomy through its underwear took some doing, and the subsequent creation of male-style underwear for women was an act of cute cultural transgression wholly characteristic of late twentieth-century sensibility.

The commodification of fetishized body parts is very much part of the contemporary discursive and visual landscape. The relation that this commercially created fictional landscape bears to reality is problematic. The "liberation" seemingly represented by the promotional images that surround us may have had little effect on the ways that people continue to view and to use their own and others' bodies. Continuing struggles over definitions of pornography and obscenity, over what can be shown on prime-time television and how cinema ratings are to be used, suggest that the commercial commodification of erotic bodily zones is still seen to be culturally separate from, and more "innocent" than, more direct representations of the erotic body. The debate suggests also that still photography has freed itself of inhibitions that still apply to (non-pornographic) cinema and to television, in which the body is narratively engaged and capable of performances. The "frenzy of the visual" characteristic of postmodern culture distinguishes between bodies that are fixed or stilled, and those in action.[2]

The body in action evokes a large domain of artistic activity that is highly characteristic of the modern: dance, which offers the body in performance, disciplined by music, as an object of visual contemplation. Ballet comes into its own in the Romantic age, with *La sylphide* (1832), with a libretto derived from the work of Charles Nodier (chief of the first Romantic *cénacle* in Paris), and then *Giselle* (1841), based on a text by that journeyman of all Romantic genres, Théophile Gautier. As ballet developed in the nineteenth century, into the more or less canonical form given it by Marius Petipa in Saint Petersburg, it offered a body that itself carried a narrative line, or, more accurately, a body that gave an expressive interpretation to a stated narrative line, enacted a narrative program. In this sense, ballet develops from the mute action of pantomime and melodrama—themselves accompanied by music—but with a much more highly codified set of conventions, resulting in a much greater abstraction from the expressionism of pantomime and melodrama.

The ballet from its inception was focused on the public performance and display of the female body. Prima ballerinas such as Marie Taglioni, Fanny Elssler, and Carlotta Grisi were the toast of a male-dominated nineteenth-century audience and the object of male adoration and desire. Dancers, from the most famous—like Mathilde Kschessinska, who became the mistress of Tsar Nicholas II of Russia—to the humblest member of the *corps de ballet,* the lowest *rat d'opéra,* were considered to be available to men, for the price of their upkeep. Their display on stage, particularly the display of their legs in a period when bourgeois women kept legs well hidden, put them into a erotic-commercial relation to the male spectator. The writings of Gautier, Balzac, and others are charged with the erotics of looking: Lucien de Rubempré, to take just one example, is seduced by Coralie onstage, and particularly by her black net stockings. Yet the dancing woman onstage would also become, particularly in late Romantic writing, the very symbol of poetry, of symbol-making itself, perhaps most famously in Stéphane Mallarmé's reflections on Loïe Fuller, the American dancer who created a sensation in Paris in her solo performances, where she used yards of silk, attached to her arms by batons, to create a swirling effect of elemental forms. Mallarmé summarized his reaction to another *danseuse,* La Cornalba, by saying that in performance she became, not a woman dancing, but a "metaphor."[3] W. B. Yeats would return again and again to the dancer as the most perfect symbol combining visual realization and idea in a moment of "bodily thought," a moment in which intellection is so thoroughly fused in sensuous embodiment that idea ceases to be a separate realm from image, to become rather something immediately apprehensible through its embodiment. The famous final lines of "Among School Children"—"O body swayed to music, O brightening glance, / How can we know the dancer from the dance?"—suggest the momentary enactment of this fusion. But the poem as a whole indicates that such fusion may not be durably available here below.

The late Romantic version of the dancer's body as the incarnation of something ineffable is marked by a certain desperation, and much twentieth-century art of the body to a degree reacts against this by affirming the bodiliness of the body. The paintings of Gauguin and Matisse are examples of a claim that the body itself, in repose and in movement, is a sufficient object of contemplation without any postulation of narrative or ideational content. And it would seem that spectatorship in the twentieth century has learned more and more to do without narrative, idea, or program: to find its pleasures in contemplation of the body itself in performance—disciplined, reaching beyond its normal constraints, expressive, yes, but not necessarily of anything but its own capacities for grace, prowess, and beauty. Ours is in many ways an age of what Richard Poirier has called "the performing self," and what is put into play in performance is perhaps most of all the body as an irreducible integer to be celebrated.[4]

I shall return at the end of this chapter to our contemporary "frenzy of the visual." But I want first to consider once more the body represented in language. Here, too, one could see the modern as characterized by a breaking of reticence, a greater openness, about the body. Some of the notable instances of this process have encountered censorship and prosecution: whereas central issues in freedom of representation versus social conventions reach a crisis in the nineteenth century in the prosecution of Flaubert's *Madame Bovary* and Baudelaire's *Les fleurs du mal,* the twentieth century has its emblematic moments in the censorship imposed on, and eventually lifted from, Joyce's *Ulysses* and Lawrence's *Lady Chatterley's Lover.* What was considered most offensive to community standards in both books, in their different ways, was their presentation of the body. In the case of *Ulysses,* the body is seen in intimate detail that even the most thorough realism of the nineteenth century did not attempt: Leopold Bloom seated over his rising stench in the outhouse; his masturbatory voyeurism with Gerty McDowell; Molly's monologue, which consists in good part of reveries on her lovers' bodies and her own, including reflections on urination and menstruation—none of which had been the object of serious literary representation in the novel. While it is in many ways the epitome of high modernist formal experimentation, *Ulysses* is also a summation (and a critique) of the realist tradition, insisting upon filling in the blanks left by its conventional reticence. I can remember as an adolescent reader asking myself, with a certain prurient annoyance, why no one in the great realist novels ever seemed to have bladder or bowels. Joyce takes pleasure in showing up convention, somewhat in the manner of his naturalized compatriot Jonathan Swift: "Oh! *Celia, Celia, Celia* shits!" Swift writes, with a pugnacious insistence on exposing convention and hypocrisy. Joyce might also be thought of as the next step beyond Zola. Yet his parodic and satiric stance differs notably from Zola's solemnity. The body for Joyce is matter-of-fact, it is a tragically rebellious servant, and it is also comic. He reaches back beyond the nineteenth-century tradition to Shakespeare and Rabelais, and he makes possible such later versions of bodiliness as Samuel Beckett's and Philip Roth's.

Lawrence's infractions are more classical, one might say, in that they concern the sexual body, and thus classic problems of obscenity and pornography. *Lady Chatterley's Lover* remains even today unsurpassed as an attempt to represent sexuality and the sexualized body in serious literature. Lawrence's efforts to render the poetry of the sexually aroused body, the urgency and tenderness of passion as it transforms the body, and to describe orgasm, male and female, may strike us variously as noble failures or as wholly unreadable foolishness. Lawrence's extended metaphorical flights rarely persuade. Traditional erotic writing—in the eighteenth century, for instance—also deployed an imagistic web to speak of the sexual. But the tone was quite different, and the kind of knowledge sought in and from the sexual encounter was, if at times no less complex and metaphysical, not marked by the turgid Edwardian late-Romantic temper that insists that the sexual is the ineffable, and then insists upon translating this ineffable into language. Yet even though the Lawrentian sexual sublime is virtually unreadable, one may acknowledge a certain admirable ambition in the attempt to see and to represent sexuality as a cognitive activity (though for Lawrence it becomes too exclusively "phallic knowledge"): he tries to extend further the long tradition of sexual difference as the impetus of an epistemophilic project. We may find that there are other, apparently more modest, efforts within this project—such as the fiction of Marguerite Duras—that are more successful.

Another famous case of twentieth-century censorship, this time in France, concerned the post–World War II publication of the complete works of the Marquis de Sade, provoking a controversy that contributed to Sade's writings' achieving in our time the curious status of an infernal classic, perhaps the only *oeuvre* in literature at once authentically horrible and canonical. Edmund Wilson once remarked that Sade was the only author who made impossible his practice of reading at breakfast; while Sade can often appear merely silly, he does still have a sulphurous effect. What is so corrosive about Sade is not only his sadism but the

logic of his project of using the body against nature to demonstrate that nothing can outrage nature. Nature, in Sade, finally is a non-principle, an impassible force. The more one works outrages on the natural body, including its destruction, the more one simply does the work of nature, which itself ultimately operates by way of destruction. Sade's libertines both adore the body and finally detest it for its limitations, for its incapacity to go beyond nature. All they can offer in the place of transcendence is an uninterrupted discourse that attempts to speak the body through the pleasure and pain elicited from it and inflicted on it. For Sade himself, this results in a massive writing project that can never reach a conclusion, that must be endlessly repeated to show that one is both in revolt against those limitations and eventually subject to them.

The mention of Sade serves to remind us that the experience of the body in twentieth-century literature is by no means exclusively a happy one: our century has more than most provided instances of the body threatened, extinguished, or in pain.[5] The overwhelming historical experiences of the twentieth century have been total warfare, mass destruction, and genocide. In his reflections on the fate of storytelling in the modern world, Walter Benjamin claims that experience is fast becoming incommunicable, and that the wisdom that comes from the communication of personal experience, from one individual to another, is being replaced by simple information, what is purveyed by the mass media. For Benjamin, personal experience has been negated in a radically new way by the total warfare of World War I: "A generation that had gone to school on a horse-drawn streetcar now stood under the open sky in a countryside in which nothing remained unchanged but the clouds, and beneath these clouds, in a field of force of destructive torrents and explosions, was the tiny, fragile human body."[6] The experience of the body in modern warfare comprehends a degradation, a devaluation, a waste which sorely test humanistic assumptions. Ernest Hemingway's novels, particularly *A Farewell to Arms,* offer a typical and influential dissent from ideas of heroism and value in the context of the First World War. One of the first and most powerful representations of man in this new species of unheroic war comes in Louis-Ferdinand Céline's *Voyage au bout de la nuit,* where the body becomes a thing of misery, cold, wet, hungry, terrified, incontinent, doomed to decay and destruction. The whole of *Voyage au bout de la nuit* is a howl of despair against the human condition, and particularly against the vicissitudes of the human body. That Bardamu (like his creator) becomes a medical doctor, thus dedicated to the saving of life, only emphasizes how little there is to save, how despairing the attempt to patch and repair the flesh can be.   263

In many ways the fullest Modernist discussion of the body comes in a novel in which war—again, the First World War—stands as epilogue rather than ostensible subject: Thomas Mann's *Magic Mountain (Der Zauberberg)*. Mann consciously sets out to provide an emblem and epitome of European society on the eve of its self-immolation in the Great War. The closed society of the Berghof Sanatorium is wholly absorbed (in Mann's ostensible view, morbidly so) with the body—its symptoms, its functioning, its preservation, its impending decay. Hans Castorp, the young man who comes to Berghof simply as visitor to his tubercular cousin Joachim Ziemssen, becomes so fascinated by the rituals of bodily care—the enforced "horizontality" of rest, the four-times-daily temperature measurements, the comparison to others' symptoms—that he comes to consider himself ill and to spend seven years in the sanatorium, until the coming of the Great War forces his return to the "flatlands" and his re-engagement with life. Hans Castorp's fascination with disease and medicine leads to his research into anatomy, physiology, biochemistry, and to the creation of a new lyricism of the body.

A moment of great significance in the novel comes with Hans Castorp's first visit to the X-ray room, where he is photographed, and where he views Joachim's body through the "lighted window" that displays the "empty skeleton." As the Hofrat explains the interior topography to him, Castorp's attention is drawn

by something like a bag, a strange, animal shape, darkly visible behind the middle column, or more on the right side of it—the spectator's right. It expanded and contracted regularly, a little after the fashion of a swimming jelly-fish.

"Look at his heart," and the Hofrat lifted his huge hand again from his thigh and pointed with his forefinger at the pulsating shadow. Good God, it was the heart, it was Joachim's honour-loving heart, that Hans Castorp saw!

"I am looking at your heart," he said in a suppressed voice.[7]

I don't know if this is the first moment in literature that the heart is viewed in X-ray. Mann in any event uses the relatively new technology to rewrite an age-old trope of the heart as the seat of emotions and character. As "swimming jelly-fish" and "honour-loving" in conjunction make plain, the heart viewed here is both a piece of anatomy and a moral concept, the heart in both physiology and poetry. Hans Castorp's awed reaction to the "pulsating shadow" indicates his sense of penetration into forbidden knowledge. What he sees is both technological marvel and *memento mori,* and he feels his position as looker to be nearly illegitimate, his gaze into the body of doubtful innocence: "his itch to commit the indiscretion conflicted in his bosom with religious emotion and feelings of concern." The passage extends remarkably the traditional realist viewing of the body by taking the gaze within, to turn what is usually conceived as moral and spiritual—indeed, religious—into something bodily. The tone of Hans Castorp's reaction suggests that there is a loss as well as a gain associated with this demystification of the heart: a realm held to be sacred has been penetrated and secularized; it has been drained of transcendence.

It is in the logic of romance at Berghof that X-ray plates should become precious keepsakes, and Hans Castorp preserves not only his own, but that of his adored Clavdia Chauchat, which he regularly takes from its case and views: "It was Clavdia's x-ray portrait, showing not her face, but the delicate bony structure of the upper half of her body, and the organs of the thoracic cavity, surrounded by the pale, ghostlike envelope of flesh. How often had he looked at it, how often pressed it to his lips, in the time which since then had passed and brought its changes with it—such changes as, for instance, getting used to life up here without Clavdia Chauchat" (348–49). The X-ray portrait of the beloved offers an interesting new conceit for the male gaze, in that the "envelope of flesh" that is the normal object of the gaze has here become "ghostlike," burned away to present woman as delicate skeleton. The penetrating observation of the body, a repeated metaphor of realist fiction, here is literalized, passing through the body as we normally conceive it to something at once more ethereal and more morbid: the body of the beloved in league with the forces of fleshly destruction. If the photographic souvenir normally records an absence—making it present as reproduction—here the souvenir itself appears as absence, as ghostly non-presence.

Hans Castorp's researches into the body culminate in his declaration of passion to Clavdia, during the Shrove Tuesday party that the novel calls *Walpurgisnacht.* This declaration takes place in French, a language which Hans Castorp masters uneasily; it disorients him from himself and allows him to overcome his inhibitions, and to address Clavdia with the intimate *tu*. He comes eventually to praise of the body, death, and love, and to one of the most extraordinary paeans to the body in literature. The passage runs, in small part:

Oh, enchantante beauté organique qui ne se compose ni de teinture à l'huile ni de pierre, mais de matière vivante et corruptible, pleine du secret fébrile de la vie et de la pourriture! Regarde la symétrie merveilleuse de l'édifice humain, les épaules et les hanches et les mamelons fleurissants de part et d'autre sur la poitrine, et les côtes arrangées par paires, et le nombril au milieu dans la mollesse du ventre, et le sexe obscur entre les cuisses! . . . Quelle fête immense de les caresser, ces endroits délicieux du corps humain! Fête à mourir sans plainte après! . . . Laisse-moi ressentir l'exhalation de tes pores et tâter ton duvet, image humaine d'eau et d'albumine, destinée pour l'anatomie du tombeau, et laisse-moi périr, mes lèvres aux tiennes! (342–43)

One suspects that Mann, as much as his fictional creation, would have been incapable of composing this strange *Liebestod* in German: its unseemliness can be carried off only in a foreign language, and specifically in French, the language of love.[8] Here love is translated through physiology, anatomy, and chemistry, the sciences of the body, into the discourse of its interior and its functioning. The lover's discourse conceives the body in terms of natural processes, as the composite of substances and processes discerned by science, and in so doing he both celebrates and decomposes the body. As an object of love, the body is also in thrall to death.

The anatomy of the beloved is the "anatomy of the tomb," and love of the body love of death. Although Mann ostensibly holds Hans Castorp's sensibility here to be diseased and decadent, his vision of Clavdia's body is within the logic of the realist gaze. It seems in fact simply to be one small step beyond Muffat's gaze at Nana, in Zola's novel. The nineteenth-century biology and physiology from which Zola sought inspiration, and which form much of the metaphorical tissue of his novels, have been superseded by a more precise naming of parts and processes. The phallic realist gaze decomposes the female body. If Mann's rewriting of the Wagnerian *Liebestod* makes reference to late-Romantic tradition, associated with Symbolists and Decadents, it reflects also on the very premises of the naturalist attitude toward the body, its ways of looking and naming. When *The Magic Mountain* ends amidst scenes of wartime destruction, the "cure" for the kind of vision in which its characters have indulged becomes the destruction of the society that the nineteenth-century novel depicted. Moral health seems for Mann to be regained by the return of aggressive impulses and the practice of death in another form. Mann, like Benjamin, sees war as an insult to the human body, yet he comes close to suggesting that the decadent vision of the body can be cleansed only in violence.

Looking at *The Lover* Looking

The body quickened through sexuality remains the object of most intense interest for our culture. It is worth dwelling on one example that will serve to draw attention, once again, to the problematics of the gaze directed at a body which is conceived as the object of a writing project, this time by a woman. The author, Marguerite Duras, is particularly sensitive to issues of looking, and has indeed worked successfully in the cinema, as well as in the theater and narrative fiction. Duras accepts the tradition of the body in the visual field but works subtle and subversive displacements within it. Although any and all of her work would be pertinent to this discussion, I shall focus on the novel that transformed her from an avant-garde novelist into a best-seller: *L'amant (The Lover)*, which is a narrative of somewhat deceptive limpidity.

L'amant tells the story of a fifteen-year-old girl in French Indochina in the 1930s who has her first sexual relationship with a Chinese financier. The affair is thoroughly scandalous from all points of view: the transgression of racial lines, the youth of the girl, and the girl's refusal to delude herself with romance. She knows from the outset that she is not in love with her lover (who is very much in love with her) but only with love itself, with the erotic transaction, and with the pleasure experienced by her body. In the social isolation that her transgression brings—other girls in the lycée are forbidden to associate with her—she makes an imaginary identification with the "woman of Vinh Long," whose young lover killed himself in despair when she announced the end of their liaison. The identification of the girl with the isolated and stigmatized woman of Vinh Long comes from the experience of their bodies: "Alone, queens. Their disgrace is a matter of course. Both of them destined to disgrace because of the kind of body they have, caressed by lovers, kissed by their mouths, given over to the infamy of a pleasure to die from, as they call it, to die from in this mysterious death of lovers without love."[9]

What particularizes the girl, from the moment she is observed by her future lover while crossing the Mekong River on the ferry, is the capacity of her body for erotic pleasure—*jouissance,* or orgasmic bliss.[10] It separates her from her mother: as soon as she has been to bed with her lover, she knows that her mother has never known this pleasure. It separates her from her family, and the tyrannical law of her elder brother. It gives a special destiny to her body, as removed from the contingencies, indignities, and displeasure of her everyday existence. She becomes the body of the beloved, and this confers on her a special status.

This status is created by the desiring gaze of the other, the lover. A key moment of the novel comes when the lover, in bed, looks at her: "*Il la regarde*" (121), and the text continues to describe her observation of his observation of her:

I used to watch what he was doing with me, how he made use of me, and I had never thought that one could do anything like that, he went beyond my hope and in accordance with my body's destiny. Thus I had become his child. He had also become something else for me. I began to recognize the inexpressible softness of his skin, of his sex, beyond himself . . . Everything worked to his desire and made him take me . . .

He takes her as he would take his child. He would take his child in the same way. He plays with his child's body, he turns it over, he covers his face, his mouth, his eyes with it. And she, she continues to abandon herself in the very direction that he took when he began to play. And suddenly it's she who begs him, she doesn't say what for, and he who yells at her to be quiet, who cries that he doesn't want her anymore, that he doesn't want to take pleasure in her anymore, and there they are again caught between themselves, locked between themselves in terror, and then this terror undoes itself again, and they give in again, in tears, in despair, in happiness. (122–23)

If she is her lover's child, it is because she is to a degree his creation, something created in the act of lovemaking, a body fashioned for his pleasure which is also a body fashioned for its own pleasure and destiny: her body become what it was supposed to become. In response, she is able to espouse the direction of his desire, and her body follows the inflections given to it by his caresses toward its own pleasure. The body is here both hyper-conscious—"I used to watch what he was doing with me"—and the place of a knowledge of inexpressible pleasure.

The passage quoted bears witness to a narrative peculiarity of *L'amant* that is closely related to the status of the body as I have been attempting to describe it. The first of the two paragraphs is in the first person, a retrospective narrative in which the girl, now a woman of some years, and explicitly a writer (and indeed, explicitly Marguerite Duras), recalls her youth. The second paragraph is in the third person: the "I" has become "she." The shift between first and third person in *L'amant* doesn't necessarily take place between paragraphs; it can happen from one sentence to another. And the play of the subjective and objective perspectives is not limited to presentation in these two pronominal modes. Consider, for instance, her reflections on the desirable body of her friend Hélène Lagonelle: "These flour-white forms, she bears them without any knowledge, she shows these things for hands to knead them, for the mouth to eat them, without holding them back, without knowledge of them, without knowledge also of their fabulous power. I would like to eat the breasts of Hélène Lagonelle as he eats the breasts of me in the room in Chinatown where I go each evening to deepen the knowledge of God. To be devoured by these flour-white breasts that are hers" (91). Translating Duras is extremely difficult: her style is deceptively limpid and simple, achieving astonishing effects by slight distortions of normal diction. In this passage, for instance, "elle montre ces choses pour les mains les pétrir, pour la bouche les manger" resorts to an almost childish syntax to express the value of Hélène Lagonelle's breasts in terms of their pleasurable use by a putative lover. "Je voudrais manger les seins d'Hélène Lagonelle comme lui mange les seins de moi" skews normal usage ("mes seins") in order to suggest her own bodily parts as experienced by her own lover. What is at issue in such moments is precisely the body known as the site of pleasure by way of the pleasure that a lover takes in it. By experiencing her own desire for Hélène Lagonelle's body, she can experience her own body as the object of the lover's desire. Point of view, the use of pronouns and perspectives, the place of the subject and the object, have to do with positions in respect to desire.

One of the prime effects of desire, in this novel, seems to be to make subject into object, to allow or to force the subject to grasp itself as it is for the desire and in the perspective of the other. Marguerite Duras' fiction has been praised by Jacques Lacan as a confirmation of his doctrine, and the view of desire presented in *L'amant* is in fact quite

Lacanian. For Lacan, the unconscious is "the discourse of the Other," which means, *inter alia,* that the individual's desire is always structured for him or her by that impersonal Other that defines the individual's ego, at the mirror stage, as alienated, that is, as the product of others' gazes and perspectives. In Lacan's conception, the demand for love is always absolute, a demand for recognition that never can be fulfilled, based on infantile scenarios of original lack. Desire, born in the discrepancy or lack between need and demand, is thus not desire for this or that, but desire *tout court,* driven by radical unsatisfaction, for which any given object is a stand-in, an "imaginary" and hence deceptive simulacrum. What a lover desires is "the desirer in the other," that the lover be "called to as desirable" by the person chosen as the object of desire.[11]

269

The Chinese lover resembles Lacan's "*objet petit a*"—the other, not the Other—in that he is simply in the place where desire seeks an object. He is an imaginary object, as he himself understands after he has first made love to the girl, when he tells her that he has known from their first meeting on the ferry that she would "love love," and that she will deceive him and all the men who will be her lovers in the future (54). And she understands "that he does not know her, that he will never know her, that he has no way of understanding such perversity" (48)— the "perversity" being her desire for desire, without regard for the person that is its pretext. "There is no such thing as a sexual relationship," Lacan says in one of his famous dicta. The knowledge that she obtains— that she "deepens"—in her erotic encounters is expressed, in the passage quoted above, as the "knowledge of God": that is, of something trans-individual, impersonal, desire in itself.

The discourse of desire in *L'amant* is especially about the place of the body in the economy and discourse of desire. The girl's place in the economy of desire is originally and insistently a product of the gaze. The first encounter with the lover, on the ferry, is initially presented by way of a photograph that might have been taken and wasn't. The girl's mother regularly arranges for photographs to be made of the family, as testimonials to its existence, somewhat in the manner that the Indochinese have themselves photographed in old age in order to be remembered after their deaths and, through the effects of age and the photographer's retouching, all end up looking the same. That the decisive encounter with the girl's lover was not photographed gives the image of their meeting its "virtue, that of representing an absolute" (17). The lacking photograph subtends the presentation of the scene as insistently visual. In the visual field thus established, our attention is insistently called to a single detail: the men's felt hat worn by the girl which, by its "determining ambiguity," transforms her looks and her very identity. Her "awkward thinness of form" becomes something else: "It ceased to

be a brutal, fatal, given of nature. It became quite the opposite, a choice against the grain of nature, a choice of the mind. Suddenly, here's what one wanted. Suddenly, I see myself as an other, as an other would be seen, from the outside, made available to all, made available to all gazes, put into the economy of towns, roads, desire [*mise dans la circulation des villes, des routes, du désir*]" (20).

In the following pages, the narrator develops this awareness of the gaze of others (essentially, of other men) as an experience of the girl's adolescence; the gaze by definition conveys an understanding of the potential for erotic encounter with its object: "It wasn't a matter of attracting desire. It was in her, the woman who provoked it, or it didn't exist. It was already there from the first glance or else it had never existed. It was the immediate understanding of sexual relation or else it was nothing" (28). Thus the girl, marked by the hat that transforms her into the object of the erotic gaze, has already entered the circulatory economy of desire when she is approached by the Chinese financier— who immediately comments on the hat. She conceives of her body as that which will henceforth be defined by that economy, and no longer by the domestic economy of the family. When she enters the Chinese financier's black limousine, she knows that her "obligations toward herself" mean that she will now have to deal with an exogamous system, that she has passed—in the direction that the hat has made her appearance pass—as it were from nature to culture, where culture is defined as the positions assigned by desire. The Chinese financier's approach to her is the first time in the text where the first person is replaced by the third, where she does not directly assume her subjectivity but rather sees herself as seen by the other: "He looks at the girl with the man's hat and the gold shoes. Slowly he comes toward her. It's evident that he is intimidated" (42).

The play of gazes in *L'amant* subtly displaces the traditional field of vision of novels in the realist tradition . Woman is the object of the male gaze. She is defined by her position in relation to desire, which is expressed by way of the male gaze. She assumes that defining property of the male gaze, adopts her identity in relation to it. And yet, the capacity of the girl in *L'amant* to assume her identity in relation to male desire consciously and deliberately, and to manipulate desire in order to realize the "destiny" of her own body, subverts the traditional model. The play of subjective and objective narrative perspectives suggests that she controls positions in regard to desire: she is no longer the passive object of the gaze (as postulated in much film theory) but actively exhibitionist. Lacan claims that woman's sexuality is inseparable from the representations through which she comes to know it: "images and symbols *for* the woman cannot be isolated from images and symbols *of* the woman . . . It is . . . the representation of feminine sexuality, whether repressed or not, which conditions how it comes into play."[12] By assuming control of representation of her sexuality—by becoming the scenarist of her own body as it comes into play—the girl of *L'amant* makes woman's relation to the displayed body active and conscious, and indeed complicates accepted notions about activity and passivity in spectatorship.[13]

One might say that Duras seems both to espouse and to subvert Freud's declaration that there is only one libido, and that it is male. Freud's somewhat cryptic statement appears to mean that there is no separate libido for women since libido is signified by the phallus as the marker of desire, and perhaps also that libido has been defined throughout history as male. Woman's freedom, on this model, is her capacity to understand and to use libido so defined, to make its masculine definition serve her own pleasure and thus to make the lover only the excuse for love, an impersonal goal. The girl in *L'amant* bears affinities with such earlier (male-created) heroines as the Marquise de Merteuil, in *Les liaisons dangereuses,* and the adolescent protagonist of Stendhal's *Lamiel.* All three work a reversal of perspectives within the male-generated and male-dominated system. Men, in the words of the Marquise de Merteuil, are "dethroned tyrants become my slaves."[14]

The liaison of the girl in *L'amant* with the lover develops, then, as a realization of the desire of the other, experienced as the true "destiny" of her own body as part of an erotic economy in which she has found her place, precisely by being displaced from the subjectivity, and the familial economy, in which she began. Upon her first assignation with the lover in his apartment, we have the comment: "She is there where she must be, displaced there" (47). Displacement, like the "perversity" she finds characteristic of her emotions a few pages later, marks a new position in regard to desire. And after her first experience of sex with the lover, as they lie together in bed: "I realize that I desire him" (*Je m'aperçois que je le désire*) (51). Desire comes as a realization, a perception, as it were as the result of a mental operation on the body which now has entered into the system of desire. The erotic, one might say, is the intelligence of the body. It is the body become sentient and self-aware by way of the other.

It is illuminating to return, in this context, to the passage that evokes her desire for the body of her friend Hélène Lagonelle. "I am prostrated by the beauty of Hélène Lagonelle's body stretched out against mine . . . Nothing is more extraordinary than this surface roundness of the breasts she carries, this exteriority held out toward the hands. Even my younger brother's little coolie body disappears next to this splendor. Men's bodies have stingy, internalized forms" (89). Then follows the passage cited earlier ("These flower-white forms, she carries them without any knowledge . . ."), which leads to a phantasy scenario in which she would take Hélène with her to the place where every evening "I have myself given the pleasure that makes one cry aloud." The passage continues:

> I would like to give Hélène Lagonelle to the man who does that to me so that he might to do it in turn to her. This in my presence, so that she do it according to my desire, that she give herself there where I give myself. It would be by way of Hélène Lagonelle's body, by the passage across her body, that pleasure would come from him to me, in its definitive form.
>
> Pleasure to die from. (92)

As I understand this difficult passage, it is about the intellection of desire, about desire becoming knowledge. Hélène Lagonelle's body as intermediary between the lover and the narrator—as the medium through which his desire is transmitted—serves, in phantasy, as a vehicle for the expression of desire in a form that she can see, realized before her eyes, and thus understand. Her lover's desire and her own would meet and become visible when acted out on Hélène Lagonelle's body. One is reminded of Balzac's *La fille aux yeux d'or*, where the body of Paquita Valdès becomes the place where the desires of Henri de Marsay and the Marquise de Saint-Réal are inscribed, in a way that represents the "infinitude" of their (ultimately incestuous) desire, and murders Paquita. It is as if another body had to be in place in order to realize fully the eroticism of the visual that is so much the definition of desire in the novel. To be "definitive," pleasure, orgasm, must be seen.

Pleasure and knowledge are products of positioning the body in relation to desire. So are suffering, sadism, and the imposition of the law. The girl's affair with her Chinese lover violates the social taboos of the

European colony in Indochina, and in particular disqualifies her for the colony's marriage market. She has lost status; she risks never being able to "place" herself in society. This realization periodically drives her mother into a rage in which she locks the girl in her room and strips her, seeking the smells and signs of the lover's body on her underwear and her body, and then strikes and beats her. As she is beaten, her elder brother is listening through the walls, with pleasure. He encourages the mother to strike, in the name of the need to discover the truth, and in the name of the law according to whose standards the girl stands condemned. Meanwhile, the younger brother begs the mother to stop; he is afraid his sister will be killed, and afraid also of his older brother. His fear finally calms the mother, rage dissolves in tears. The girl cries with her, and denies that she is having sex with the Chinese financier. The account of this repeated incident ends: "I know that my older brother is riveted to the door, listening, he knows what my mother is doing, he knows that his younger sister is naked, and being beaten, he would like that to go on and on, till it became dangerous. My mother is not unaware of this obscure and terrifying intention on the part of my brother" (74).

273

The scene bears a close resemblance to a typical scenario analyzed by Freud in his essay "A Child Is Being Beaten" ("Ein Kind wird geschlagen," 1919). Here, Freud also emphasizes positions in relation to desire and its repression. A girl will typically move through three positions, the first and third sadistic—another child is being beaten—the second masochistic, erotic, and deeply repressed: she is the child being beaten, by her father. For a boy, in a yet more complicated process of transformation, a first phantasy, "I am loved by my father," is transformed into the conscious phantasy "I am being beaten by my mother."[15] Without attempting to find direct correspondences between Freud's scenarios and Duras' beating scene, one can note a general resemblance of the positions of the three children in relation to the beating and the various positions that can be assumed by one child according to Freud. In particular, the older brother's excitement at his naked sister's beating suggests both sadistic and masochistic urges, and the desire to be in the places both of beater and beaten. As in Freud's essay, positions in relation to desire in L'amant are virtually a matter of grammatical transformations. The subject finds and takes up positions in relation to desire, active and passive, sadistic and masochistic, in processes capable of reversal and contradiction. Freud's essay, read in conjunction with the beating episode of L'amant, suggests again the crucial importance of where one stands in relation to desire, including its negative transformations. Desire is always desire of the other, and of the other's desire; there is no such thing as a simple, unmediated, unproblematic desire on the part of the subject. The girl creates desire on the part of her future lover from the moment he looks at her, while his desire creates her, as part of that circulatory system which, in the description given by Freud in this essay, allows the subject to take up multiple positions within it.

To return once again to the girl's lovemaking, and particularly to the moments that describe her lover's gaze at her, one further passage needs quotation:

> He looks at her. His eyes closed he looks at her still. He inhales her face. He breathes in the child, his eyes closed he breathes in her breathing, the warm air that comes from her. He discerns less and less clearly the limits of this body, this one is not like the others, it is not finite, in the room it keeps growing, it is still without fixed forms, being made at every moment, it's not only there where he sees it, it is also elsewhere, it extends beyond his view, toward risk, death, it's supple, it embarks whole into pleasure as if it were grown up, adult, it is without guile, it has a frightening intelligence.   (121)

Besides offering a remarkable view of herself in terms of the desiring gaze directed at her, and an understanding of her own capacity to serve as the object of desire, this passage suggests the importance of desire and the erotic as potential transgressions of human finitude.

For Georges Bataille, in *L'érotisme,* the erotic is fundamentally transgressive of taboos and limitations. Human beings are "discontinuous"— finite, closed, incapable of deep communication with others because the bodies of others are closed to them. In the erotic encounter discontinuity and finitude are breached, if only momentarily. One body accedes to another, breaches its walls, enters its bodily orifices. Bataille writes:

> All the work of eroticism has as its principle a destruction of the structure of the closed being that each partner in the game is in the normal state.
>
> The decisive action is making naked. Nudity is opposed to the closed state, in other words, to the state of discontinuous existence. Nudity is a condition of communication, which reveals the quest for a possible continuity of being, beyond the closing in on oneself. Bodies open to continuity by these secret passages that give us the feeling of obscenity. Obscenity signifies the trouble that disorders a

condition of bodies in possession of themselves, a possession of a durable and affirmed identity . . .

What is at stake in eroticism is always a dissolution of constituted forms . . . But in eroticism, even less than in reproduction, discontinuous life is not doomed, despite Sade's claim, to disappear: it is simply put into question. It must be troubled, maximally disordered.[16]

Putting one's body at risk in this manner creates a disequilibrium in which one consciously puts oneself into question. The erotic thus offers a momentary transcendence of limits, of discontinuity. It is comparable to sacrifice, as the revelation—and creation—of the sacred. "The sacred is precisely the continuity of being, revealed to those who fix their attention, in a solemn rite, on the death of a discontinuous being" (92). Death offers the final transgression or transcendence of the closed body. Eroticism as an act of transgression indicates that "the sacred and prohibition are bound up together, and that access to the sacred takes place in the violence of an infraction" (139). Bataille thus redefines the age-old intimacy of love and death: eroticism is "the affirmation of life all the way unto death" ("l'approbation de la vie jusque dans la mort").

I cite Bataille because he so well captures the trans-personal state achieved in erotic realization by the protagonist of *L'amant,* and how this state opens onto a sacred state ("the knowledge of God," she calls it) that is also akin to death. For both Bataille and Duras, the erotic is a state of expenditure and excess. These are key terms for Bataille, since they underlie his attempt—given its fullest statement in *La part maudite*—to found a social economy based not on saving and capitalization but on expenditure *(la dépense),* waste, and unproductiveness, which are necessary to regain a sense of the sacred beyond the utilitarian. Art is in this sense also expenditure, waste, excess. Poetry, says Bataille, is "creation by means of loss . . . the pursuit of inconsistent shadows that provide nothing but vertigo and rage. The poet frequently can use words only for his own loss."[17] The view of writing advanced in *L'amant* is quite similar.

L'amant closes with a phone call from the Chinese lover to the girl, now married and divorced, and a mother, many years after her return to France, during his visit to Paris. The call ends with his avowal that he loves her still, that he could never stop loving her, that he will love her unto death. The desire created in *L'amant* is absolute, beyond the specific circumstances in which it is enacted. The episode of the phone call is immediately preceded by the narrative of the lover's arranged marriage with the Chinese wife chosen by his father—events which the girl did not witness and could not know. According to her account, the lover must for a long time have been impotent with his new wife, unable to consummate the marriage because of his memory of the white girl, as if her body stretched sideways across the marriage bed:

> She must have remained for a long time the ruler of his desire, the personal reference of his emotion, of the immensity of his tenderness, of somber and terrible carnal depth. Then the day came when it must have been possible. Precisely when desire for the white girl must have been so strong, so unbearable that he could recall her image in its totality as in a raging fever and could penetrate the other woman with this desire for her, the white girl. It must have been by way of a lie that he found himself inside this woman, and by a lie that he engendered what the two families, Heaven, his ancestors in the North, all expected from him, that is, an heir to his name. (140–41)

In the manner of the phantasmatic scenes played out on the body of Hélène Lagonelle, the body of the girl serves as intermediary in the realization of desire, indeed takes on the role of the phallus: it is with this desire that the lover finally succeeds in entering his bride. But whereas the phantasmatic body of Hélène Lagonelle serves the intellectual comprehension of desire, here the hallucinated body of the girl—invoked as in a fever—serves rather the lie, the substitution of sexual objects. One may then ask which kind of phantasy or hallucination presides at the writing of this passage, which narrates not what the girl has witnessed and knows to be the case, but rather the way things "must have been." Is this a lie? Or is it the kind of phantasy that creates truth, the truth dictated by desire? Is it, in this sense, an emblem of the very fiction-making process, of the capacity to narrate not only events but also the history of desire underlying events, the history in which events are merely symptoms of a determinative, hidden narrative? It is not to cast doubt on the truth of the events recounted in *L'amant* to suggest that the guiding thread of the narrative, and the dynamic of the plot, have less to do with the relatively sparse and simple events of the novel than with the force of desire, as the source of hallucinated and phantasized bodies, of bodies that have a corporeal reality but become significant in their placement in relation to desire. The writing of the book also has to do with positions in relation to desire. The writing body retraces the eros of the story in a state of deprivation and hallucination.

There is a moment in the novel, following the girl's fantasy of Hélène Lagonelle in the arms of her lover, when the place of erotic encounter with the lover, the Cholon apartment, is analogized to the place of writing. Within the aridity and hardness of her family the girl gains her essential conviction that she will be a writer. She has come to understand her family in a new light because of the hours she spends in the Cholon apartment. "It is an unbearable place, it borders on death, a place of violence, of pain, of despair, of dishonor. And such is the place in Cholon" (93). That is, the place of writing, its spiritual space, is one of agony and despair, also of eroticism and death. We are reminded of a passage early in the novel where the narrator refers to her vocation of writing, which she discovers along with eroticism at age fifteen, as characterized by an "inconvenance fondamentale," a fundamental impropriety. Writing is a violation of accepted norms, a transgression of limits, an experience of pain and of orgasmic pleasure. Writing indeed (as I have suggested) may originate in the erotic. And the erotic espouses the mission of writing when it is the source and the object of an act of intelligence, when it is seized intellectually as a testing of limits.

Writing for Bataille is linked in much the same manner to the lucid, willed transgression of proprieties and prohibitions, the creation of value through the experience of infraction and loss. Bataille's essays in literary criticism, in *La littérature et le mal*, turn around the issue posed in Baudelaire's phrase, from the poem "L'irrémédiable," "la conscience dans le mal," consciousness of evil and consciousness within evil, the transgressor's awareness at the moment of transgression. It is not so much that wrongdoing is pleasurable, as that taking pleasure is seen as evil. "Evil is not transgression, it is transgression condemned. It is precisely sin."[18] The importance of sin lies in its conceptualization, as that kind of transgressive act that changes one's spiritual condition and entails sanctions. In sinning, one may choose the state of damnation, and therefore know it in full lucidity. Eroticism, for both Bataille and Duras—as also for Baudelaire—offers the most direct experience of *mal*: transgression condemned, turned into sin. The act of erotic transgression is a moment of heightened consciousness beyond the normal limits and conventions. The transgression of writing—another form of "communication"—is fundamentally similar; it assumes the impossible, as place and as state of being, a condition akin to mortal sin where pleasure is derived from the knowledge of *mal,* of one's wrongdoing, and knowledge itself is that pleasure.

The Body and the "Frenzy of the Visible"

L'amant, like Bataille's writings on eroticism, belongs very much to the epistemophilic project that we have repeatedly encountered in stories of the body: the project of knowing the body and knowing through the body, essentially by way of erotic experience, since eroticism makes the body most fully sentient and also most "intellectual," the most aware of what it is doing and what is being done to it.

The tradition of the intellectual-erotic, as one might call it, is of course very old (Ovid's arts of love are part of it), but it is particularly pertinent in the eighteenth century, especially in France, and in the mid-to-late twentieth century—which has discovered many affinities with the eighteenth. Yet at present the project of knowing the body appears to be pursued less in writing than in the visual arts. The postmodern age is intensely visual, defined by film, video, dance, performance art, blockbuster museum shows. As Jean-Louis Comolli suggests, since the late nineteenth century we have lived in a "frenzy of the visible," and certainly our own time has seen only an intensification of the frenzy.[19] Even though George Eliot and Freud taught us, in different ways, to listen to the body, our knowing of the body still seems to be obsessed with viewing it, striving to see it in its moments of most intense sensation. Linda Williams has discussed the pornographic film as an example of Michel Foucault's "knowledge of pleasure": the apparently insatiable need to see the body perform erotically, organized around moments of orgasm—especially male orgasm, which is visually demonstrable, the orgasm that cannot be faked.[20] Although pornography remains a special realm, its demarcations from acceptable artistic expression have been repeatedly questioned, in ways that define some of the issues of the body and knowledge in our time. Two examples deserve brief mention here.

The first is the controversy sparked by the posthumous show of photographs by Robert Mapplethorpe in 1989. The cancellation of the show by the Corcoran Gallery in Washington, D.C., after Senator Jesse Helms and others objected to its contents, the subsequent protest by the arts community, and the continuing attempts in Congress to police on the grounds of "decency" and "offensiveness" the grants made by the National Endowment for the Arts brought into focus one of the last prohibitions of public display in our culture. For what was deemed offensive and censorable in Mapplethorpe's work was essentially the penis, and in particular the erect penis (to which one might add that many of the organs so photographed belonged to black men). A moment's reflection is sufficient to assure us that if the genitals displayed had been those of women, the scandal would not have existed. In film, advertising, and art, the woman's sex, attenuated or not, has become acceptable for public display. It may shock, it may be displayed in ways that make the image pornographic, but it is clearly not censorable. One could argue, in the manner of Linda Williams, that the penis is in this manner the object of visual frenzy because it makes sexual excitation and orgasm visible in a way that is not the case for women. Another argument would have it that the penis must be covered because uncovered it is never adequate to the imaginary standard of power, the phallus. Or one could invoke the Lacanian position that the phallus is the "the privileged signifier of that mark where the share of the logos is wedded to the advent of desire," and thus surmise that its display uncovers unacceptably the complex intertwining of body, language, and sexuality.[21]

These arguments are all plausible. But one might also say, more simply, that the unacceptable display is of the organ of patriarchy, which in a culture where patriarchy is the basis of knowledge and power, and the gaze is phallic, must be veiled. To display the penis is to turn subject into object, a twist or per-version which is of course also part of Mapplethorpe's explicitly homoerotic work. As Barthes argues, the nakedness of the drunken patriarch Noah is taboo, a nakedness that his sons must veil in order to maintain the Law of the Father. Mapplethorpe's photographs, glossy and fashionable in the manner of *Vogue* magazine, often turn the penis into something of a joke, a camp object deprived of the *mysterium tremendum* which ought, in patriarchy, to accompany this most sacred object.[22] Mapplethorpe's photographs, then, do not overwhelm us with the tremendous presence of the phallus, but rather they offer for bemused, even amused, inspection the penis doing its thing. These photographs are ultimately demystifying, something that much of our culture apparently is not yet ready to accept.

The other example is "super-realist" art ("hyper-realist" and "photo-realist" are other labels) created in the 1970s, particularly the sculpture of John De Andrea. In distinction to such super-realist painters of the body as Philip Pearlstein or William Beckman, De Andrea offers bodies in full, life-size volume; and in distinction to the sculptures of Duane Hanson, which depend for their social and often satiric statement on detailed clothing, De Andrea's bodies are nude. By the idealizing standards of classical nude sculpture, one would say instead that they are naked: they are detailed and particularized. Indeed, since they are cast from life, they take the form of particular people (and often bear their names). Thus they offer the kind of nakedness that one might see in the bedroom, or at a nude beach. They constitute an invasion of privacy. They also pose the problem of how they are to be looked at. Any art object that offers itself to spectatorship calls for inspection, an intensified kind of looking. And looking at a De Andrea sculpture is for most people an uncomfortable experience, precisely because the kind of inspection involved seems to violate normal artistic canons of contemplation and to approach an almost illicit voyeurism.

I remember attending the opening of a De Andrea show (at Issy Brachot Gallery in Paris) at which it became evident that the spectators, myself included, were embarrassed by their own looking. Here were a dozen or so sculptures of nudes, mostly women. The poses were casual, everyday postures, the bodies young and attractive. They were reproduced with astonishing fidelity: flesh tones, folds of the skin, fingernails, pubic hair (Figure 39). Much of one's attention was focused on the *techne* of these recreations of the body, on how it could be reproduced in these materials with such illusionistic fidelity. This art reminded one of Madame Tussaud's waxworks, but without the illustrational, anecdotal aim of the waxworks—though there are some narrative elements, particularly in the representations of couples. Our interest in the De Andrea sculptures seemed to be a manner of saying to ourselves: yes, that's what it looks like—a judgment of conformity to the thing imitated. Such was not, of course, the standard of judgment for classical sculpture, where the body is conceived to be the vehicle of expression—even simply expression of itself, the body grasped as form, volume, and movement. De Andrea's figures are curiously inexpressive, though often beautiful and erotic. Their very simulacrum of the real body makes you ask what you are supposed to do with them. They almost appear to be full-sized dolls for some sort of regressive adult play. (Consider here De Andrea's version of Pygmalion and Galatea, in his *Self-Portrait with Sculpture* of 1980 [Figure 40].) But their setting in the space of the art gallery negates that response. They are simply to be looked at, inspected; the spectators come away with the conclusion, that's what the body looks like, that's what it's like to rebuild the body, from scratch, and to have it come out looking just like the real thing.

De Andrea's project is not unlike that attributed by Jorge Luis Borges to his invented writer Pierre Menard, who sets out to rewrite *Don*

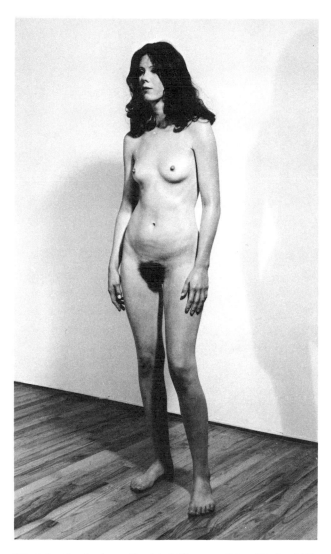

39. John De Andrea, *Freckled Woman*. (New York: ACA
  Galleries. Photo: Eric Pollitzer)

Quixote in the twentieth century. Menard does not simply copy the
existing work by Cervantes. He undertakes the much more astonishing
feat of making himself—a twentieth-century Frenchman—write anew a
work in Golden Age Spanish prose, in the mental framework of the
time, and having it result in a text that "would coincide—word for
word and line for line" with the original. He proposes a work "verbally
identical" to the *Quixote,* but utterly changed by the context of its

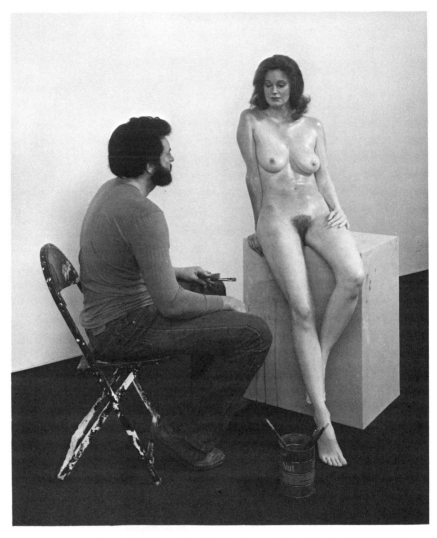

40. John De Andrea, *Self-Portrait with Sculpture*. (New York: ACA Galleries. Photo: D. James Dee)

writing and its reading, which "denaturalizes" all the moral, psychological, historical, and stylistic assumptions of the original.[23] The hypernaturalism of De Andrea has something of this denaturalizing effect. The very banality of his beautifully rendered bodies makes us look anew, and makes us ask questions about our continuing interest in inspecting the body. In a sense, De Andrea reduces the epistemophilic project exercised on the body to a kind of tautology, or a mere gesture of pointing: *that* is the body. The project of making the body signify thus issues in a lovingly detailed impasse.

The problems of looking suggested by Duras, Mapplethorpe, and De Andrea offer the occasion for a final reflection on the issue of spectatorship and gender. Feminist film theory has led us to a perception of the long tradition of a male gaze exercised on women coded for display, and certainly most of the works of literature and art I have mentioned in the course of this study belong to that tradition. Even so, to describe and define them as exclusively examples of phallic vision dominating its objects seems to me to do less than justice to the actual pleasures of reading and viewing. The realm of imaginative works may be the area in which rigid gender distinctions, like other "laws" of social existence, are relaxed, where we are free to explore some of the polymorphousness and bisexuality which have been subject to repression, in greater or lesser degree, in human development. Freud's inadequate but suggestive model of aesthetic pleasure, in his essay "Creative Writers and Daydreaming" (1908), indicates that art may work on us through a relaxation of ego defenses, and his much more complex "A Child Is Being Beaten" suggests that the individual is capable of assuming a variety of positions, active and passive, female and male, in relation to desire.[24] However well-defined our gender and our sexual preferences may be in the practice of our social lives, we are, I believe, capable of responding— and responding erotically—to depictions of male and female bodies in a great variety of ways, as seer and seen, as voyeur and actor, in objectification and participation. Although the male gaze is inscribed in our cultural ideologies, its privilege is precarious—merely ideological—and subject to imaginative twists and reversals.

I want to conclude by returning from the visual body to the written body, in an emblematic tale literally about writing on the body, in this case not in pleasure but in pain: Franz Kafka's "In the Penal Colony" ("In der Strafkolonie") of 1916. The story concerns an explorer's invitation to witness the execution of a soldier, condemned for disobedience and insulting behavior to a superior, in a penal colony ruled by a Commandant who apparently does not believe in the exemplary punishments so important to the former Commandant. The explorer's witnessing of the punishment may indeed serve the new Commandant's intention to abolish the practice: such, at least, will be the conclusion of the officer charged with the execution, a devoted admirer of the old Commandant who seeks to perpetuate his practices. The centerpiece of the story is the apparatus used for executions, explained in detail by the officer to the explorer—in French, a language which the condemned man and his guard do not understand, though the condemned man makes an effort to follow the naming of the machine's parts. The guilty person is strapped onto the Bed, under the Harrow, controlled by the Designer above it. The apparatus when set in motion proceeds to inscribe with needles on the condemned man's body the sentence passed on him—in this case the sentence HONOR THY SUPERIORS! Since the Harrow is made of glass, one can look through it and follow the inscription forming on the body. And since the punishment takes twelve hours, the script of the simple sentence takes on "flourishes" and "embellishments." The explorer asks:

> "Does he know his sentence?" "No," said the officer, eager to go on with his exposition, but the explorer interrupted him: "He doesn't know the sentence that has been passed on him?" "No," said the officer again, pausing a moment as if to let the explorer elaborate his question, and then said: "There would be no point in telling him. He'll learn it on his body."[25]

The judicial sentence—a sentence to death—is to be learned as a sentence written—also to death—on the body. Learning one's sentence on the body presents a chilling literalization of Roland Barthes' claim that the ultimate field of symbolism is the human body.[26] Here the distance between symbol and symbolized has collapsed; the animating tension between writing and the body has simply been abolished. The body itself has become literally the place for the inscription of the letter. And here the letter killeth, literally.

The old Commandant's apparatus reverses the Freudian production of symptoms, which are inscriptions on the body of the dictates of repressed desire. Here, the inscriptions of the law on the body are supposed to produce an inner conversion. As the officer explains:

> "But how quiet he grows at just about the sixth hour! Enlightenment comes to the most dull-witted. It begins around the eyes. From there it radiates. A moment that might tempt one to get under the Harrow oneself. Nothing more happens than that the man begins to understand the inscription, he purses his mouth as if he were listening. You have seen how difficult it is to decipher the script with one's eyes; but our man deciphers it with his wounds. To be sure, that is

a hard task; he needs six hours to accomplish it. By that time the Harrow has pierced him quite through and casts him into the pit, where he pitches down upon the blood and water, and the cotton wool." (204)

Enlightenment is a product of the body's having received the sentence unto death, so that it is entirely marked with the sentence of the law.

When it becomes evident to the officer that the explorer does not find the justice apparatus "convincing," and will no doubt present a negative report to the Commandant, the officer frees the condemned man from the apparatus and puts himself under the Harrow. But as the machine starts to write on his body the new sentence he has programmed into the Designer—BE JUST!—it begins to self-destruct. Cogwheels rise from the Designer and fall to the ground. The Harrow ceases to write, it only jabs; the bed no longer rotates the body but brings it up quivering against the needles. Then the Harrow rises with the body spitted on it, as if to drop it in the pit—as it is supposed to do only at the twelfth hour—but the body remains hanging. And now the explorer sees the dead officer's face: "It was as it had been in life; no sign was visible of the promised redemption; what the others had found in the machine the officer had not found; the lips were firmly pressed together, the eyes were open, with the same expression as in life, the look was calm and convinced, through the forehead went the point of the great iron spike" (224–25).

The promise of redemption or enlightenment through inscription on the body never is fulfilled for the man who most believed in the power of the script. The message "Be just!" never is written. No illumination comes. We are left with an impaled body that is just that, a body, without transcendence or signification. It is as if the promise of a body recovered for the law and for meaning by writing were untenable, false. To the extent that the writing project is imposed by a totalitarian ideology, one may see in the officer's untranscendent death an affirmation of the body's resistance to claims of correction, ennoblement, and conversion asserted upon it. The tortured body here refuses to give satisfaction to the torturing regime; indeed it betokens the moral bankruptcy of that regime. In a less optimistic interpretation—and nothing in Kafka's chilling story encourages the least optimism—one can say that the body simply resists any attempt to write messages on it. The sixth hour—*nel mezzo del cammin*—brings no enlightenment, and the twelfth hour brings bloody death, period. In this manner, Kafka's tale may warn against all our attempts to redeem the body for the signifying process, to make its naturalness into a cultural product. The body remains the body, fragile, subject to pain and to mortality.

286 But it is not in an impasse, even one so emblematic of the project of inscribing the body, that I want to conclude, since the project of making the body signify—making it the protagonist of stories and the scene of stories—has not ended and will not end. Even though we acknowledge the meaningless mortality of the body, we continue to celebrate and emblazon the body while we are alive. We have banalized the body, demystified it, displayed it to the point that there may be no more to learn about it—at least, about its exterior. We have listened to its talk, in an effort to penetrate to its most reticent messages. But we still don't know the body. Its otherness from ourselves, as well as its intimacy, make it the inevitable object of an ever-renewed writing project.

Notes
Index

Notes

1. Narrative and the Body

1. *The Odyssey,* trans. Robert Fitzgerald (Garden City, N.Y.: Anchor Books, 1963), Book 19, ll. 388–93. The classic study of this episode is in Erich Auerbach, *Mimesis: The Representation of Reality in Western Literature,* trans. Willard Trask (Garden City, N.Y.: Anchor Books, 1957). It is significant that the "flashback" narrative of the wound also recounts how Odysseus received his name, from his maternal grandfather, Autolykos (who later leads the boar hunt), thus reinforcing the sense that the scarring of his body is fundamentally linked to his identity.

2. On this scene, and these questions generally, see Terence Cave, *Recognitions: A Study in Poetics* (Oxford: Clarendon, 1988). Cave comments that Odysseus' scar "composes his identity by calling up retrospectively a fragment of narrative" (p. 23). Cave also discusses Aristotle's types of recognition (from Chapter 16 of the *Poetics*), which include recognition by signs *(sêmeia),* which may be congenital (birthmarks), acquired (scars) or worn (such as *la croix de ma mère);* see pp. 38ff. Shakespeare's *Cymbeline* offers a particularly interesting instance of the birthmark: the mole on Imogen's left breast—in a place not supposed to be seen—offers a false sign of her infidelity.

3. See Sheila Murnaghan, "Body and Voice in Greek Tragedy," *Yale Journal of Criticism* 1:2 (Spring 1988), pp. 23–43, who notes that the warriors' bodies and body parts in the *Iliad* are named in the greatest detail as they are "assaulted, pierced, traversed by spears, ground into the dust" (p. 24); on the signs used in Greek tragedy, see the discussions in Cave, *Recognitions.*

4. Northrop Frye, *Anatomy of Criticism* (Princeton: Princeton University Press, 1957), p. 214.

5. Francis Barker, *The Tremulous Private Body: Essays on Subjection* (London and New York: Methuen, 1984), p. 24. See also Mikhail Bakhtin, *Rabelais and His World* (Bloomington: Indiana University Press, 1984). For a useful summary of recent work on the body, see Leslie Rado, "On the Recent Intellec-

tual Interest in the Body" (unpublished paper presented at the Northeastern American Studies Association Conference, Lexington, Mass., 1988).

6. Roland Barthes, *S/Z* (Paris: Editions du Seuil, 1970), p. 220; English trans. Richard Miller, *S/Z* (New York: Hill and Wang, 1974). Translations from the French, here and elsewhere in the book, are my own unless otherwise specified.

7. See Sigmund Freud, "On Narcissism: An Introduction," *Standard Edition of the Complete Psychological Writings of Sigmund Freud* (London: Hogarth Press, 1953–1974), 14:77; see also *Three Essays on the Theory of Sexuality,* ibid., 7:181–83. See Melanie Klein, "Early Stages of the Oedipus Conflict," *Contributions to Psycho-Analysis, 1921–1945* (London: Hogarth Press, 1950), pp. 202–226.

8. Melanie Klein, "The Importance of Symbol Formation in the Development of the Ego," in *Contributions to Psycho-Analysis,* p. 237; see also, in the same volume, "The Psychological Principles of Infant Analysis." On the thought of Melanie Klein, I have found very helpful the introduction and notes by Juliet Mitchell in *The Selected Melanie Klein,* ed. Juliet Mitchell (Harmondsworth: Penguin, 1986).

9. See Georges Bataille, *L'érotisme* (1957; Paris: Union Générale d'Editions, 1965), especially pp. 15–30; English trans. Mary Dalwood, *Erotism* (New York: Boyars, 1987).

10. Luce Irigaray, *Speculum de l'autre femme* (Paris: Editions de Minuit, 1974), p. 53; English trans. Gillian C. Gill, *Speculum of the Other Woman* (Ithaca: Cornell University Press, 1985). I discuss Freud's discussions of scopophilia and the visuality of the epistemophilic urge in Chapter 4.

11. Edith Jacobsen, *The Self and the Object World* (Madison, Conn.: International Universities Press, 1964), p. 71.

12. On this scenario, see also Sándor Ferenczi, *Thalassa: A Theory of Genitality,* trans. Henry Alden Bunker (New York: Norton, 1968), where he speculates that olfaction is the "biological prototype of ideation."

13. William Irwin Thompson: "The shift from estrus to a receptivity for intercourse at all times represents an eroticization of time; sexuality becomes an orientation to all experiences rather than a perfunctory ten-second interlude in a way of life oriented around status and power." *The Time Falling Bodies Take to Light: Mythology, Sexuality, and the Origins of Culture* (New York: St. Martin's Press, 1981), p. 72. The erect posture also entails the possibility of face-to-face copulation in humans, rather than *a tergo,* as in most animals, which leads Jacques Lacan to some tantalizing but fragmentary reflections on the fact that objects of desire come to humans in a face-to-face relation; see Lacan, *Le séminaire, Livre VII: Le transfert* (Paris: Editions du Seuil, 1991), p. 443.

14. *Oeuvres complètes de Duclos* (Paris, 1820–21), 9:424.

15. Freud, "Medusa's Head" (1922), *Standard Edition* 18:273. This is not the whole of Freud's story of the male's perception of the female genitals,

however; a more complex view emerges from his essay "The Uncanny" ("Das Unheimliche," 1919).

16. Jacqueline Rose, "Introduction-II," in *Feminine Sexuality: Jacques Lacan and the Ecole Freudienne,* ed. Juliet Mitchell and Jacqueline Rose (London: Macmillan, 1982), p. 43. This volume, including Lacan's essential essays on the subject and extraordinarily helpful introductory essays by Mitchell and Rose, offers the best current thinking on questions of "castration" as well as feminine sexuality. On these questions, see also Sarah Kofman, *L'énigme de la femme* (Paris: Editions Galilée, 1980); English trans. Catherine Porter, *The Enigma of Woman* (Ithaca: Cornell University Press, 1985).

17. Juliet Mitchell, "Introduction-I," in *Feminine Sexuality,* p. 24.

18. Juliet Mitchell, "From King Lear to Anna 'O' and Beyond: Some Speculative Theses on Hysteria and the Traditionless Self," *Yale Journal of Criticism* 5:2 (1992), p. 93.

19. Gregorio Kohon, "Reflections on Dora: The Case of Hysteria," in *The British School of Psychoanalysis: The Independent Tradition,* ed. Gregorio Kohon (New Haven and London: Yale University Press, 1986), p. 371, pp. 372–73. Italics are Kohon's. In a note to the second passage quoted, Kohon refers his reader to O. Masotta, *Lecciones de introducción al psicoanálisis,* vol. 1 (Barcelona: Gedisa, 1977).

20. See Jacques Lacan, "Le stade du miroir comme formateur de la fonction du Je," *Ecrits* (Paris: Editions du Seuil, 1966), pp. 93–100; English trans. Alan Sheridan, *Ecrits* (New York: Norton, 1977). The "anecdote" of the infant in front of the mirror need not be literal: the mirroring can come from other people.

21. See Norbert Elias, *The Civilizing Process,* trans. Edmund Jephcott, vol. 1, *The History of Manners* (New York: Pantheon, 1978); vol. 2, *Power and Civility* (New York: Pantheon, 1982),

22. See Philippe Ariès, *L'enfant et la vie familiale sous l'ancien régime* (Paris: Plon, 1960); English trans. Robert Baldick, *Centuries of Childhood* (New York: Vintage Books, 1962); see also *Histoire de la vie privée,* ed. Philippe Ariès and Georges Duby, vol. 3: *De la Renaissance aux Lumières,* ed. Roger Chartier (Paris: Editions du Seuil, 1986); English trans. Arthur Goldhammer, *The History of Private Life* (Cambridge, Mass.: Harvard University Press, 1988).

23. See Michel Foucault, *Histoire de la sexualité: I. La volonté de savoir* (Paris: Gallimard, 1976); trans. Robert Hurley, *The History of Sexuality, 1* (New York: Pantheon, 1978).

24. Roland Barthes, *Le plaisir du texte* (Paris: Editions du Seuil, 1973), p. 20; English trans. Richard Miller, *The Pleasure of the Text* (New York: Hill and Wang, 1975). Barthes may suggest here that the attention to female nudity is something of a coverup for the more deeply feared nudity, though this would seem to run counter to the Freudian scenarios of castration. The question of the ultimately most scandalous nudity seems to me undecidable.

25. For a probing discussion of pornographic cinema, see Linda Williams,

Hard Core: Power, Pleasure, and the "Frenzy of the Visible" (Berkeley and Los Angeles: University of California Press, 1989). Williams suggests that the prominent attention to the erect and ejaculating penis in hard-core cinema is related to the impossibility of visually "proving" woman's sexual pleasure.

26. See Kenneth Clark, *The Nude: A Study in Ideal Form* (1956; Garden City, N.Y.: Doubleday Anchor Books, 1959), pp. 112 ff. See also Gill Saunders, *The Nude: A New Perspective* (New York: Harper and Row, 1989); Edward Lucie-Smith, *Sexuality in Western Art* (New York: Thames and Hudson, 1991); Susan R. Suleiman, ed., *The Female Body in Western Culture* (Cambridge, Mass.: Harvard University Press, 1986); and Margaret Walters, *The Nude Male* (1978; Harmondsworth: Penguin Books, 1979).

27. Candace Clements makes the interesting argument that the exclusion of female models from the Académie Royale in the eighteenth century meant that young artists learned to paint the female nude in private, intimate, domestic spaces, thus establishing a separate—and eroticized—tradition. See Clements, "The Academy and the Other: *Les grâces* and *le genre galant,*" *Eighteenth Century Studies,* 25:4 (1992):469–94.

28. Kenneth Clark, discussing Ingres and the female nude: "Fifty years earlier Winckelmann had asserted that whereas the male nude might achieve character, the female nude alone could aspire to beauty: an assertion uninfluenced by personal preferences but by his theory that beauty consists in smoothness and continuity. It was largely because Ingres for so long dominated the center of the academic system that his theory became reality, and naked women took the place of men as the models in art schools" (*The Nude,* pp. 218–19). Concerning Girodet's *Sleep of Endymion:* Thomas Crow, comparing the painting to David's unfinished *Death of Bara* (1794), argues a political/heroic significance for this kind of male beauty, which he derives from Winckelmann's aesthetics. See Crow, "Revolutionary Activism and the Cult of Male Beauty in the Studio of David," in *Fictions of the French Revolution,* ed. Bernadette Fort (Evanston, Ill.: Northwestern University Press, 1991), pp. 55–83.

29. For an interesting discussion of this question, see Anne Hollander, *Seeing through Clothes* (New York: Viking, 1978), pp. 136–48.

30. See Foucault, *La volonté de savoir,* pp. 193–96. On some of the questions raised by privacy, display, spectatorship, and commodification, see Abigail Solomon-Godeau, "Reconsidering Erotic Photography: Notes for a Project of Historical Salvage," *Journal: A Contemporary Art Magazine,* 47:5 (Spring 1987), pp. 51–58.

31. See Barthes, *Le plaisir du texte,* pp. 19–20; see also *S/Z* on Barthes' model of narrative, and, on these general questions of narrative, my *Reading for the Plot* (New York: Knopf, 1984; Cambridge, Mass.: Harvard University Press, 1992).

32. I quote from the translation of *Metamorphoses* 10:253–58 by Mary M. Innes (Harmondsworth: Penguin Books, 1955), p. 231.

33. The story of Pygmalion and Galatea can of course be considered exclusively a male wish-fulfillment, in which the female body is created according to

the man's desire. Yet given that the epistemophilic urge develops in both men and women originally from the experience of the mother's body, perhaps this emblematic story could concern only the creation of a woman's body.

34. See Alain Corbin, "Coulisses," in *Histoire de la vie privée,* ed. Philippe Ariès and Georges Duby, vol. 4: *De la Révolution à la Grande Guerre,* ed. Michelle Perrot (Paris: Editions du Seuil, 1987), especially pp. 419–436, "l'individu et sa trace"; English trans. Arthur Goldhammer, *From the Fires of the Revolution to the Great War* (Cambridge, Mass.: Harvard University Press, 1990). On marks of identity and narrative, see also the remarkable essay by Carlo Ginzburg, "Spie: radici di un paradigma indizario," in *Miti, emblemi, spie* (Turin: Einaudi, 1986); English trans. John and Anne C. Tedeschi, "Clues: Roots of an Evidential Paradigm," in *Clues, Myths, and the Historical Method* (Baltimore: Johns Hopkins University Press, 1989).

2. Invasions of Privacy

1. See Ian Watt, *The Rise of the Novel* (Berkeley and Los Angeles: University of California Press, 1957), esp. chap. 6, "Private Experience and the Novel." On the new valuation of privacy, see also Philippe Ariès, *L'enfant et la vie familiale sous l'ancien régime* (Paris: Plon, 1960), and Philippe Ariès and Georges Duby, eds., *Histoire de la vie privée* (Paris: Editions du Seuil, 1986), vol. 3, *De la Renaissance aux Lumières,* ed. Ariès and Roger Chartier, especially the chapter by Orest Ranum, "Les refuges de l'intimité," pp. 211–65; English trans. Arthur Goldhammer, *Passions of the Renaissance* (Cambridge, Mass.: Harvard University Press, 1989). Ranum notes that what were originally pieces of furniture— *bibliothèque, cabinet, étude*—tended to become separate rooms. This and other work by social historians has more and more confirmed that the crucial development of the modern sense of privacy took place in the eighteenth century. Recent work has suggested the importance of conceptions of the body in this development: see in particular Thomas Laqueur, *Making Sex: Body and Gender from the Greeks to Freud* (Cambridge: Harvard University Press, 1990).

2. See Stendhal, "La comédie est impossible en 1836," in *Mélanges de littérature,* ed. Henri Martineau (Paris: Le Divan, 1933), 3:431; on the revolutionary importance of silent reading, see Roger Chartier, "Les pratiques de l'écrit," in *Histoire de la vie privée* 3:113–60; for a good example of the connections among privacy, writing, and the body, see the discussion of Samuel Pepys' diary in Francis Barker, *The Tremulous Private Body* (London and New York: Methuen, 1984), especially pp. 3–9.

3. On these questions, see the excellent exposition in Walter J. Ong, *Orality and Literacy: The Technologizing of the Word* (London and New York: Methuen, 1982), esp. chap. 4.

4. Walter Benjamin, "The Storyteller" ("Der Erzähler"), in *Illuminations,* trans. Harry Zohn (New York: Schocken Books, 1969), p. 100.

5. Francis Jeffrey's article, published in 1804, is cited by Watt, *The Rise of the Novel,* p. 175.

6. Jean-Marie Goulemot, in "Les pratiques littéraires ou la publicité du privé," in *Histoire de la vie privée* 3:371–405, working from a different perspective and with different intentions, provides analyses that often converge with my own.

7. On the privatization of the body in the nineteenth century, see Philippe Perrot, *Le travail des apparences* (Paris: Editions du Seuil, 1984) and Alain Corbin, "Coulisses," in Ariès and Duby, eds., *Histoire de la vie privée*, vol. 4, *De la Révolution à la Grande Guerre*, ed. Michelle Perrot (Paris: Editions du Seuil, 1987), pp. 413–610; English trans. Arthur Goldhammer, *From the Fires of the Revolution to the Great War* (Cambridge, Mass.: Harvard University Press, 1990). On many aspects of intimate experience in the nineteenth century, see Peter Gay, *The Bourgeois Experience: Victoria to Freud*, vol. 1, *Education of the Senses*, and vol. 2, *The Tender Passion* (New York: Oxford University Press, 1984–86).

8. See Terry Eagleton, *The Rape of Clarissa* (Oxford: Basil Blackwell, 1982), and Terry Castle, *Clarissa's Ciphers* (Ithaca: Cornell University Press, 1982).

9. See Orest Ranum on how certain paintings by Watteau turn the spectator into a voyeur, in "Les refuges de l'intimité," *Histoire de la vie privée*, 3:226. For a brilliant and persuasive argument concerning the importance of the subject's represented unconsciousness of the observing gaze in eighteenth-century painting, see Michael Fried, *Absorption and Theatricality: Painting and Beholder in the Age of Diderot* (Berkeley and Los Angeles: University of California Press, 1979).

10. Denis Diderot, "Salon de 1765," in *Oeuvres esthétiques*, ed. Paul Vernière (Paris: Garnier, 1959), p. 533. Diderot's reviews of the Paris salons, from 1759 to 1781, were composed for Melchior Grimm's *Correspondance littéraire*, and were thus conceived as descriptive and critical commentaries on the state of French art directed to an elite public in other European countries. His sustained attention to the careers of the major French artists of his time makes Diderot in some measure the first "professional" art critic.

11. On Diderot's empathetic, participatory reaction to the situations of Richardson's characters, see his "Eloge de Richardson," in *Oeuvres esthétiques*, pp. 29–48.

12. Jean-Jacques Rousseau, *Les confessions; Autres textes autobiographiques* (Paris: Bibliothèque de la Pléiade, 1962), p. 18. Page references to the *Confessions* hereafter are given in parentheses in the text.

13. Jacques Derrida, *De la grammatologie* (Paris: Editions de Minuit, 1967); English trans. Gayatri Chakravorty Spivak, *Of Grammatology* (Baltimore: Johns Hopkins University Press, 1976).

14. *Confessions*, p. 445. The language here is indirect—as it always is when Rousseau is discussing auto-eroticism—but a careful reading makes it clear what happens during his journeys on foot from the Ermitage to Eaubonne.

15. Rousseau, *Julie, ou la nouvelle Héloïse* (Paris: Bibliothèque de la Pléiade, 1964), p. 146.

16. See Roman Jakobson, "Two Poles of Language and Two Types of Aphasic

Disturbance," in Jakobson and Halle, *Fundamentals of Language* (The Hague: Mouton, 1956).

17. See Rousseau, *Pygmalion* (new edition, Geneva, 1776), pp. 8–9. Any reader familiar with Rousseau will know that it had to be Galatea's breasts that Pygmalion touched at the moment of animation: Rousseau is more than normally fixated on breasts and (what saves him from being a mere pathological case) quite aware of his fixation.

18. Carlo Ginzburg, "Spie: Radici di un paradigma indiziario," in *Miti, emblemi, spie* (Torino: Einaudi, 1986), p. 166; my translation. English trans. John and Anne C. Tedeschi, "Clues: Roots of an Evidential Paradigm," in *Clues, Myths, and the Historical Method* (Baltimore: Johns Hopkins University Press, 1989).

19. John Cleland, *Memoirs of a Woman of Pleasure* (1749; rpt. New York: Dell, 1963), p. 37.

20. For a very brief discussion of this polymorphousness in the reading of letter 10 of the novel, see my "1782: Words and 'the Thing,'" in *A New History of French Literature,* ed. Denis Hollier (Cambridge: Harvard University Press, 1989), pp. 540–41.

3. Marking Out the Modern Body

1. Charles Baudelaire, "Notes sur *Les liaisons dangereuses*," *Oeuvres complètes* (Paris: Bibliothèque de la Pléiade, 1954), p. 996. I want to thank Sarah Maza for her many helpful comments on the parts of this chapter concerned with the body in the French Revolution. I'm aware that I haven't adequately responded to some of her pertinent queries.

2. On the performatives of Revolutionary oratory, see especially Marc Blanchard, *La révolution par les mots: Saint-Just & cie.* (Paris: Nizet 1970); in the domain of Revolutionary art, see James H. Rubin, "Disorder/Order: Revolutionary Art as Performative Representation," in *The French Revolution, 1789–1989,* ed. Sandy Petrey (Lubbock, Tex.: Texas Tech University Press, 1989), pp. 83–112.

3. Michel Foucault writes, in exposition of the actions of penal reformers of the Revolutionary period: "As soon as the crime has been committed, and without losing any time, punishment will come, putting into action the discourse of the law and showing that the penal Code, which orders ideas, orders also realities." *Surveiller et punir* (Paris: Gallimard, 1975), p. 112; English trans. Alan Sheridan, *Discipline and Punish* (New York: Vintage Books, 1977).

4. Saint-Just, "Discours concernant le jugement de Louis XVI" (13 November 1790), in *Oeuvres choisies* (Paris: Gallimard-Idées Poche, 1968), p. 78. Saint-Just was to become Robespierre's close associate during the Reign of Terror, and the most eloquent spokesman for the Jacobin ideal.

5. "Rapport sur la nécessité de déclarer le gouvernement révolutionnaire jusqu'à la paix" (10 October 1793), *Oeuvres choisies,* p. 169.

6. "Rapport sur les suspects incarcérés" (26 February 1794) *Oeuvres chois-ies,* p. 192.

7. Dorinda Outram, *The Body and the French Revolution: Sex, Class, and Political Culture* (New Haven and London: Yale University Press, 1989), p. 81.

8. It should be noted as well that Revolutionary legislation instituted certain protections of the private space of the private body, giving concrete form to the Enlightenment ideals mentioned in the last chapter: for instance, the declaration that a person's domicile was inviolable (1792), the prohibition of nocturnal searches (1795), as well as the abolition of most "peines infamantes"—punish-ments in which parts of the body were mutilated. As Michelle Perrot comments, "Home and night sketch out a space-time of privacy around the body, whose dignity is recognized (abolition of most of the 'peines infamantes') and liberty. Homosexuality, for instance, is no longer an offense except when it is accom-panied with public violation of modesty." *Histoire de la vie privée,* ed. Philippe Ariès and Georges Duby, vol. 4, *De la Révolution à la Grande Guerre,* ed. Michelle Perrot (Paris: Editions du Seuil, 1987), p. 413; English trans. Arthur Goldhammer, *From the Fires of the Revolution to the Great War* (Cambridge, Mass.: Harvard University Press, 1990).

9. See Simon Schama, *Citizens* (New York: Knopf, 1989), esp. chap. 17.

10. I am indebted here to the account of this episode given by Emmet Kennedy in *A Cultural History of the French Revolution* (New Haven, Conn.: Yale University Press, 1989), pp. 206–212. Kennedy has the great merit of seeing the symbolic significance of this episode.

11. Outram, *The Body and the French Revolution,* p. 127. See also Lynn Hunt, *Politics, Culture, and Class in the French Revolution* (Berkeley and Los Angeles: University of California Press, 1984); and Joan B. Landes, *Women and the Public Sphere in the Age of the French Revolution* (Ithaca, N.Y., and London: Cornell University Press, 1988); Sarah Maza, "Representing the French Revo-lution," Yale Symposium, October 7, 1989 (unpublished paper).

12. *Le Moniteur Universel,* 19 November 1793, translated and cited in Chan-tal Thomas, "Heroism in the Feminine: The Examples of Charlotte Corday and Madame Roland," in *The French Revolution, 1789–1989,* ed. Petrey, pp. 79–80.

13. Cited in Marvin Carlson, *The Theater of the French Revolution* (Ithaca, N.Y.: Cornell University Press, 1966), p. 177.

14. Charles Nodier, preface to Guilbert de Pixerécourt, *Théâtre choisi,* 4 vols. (Paris and Nancy, 1841–1843).

15. Saint-Just, *Oeuvres choisies,* p. 327.

16. I quote from the first published edition of *Le jugement dernier des rois* (Paris: C.-F. Patris, L'an second de la République Française, une et indivisible). Translations are my own. My complete translation of the play is printed in *Yale Review* 78:4 (1990), pp. 583–603.

17. Marmontel, *Supplément* to the *Encyclopédie,* vol. 4 (Paris and Amster-dam, 1777), s.v. "Pantomime." On these questions, see my *The Melodramatic*

Imagination (1976; rpt. New York: Columbia University Press, 1985), chap. 3, "The Text of Muteness."

18. Oscar Wilde, "The Decay of Lying," in *Intentions* (1891) (Garden City, N.Y.: Dolphin Books, n.d.), p. 31.

19. Honoré de Balzac, *Illusions perdues* (Paris: Bibliothèque de la Pléiade, 1977), 5:164. Subsequent references to *La comédie humaine* are to this edition, and are given in parentheses in the text. Translations are my own. On the bodies of some of Balzac's spectacular young protagonists, see D. A. Miller, "1839: Body Bildung and Textual Liberation," in *A New History of French Literature,* ed. Denis Hollier (Cambridge, Mass.: Harvard University Press, 1989), pp. 681–87.

20. Albert Béguin, *Balzac visionnaire* (Geneva: Skira, 1946), pp. 151–79.

21. On the narrative potential of the prostitute, and some of its nineteenth-century realizations, especially in Eugène Sue's *Les mystères de Paris,* see my *Reading for the Plot* (New York: Knopf, 1984; rpt. Cambridge, Mass.: Harvard University Press, 1992), chap. 6, "The Mark of the Beast."

22. As I noted in Chapter 1, this anxiety led to various attempts to find systematic means to identify habitual criminals, including "bertillonage," and, much later, the practice of fingerprinting. See Alain Corbin, "Coulisses," in *Histoire de la vie privée* 4:430–36.

23. See Terence Cave, *Recognitions: A Study in Poetics* (Oxford: Clarendon, 1988), p. 251; Carlo Ginzburg, "Spie: Radici di un paradigma indiziario," in *Miti, emblemi, spie* (Turin: Einaudi, 1986).

24. For a more extended discussion of the body metonymized and fetishized, see Chapter 4.

25. The Pléiade edition regrettably omits titles of chapters and parts in Balzac's novels. In a text with the chronological complexities of *La Duchesse de Langeais*—it opens with Montriveau's coming to the convent where the Duchess has sequestered herself, then moves back to their meeting and his courtship, including the scene of proposed marking, then jumps forward to the attempted abduction and the dénouement—this is especially unfortunate. For the four divisons and their titles, see *La Duchesse de Langeais* in *Histoire des Treize,* ed. P.-G. Castex (Paris: Garnier, 1966).

26. As Patrick Berthier notes in his introduction to the Pléiade edition of the tale, Henri Martin was reputed to tame his wild beasts in this way, apparently through masturbation, before performances. This alleged practice may have worked for the male beasts, but the periodicity of estrus in female mammals makes it appear less than constantly applicable to Balzac's female panther. The thematic marker is thus perhaps not without ironies. But readers of Balzac's tale would no doubt have been prepared for the story of a sexual relation of some kind between soldier and panther, as Janet L. Beizer notes in her excellent study of this tale in *Family Plots: Balzac's Narrative Generations* (New Haven, Conn.: Yale University Press, 1986), p. 53. Beizer's own source for information on Martin is Léon-François Hoffmann, "Eros camouflé: En marge d'*Une passion*

dans le désert," *Hebrew Studies in Literature* 5:1 (1977), pp. 19–36. Beizer's chapter on *Une passion dans le désert* is constantly illuminating.

27. Beizer, *Family Plots,* p. 75. Beizer also points out the connections among the tail, the amputated leg, and the patriarchal palm tree—this "king of the desert"—which the soldier fells in an act with strong Oedipal resonances.

28. If we consider that Martin's "secrets" applied only to male beasts, we may find in the irony a further male reflection on female sexuality, as precisely that which cannot be tamed.

29. Balzac, "Traité de la vie élégante," in *Oeuvres diverses* (Paris: Conard, 1938), 2:180. For a semiotic study of Balzac's descriptive presention of characters, see Bernard Vannier, *L'inscription du corps: Pour une sémiotique du portrait balzacien* (Paris: Klincksieck, 1972).

30. Balzac, "Préambule" to the "Traité des excitants modernes," in *Oeuvres complètes* (Paris: Les Bibliophiles de l'originale, 1969), 19:545–46.

31. See D. A. Miller, *The Novel and the Police* (Berkeley and Los Angeles: University of California Press, 1988), esp. chap. 1. Miller's starting point is of course Michel Foucault's *Surveiller et punir.*

32. In Balzac, *Pensées, sujets, fragments,* ed. J. Crépet (Paris: Blaizot, 1910), p. 45, cited by Vannier, *L'inscription du corps,* p. 174.

33. "La femme sans coeur" is the title of the middle section of the novel, in which the scene discussed occurs; "athée en amour": p. 161.

34. On these details, see the very helpful notes and variants by Maurice Allem in his edition of *La peau de chagrin* (Paris: Garnier, 1967), pp. 396–97.

4. The Body in the Field of Vision

1. For discussion of some examples that do dissent from the main tradition, see Chapters 7 and 8. On the question of gender and the difference of the sexesin the nineteenth century, see Thomas Laqueur, *Making Sex: Body and Gender from the Greeks to Freud* (Cambridge: Harvard University Press, 1990). For a subtle and convincing argument that many key nineteenth-century novels are indeed about gender as defining character and experience, see Evelyne Ender, *Le roman de l'identité sexuelle* (Ph.D. diss., University of Geneva, 1991; forthcoming in English translation from Cornell University Press). The contrast between the nineteenth-century and Renaissance traditions was brought to my attention by Jonathan Crewe, in some very pertinent questions following a lecture I gave at Dartmouth College in 1990.

2. Gustave Flaubert, *Madame Bovary* (Paris: Gallimard/Folio, 1972), p. 87. Subsequent references are to this edition, and are given in parentheses in the text. For an interesting discussion of the body in Flaubert, see Roger Kempf, *Sur le corps romanesque* (Paris: Editions du Seuil, 1968), pp. 101–130.

3. Of the many uses of the mirror metaphor, one of the best known is Stendhal's: "A novel is a mirror that one carries along a road." See, among other places where the phrase is used, *Le rouge et le noir* in Stendhal, *Romans* (Paris: Bibliothèque de la Pléiade, 1952), 1:288.

4. See "Honoré de Balzac," in Henry James, *Literary Criticism: French Writers; Other European Writers; The Prefaces to the New York Edition* (New York: The Library of America, 1984), p. 113.

5. This is one of the sources of Henry James's strictures on Flaubert. See, for instance, his comment that Flaubert "never approached the complicated character in man or woman"; "Gustave Flaubert" (1902), in *Literary Criticism*, p. 338.

6. See Naomi Schor's apt comment: "[Flaubert's] descriptions are notable for their juxtaposition of heterogeneous details which, in extreme cases, work to reduce the objects of referential reality to inert and stupid matter." *Reading in Detail: Aesthetics and the Feminine* (New York and London: Methuen, 1987), p. 41. Schor's book provides a valuable reflection on the importance of the detail in the creation of modern aesthetics.

Roland Barthes' celebrated "effet de réel"—the inclusion of thematically superfluous details to "make real" the world described—offers one way to think about Flaubertian detail. But as a number of critics have shown, often using Barthes' own example of the barometer in Madame Aubain's house in *Un coeur simple*, details can always be thematically rationalized in some perspective of reading. What interests me is less the apparent thematic irrelevance of certain details than their lack of cohesion into a whole. On Barthes' project, rethought in historical perspective, see Schor's fine discussion in *Reading in Detail*, chap. 5.

7. See Roman Jakobson, "Two Types of Language and Two Types of Aphasic Disturbances," in Jakobson and Morris Halle, *Fundamentals of Language* (The Hague: Mouton, 1956). *L'education sentimentale* presents a yet more radical metonymization and commodification of the woman's body when, late in the novel, Madame Arnoux's personal effects, including undergarments, are auctioned off following Arnoux's bankruptcy: we no longer have before us parts of the body, but only the clothes and accessories associated with them.

8. A comparison of two lengthy descriptions of horse races at the Champ de Mars, one in Flaubert's *L'éducation sentimentale*, the other in Zola's *Nana*, offers an instructive contrast between the results of visual observation in the two novelists.

9. Hans Jonas, "The Nobility of Sight: A Study in the Phenomenology of the Senses," in *The Phenomenon of Life* (New York: Harper and Row, 1966), p. 135. The work of Walter J. Ong and other scholars of "orality" might suggest that that the primacy of the visual was established only with the invention of writing, then reinforced by the invention of printing when, according to Ong, "Hearing-dominance yields to sight-dominance"; see Ong, *Orality and Literacy: The Technologizing of the Word* (London and New York: Methuen, 1982), p. 117. But the psychoanalytic account of "sight-dominance," as I shall develop it, may suggest that it does have a primordial role, particularly in regard to the body.

10. Jean-Paul Sartre, *L'être et le néant* (Paris: Gallimard, 1943), p. 667; English trans. Hazel Barnes, *Being and Nothingness* (Philadelphia: Philosophical Library, 1956). Sartre curiously does not mention the punishment of Actaeon,

torn apart by his hounds—whereas Jacques Lacan makes Actaeon's fate an emblem of Freud's relation to the object of knowledge. See the interesting discussion of Lacan on Freud as Actaeon in Malcolm Bowie, *Freud, Proust and Lacan: Theory as Fiction* (Cambridge: Cambridge University Press, 1987), pp. 168–72.

300

11. Friedrich Nietzsche, *Beyond Good and Evil,* trans. Walter Kaufmann (New York: Vintage Books, 1966), p. 2. For a discussion of woman in Nietzsche's philosophy, see Jacques Derrida, *Eperons: Les styles de Nietzsche* (Venice: Corbo e Fiore, 1976).

12. Charles Pinot Duclos, *Oeuvres complètes* (Paris, 1820–1821), 9:424.

13. "Mes pensées, ce sont mes catins." Denis Diderot, *Oeuvres romanesques,* ed. Henri Bénac (Paris: Garnier, 1959), p. 395.

14. See Steven Marcus, *The Other Victorians* (New York: Basic Books, 1964), pp. 172–73. The author of *My Secret Life* writes: "some men—and I am one—are insatiable and could look at a cunt without taking their eyes off it for a month." In Freud, see particularly "Some Psychical Consequences of the Anatomical Distinction between the Sexes," "The Infantile Genital Organization of the Libido," and "Medusa's Head." See also Alain Roger, "Vulva, Vultus, Phallus," *Communications* 46 (1987), pp. 181–98.

15. René Descartes, *Méditations métaphysiques* (Paris: J. Vrin, 1976), p. 17.

16. Luce Irigaray, *Speculum de l'autre femme* (Paris: Editions de Minuit, 1974), p. 53. See Freud, "The Uncanny" (1919), *Standard Edition* 17:219–56.

17. Freud, *Three Essays on the Theory of Sexuality* (1905), *Standard Edition* 7:191–92 and 194. For a concise discussion of this association, see Malcolm Bowie, *Freud, Proust and Lacan,* pp. 42–43 and p. 185, n. 41.

18. Freud, "The Infantile Genital Organization" (1923), *Standard Edition* 19:143. I give here a kind of amalgam of Freud's thought, which evolves from the *Three Essays on the Theory of Sexuality* (in a section added to that work in 1915), where he stresses the primacy of the question, "Where do babies come from?" to such later essays as "The Infantile Genital Organization" and "Some Psychical Consequences of the Anatomical Distinction between the Sexes" (1925), where he urges the primacy of the perception of anatomical difference. He writes in a footnote to the latter essay: "This is an opportunity for correcting a statement which I made many years ago. I believed that the sexual interest of children, unlike pubescents, was aroused, not by the difference between the sexes, but by the problems of where babies come from. We now see that, at all events with girls, this is certainly not the case. With boys it may no doubt happen sometimes one way and sometimes the other; or with both sexes chance experiences may determine the event" (*Standard Edition* 19:252). In essence, of course, the two questions are the same, even if the child does not consciously recognize this to be the case.

19. See Toril Moi, "Patriarchal Thought and the Drive for Knowledge," in Teresa Brennan, ed., *New Directions in Psychoanalysis and Feminism* (London and New York: Routledge, 1989), pp. 189–205. See Freud, *Notes Upon a Case*

of *Obsessional Neurosis* ("The Rat Man"), *Standard Edition* 10:158–249, especially p. 245.

20. Laura Mulvey, "Visual Pleasure and Narrative Cinema," *Screen* 16:3 (1975), reprinted in Mulvey, *Visual and Other Pleasures* (London: Macmillan, 1989), p. 25. Following Mulvey's essay, many other film theorists have followed and extended her analysis; see, among others, Stephen Heath, "Difference," *Screen* 19:3 (1978); E. Ann Kaplan, "Is the Gaze Male?" in *Women and Film: Both Sides of the Camera* (New York and London: Methuen, 1983); Teresa de Lauretis, *Alice Doesn't* (Bloomington: Indiana University Press, 1984); Jacqueline Rose, *Sexuality in the Field of Vision* (London: Verso, 1986).

21. Laura Mulvey, "Afterthoughts on 'Visual Pleasure and Narrative Cinema' Inspired by King Vidor's *Duel in the Sun* (1946)," in *Visual and Other Pleasures,* pp. 29–38. For a detailed critique of Mulvey's position, and an argument that Freud's understanding of positions taken up in regard to the gaze are more complicated than she allows, see D. N. Rodowick, *The Difficulty of Difference* (New York and London: Routledge, 1991), especially pp. 4–17. See also Edward Snow, "Theorizing the Male Gaze: Some Problems," *Representations* 25 (1989), pp. 30–41.

22. Roland Barthes, *La chambre claire* (Paris: Cahiers du Cinéma/Gallimard/ Seuil, 1980), esp. pp. 56 and 144ff; English trans. Richard Howard, *Camera Lucida* (New York: Hill and Wang, 1981). On early erotic and pornographic photography, see the interesting essay by Abigail Solomon-Godeau, "Reconsidering Erotic Photography," *Journal: A Contemporary Art Magazine* (Spring 1987), pp. 51–58.

23. For a more detailed study of these questions, see my *Reading for the Plot* (1984; rpt. Cambridge, Mass.: Harvard University Press, 1992), esp. chap. 4.

24. Roland Barthes *Le plaisir du texte* (Paris: Editions du Seuil, 1973), pp. 19–20. For a study of fetishism in some late nineteenth-century French texts, see Emily Apter, *Figures of Fetishism: Pathology, Gender and Narrative Obsession in Turn-of-the-Century France* (Ithaca, N.Y.: Cornell University Press, 1991).

25. See in particular Philippe Perrot, *Le travail des apparences* (Paris: Editions du Seuil, 1984); Jean-Claude Bologne, *Histoire de la pudeur* (Paris: Olivier Orban, 1986); Alain Corbin, "Coulisses," in Philippe Ariès and Georges Duby, eds., *Histoire de la vie privée* (Paris: Editions du Seuil, 1987), vol. 4, *De la Révolution à la Grande Guerre,* pp. 419–614; English trans. Arthur Goldhammer, *From the Fires of the Revolution to the Great War* (Cambridge, Mass.: Harvard University Press, 1990).

26. Georges Bataille, *L'erotisme* (Paris: Union Générale des Editions, 1957), p. 22.

27. See Michel Foucault, *Surveiller et punir* (Paris: Gallimard, 1975); and the most intelligent discussion of nineteenth-century narrative in a Foucauldian perspective, D. A. Miller, *The Novel and the Police* (Berkeley and Los Angeles: University of California Press, 1988).

28. Moi, "Patriarchal Thought and the Drive for Knowledge," p. 203.

29. Henry James, *The Sacred Fount* (1901; rpt., New York: Grove Press, 1953), p. 9.

30. See Claude Lévi-Strauss, *La pensée sauvage* (Paris: Plon, 1962), pp. 26–47; English trans. *The Savage Mind* (Chicago: University of Chicago Press, 1966). One may note in passing that the matrix in a general way resembles what Claude Lévi-Strauss calls a "four-part homology," and also the diagram that A. J. Greimas provides as the "matrix structure" from which a narrative can be generated. See Claude Lévi-Strauss, "La structure et la forme," *Cahiers de l'Institut de Science économique appliquée* 99, series M, no. 7 (1960); A. J. Greimas, *Sémantique structurale* (Paris: Larousse, 1966).

31. The search for the "victim" necessary to explain Gilbert Long's positive transformation has led the narrator, in various dialogues with Ford Obert, Grace Brissenden, and Lady John, to the person of May Server, giving the first revision of the matrix:

| Grace Brissenden | + | Guy Brissenden | − |
| Gilbert Long | + | May Server | − |

Later, the association of the two "victims" will lead the narrator to work a transformation of his scheme, one that is confirmed when he finds the two "profiteers," Grace Bissenden and Gilbert Long, in familiar colloquy, giving, as he puts it, a "full roundness of my theory" (181). The roundness is achieved by a chiasmus, a kind of cross-multiplication, thus:

| Guy Brissenden | − | May Server | − |
| Gilbert Long | + | Grace Brissenden | + |

32. *Secrets d'alcôve:* see Freud, "On the History of the Psychoanalytic Movement," *Standard Edition* 14:13. An excellent study of the "secrets of the alcove" in relation to nineteenth-century fiction can be found in Evelyne Ender, *Le roman de l'identité sexuelle.*

33. See Freud, "From the History of an Infantile Neurosis," *Standard Edition* 17:7–122, and my discussion of this case history in *Reading for the Plot,* chap. 10.

34. The draped piano legs may be apocryphal, the satirical creation of Captain Frederick Marryat; see Peter Gay, *The Bourgeois Experience: Victoria to Freud,* vol. 1, *Education of the Senses* (New York: Oxford University Press, 1984), pp. 341 and 495. They have gained such currency, however, that they have the cultural authority of myth.

35. Henry James, *The Ambassadors* (New York: Scribner's, 1909), 2:284.

36. Malcolm Bowie provides a good discussion of jealousy as the quest for knowledge in Proust; see *Freud, Proust and Lacan,* chap. 2.

37. I use the name "Marcel" to refer to the narrator-as-protagonist, that is, within the narrative, rather than the narrator-as-narrator, he who proffers the narrative discourse. The name is given only once in the *Recherche,* and then only as a substitute, an "as-if" name: see note 38, below. "Marcel" should properly be used only in quotes, but to do so is distracting.

38. Marcel Proust, *A la recherche du temps perdu,* ed. Pierre Clarac et André Ferré (Paris: Bibliothèque de la Pléiade, 1954), 3:70. The passage under consideration runs from p. 69 to p. 80, and includes the one moment in the novel where the narrator names himself as protagonist of the action as "Marcel," in a hypothetical construction: Albertine calls him "my dear" *(mon chéri),* followed with his forename, "which, in giving to the narrator the same name as the author of this book, would have given 'My dear Marcel'" (p. 75). This allows us to speak of the protagonist as "Marcel," understanding that the identity of this forename with that of Marcel Proust is only an "as-if," and not an identity.

39. See Freud, "The Theme of the Three Caskets" ("Das Motiv der Kästchenwahl") (1913), *Standard Edition* 12:299; and "The Uncanny" ("Das Unheimliche") (1919), *Standard Edition* 17:245.

5. Nana at Last Unveil'd?

I wish to thank Helen Chillman, librarian of the Yale slides and photographs collection, for her help in assembling the illustrations accompanying this chapter.

1. See Eve Kosofsky Sedgwick, *Between Men: English Literature and Male Homosocial Desire* (New York: Columbia University Press, 1985).

2. Emile Zola, *Nana,* in *Les Rougon-Macquart* (Paris: Editions du Seuil, 1970), 3:204. Further references to Zola's novels are to this edition.

3. Emile Zola, "Nos peintres au Champ-de-Mars," *Oeuvres complètes,* ed. Henri Mitterand (Paris: Cercle du Livre Précieux, 1969), 12:852.

4. Ibid., p. 854.

5. Zola, "Le Salon de 1875," *Oeuvres,* 12:918.

6. Zola, "Lettres de Paris: Une exposition de tableaux à Paris" [Salon de 1875], *Oeuvres,* 12:930.

7. Zola, "Lettres de Paris: L'école française de peinture à l'exposition de 1878," *Oeuvres,* 12:985.

8. Caricature by Gill, *La Lune Rousse,* vol. 3, no. 150 (19 October 1879). Thanks to my colleague Martine Reid for bringing this caricature to my attention.

9. Zola, "Edouard Manet," *Oeuvres,* 12:839.

10. Ibid., p. 837.

11. See T. J. Clark, "Olympia's Choice," in *The Painting of Modern Life* (New York: Knopf, 1985), p. 122. On these questions, see also Rozsika Parker and Griselda Pollock, *Old Mistresses* (New York: Pantheon, 1981).

12. Beatrice Farwell, *Manet and the Nude: A Study in Iconography in the Second Empire* (New York: Garland Publishers, 1981), p. 39.

13. Ibid., p. 220. On the uses of the nude in Victorian England, and especially the doctrine of aesthetic "distance" to make nudity acceptable, see Peter Gay, *The Bourgeois Experience,* vol. 1, *Education of the Senses,* pp. 379–402.

14. "Je sais bien qu'on ne peut pas faire déshabiller un modèle dans la rue.

Mais il y a les champs et, tout au moins l'été, on pourrait faire des études de nu dans la campagne, puisque le nu est, paraît-il, le premier et le dernier mot de l'art." Manet, as quoted in A. Proust, *Edouard Manet: Sources* (Paris: H. Barthélemy, 1919), p. 12; cited in Farwell, *Manet and the Nude*, p. 219.

304

15. On the social, political, and economic context of art in this period, see also Patricia Mainardi, *Art and Politics in the Second Empire: The Universal Expositions of 1855 and 1867* (New Haven and London: Yale University Press, 1987).

16. Zola, "Salon de 1879," *Oeuvres*, 12:1005. There is some evidence that Gervex added the pile of discarded clothes to *Rolla* at the suggestion of Degas, who of course was himself intent upon breaking from the academic tradition of the nude.

17. See Jean Borie, *Zola et les mythes* (Paris: Seuil, 1971); Naomi Schor, *Zola's Crowds* (Baltimore: Johns Hopkins University Press, 1978), pp. 101-102; Janet L. Beizer, "Uncovering *Nana*: The Courtesan's New Clothes," *L'Esprit Créateur*, vol. 25, no. 2 (1985), pp. 52–53. See also Chantal Bertrand-Jennings, *L'éros et le femme chez Zola* (Paris: Klincksieck, 1977).

18. Beatrice Farwell, "Courbet's 'Baigneuses' and the Rhetorical Feminine Image," in *Woman as Sex Object*, ed. Thomas B. Hess and Linda Nochlin (New York: Newsweek, 1972), p. 75.

19. Camille Lemonnier, *Salon de Paris 1870* (Paris, 1870), pp. 80–81; cited in Clark, *The Painting of Modern Life*, pp. 128–29.

20. For Clark's discussion of the problem, see *The Painting of Modern Life*, p. 135ff.

21. Zola, "Les Chutes" [Salon of 1866], *Oeuvres*, 12:811.

22. The review by Ferragus, in *Le Figaro*, and Zola's reply, are reprinted in many modern editions, including the "Folio" (Paris: Gallimard, 1979). On the relation of Zola's fiction and Courbet's painting, see Denis Hollier, "How to Not Take Pleasure in Talking about Sex," *Enclitic* 8, no. 1–2 (1984), pp. 84–93. See also Linda Nochlin, "Courbet's *L'origine du monde*: The Origin without an Original," *October* 37 (1986), pp. 77–86.

Anne M. Wagner, in a superb discussion of Auguste Rodin's sculpture, *Iris, Messenger of the Gods* (ca. 1890), which represents Iris with her legs thrust apart and vulva open, notes that "neither the body's substance nor its activity have anything to do with the sculpted vocabulary of the feminine current at the time," and considers whether, despite the frankly phallocentric rhetoric of the image, it might be susceptible to a feminist reading which sees it as enabling women to "repossess their sexuality, understand and savor it." Anne M. Wagner, "Rodin's Reputation," in *Eroticism and the Body Politic*, ed. Lynn Hunt (Baltimore: Johns Hopkins University Press, 1991), pp. 191–242. Could something similar be said in favor of *L'origine du monde*, despite its origins as a "special" painting for a male voyeur? This is suggested in Michael Fried's essay "Courbet's Femininity"—where he argues, in essence, that Courbet has incorporated himself in some of his nudes, rather than maintaining the distanced and dominating postures of more "theatrical" representations of the nude—in *Courbet's Realism* (Chicago: University of Chicago Press, 1990), pp. 209–222.

23. For Clark's acute discussion of the place of the viewer in this painting, see *The Painting of Modern Life*, p. 250.

24. On "The Uncanny" ("Das Unheimliche"), *Standard Edition* 17:219–56), see Chapter 4. See also "Some Psychical Consequences of the Anatomical Distinction between the Sexes," *Standard Edition* 19:248–58, and "Medusa's Head," *Standard Edition* 18:273–74. On the narcissistic woman, see Sarah Kofman, *L'énigme de la femme* (Paris: Editions Galilée, 1980), pp. 60–77.

25. For this information, I am indebted to the Montreal Museum of Fine Arts catalogue *William Bouguereau*, prepared for the Bouguereau exhibition in 1984–85 at the Petit-Palais, the Montreal Museum of Fine Arts, and the Wadsworth Atheneum. There are many good examples of Bouguereau's painting in the United States, in part because he established a profitable "mail-order" trade with American collectors: a customer would write to order a nude, or a Madonna, or a peasant scene, Bouguereau would send back a sketch, and when this was approved he would execute the finished canvas.

26. See Michel Serres, *Feux et signaux de brume, Zola* (Paris: Grasset, 1975).

27. On the history of the Bon Marché, see Michael Miller, *The Bon Marché: Bourgeois Culture and the Department Store, 1869–1920* (Princeton: Princeton University Press, 1981); on shopping and the novel, see the stimulating study by Rachel Bowlby, *Just Looking: Consumer Culture in Dreiser, Gissing and Zola* (New York and London: Methuen, 1985).

28. The social historian Alain Corbin confirms the impression given in Zola's novel that the late nineteenth century marked a "hypertrophy" of women's lingerie, decorated with a new richness of lace and embroidery. See *Histoire de la vie privée*, ed. Philippe Ariès and Georges Duby, vol. 4, *De la Révolution à la Grande Guerre*, ed. Michelle Perrot (Paris: Editions du Seuil, 1987), p. 447; English trans. Arthur Goldhammer, *From the Fires of the Revolution to the Great War* (Cambridge, Mass.: Harvard University Press, 1990).

29. Jacques Lacan, *Ecrits* (Paris: Editions du Seuil, 1966), p. 732.

30. See Charles Bernheimer, *Figures of Ill Repute* (Cambridge, Mass.: Harvard University Press, 1989).

31. Jules Barbey d'Aurevilly, "A un dîner d'athées," in *Les diaboliques* (Paris: Garnier/Flammarion, 1967), p. 261.

32. Zola to Cézanne, 16 January 1860. *Correspondance,* in *Oeuvres,* 14:1201. See Joanna Richardson, *Zola* (New York: St. Martin's Press, 1978), p. 8.

33. See O. Mannoni, "Je sais bien mais quand même," in *Clefs pour l'imaginaire ou l'Autre Scène* (Paris, Seuil, 1969).

6. Gauguin's Tahitian Body

1. See *Guide illustré de l'Exposition Universelle publié par le Bulletin Officiel* (Paris: Imprimerie de l'Exposition, G. Robert, 1889), p. 138; and Gauguin to

Emile Bernard, March 1889, in *Lettres de Gauguin à sa femme et à ses amis,* ed. Maurice Malingue (Paris: Grasset, 1946), p. 157 (hereafter cited as *LFA.*) In writing this chapter, I had the benefit of helpful dialogue and criticism from several sources: Eliza Nichols, Natasha Staller, Abigail Solomon-Godeau, Sara Suleri, and James Clifford.

306

2. On the guidebook—L. Enrique, *Les colonies françaises* (Paris, 1889)—see Bengt Danielsson, *Gauguin in the South Seas* (Garden City, N.Y.: Doubleday, 1966), p. 33.

3. To Mette Gauguin, February 1890. *LFA,* p. 184.

4. To J. F. Willumsen, late 1890, in Gauguin, *Oviri, écrits d'un sauvage,* ed. Daniel Guérin (Paris: Gallimard, 1974), p. 68.

5. See Edward Said, *Orientalism* (New York: Vintage Books, 1979).

6. See Danielsson, *Gauguin in the South Seas,* p. 33.

7. To Emile Bernard, June 1890. *LFA,* p. 192.

8. Charles Baudelaire, "Parfum exotique" (lines 5–8) in *Les fleurs du mal:* "A lazy isle where nature gives / Singular trees and savorous fruits / Men whose bodies are slim and vigorous / And women whose eyes astound in their frankness."

9. Louis-Antoine de Bougainville, *Voyage autour du monde, suivi du Supplément de Diderot,* ed. Michel Hérubel (Paris: Union Générale des Editions, 1966), p. 185. This edition also includes excerpts from the journal of Philibert de Commerson. Subsequent references are given in the text. On the first, brief *Relation* of Bougainville's discovery, see L. Davis Hammond, ed., *News from New Cythera: A Report of Bougainville's Voyage* (Minneapolis: University of Minnesota Press, 1970).

10. Jean-Jacques Rousseau, *Discours sur cette question proposée par l'Académie de Dijon: Quelle est l'origine de l'inégalité parmi les hommes et si elle est autorisée par la loi naturelle?,* in *Du contrat social . . .* (Paris: Garnier, 1962), p. 72. Bougainville speaks directly to Rousseau's *Discours* in his final journal entry before leaving the island: "Législateurs et philosophes, venez voir ici, tout établi, ce que votre imagination n'a pu même rêver. Un peuple nombreux, composé de beaux hommes et de jolies femmes, vivant ensemble dans l'abondance et la santé, avec toutes les marques de la plus grande union, connaissant assez le mien et le tien pour qu'il y ait cette distinction dans les rangs nécessaires au bon ordre, ne le connaissant pas assez pour qu'il y ait des pauvres et des fripons." Bougainville, *Journal* (unpublished), quoted in Jean-Etienne Martin-Allanic, *Bougainville navigateur et les découvertes de son temps,* 2 vols. (Paris: Presses Universitaires de France, 1964), 1:683.

11. Diderot, "Supplément au Voyage de Bougainville," in Bougainville, *Voyage,* p. 444.

12. Samuel Wallis, in John Hawkesworth, ed., *An Account of the Voyages Undertaken by the order of his Present Majesty for Making Discoveries in the Southern Hemisphere . . . and successively performed by Commodore Byron, Captain Wallis, Captain Carteret, and Captain Cook. From the Journals that were kept by the several Commanders, and from the Papers of Joseph Banks,*

Esq., 3 vols. (London: W. Strahan and T. Cadell, 1773), 1:458–59. On the first discoverers of Tahiti, I have have consulted with profit Alan Moorehead, *The Fatal Impact: An Account of the Invasion of the South Pacific, 1767–1840* (New York: Harper and Row, 1966); David Howarth, *Tahiti: A Paradise Lost* (New York: Viking, 1983); Bernard Smith, *European Vision and the South Pacific,* 2nd. ed. (New Haven and London: Yale University Press, 1985); and Michèle Duchet, *Anthropologie et histoire au siècle des lumières* (Paris: François Maspero, 1971).

307

13. George Robertson, *An Account of the Discovery of Tahiti, from the Journal of George Robertson, Master of HMS Dolphin,* ed. Oliver Warner (London: Folio Press/J. M. Dent, 1973), p. 73.

14. Compare Rousseau's view: "Pour le philosophe, ce sont le fer et le blé qui ont civilisé les hommes et perdu le genre humain. Aussi l'un et l'autre étoient-ils inconnus aux sauvages de l'Amérique, qui pour cela sont demeurés tels; les autres peuples semblent même être restés barbares tant qu'ils ont pratiqué l'un de ces arts sans l'autre." *Discours,* p. 73. The Tahitians of course did practice agriculture, and reared domestic animals. The importance of iron to the Tahitians is confirmed by James Morrison, boatswain's mate on the *Bounty,* who spent nearly two years on the island—August 1789 to May 1791—and left one of the most thorough accounts of Tahitian society: "The grand object of these people is Iron and like us with Gold it matters not by what means they get it or where it comes from if they can but get it." James Morrison, *Journal* (London: The Golden Cockerel Press, 1935), p. 52.

15. See Douglas L. Oliver, *Ancient Tahitian Society* (Honolulu: University of Hawaii Press, 1974), 1:350–74; Marshall Sahlins, "Supplement to the Voyage of Cook; or, *le calcul sauvage,*" in *Islands of History* (Chicago: University of Chicago Press, 1985), pp. 1–31. The "calculus" may also have had something to do with an apparent Tahitian valuation of light skin. Vivès, the ship's doctor of the *Boudeuse,* reports: "La blancheur de notre peau les enchante, ils témoignent leur admiration à cet égard de la manière la plus expressive" (cited in Martin-Allanic, *Bougainville navigateur,* p. 668); and his report is confirmed by that of the Prince de Nassau-Siegen, who appears to have spent as much time as anybody making love to Tahitian women, and who mentions in the course of an account of an afternoon spent with three of them that "la blancheur du corps européen les ravit" (cited in ibid., p. 670).

16. James Cook, *A Journal of a Voyage Around the World in His Majesty's Ship Endeavour in the Years 1768, 1769, 1770, 1771* (London: T. Becket and P. A. De Hondt, 1771), p. 44. This journal is not in fact Cook's, and it is uncertain which member of the crew was responsible for it; see J. C. Beaglehole, ed., *The Journals of Captain James Cook on His Voyages of Discovery* (Cambridge: The Hakluyt Society, 1955), vol. 1, pp. cclvi–cclxiv. For Cook's own observations on the practice of tattooing—more extensive than those quoted, but without the mention of the Tahitians' comparison to writing—see Beaglehole, *Journals of Captain Cook,* 1:125. Sir Joseph Banks also described the practice in detail in his journal.

17. On this point, see the wise comment by James Morrison: "And here it may not be improper to remark that the Idea formed of this Society and of the Inhabitants of this Island in general by former Voyagers could not possible extend much farther than their own Oppinion, None having remained a sufficient length of time to know the manner in which they live and as their whole system was overturned by the arrival of a Ship, their Manners were then as much altered from their Common Course, as those of our own Country are at a Fair, which might as well be given for a specimen of the Method of living in England— which was always their situation as soon as a ship Arrived their whole thought being turned toward their Visitors, & all Method tryd to win their Friendship" (*Journal*, p. 235).

18. Paul Gauguin, *Noa Noa,* ed. Pierre Petit (Paris: Jean-Jacques Pauvert et Cie, 1988), p. 37. This edition reprints the original Gauguin manuscript, without the additions made by Charles Morice for the first published edition, and without the later revisions made by Gauguin to the published text. Petit's critical edition in my view deserves its billing as the "première édition authentique" of the text.

19. On the archaizing strategy in ethnographic writing, see James Clifford, "On Ethnographic Allegory," in *Writing Culture,* ed. Clifford and George E. Marcus (Berkeley: University of California Press, 1986); Renato Rosaldo, "Imperialist Nosatalgia," in *Culture and Truth: The Remaking of Social Analysis* (Boston: Beacon Press, 1989); and Johannes Fabian, *Time and the Other: How Anthropology Makes Its Object* (New York: Columbia University Press, 1983).

20. For Huysmans' remarks on the *Etude de nu,* see "L'exposition des indépendants en 1881," in *L'art moderne* (Paris: G. Charpentier, 1883), p. 238. On Gauguin's iconographic sources for several of the Tahitian paintings, see Richard Field, *Paul Gauguin: The Paintings of the First Trip to Tahiti* (New York and London: Garland, 1977).

21. Letter of 5 February 1895. *LFA,* p. 263.

22. Interview with Eugène Tardieu, *L'echo de Paris,* 13 May 1895, in Paul Gauguin, *Oviri, écrits d'un sauvage,* ed. Daniel Guérin (Paris: Gallimard, 1974), p. 140.

23. Abigail Solomon-Godeau, "Going Native," *Art in America* (July 1989), pp. 123–24. One's view of these matters depends very much on how one reacts to Gauguin's paintings. Solomon-Godeau writes: "to contemplate Gauguin's strangely joyless and claustral evocations of Tahiti and the Marquesas is to be, in the final instance, not at all far from Loti" (p. 125). I cannot agree with this characterization of the painting, nor the implied similarity to Loti's purple prose.

24. See Danielsson, *Gauguin in the South Seas.*

25. Letter of 25 August 1902, *Lettres à Daniel de Monfried,* ed. Mme. Joly-Segalen (Paris: Georges Falaize, 1950), p. 191.

26. Victor Segalen, in his "Hommage à Gauguin," discusses this androgyny at length: "From the shoulder to the fingertips, the Maori woman presents, moving or bent, a continuous line. The volume of the arm is very elegantly rounded. The thigh is discreet and naturally androgynous . . . The entire leg is another moving column; or, when still, two powerful columns," etc. See Victor

Segalen, *Gauguin dans son dernier décor et autres textes de Tahiti* (Fontfroide: Bibliothèque artistique et littéraire, 1986), p. 99.

27. See J. A. Moerenhout, *Voyages aux îles du grand océan* (Paris: A. Bertrand, 1837), 2:206–211.

28. From the Louvre manuscript of *Noa Noa*, 109–110, cited in *The Art of Paul Gauguin*, by Richard Brettell, Françoise Cachin, Claire Frèches-Thory, and Charles F. Stuckey (Washington: The National Gallery of Art; Chicago: The Art Institute, 1988), p. 280.

29. See Marcel Mauss, "Essai sur le don" (1925), in *Sociologie et anthropologie* (Paris: Presses Universitaires de France, 1968), pp. 145–279; English trans. W. D. Hall, *The Gift* (London: Routledge, 1990); Georges Bataille, "The Notion of Expenditure," in *Visions of Excess: Selected Writings, 1927–1939*, ed. Allan Stoekl (Minneapolis: University of Minnesota Press, 1985), pp. 116–129. In my discussion of this painting, I am indebted to the perceptive comments offered by Hilary Schor, of the University of Southern California, when I presented an early version of this paper as a lecture. James Clifford has pointed out to me that Mauss's interpretation of the actual potlatch was probably incorrect, but this does not alter the way the term has come to be used.

30. See Richard Field, "Gauguin, plagiaire ou créateur?" in *Paul Gauguin* (1961; Paris: Editions du Chêne, 1986), pp. 123–24.

31. See in particular letters of June 1892, 8 December 1892, and 14 February 1897, in *Lettres à Daniel de Monfried*, pp. 57, 63, 101.

32. See Brettell et al., *The Art of Paul Gauguin*, pp. 398–99.

33. Letter of 14 February 1897, in *Lettres à Daniel de Monfried*, p. 101.

34. Victor Segalen, "Gauguin dans son dernier décor," in *Gauguin dans son dernier décor*, pp. 28–29.

35. Segalen, "Hommage à Gauguin," in *Gauguin dans son dernier décor*, p. 101.

36. The Gauguin-Tahiti myth has, of course, been commercialized in our own time: the major retrospective of his work in 1989 produced in Paris not only a run of Gauguin shopping bags, but Gauguin-inspired bathing suits, lipstick, and so on. It is perhaps typical of postmodern society that myth almost instantaneously turns into its commercial parody.

7. What Is a Monster?

1. A diagram of the narrative structure would look like this: { [( )] }.

2. Mary Shelley, *Frankenstein; or, The Modern Prometheus* (New York: NAL/Signet, 1983), pp. 92–93. Susequent references are to this edition, which reprints the revised text of 1831. I have also consulted the helpful critical edition by James Rieger (Indianapolis and New York: Bobbs-Merrill, 1974), which prints the original text of 1818 (with the corrections of 1823) and indicates the variants occurring in the revised edition.

3. For the reader, the contradiction between the visual and the verbal appears also as a clash of generic expectations, between the Gothic novel and the

philosophical tale: the Monster's hideous body and frightful crimes belong the Gothic tradition, whereas his autobiograpical narrative and the issues it raises suggest an eighteenth-century philosophical tale.

4. See Roland Barthes, *S/Z* (Paris: Editions du Seuil, 1970), pp. 95–96. For some comments on the model of the "narrative contract," and the need to extend it toward a more dynamic concept of narrative transaction, see my "Narrative Transaction and Transference," in *Reading for the Plot* (1984; rpt. Cambridge, Mass.: Harvard University Press, 1992), pp. 216–37.

5. On these questions, see the classic essay by Emile Benveniste, "De la subjectivité dans le langage," in *Problèmes de linguistique générale* (Paris: Gallimard, 1967), pp. 258–66.

6. On the Lacanian terms used here see in particular Jacques Lacan, "Le stade du miroir" and "L'instance de la lettre dans l'inconscient ou la raison depuis Freud," in *Ecrits* (Paris: Editions du Seuil, 1966), pp. 93–100 and 493–528.

7. See Jean-Jacques Rousseau, *Essai sur l'origine des langues* (Paris: Bibliothèque du Graphe, 1973), reprinted from the 1817 edition of Rousseau's works published by A. Belin. For a thorough and subtle discussion of Rousseau's presence throughout *Frankenstein,* see David Marshall, "*Frankenstein,* or Rousseau's Monster: Sympathy and Speculative Eyes," in *The Surprising Effects of Sympathy* (Chicago: Unversity of Chicago Press, 1988), pp. 178–227. Marshall's comments on the *Essai sur l'origine des langues* start from my own evocation of the pertinence of that text in a very early version of this chapter, "'Godlike Science/Unhallowed Arts': Language and Monstrosity in *Frankenstein,*" *New Literary History* 9:3 (1978), reprinted (slightly modified) in *The Endurance of Frankenstein,* ed. George Levine and U. C. Knoepflmacher (Berkeley: University of California Press, 1979)—but Marshall treats the subject far more fully than I did.

8. Several critics have pointed to the importance of the absence of mothers, and the search for a mother, in *Frankenstein:* see in particular Marc A. Rubenstein, "'My Accursed Origin': The Search for the Mother in *Frankenstein,*" *Studies in Romanticism* 15 (1976), pp. 165–194; Sandra M. Gilbert and Susan Gubar, "Horror's Twin: Mary Shelley's Monstrous Eve," in *The Madwoman in the Attic* (New Haven: Yale University Press, 1979), pp. 213–47; Mary Jacobus, "Is There a Woman in This Text?" in *Reading Women: Essays in Feminist Criticism* (New York: Columbia University Press, 1986), esp. p. 101; and Margaret Homans, "Bearing Demons: Frankenstein's Circumvention of the Maternal," in *Bearing the Word* (Chicago: University of Chicago Press, 1986), pp. 100–119. On the biographical resonances of some of these issues—particularly the relation of Mary Shelley to her mother, Mary Wollstonecraft, who died shortly after giving birth to her, and her father, William Godwin, and her children, especially William—see, in addition to the studies just mentioned, Ellen Moers, "Female Gothic," U. C. Knoepflmacher, "Thoughts on the Aggression of Daughters," and Kate Ellis, "Monsters in the Garden: Mary Shelley and the Bourgeois Family," all in *The Endurance of Frankenstein.* See also Barbara

Johnson, "My Monster/My Self," in *A World of Difference* (Baltimore: Johns Hopkins University Press, 1987), pp. 144–54. The fullest and most useful biography of Mary Shelley is Emily W. Sunstein, *Mary Shelley: Romance and Reality* (Boston: Little, Brown, 1989).

9. On the "anaclitic" or "attachment type" *(Anlehnungstypus)* of object choice, see Freud, "On Narcissism: An Introduction," *Standard Edition* 14:87. The attachment is that of the sexual instincts to the ego instincts, with the result of a choice of love objects that takes the subject back to the mother.

10. "Qu'est-ce qui est désiré? C'est le désirant dans l'autre—ce qui ne peut se faire qu'à ce que le sujet lui-même soit convoqué comme désirable. C'est ce qu'il demande dans la demande d'amour." Lacan, *Le séminaire*, vol. 8, *Le transfert* (Paris: Editions du Seuil, 1991), p. 415.

11. Note in this context the curious scenario leading to the death of Clerval: Frankenstein rows out to sea in his skiff and throws the mangled pieces of the female monster overboard; a storm comes up and blows him off course; he lands on a strange shore—it is Ireland—and is at once arrested as a murderer, and taken to see the body of his supposed victim, Clerval. Thus there is a direct exchange between the body of the female monster and that of Clerval.

12. Rubenstein, "My Accursed Origin," p. 165.

13. In the Wolf Man's dream, "suddenly the window opened of its own accord," and the terrified child sees the wolves sitting in a tree in front of the window, looking at him attentively. Freud's patient then interprets the window opening to mean "My eyes suddenly opened." See Freud, "From the History of an Infantile Neurosis," *Standard Edition* 17:29–47. On "primal phantasies," see this case history and also *Introductory Lectures on Psycho-Analysis, Standard Edition* 16:367–71. David Marshall, working from Marc Rubenstein's suggestions, gives a fine analysis of these scenes, in *The Surprising Effects of Sympathy,* pp. 222–26.

14. It is worth mentioning in this context that during the evenings of reading ghost stories in the Villa Diodati, on the shores of Lake Geneva, that brought together the Shelleys with Lord Byron, his personal physician Dr. Polidori, and Claire Clairmont (Byron's mistress and Mary's stepsister) and led to the ghost story writing "contest" that produced *Frankenstein*, P. B. Shelley had a hallucination: "Byron repeated some verses of Coleridge's *Christabel,* of the witch's breast; when silence ensued, and Shelley, suddenly shrieking and putting his hands to his head, ran out of the room with a candle. Threw water in his face and after gave him ether. He was looking at Mrs. Shelley, and suddenly thought of a woman he had heard of who had eyes instead of nipples, which taking hold of his mind, horrified him" (*The Diary of Dr. John William Polidori,* ed. W. M. Rossetti [London: Elkin Matthews, 1911], pp. 128–29, quoted by Rubenstein, p. 184). The woman with eyes in the place of nipples effectively sexualizes vision, and turns the male's scopic fixations back on the voyeur, with hallucinatory results.

15. Laura Mulvey, "Visual Pleasure and Narrative Cinema," in *Visual and Other Pleasures* (London: Macmillan, 1989), p. 19.

16. See Gilbert and Gubar, who suggest that the Monster's "intellectual similarity to his authoress (rather than his 'author')" indicates that he may be "a female in disguise" (*The Madwoman in the Attic,* p. 237). Mary Jacobus notes the "bizarre pun" in which Frankenstein describes the Monster as "a mummy again endued with animation" (*Reading Women,* p. 101). Margaret Homans, citing my own argument (in my earlier essay on the novel) about the Monster's failure to gain his place in the symbolic order, states: "I would argue that in its materiality and its failure to acquire an object of desire, the demon enters the symbolic primarily as the (dreaded) referent, not as signifier. The negative picture of the demon's materiality is a product of its female place in the symbolic, and not of any lingering in the realm of the imaginary (which Brooks, with other readers of Lacan, views as tragic)" (*Bearing the Word,* pp. 304–305, n. 18). I would agree with this to the extent that the materiality of the Monster continually vitiates his assumed place—the place he would assume—in the symbolic. But doesn't that status as dreaded referent continually throw him back into the imaginary?

17. The Monster, we have noted, is often the observer in the novel, which is the male role. When he is looked at, however, he takes on aspects of the Medusa, who turns (male) observers to stone, and who for Freud represents the terror of the female genitals to the (childish) male observer: see Freud, "Medusa's Head," *Standard Edition* 18:273–74. Note, in this context, Walton's reaction when he first meets the Monster: "Never did I behold a vision so horrible as his face, of such loathesome yet appalling hideousness. I shut my eyes involuntarily" (207).

18. See Freud, "Psychoanalytic Notes upon an Autobiographical Account of a Case of Paranoia (Dementia Paranoides)" (1911), *Standard Edition* 12:9–82.

8. Talking Bodies, Delicate Vessels

1. Michel Foucault, *Naissance de la clinique* (Paris: Presses Universitaires de France, 1963); English trans. Alan Sheridan, *Birth of the Clinic* (London: Tavistock Press, 1973).

2. Cynthia Eagle Russett, *Sexual Science: The Victorian Construction of Womanhood* (Cambridge, Mass.: Harvard University Press, 1989), p. 48.

3. My information on Pinel is derived almost entirely from the excellent study by Jan Goldstein, *Console and Classify: The French Psychiatric Profession in the Nineteenth Century* (Chicago: University of Chicago Press, 1987).

4. The case is summarized in Goldstein, *Console and Classify,* p. 83.

5. I have discussed Balzac's novella *Adieu* in relation to Freud's conception of transference in "Psychoanalytic Constructions and Narrative Meanings," *Paragraph* No. 7 (Oxford: Oxford University Press, 1986).

6. See Goldstein, *Console and Classify,* pp. 82–83.

7. Hysteria has been the subject of a number of studies: see in particular Ilza Veith, *Hysteria: The History of a Disease* (Chicago: University of Chicago Press, 1965); Elaine Showalter, *The Female Malady* (New York: Pantheon, 1985), esp. chap. 6, "Feminism and Hysteria: The Daughter's Disease"; Charles Bernheimer

and Claire Kahane, eds., *In Dora's Case: Freud-Hysteria-Feminism* (New York: Columbia Unversity Press, 1985); Evelyne Ender, *Le roman de l'identité sexuelle* (Ph.D. diss., University of Geneva, 1991; English trans. forthcoming from Cornell University Press). I am particularly indebted to Janet Beizer's careful reading of nineteenth-century French medical treatises in her forthcoming study *Ventriloquized Bodies: The Narrative Uses of Hysteria in France (1850–1900)*.

313

8. A selection of the Salpêtrière photographs can be found in Georges Didi-Hubermann, *L'invention de l'hystérie* (Paris: Macula, 1982).

9. See Stephen Heath, *The Sexual Fix* (London: Macmillan, 1982), pp. 37–38.

10. See Breuer and Freud, *Studies on Hysteria* (1895), *Standard Edition* 2:30. The phrase is in English in the original.

11. See Jacques Lacan, "L'instance de la lettre dans l'inconscient, ou la raison depuis Freud," *Ecrits* (Paris: Editions du Seuil, 1966), pp. 506–509; on the metonymical contamination of metaphor, see Gérard Genette, "Métonymie chez Proust," in *Figures III* (Paris: Editions du Seuil, 1972), pp. 41–63.

12. Charles Darwin, *The Expression of the Emotions in Man and Animals* (1872; rpt. New York: Greenwood Press, 1969), p. 42.

13. Ralph Waldo Emerson, "Nature," in *The Complete Essays and Other Writings of Ralph Waldo Emerson*, ed. Brooks Atkinson (New York: Modern Library, 1940), pp. 14–15. Emerson continues: "We say the *heart* to express emotion, the *head* to denote thought; and *thought* and *emotion* are words borrowed from sensible things, and now appropriated to spiritual nature"; Johann Gottfried Herder, "Essay on the Origin of Language," in *On the Origin of Language*, trans. and ed. Alexander Gode (New York: Frederick Ungar, 1966), pp. 134–35.

14. Arthur Conan Doyle, "The Adventure of the Speckled Band," in *The Adventure of the Speckled Band and Other Stories of Sherlock Holmes* (New York: NAL/Signet, 1965), p. 18.

15. "The Naval Treaty," in *Adventure of the Speckled Band*, p. 145.

16. We are told of Freud's interest in Sherlock Holmes by his celebrated patient known as the Wolf Man, the subject of *From the History of an Infantile Neurosis* (*Standard Edition* 17:7–122). See *The Wolf-Man by the Wolf-Man*, ed. Muriel Gardiner (New York: Basic Books, 1971), p. 146. For a further discussion of Holmes and Freud, see my *Reading for the Plot* (New York: Alfred A. Knopf, 1984; rpt. Cambridge, Mass.: Harvard University Press, 1992), pp. 269ff.; and for analysis of the structure of the detective story, chap. 1 of that book.

17. On the *secrets d'alcôve*, see Freud, "On the History of the Psychoanalytic Movement," *Standard Edition* 14:13.

18. The critical literature on Dora's case history is very rich: see in particular, Philip Rieff's introduction to *Dora* (New York: Collier Books, 1963), pp. 7–20; and Steven Marcus, "Freud and Dora: Story, History, Case History," in *Representations: Essays on Literature and Society* (New York: Random House, 1976), reprinted in Bernheimer and Kahane, *In Dora's Case*, which contains a

number of other interesting essays on the case, especially those by Suzanne Gearhart, Jacqueline Rose, Maria Ramas, Madelon Sprengnether, and Toril Moi.

19. See in particular the sensitive analyses of Dora's situation by Philip Rieff and Steven Marcus cited in the previous note.

20. Lacan writes: "Woman is the object which it is impossible to detach from a primitive oral desire, and yet in which she must learn to recognize her own genital nature. (One wonders here why Freud fails to see that the aphonia brought on during the absences of Herr K is an expression of the violent appeal of the oral erotic drive when Dora was left face to face with Frau K, without there being any need for Freud to evoke her awareness of the fellatio undergone by her father when everyone knows that cunnilingus is the artifice most commonly adopted by 'men of means' whose powers begin to abandon them.) For Dora to gain access to this recognition of her femininity, she would have to take on this assumption of her own body, failing which she remains open to the functional fragmentation (to refer to the theoretical contribution of the mirror stage) that constitutes conversion symptoms." "Intervention sur le transfert," *Ecrits,* p. 221; cited in the translation by Jacqueline Rose, as printed in Bernheimer and Kahane, *In Dora's Case,* p. 98.

21. Lacan, "Intervention sur le transfert," *Ecrits,* p. 220. Lacan writes elsewhere: "Frau K is for her the incarnation of this question, *what is a woman?*" *Le séminaire,* vol. 8, *Le transfert* (Paris: Editions du Seuil, 1991), p. 288.

22. Serge Leclaire, "Jérôme, ou la mort dans la vie de l'obsédé," in *Démasquer le réel* (Paris: Editions du Seuil, 1971), pp. 121–46. On the hysteric's confusion about sexual identity, see also Freud, "Hysterical Phantasies and Their Relation to Bisexuality," *Standard Edition* 9:159–66; Gregorio Kohon, "Reflections on Dora: The case of hysteria," in *The British School of Psychoanalysis: The Independent Tradition,* ed. Gregorio Kohon (New Haven: Yale University Press, 1986), pp. 362–80; and Juliet Mitchell, who writes: "The hysteric (in this Oedipal constellation more typically 'she' than 'he') will not acknowledge the Law of the castration complex, will oscillate between the two desired positions of the Oedipus complex—being mother or being father—and will be unable unconsciously to acknowledge that the polymorphous delights of infantile sexuality must be forgotten and repressed if past, present and future—traditions—are to be established in the mind. Not properly internalizing the representative of the law (the 'superego') in fantasy, she will be an incestuous Oedipus before his discovery of his origins, a self without a history." "From King Lear to Anna O. and Beyond: Some Speculative Theses on Hysteria and the Traditionless Self," *Yale Journal of Criticism* 5:2 (1992), p. 93.

23. The pioneering work here was Susan Gubar and Sandra Gilbert, *The Madwoman in the Attic* (New Haven: Yale University Press, 1979); more specifically on hysteria, see Evelyne Ender, *Le roman de l'identité sexuelle;* and Jacqueline Rose, "George Eliot and the Spectacle of Woman," in *Sexuality in the Field of Vision* (London: Verso, 1966), pp.105–122. My discusssion of George Eliot's *Daniel Deronda* is indebted to Rose's essay and, especially, to Ender's chapter on that novel.

24. Baudelaire, "Madame Bovary," in *Oeuvres complètes* (Paris: Bibliothèque de la Pléiade, 1976), 2:83.

25. George Eliot, *Daniel Deronda* (Harmondsworth: Penguin Books, 1986), p. 91. Note that Gwendolen's reaction to seeing the picture behind the panel for the first time, the day of her family's arrival at Offendene, is already hysterical: she turns in anger on her half-sister who has opened the panel and demands that it be locked up, and the key entrusted to her. The picture of "the upturned dead face" may be the first Medusa face of the novel.

26. On these scenes, see Jacqueline Rose, *Sexuality in the Field of Vision*, pp. 105ff.

27. My starting point in analysis of this scene is the excellent discussion of it by Evelyne Ender in *Le roman de l'identité sexuelle*, pp. 253–63.

28. Laura Mulvey, "Pandora: The Mask, the Box, and Curiosity," in *Space and Sexuality* (Princeton: Princeton University Press, 1992).

29. Angela Carter, "The Bloody Chamber," in *The Bloody Chamber and Other Stories* (Harmondsworth: Penguin, 1981), pp. 16–17.

30. See Walter Benjamin, "The Storyteller," in *Illuminations,* trans. Harry Zohn (New York: Schocken Books, 19), p. 91.

31. F. R. Leavis, in *The Great Tradition* (London: Chatto & Windus, 1948), pp. 79–125, argues in detail the inheritance of James from Eliot, especially in *The Portrait of a Lady.* But the greater subtlety in representation of woman's moral consciousness comes in the later novels I mentioned—which Leavis dislikes. James himself makes clear his appreciation of *Daniel Deronda*, especially the portrayal of Gwendolen, in *"Daniel Deronda*: A Conversation" (1888), in *Literary Criticism* (New York: The Library of America, 1984), pp. 974–992.

32. On these questions, see my *Reading for the Plot,* esp. pp. 20–23 , and Georg Lukács, *Theory of the Novel,* trans. Anna Bostock (Cambridge, Mass.: MIT Press, 1971).

33. James, *Literary Criticism,* p. 990.

34. See, for example, George Steiner, "Eros and Idiom," in *On Difficulty and Other Essays* (Oxford: Clarendon, 1978), p. 105; Ellen Moers, *Literary Women* (London: The Woman's Press, 1986), p. 253; and Ender, *Le roman de l'identité sexuelle,* pp. 257–58.

9. Transgressive Bodies

1. See Walter Benjamin, "The Work of Art in the Age of Mechanical Reproduction," in *Illuminations,* trans. Walter Zohn (New York: Schocken Books, 1969), pp. 217–251. Our supposedly liberated age is of course in some ways less familiar with the body than the nineteenth century, when many routines of the body, including childbirth and death, took place at home, not in hospitals. The medicalization of the body has to a degree alienated it from the domestic sphere. See Peter Gay, *The Bourgeois Experience,* vol. 1, *Education of the Senses* (New York: Oxford University Press, 1984), esp. pp. 336–58.

2. I adopt and alter Jean-Louis Comolli's phrase "the frenzy of the visible"

in "Machines of the Visible," in Teresa de Lauretis and Stephen Heath, eds., *The Cinematic Apparatus* (New York: St. Martin's Press, 1980), pp. 122–23.

3. Stéphane Mallarmé, "Crayonné au théâtre," *Oeuvres complètes* (Paris: Bibliothèque de la Pléiade, 1945), p. 304. On these questions, see Frank Kermode, *Romantic Image* (London: Routledge, 1957). See also Paul Valéry, *Degas, Danse, Dessin,* in *Oeuvres complètes* (Paris: Bibliothèque de la Pléiade, 1960), 2:1163–1240.

4. Richard Poirier, *The Performing Self* (New York: Oxford University Press, 1971).

5. On these questions, see the remarkable study by Elaine Scarry, *The Body in Pain* (New York: Oxford University Press, 1985).

6. Walter Benjamin, "The Storyteller," in *Illuminations,* p. 84.

7. Thomas Mann, *The Magic Mountain,* trans. H. T. Lowe-Porter (1927; New York: Vintage Books, 1969), pp. 217–18.

8. Mann does not translate the French passages into German. An approximate English translation: "Oh, enchanting organic beauty which is composed neither of oil paint nor stone but of living and corruptible matter, full of the febrile secret of life and decomposition! Behold the marvelous symmetry of the human edifice, the shoulders and the hips and the nipples flourishing on each side of the chest, and the ribs arranged in pairs, and the navel in the middle in the softness of the belly, and the obscure sex between the thighs! . . . What a great feast to caress them, these delicious parts of the human body! A feast to die from afterward without complaint! . . . Let me breathe in the exhalation of your pores and touch your bush, human image made of water and albumin, destined for the anatomy of the tomb, and let me perish, my lips on yours!"

9. Marguerite Duras, *L'amant* (Paris: Editions de Minuit, 1985), p. 111; English trans. Barbara Bray, *The Lover* (New York: Pantheon, 1985). The translation of this stylistically challenging text by Barbara Bray is excellent. I have preferred to give my own translations, however, in an attempt to remain closer to the peculiar syntax of the original, although this often results in an English version less fluent and graceful than Bray's. Duras in 1991 published another, very different version of her story, *L'amant de la Chine du Nord* (Paris: Gallimard, 1991), which apparently was begun as a screenplay for the film of *L'amant* and, not used in this capacity, developed into a novel, though one with indications to the maker of a possible film of the original novel. It is a strange performance, much less subtle and compelling than *L'amant.*

10. In the wake of of Roland Barthes' use of *jouissance* in distinction to *plaisir,* it has been usual to translate the former term as "bliss." But the connotations of "bliss" strike me as hopelessly wrong for designating intense, orgasmic bodily pleasure. I note that Barbara Bray also uses "pleasure" to translate *jouissance.*

11. See Jacques Lacan, "Hommage fait à Marguerite Duras du ravissement de Lol V. Stein," in François Barat and Joël Farges, eds., *Marguerite Duras,* rev. ed. (Paris: Editions Albatros, 1979), pp. 131–37. Lacan writes, "Marguerite Duras s'avère savoir sans moi ce que j'enseigne" (p. 133). Lacan's piece was

316

originally published in the *Cahiers Renaud-Barrault* (December 1965). I adapt here especially material from Lacan, *Le séminaire*, book 8, *Le transfert* (Paris: Editions du Seuil, 1991), p. 415.

12. Lacan, "Propos directifs pour un Congrès sur la sexualité féminine," in *Ecrits* (Paris: Editions du Seuil, 1966), pp. 725–36; I quote from the translation by Jacqueline Rose, "Guiding Remarks for a Congress on Feminine Sexuality," in *Feminine Sexuality: Jacques Lacan and the Ecole Freudienne*, ed. Juliet Mitchell and Jacqueline Rose (London: Macmillan, 1982), p. 70. For Rose's comments on this passage, see p. 43.

13. Sharon Willis makes a similar point in the context of feminist theory: "The figure of an exhibitionist female subject should have special force for feminist readers . . . [Duras'] work centers on issues of concern to most feminist theoretical enterprises: desire and sexuality, gender and biology, the relation of the body to language. *The Lover* reinscribes the exhibitionist scenario in a woman's active self-display, a presentation of her life as spectacle—active, that is, as opposed to the passive form of woman as object of/spectacle for a mastering gaze, that of reader or spectator." *Marguerite Duras: Writing on the Body* (Urbana and Chicago: University of Illinois Press, 1987), p. 7.

14. Choderlos de Laclos, *Les liaisons dangereuses*, in *Oeuvres complètes* (Paris: Bibliothèque de la Pléiade, 1979), Letter 81, p. 169.

15. Sigmund Freud, "A Child Is Being Beaten," *Standard Edition* 17:179–204.

16. Georges Bataille, *L'érotisme* (1957; Paris: Union Générale d'Editions/10/18, 1965), pp. 22–23. The evident affinities of Bataille's thinking about eroticism with Lacan's are not accidental: Lacan was much influenced by Bataille.

17. "The Notion of Expenditure," in Georges Bataille, *Visions of Excess: Selected Writings, 1927–1939*, ed. Allan Stoekl, trans. Allan Stoekl with Carl R. Lovitt and Donald M Leslie, Jr. (Minneapolis: University of Minnesota Press, 1985), p. 120.

18. Bataille, *L'érotisme*, p. 140.

19. Comolli, "Machines of the Visible," in Lauretis and Heath, *The Cinematic Apparatus*, pp. 122–23.

20. Linda Williams, *Hardcore: Power, Pleasure, and the "Frenzy of the Visible"* (Berkeley and Los Angeles: University of California Press, 1989). Williams makes the pertinent argument that hard-core cinema is preoccupied with filming male orgasm precisely because it is baffled by the invisibility of female orgasm: "Hard core desires assurance that it is witnessing not the voluntary performance of feminine pleasure, but its involuntary confession. The woman's ability to fake the orgasm that the man can never fake (at least according to certain standards of evidence) seems to be at the root of the genre's attempts to solicit what it can never be sure of: the out-of-control confession of pleasure, a hard-core 'frenzy of the visible.' The animating fantasy of hard-core cinema might therefore be described as the (impossible) attempt to capture visually this frenzy of the visible in a female body whose orgasmic excitement can never be objectively measured" (p. 50).

NOTES TO PAGES 271–278

21. Jacques Lacan, "La signification du phallus," in *Ecrits*, pp. 685–95. I quote from the translation by Jacqueline Rose, "The Meaning of the Phallus," in Mitchell and Rose, *Feminine Sexuality*, p. 82. Lacan continues: "One might say that this signifier is chosen as what stands out as most easily seized upon in the real of sexual copulation, and also as the most symbolic in the literal (typographical) sense of the term, since it is the equivalent in that relation of the (logical) copula." This preserves and perpetuates the ambiguities of the Freudian and Lacanian concepts of the phallus, as on the one hand the anatomical symbol of difference, and on the other the piece of anatomy in which difference—as a prior concept—finds its symbol. On some of the general issues raised by the conjunction of the body, sexuality, and language, see Jane Gallop, *Thinking through the Body* (New York: Columbia University Press, 1988).

22. On the *mysterium tremendum* as a definition of the sacred, see Rudolph Otto, *The Idea of the Holy*, trans. John W. Harvey (London: Oxford University Press, 1923). Compare Moustafa Safouan: "And what, precisely, does [analytic experience] teach us about the phallus, if not that it makes a joke of phallicism?" Quoted in Lacan, "Meaning of the Phallus," in Mitchell and Rose, *Feminine Sexuality*, p. 134. I note also the significance of another kind of breakthrough of taboo in the film *Europa Europa* (1990), in which the circumcised penis of the Jewish hero struggling to survive among Nazis is a key element in the story, and treated with a notable matter-of-factness.

23. Jorge Luis Borges, "Pierre Ménard, author of *Don Quixote*," trans. Anthony Bonner, in *Ficciones*, ed. Anthony Kerrigan (New York: Grove Press, 1962), pp. 45–55.

24. See "Creative Writers and Daydreaming," *Standard Edition* 9:147–53. "A Child Is Being Beaten" is very perceptively discussed by D. N. Rodowick in *The Difficulty of Difference* (New York and London: Routledge, 1991), pp. 69–83, who derives from it a model of spectatorship and gendering far more complex than most of those current in film theory. For an argument against the simple dominance of the phallic gaze in the spectatorship of painting, see Edward Snow's discussion of Velázquez' *Rokeby Venus* in "Theorizing the Male Gaze: Some Problems," *Representations* 26 (1989), pp. 30–41.

25. Franz Kafka, "In the Penal Colony," in *The Penal Colony: Stories and Short Pieces*, trans. Willa and Edwin Muir (New York: Schocken Books, 1961), p. 197. This story is also discussed by Gabriel Josipovici in *Writing and the Body* (Brighton: Harvester Press, 1982), pp. 112–14. Josipovici's book as a whole is a subtle and interesting reflection on the relations of writing, rhetoric, and the body, from a perspective quite different from my own.

26. Roland Barthes, *S/Z* (Paris: Editions du Seuil, 1970), p. 220.

Index

320

321

323

325